THE ILLUSTRATED
—BOOK OF—
INSECTS

THE ILLUSTRATED —BOOK OF— INSECTS

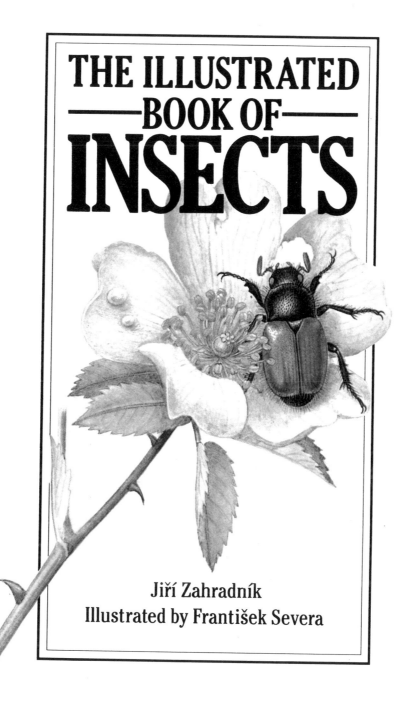

Jiří Zahradník
Illustrated by František Severa

CHARTWELL
BOOKS, INC.

Text by Jiří Zahradník
Illustrations by František Severa
Line drawings by Jiří Moravec, Jiří Zahradník and Miloš Váňa
Graphic design by Eva Adamcová
Translated by Margot Schierlová

Published in 1991 by
CHARTWELL BOOKS, INC.
A Division of
BOOK SALES, INC.
110 Enterprise Avenue
Secaucus. New Jersey 07094

ISBN 1-55521-651-X
Printed in Czechoslovakia by Neografia, š. p., Martin
3/13/14/51-01

Contents

Insects and their appearance

Most insects can be distinguished quite easily from other arthropods. It is more complicated to define insects exactly, however; every definition has its exceptions because nature does not allow herself to be compartmentalised, however much experts might wish that she would.

According to a concise definition, an insect's body is composed of three parts – the head, the thorax and the abdomen. The head is the seat of important sensory organs (mouthparts, antennae, palps, eyes), while the thorax carries two pairs of wings and three pairs of segmented limbs. Even these details have their exceptions, however, since the various parts of the body may not be clearly differentiated or even separate. The mouthparts, antennae and palps may be rudimentary and the eyes may be missing. One or both pairs of wings may also be missing. The three pairs of limbs are usually present, although often much modified for different functions.

Let us take a closer look at the size and organisation of the typical insect body, together with the most striking exceptions. The majority of insects in the temperate areas of the world tend to be small, with a length of only a few millimetres, while the tropics are inhabited by large species with brighter colours and more bizarre forms. The tiny wasps of the Scelionidae family are only some 0.2 mm long (five wasps placed end to end measure just 1 mm) and spider beetles – the smallest of the beetles – are often no longer than 0.5 mm, yet all of these insects must be equipped with organs essential for life and for the reproduction of their species.

The largest insects which interest us here are mainly moths and butterflies (Lepidoptera), stick- and leaf-insects (Phasmida) and beetles (Coleoptera). The wings of lepidopterans have a maximum span of about 32 cm ($12\frac{1}{2}$ in) and a maximum area of about 300 sq cm ($46\frac{1}{2}$ sq in). It is not unusual for phasmids to measure 20––30 cm (8–12 in), while the longest beetle, *Titanus giganteus,* can be over 20 cm (8 in) in length if its jaws are included.

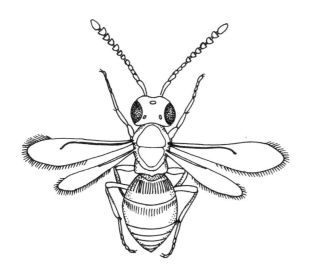

Example of the smallest insects (Hymenoptera, family Scelionidae)

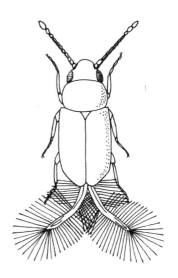

One of the smallest beetles (family Ptiliidae)

7

If we were to classify insect orders according to the size of their members, they would form three groups. The first would comprise orders with tiny species, in which there is only a small difference between the smallest and the largest species. The second would contain orders with moderately large to large species, such as dragonflies, and the third, most extensive group would be composed of orders with differences of a few to several hundred millimetres between their largest and smallest species.

Some insects have a very soft body surface (e.g. aphids), but in the majority the body is covered with hard, chitinous armour, forming a kind of outer skeleton which largely retains its shape even after death.

The head

The anterior part of an insect's body is the head. This may be more chitinised than the rest of the body. It consists of six segments, which unite during development and are not distinguishable in the adult individual. The front part, between the eyes, is called the frons. Behind or above it, right on top of the head, is the vertex, while the occiput is right at the back. The part behind the eyes, stretching down to the mouthparts, is known as the cheek or gena. Below, or in front of, the frons lies the clypeus. Although the head is actually much more complicated, this description is adequate for our requirements.

The mouthparts are situated at the front of the head, although in many insects the head is bent down so that the mouthparts are below it. Biting mouthparts, as in beetles, for example, are the basic type. They consist of two upper jaws (mandibles), two lower jaws (maxillae) and a lower lip (labium) and are protected from above by an upper lip (labrum). The mandibles are generally very hard and their function is to cut and crush food into small particles. Sometimes, however, they may also be used for other purposes, such as digging. Their inner edges are often toothed, but they do not carry any appendages. The lower jaws (maxillae) are each composed of several parts and are surmounted by the maxillary palps, which usually have five joints. The function of the maxillae is to hold the food and to help grind

it to a still finer consistency, and convey it into the mouth. Unlike the mandibles and the maxillae, the labium is not paired, but carries paired labial palps. Both maxillary and labial palps are involved in tasting the food to ensure it is suitable to eat.

Biting mouthparts are the basic type, but are by no means the only type. Suctorial, stabbing-suctorial and licking mouthparts are also widespread. The most familiar example of suctorial mouthparts is the tubular proboscis of moths and butterflies, which is often very long and is held coiled on the underside of the head. Insects with stabbing-suctorial mouthparts, such as bugs or flies, puncture plant or animal tissues and suck their juices. Licking mouthparts are also to be found in many flies. Hymenopterans have the basic type of mouthparts, but here the mandibles are often used for building the nest, kneading wax and chewing food for the offspring. Most hymenopterans live on juices, which they suck through modified mouthparts.

The antennae, which grow from the head, are important organs. Primarily they have olfactory and tactile functions and are often compared to radar. They are formed of segments, whose number may vary among insects of the same order, the same family and even the same species. Antennae have three main parts, which in some cases are clearly distinguishable and in others less so. The first segment is known as the scape. This forms a base for the next part, the pedicel, which leads to the tip of the antenna, the flagellum. Long, filiform antennae, like those found in cockroaches and crickets, for instance, are the basic type, but the number of different forms is virtually inexhaustible. In addition to filiform, pectinate, bipectinate, clavate, flabellate and geniculate antennae, there are countless other forms, many of which are positively bizarre. Some insects, however, including many scale insects, have only vestigial antennae which appear as small protuberances.

Insects have quite remarkable eyes. Most of them have two compound eyes, one on each side of the head, but in many groups there are three further simple eyes (ocelli) on the vertex. The compound eye is composed of a variable number of small elements known as ommatidia, each of

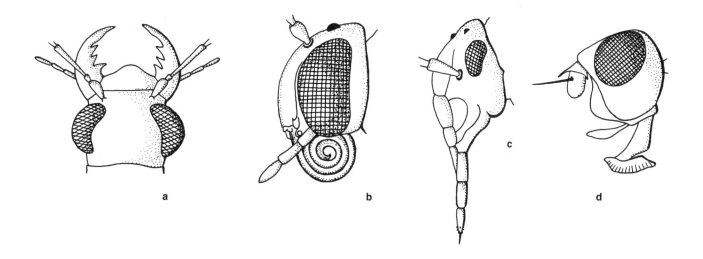

Types of mouthparts: a – biting (Coleoptera); b – suctorial (Lepidoptera); c – stabbing-suctorial (Heteroptera); d – licking (Diptera)

which possesses independent vision, so that the resultant image seen by the insect is a kind of mosaic. The compound eyes of insects which are less dependent on their vision usually have relatively few ommatidia, but the eyes of dragonflies, which hunt their prey by vision, have up to 30,000. The compound eye may be only one colour, but in many insects it glows with different colours; dragonflies have beautifully coloured eyes, and the eyes of many dipterans show all the colours of the rainbow. Iridescent eyes are to be found only in the living insects, however; after death the colours disappear.

The position of the head in relation to the rest of the body varies. The basic type is a prognathous head, i.e. one which points straight forward. If the head is held at right angles to the body axis, it is described as hypognathous, and

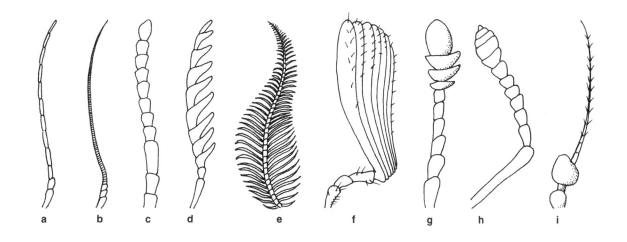

Different types of insect antennae: a – filiform; b – setaceous; c – catenate; d – pectinate; e – bipectinate, f – flabellate; g – clavate; h – geniculate; i – aristate

if it points both downwards and backwards it is opisthognathous. Ground beetles have a typically prognathous head, grasshoppers and locusts a hypognathous head and cockroaches an opisthognathous head.

The thorax

The next part of the insect body, the thorax, has three, largely distinct, parts – the prothorax (at the front), the mesothorax (in the middle) and the metathorax (behind). The second and third thoracic segments each usually carries a pair of wings. Each of the thoracic segments also bears one pair of legs. The dorsal plate of each segment (the tergite) and the ventral plate (the sternite) are joined together at the sides by pleurites. The wings sprout from the boundaries between the second and third tergites and pleurites, while the legs are attached to the pleural part of the thorax.

The first thoracic segment is often very different from the other two, and a much enlarged prothorax may form a dorsal shield (pronotum), which is a typical feature of beetles, bugs, cockroaches and earwigs. Sometimes the prothorax is strikingly long, as in snake-flies and mantids.

The wings grow from the mesothorax and metathorax. In Diptera, which have only one pair of wings, the most powerfully developed segment is the mesothorax.

In many insects (especially tropical species) spiny processes and outgrowths resembling

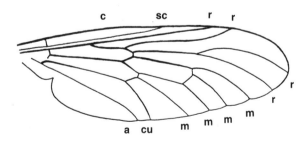

Scheme of an insect's wing. Main veins: c – costa; sc – subcosta; r – radius; m – media; cu – cubitus; a – annus

thorns or seeds are present on the thorax. The bugs of the Membracidae family and stick- and leaf-insects are good examples.

Insects generally have four wings. The insect wing is mainly membranous. It consists not of one membrane, however, but of two contiguous membranes enclosing branched tracheae (the veins). The veins run lengthwise and crosswise, forming circumscribed fields on the wings. The veins and fields have their own names. In general, the wing has the following veins: a marginal vein (costa), a submarginal vein (subcosta), a radial vein (radius), a medial vein (media), a cubital vein (cubitus) and anal veins, which sometimes form a fan (vannus). If you look at the wing of a mayfly, a dragonfly, a grasshopper, an earwig, a beetle, a butterfly, a wasp and a housefly, you can immediately see how vast the variety of insect venation is. Even experts often have difficulty in deciding which vein is which.

The wing is narrower at its base and is joined to the thorax by sclerites (pteralia). Its surface is very often covered with fine hairs or scales and however bare a wing may appear to be, a magnifying glass will often reveal the presence of minute hairs. Very often the first pair of wings has been transformed into a horny or leathery structure. This is most striking and familiar in beetles, in which the membraneous second pair of wings is usually kept folded below thick, chitinous wing-cases (elytra) showing only a few traces of venation. A similar transformation of the first pair of wings occurs in earwigs, cockroaches, crickets, grasshoppers and mantids. The modified first pair of wings of bugs is somewhat different, since part of the wing is leathery and part membraneous. Such wings are known as hemelytra.

In some insects, all four wings are roughly the same size (damselflies, dragonflies, some moths and butterflies) while in others the forewings are conspicuously larger than the hindwings (e.g. mayflies, many hymenopterans) and in others again the forewings have a smaller area than the hindwings (stoneflies, caddis flies).

All four wings do not always develop and in the subclass Apterygota (wingless insects) they do not develop at all. The best-known example of this is the Silver-fish (*Lepisma*), but even among winged insects (Pterygota) we find remarkable modifications of the number and size of the wings and also differences between the wings of males and females. It is quite common for the males of a given group to be winged and for the females to be wingless or provided only with wing stumps. Such is the case with some geometer moths for instance; while the males fly like other moths, all the females can do is crawl about on plants. The differences between male and female scale insects are greater still. The females are always wingless and only the forewings develop in the males; their rudimentary hindwings resemble the halteres of two-winged insects. The latter (Diptera) do, in fact, have only one pair of functioning wings; the hindwings have been transformed to organs of balance, known as halteres.

Wingless forms likewise occur in winged orders. This is common among hymenopterans, especially among small species of parasitic wasps (Chalcididae). Another combination is known among ants, whose males are winged for the whole of their lifetime, while the females shed their wings after the nuptial flight, and the workers are always wingless.

A search for variation in the organisation of the wings of winged insects inevitably takes us to the curious fringed wings of thrips (Thysanoptera), to winged and wingless forms of aphids and psocids (Psocoptera) and lastly to orders composed of secondarily wingless species, i.e. lice (Anoplura), bird lice (Mallophaga) and fleas (Siphonaptera).

In the vast majority of insects, the size of the wings is constant; however, there are species in which some individuals have normally developed wings and others have more or less stunted wings.

One pair of legs is attached to each thoracic segment. If we take the cursorial (running) leg as the basic type, we see that it has five distinctly separate regions – from the body outwards these are the coxa, the trochanter, the femur, the tibia and the tarsus, which is generally formed of five small segments. However, as with the wings, various aberrations occur in the legs, chiefly as regards their form and function.

The commonest type are long, slim cursorial legs used primarily for quick locomotion. We

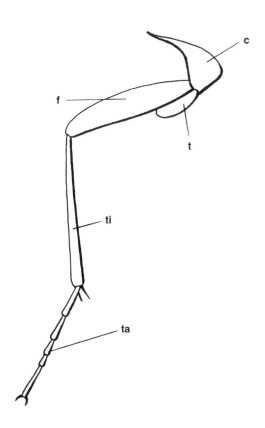

Parts of the insect limb (proximodistally): c – coxa; t – trochanter; f – femur; ti – tibia; ta – tarsus terminating in claws (unguiculi)

come across these in ground beetles, tiger beetles, cockroaches, bugs, hymenopterans, dipterans and many other insects. Saltatorial legs (for jumping), with powerfully developed hind femurs, are a different type; they are best known in grasshoppers and some leaf beetles (*Phyllotreta*).

Natatorial (swimming) legs are a fairly common type. They occur in aquatic species and are particularly highly developed in predacious diving beetles (Dytiscidae).

Many insects, in different groups, also use their legs for digging. Some insects dig to avoid the light (many beetles) or the cold (beetle-wasps – Scoliidae), while others bury themselves in the egg-laying season (female stag beetles). Digging legs are also very important for many hymenopterans, e.g. digger wasps (Sphecidae) and solitary bees, and beetles (e.g. dung beetles).

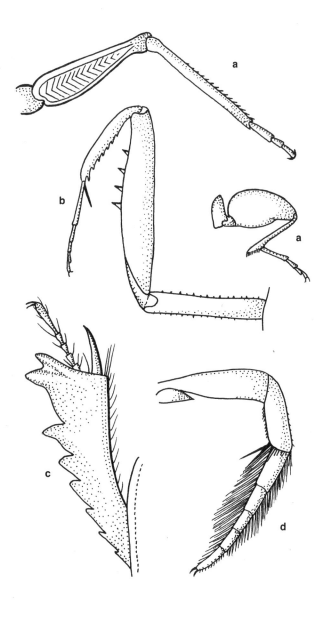

fully developed and others in which they are all reduced. For example, fritillary and vanessid butterflies (Nymphalidae) have much reduced front legs.

The abdomen

The last part of the body – the abdomen – is generally the largest. It is actually composed of eleven segments, but the full number is not discernible, since some of them, especially the terminal segments, are fused. The abdomen is usually soft. It does not bear any organs of locomotion, but contains most of the viscera and a fat body of variable size.

The viscera and their functions are much more complex than the outer chitinous skeleton. They must operate inside a minute body which is only a few tenths of a millimetre long just as reliably as in a robust organism.

Specialised insect limbs: a – for jumping; b – raptorial; c – for digging; d – for swimming

Digging legs are usually equipped with strong spines and bristles. It is usually the forelegs which are adapted for this purpose, but mining-bees of the genus *Dasypoda*, for instance, have hairy hindlegs which act as a kind of broom. Adaptation of the legs for digging can be very highly specialised, as in the case of the forelegs of the Mole Cricket.

The degeneration of legs is not very common among insects. The greatest degree of limb reduction is to be found in scale insects, which include species in which all three pairs of legs are

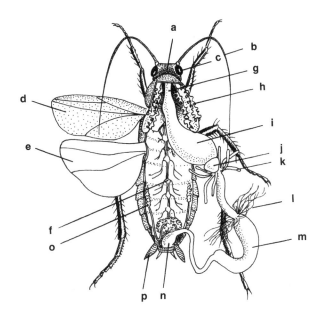

Scheme of organisation of the insect body: a – head; b – antenna; c – compound eye; d, e – first and second pair of wings; f – ventral neural cord; g – oesophagus; h – salivary gland; i – crop (ingluvies); j – muscular stomach; k – diverticula of stomach; l – Malphighian tubes; m – large intestine; n – rectum; o – gonad (male); p – cercus

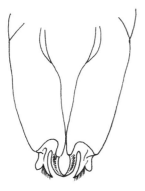

Male copulatory apparatus (wasp)

The digestive system begins with the mouth, followed by the pharynx and the oesophagus. The food then enters the crop and the stomach, and continues to the midgut, which has a number of diverticula (blind processes). The last part, the hindgut, terminates as the rectum and here the digestive system opens outwards through the anal orifice. This scheme is very general, of course, and many aberrations can be found which relate to an individual species' mode of life.

The respiratory system consists of tracheae – small tubes which divide into progressively finer branches carrying air directly to the tissues. Externally, the tracheae open through small holes known as spiracles or stigmata; there are two pairs on the sides of the thorax and eight pairs on the abdomen. This type of respiration does not apply strictly everywhere, however, and insects can also breathe through the surface of their bodies.

Insects have an open vascular system, i.e. the haemolymph does not flow through closed vessels. Blood from the abdomen is carried towards the head by the dorsal vessel. The part of the vessel lying in the abdomen is known as the heart and the thoracic part as the aorta. Openings are present in both the heart and the aorta; blood is pumped along the dorsal vessel to the front of the body where it bathes the organs and then returns, via these openings, to the heart, resulting in regular pulsation. The haemolymph may be clear and colourless, or yellowish, greenish, brown or even red, depending on pigmentation. The amount of haemolymph is relatively large; in cockroaches, for instance, it accounts for about one fifth of total body weight.

Metabolic waste is disposed of or stored by the excretory organs. Insects have several possible excretion routes, from their body tegument to the intricate Malphighian tubes opening into their digestive tract between the midgut and the hindgut. Metabolic waste is not always removed from the body, however; it may be stored in special cells or tissues, which could be described as storage kidneys.

Most insects are gonochorists; that is to say, the individual is either a male or a female. Hermaphrodites, which possess the reproductory organs of both sexes, are very rare. Gynandromorphs, i.e. individuals with the secondary characteristics of both sexes, are more common; they are particularly noticeable in species in which the male differs from the female in colouring or size.

All of the body systems are controlled and regulated by the nervous system, which consists of a series of ventrally localised nerve centres (ganglia) in the head, thorax and abdomen. The ganglia are joined together by a nerve-cord.

The space between the organs is filled by a heterogeneous muscle system and a fat body. Grasshoppers have about 900 muscles, but some caterpillars have up to 4,000. Insect muscles are remarkably resistant to fatigue.

Locomotion

The possible forms of insect locomotion are many and varied. Insects can crawl, run, jump, swim and fly. Most of them master several different ways of moving to new surroundings or of finding sources of food. For instance, some species, which crawl or swim, can also fly, but in view of the tremendous diversity of insect life it is only natural that one type of locomotion usually predominates. Many species fly as a rule, while in others running is the predominant form of movement. Only a small percentage is limited to just one type of locomotion. These are primarily or secondarily wingless insects, such as silverfish, body lice, bird-lice and worker ants, etc., which can only crawl. Quite a few insects have lost all capacity for active movement. The best known of these are the female scale insects of the Diaspididae family.

Most insects are able to fly. Many of them spend the whole of their lives in the place where they were born, but others leave for new surroundings far, or not so far, away. Locusts and hawk moths travel distances of up to several thousand kilometres and thus infiltrate new territories.

Not all insects fly in the same manner, but the movements of their wings are so quick that we miss the details. Slow-motion film, however, shows us that butterflies flap their wings ten to fifteen times a second, green lacewings 21–26 times a second, and hawk moths about 40–50 times a second. Sometimes – in dragonflies, for example – both pairs of wings can be moved independently of each other. In most insects, however, the wings are connected and move as a single pair.

Insects can often fly at remarkable speeds over short distances. The fastest species are the nostril-flies of the Oestridae family, which can reach a speed of over 100 kmph (63 mph), and hawk moths, which can fly at more than 50 kmph (31 mph). With a speed of up to 36 kmph ($22\frac{1}{2}$ mph), dragonflies are also excellent fliers. Bumblebees, which average 10–15 kmph (6–

9 mph), are slower, while cockchafers fly at only 9 kmph ($5\frac{1}{2}$ mph), whites (butterflies) at about 7 kmph (4 mph) and green lacewings (Chrysopa) at only 2 kmph ($1\frac{1}{4}$ mph). Compared with the rate of a human walking, however, these speeds are still truly remarkable.

Running is also a useful way of getting about. Cursorial legs are long, with long, slender segments. If you watch a large ground beetle running, you will see that it treads on the underside of its tarsi and uses its legs in the following sequence: left fore – right middle – left hindleg, and then right fore – left middle – right hindleg. Insects do not usually run long distances and the rate at which they run bears no comparison with the speed of their flight. Crawling, as a rule, is the slowest form of locomotion.

Numerous groups of insects proceed by leaping, in which the hind limbs, with their thickened femurs, play the main role. They include grasshoppers, crickets, cicadas, some bugs, certain beetles, hymenopterans and fleas. Here again, jumping is not the sole form of locomotion and a saltatorial species may also crawl or run. Jumping is most pronounced in crickets and grasshoppers, which also use different kinds of leaps. The leap they use if they want to move just a little way is much shorter than the leaps they take when escaping from danger. For instance, the Great Green Bush Cricket (*Tettigonia viridissima*) does not normally jump distances of more than 1 m (1 yd), but if in danger its leaps can measure 4 m ($4\frac{1}{3}$ yd).

The hind limbs are not necessarily the only means of jumping. On the underside of their bodies, click beetles (Elateridae) have a special device which enables them to spring from a supine position onto their feet.

Aquatic insects are adapted for swimming just as well as terrestrial insects are for locomotion on dry land. In aquatic species, as in saltatorial species, the hind limbs display the greatest differences from the other two pairs. Take predacious diving beetles, for example. Their hindlegs are their longest legs and are thickly overgrown with long, stiff hairs. The whole limb acts as a paddle. The imagos of some aquatic insects can 'row' about and hunt their prey on the surface of the water. They are such experts in this respect that male water-striders of the bug genus *Gerris* can hold prey weighing 40 times more than themselves without being dragged down by it. Whirligig beetles (Gyrinidae) also travel over the surface extremely fast, but quite differently from bugs; their bodies are partly submerged and they are also able to dive.

Even aquatic species are not entirely dependent on their natatorial legs, however; if they decide to 'move house' many just climb out onto the bank and fly away.

Colouring

The colour combinations on butterflies' wings and on the wing cases of beetles and other insects are often so rich and splendid that even an experienced artist would have difficulty in putting them onto canvas. Other species, however, are very plainly coloured, being inconspicuously greyish, brownish, brownish-black or black. Furthermore, splendid colours are often kept hidden to be displayed only in specific circumstances. This is the case with many moths, whose forewings blend with their surroundings, but are suddenly unfolded if the insect is disturbed to reveal the provocative colours of the hindwings. Both colour schemes are of importance to the moth – the forewings to make it invisible to inquisitive birds and the hindwings to shock its enemies.

Defenceless, unaggressive insects are often a similar colour to their more dangerous relatives. The commonest colourings of this type are wasp-like combinations of yellow and black or yellow and dark brown. Birds which have once encountered a wasp will think twice before approaching this ominous combination of colours again, so that many other hymenopterans (sawflies, horntails) and many dipterans (hover-flies, soldier-flies, thick-headed flies), beetles (longhorns) and lepidopterans (clearwings), etc., profit from their impersonation of wasps.

Insects' colouring is determined by pigment (pigmental coloration), by light ray diffraction (structural coloration) and by combinations of these two factors.

The number of insect pigments is very large and they are often very complex substances. Colourless, yellow, red and orange pterins abound in moths' and butterflies' wings. Red and reddish-brown melanins are also common insect pigments. The cherry-red pigment antrachin was made famous by the cochineal insect (*Dactylopius coccus*). Red carotenoids are very frequent in the insect epidermis; they are known in ladybirds and in the larvae of the Colorado Beetle. The presence of haemoglobin is another remarkable, although exceptional, finding; this pigment occurs in the red larvae of midges, known chiefly to anglers and aquarists.

The colouring produced by interference and the diffraction of light rays on butterflies' wings could be said to be an optical delusion. If you look at the wings of the male Purple Emperor (*Apatura*) from different angles, violet-blue patches appear on them; if the wings are moistened the beautiful colour disappears, but returns when the wings are dry again.

The principle of structural coloration is more difficult to grasp. Light rays are diffracted on the scales of the butterfly's wings, but not always in the same way. Some scales are variously grooved and folded and on these the rays are diffracted in a different manner from scales formed of a large number of layers of unequal thickness and quality. Structural coloration is not only confined to lepidopterans, but is also found among hymenopterans (especially cuckoo wasps), dipterans ('golden' flies) and beetles. Among the latter, the tropical metallic wood-borers (Buprestidae) have the most brilliant structural coloration; on their elytra they have very fine, microscopic particles which absorb and reflect light rays in different ways.

Pigmental and structural coloration are often combined. Structural colouring make take the form of just a small spot on the body. In a beetle it may decide the colour of the pronotum, while the colouring of the elytra is determined by pigments.

Sexual dimorphism and dichroism; polymorphism

This section deals with inter-sex differences in form and colouring and with the occurrence of different morphological types in the same species.

With some insects it is very difficult to distinguish between the male and the female because at first glance they appear to be identical. In many species, however, there are striking morphological differences between the sexes. One of the best examples is the Stag Beetle (*Lucanus cervus*), in which species males have huge mandibles. The related lamellicorn beetles also display marked morphological differences. The male European Rhinoceros Beetle (*Oryctes nasicornis*) is armed with a large horn, which is missing

in the female. In tropical species, e.g. the South American Hercules Beetle (*Dynastes hercules*), the differences are even more pronounced. They are not only related to the development of the horns and mandibles but have many other strik-

Chionaspis salicis, scale of male

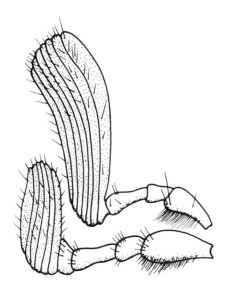

Antennae of male (above) and female (below) cockchafer

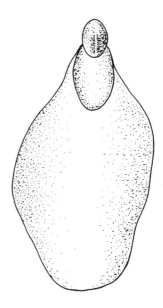

Chionaspis salicis, scale of female

ing characteristics differentiating the sexes. In predacious diving beetles, the males have suction discs on their legs; in male ground beetles some of the segments of the front tarsi are widened; the males of many species have pectinate antennae; male longhorn beetles often have much longer antennae than the females; the males of many hymenopteran species have an extra joint in their antennae.

There may also be marked differences in the shape of the wings and even in their development. Male geometrids (family Geometridae) are winged, but the females of some species have reduced wings or no wings at all. There are also pronounced differences between male winged coccids and the completely wingless females, and the same applies to velvet ants (Mutillidae) and some tiny wasp-like chalcids (Chalcididae). The female of some insects can be distinguished from the male by her ovipositor (e.g. crickets). In addition she may be different in colour (e.g. the horntail, *Urocerus gigas*).

Different coloration of the male and female (sexual dichroism) is very frequent among insects. The differences are sometimes discernible only to a practised eye, but they are equally often such that the male, seen beside the female, looks like a totally different species. Male damselflies (of the species *Calopteryx splendens*) have a bluish-violet band on each of their four wings, while the females have plain greenish wings. The male of the very common longhorn beetle *Leptura rubra* has yellowish elytra and a black pronotum, whereas the female is entirely brownish-red. Colour differences among lepidopterans are very frequent; for instance, only the male Orange-tip *(Anthocharis cardamines)* actually has large orange spots on its forewings, while only the male Brimstone Butterfly (*Gonepteryx rhamni*) is lemon-yellow, the female being whitish. Marked colour differences can also be seen in the Lycaenidae family (Blues, Coppers and Hairstreaks); the males of some species are blue, while the females are brown. There are also marked differences between the male and female Purple Emperor (*Apatura*) since the male has a bluish-violet lustre of structural origin on its wings, which the female lacks. On their forewings, male fritillaries, but not the females, have rows of scented scales.

The members of one species usually all have the same form, but in social insects, in whose communities labour is often very strictly divided, there are several, noticeably different forms. These are known as polymorphous species. Polymorphism is known, for example, in the Honeybee, whose hive houses three morphologically different types – the queen (the largest), the workers and the drones (the males). Relationships among ants (and still more among termites) are more complex, since there are more types of non-sexual individuals (workers, soldiers, etc.).

Development

During their development from the egg to the imago, most insects undergo a complete or incomplete metamorphosis. The exceptions are the silverfish, which do not have any real metamorphosis.

In incomplete metamorphosis, the nymph hatches from the egg, grows and moults a few times. When it reaches maturity, its outer skin cracks open and the adult insect emerges from the body of the nymph. This type of metamorphosis is characteristic of mayflies, dragonflies, stoneflies, earwigs, cockroaches, grasshoppers and crickets, psocids, lice, bird-lice, thrips and heteropteran and homopteran insects.

In complete metamorphosis, the young insect is called a larva. It changes into a resting stage, the chrysalis or pupa, from which the imago subsequently emerges. This type of metamorphosis is characteristic of all four of the biggest insect orders, i.e. beetles, moths and butterflies, hymenopterans and dipterans, and also of alder-flies, snake-flies, lacewings, caddis flies, scorpion flies and fleas.

The various developmental stages (instars) in

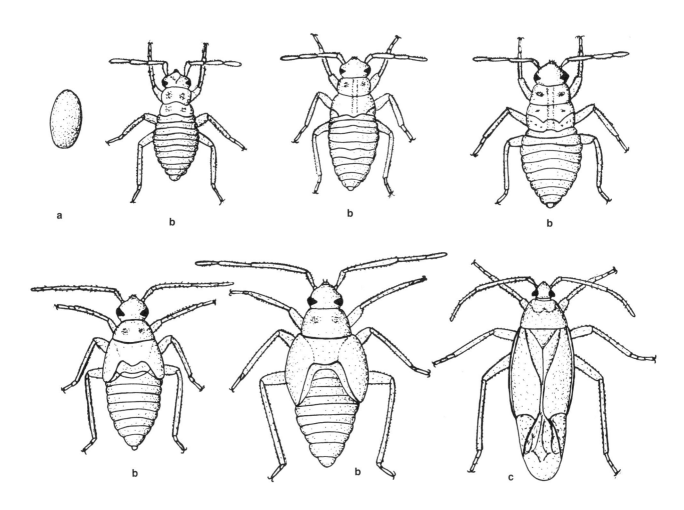

Incomplete metamorphosis (Heteroptera): a – egg; b – various nymphal instars; c – imago

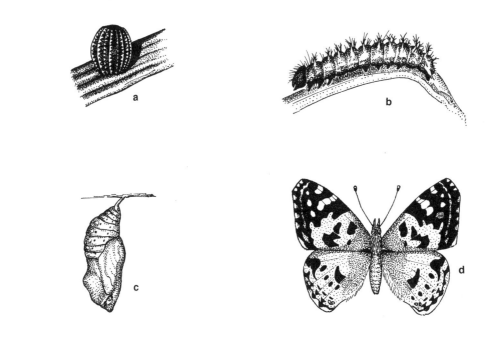

Complete metamorphosis (Lepidoptera): a – egg; b – larva (in this case caterpillar); c – pupa; d – imago

incomplete metamorphosis are not very different from one another and increasingly resemble the imago, while in complete metamorphosis the larval instars bear no resemblance to the adult insect.

In some cases, however, metamorphosis is much more complex and is complicated by the formation of a further, morphologically different larva. In this case it is termed hypermetamorphosis, which is known in beetles (oil beetles), strepsipterans and some neuropterans, hymenopterans and dipterans.

Metamorphosis begins with the egg, which in most insects is fertilised. There are, however, species whose eggs are not fertilised, but nevertheless develop. There are several reasons for non-fertilisation; either the male is unknown, or is very rare, or only a few of the total number of eggs are fertilised intentionally. This form of reproduction, in which the eggs develop without being fertilised, is known as parthenogenesis.

Parthenogenesis is not usual among insects, but in some groups of insects it is quite common. Many species of aphids and some coccids, stick insects, gall wasps and other hymenopterans, and occasionally beetles, reproduce in this way.

The alternation of sexual and parthenogenetic generations is a very complex phenomenon termed metagenesis, which is known chiefly among aphids and gall wasps. In some cases it is complicated still further by alternation of the host plants. As a rule, the individuals of the different generations differ as regards their size and certain morphological features.

The egg

Insects' eggs may be spherical, pear-shaped, oval, elongated, tapering or flattened in diverse ways. They may be fitted with a 'float', or they

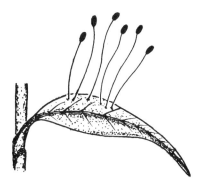

Chrysopa egg with pedicel

may be attached to a thread of some kind. Sometimes they are smooth and glossy, although they generally have a finely sculptured surface with fine ridges, ribs or dimples. The sculpturing, which can be observed best with the aid of a strong magnifying glass, is quite fascinating.

The coloration of the eggs is also very varied and frequently changes, sometimes several times, during their development.

The size of the eggs is not always proportional to the size of the female which laid them. The eggs of the biggest ground beetle measure about 11 mm ($\frac{7}{16}$ in) but the eggs of oil beetles, which are not exactly small insects, are microscopic. Similarly, the size of the beetle gives no hint as to the number of eggs laid, which depends more on the future environment of the young larvae. For instance, sexton beetles, whose larvae live underground and develop very quickly, lay only a small number of eggs, while oil beetles lay several thousand, because their development (hypermetamorphosis) is very complex and mortality among the young larvae is high.

Some females lay their eggs singly or just a few at a time, while others lay them all at once. It is not uncommon for the female to weave or stick

Examples of different shapes of lepidopteran eggs

together a protective cocoon (ootheca) for the eggs. In this respect mantids are outstanding, but earwigs, cockroaches and water scavenger beetles also care for their eggs. Some females cover the eggs with a protective layer, or 'stitch' rolled leaves together and lay the eggs inside these.

Nymphs and larvae

Nymphs are the young stage of insects that grow up without a pupal stage. They gradually assume the adult form as they grow. Larvae are the young stage of those insects that do undergo a pupal stage.

All of an insect's growth takes place during the nymphal or larval stages. Adult insects do not grow any more.

Nymphs and larvae inhabit both dry land and water. They may be free-living or parasitise plants or animals. In water we not only find the young of aquatic insects (e.g. predacious diving beetles, water scavenger beetles and aquatic bugs), but also those of species whose imagos live on dry land (mayflies, dragonflies, caddis flies, etc.).

Nymphs very often look quite like the adults, especially in their later stages, but larvae look nothing like the adults and have no sign of wings.

The better known larvae can be divided into three major groups, according to their form and the development of their body appendages. The first comprises oligopodous larvae. This term is taken from the Greek and means that the larvae have only a few legs. These larvae have only thoracic legs. They are known among beetles, neuropterans and caddis flies.

The next group contains polypodous larvae. This term is again taken from the Greek and means that an animal has many feet. In addition to thoracic legs, these larvae have abdominal legs (prolegs), or, in aquatic larvae, tracheal gills (bronchial appendages with tracheae, which spring from the body wall). The best known of these larvae are caterpillars, the larvae of leaf-rolling sawflies and scorpion fly larvae. Caterpillars have differing numbers of pairs of prolegs and extra processes on their terminal segment.

Apodous (legless) larvae are likewise very common (the Greek prefix 'a' means 'not' or 'without'). They have a soft body and are usually white. They live only in places where they can find enough food without having to move about, and include the larvae of many beetles (weevils, bark beetles), hymenopterans, flies and fleas.

Nymphs and larvae moult several times, as

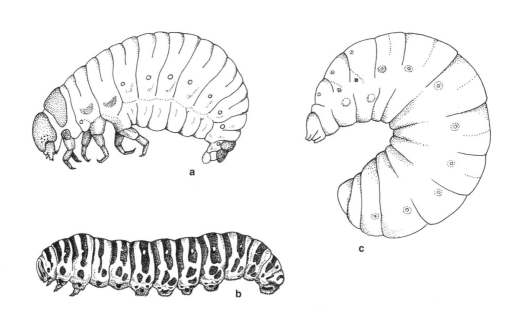

Basic types of insect larvae: a – oligopodous (beetle); b – polypodous (lepidopteran); c – apodous (bumblebee)

their skin becomes too tight. This is known as ecdysis. When the skin has been shed the body tegument becomes elastic for a while, so that the insect can eat its fill and grow again.

After a given time, the youngster stops growing and is either transformed into the imago (in incomplete metamorphosis), or pupates (in complete metamorphosis). Larvae either pupate on the plant on which they have previously lived, retire below bark, or pupate in moss or on the ground. Very often they leave their previous environment. The aquatic larvae of predacious diving beetles leave the water before pupating and bury themselves in the ground on the bank. At the end of their development, many larvae make themselves a case of various materials (sand, soil, fragments of plants) stuck together with saliva, wrap themselves in a silken cocoon or weave a few leaves together and pupate in the resultant sheath.

The pupa

The pupa, the penultimate stage of complete metamorphosis, is very vulnerable and in constant danger. As a rule, it is not capable of active movement, except for the pupae of ant-lions, snake-flies, scorpion flies and caddis flies, which have movable mandibles and bite their way out

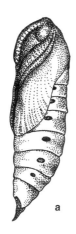
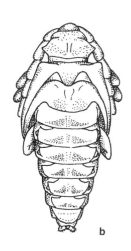

Two of the most common types of insect pupae: a – mummiform pupa or pupa obtecta (Lepidoptera); b – exarate pupa or pupa libera (Coleoptera)

of hiding towards the end of the pupal period. There are many types of pupae, but the commonest are the mummiform pupa (*pupa obtecta*) and the exarate or free pupa (*pupa libera*).

In the mummiform pupa, the future antennae, legs and wings are partly distinguishable, but are all attached to the trunk; lepidopteran pupae are a typical example. Some of them (e.g. fritillary pupae) hang head downwards on a plant. Dipterans and some beetles also have mummiform pupae. The most familiar of these are the brightly coloured pupae of ladybirds, which are likewise attached to plants.

All the body appendages, i.e. the future antennae, legs and wings, are very clearly discernible on the pupa libera. They are not freely movable, but neither are they firmly attached to the trunk, as they are in the pupa obtecta. The pupa libera is the commonest type among beetles and the sex of the future adult can often be determined from the development of the appendages. The Longhorn Timberman Beetle has a very striking pupa, for instance, and if it belongs to a male, it will also already have very long antennae. From the size of the mandibles on the stag beetle's pupa we can also tell whether the imago will be a male or a female. Most hymenopterans, together with fleas and strepsipterans, likewise have a pupa libera.

Very often the pupa lies in a mud or wooden case (many beetles), in a silken cocoon (many moths and butterflies, the best known of which is the silkworm moth), or in a puparium (some dipterans).

The pupa is a remarkable stage of development, during which tremendous transformations take place. In the pupa, the former larval tissues are broken down (histolysis) and the new tissues of the future imago are formed (histogenesis).

The imago

The last stage of development, completing metamorphosis, is that of the adult insect or imago. When it leaves the nymph or crawls out of the pupa the imago has a very soft body. It takes some time before its body tegument hardens and acquires its definitive coloration. The imago

Odonata

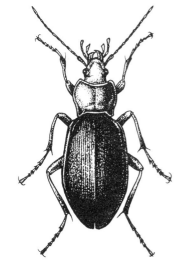

Coleoptera

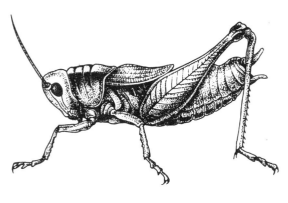

Caelifera

Hymenoptera

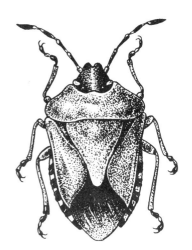

Heteroptera

Lepidoptera

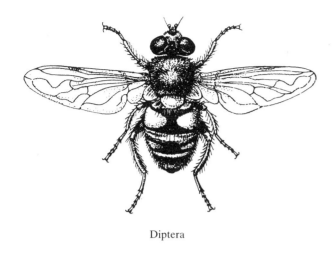

Diptera

which leaves a 'case' attached to a plant, among fallen leaves or lying open on the ground, has a much easier time than the imago which emerges underground or under bark or wood. The skin of a pupa hanging from a plant (e.g. the pupae of many lepidopterans) or of a nymph attached to

a leaf (e.g. dragonflies) splits at the outset of emergence and the young imago then vigorously forces its way out. Newly emerged moths, butterflies and dragonflies need to catch hold of a branch or some other object to give themselves time to spread their wings slowly, fill them with air and thus aid their necessary development. Imagos which emerge in the ground usually need first of all to bite their way through the wall of a protective cocoon and will then still have to dig their way out to the surface. Imagos which emerge in wood are separated from the outside world by a layer of wood and bark, but nature thinks of everything. In the last phase of their development, the larvae of xylophagous (wood-eating) insects return to the outermost layer of the wood and then all the imago usually has to do is overcome a relatively thin barrier cutting it off from the light of day.

Insect imagos are characterised by a huge quantity of forms, sizes and colours. No less varied or ingeniously organised is their mode of life and the manner in which they care for their offspring.

Age

A phylogenetic comparison of the age of insects with the age of various other groups of animals would arrive at the following conclusion: insects are about 100 million years older than reptiles. If we compare insects with human beings, we find that insects are about 1,000 times older than the first 'modern' human.

During past epochs many groups of insects appeared and disappeared, but their remains have been preserved in various rocks and resins; fossil insect remains can be traced right back to the Palaeozoic Era. The richest and best preserved finds come from amber, a fossil conifer resin in which the insects became hermetically sealed and can therefore be studied much more satisfactorily than earlier fossil remains.

Until quite recently, the wingless springtails, which already lived in the Devonian period, over 400 million years ago, were considered to be the

oldest insects. However, since springtails, according to modern systematics, are no longer classified among the insects, the precursors of the cockroaches are now regarded as the oldest insect representatives. These fossil forms closely resemble recent cockroaches and their existence has been confirmed by fossil remains found in carboniferous rocks in the British Isles and in Germany.

The precursors of our present-day insects often grew to considerable proportions. For example, *Meganeura monyi,* a member of the Meganisoptera order and related to the dragonflies, lived in the Carboniferous period and had a wing span of about 70 cm ($27\frac{1}{2}$ in).

The study of fossil insects has brought to light forms now long extinct all over the world. Finds of many warmth-loving species in Baltic amber, dating from the Oligocene period, testify that

A precursor of recent insects: *Meganeura monyi*

these species inhabited northern Europe, which in those days had a warm climate. As the climate grew colder, the warmth-loving fauna disappeared. Species which once lived in northern Europe can now be found in tropical America – for example, the tiger beetle, *Tetracha carolina*. This can be found in Baltic amber but occurs live today in the southern parts of the USA.

Life span

Much of our knowledge of insects' length of life comes from laboratory breeding, and may be largely inaccurate. However, the length of life of a given species is more or less stable and shows no important deviations. Mayfly imagos are very short-lived; it is not for nothing that they are named Ephemeroptera (in Greek *ephemera* meaning 'short-lived' or 'living for a day'). Mayflies would not live longer even if given better conditions than those provided by nature. The brevity of their imaginal life is compensated for by the length of their pre-imaginal life, which lasts for between one and three years. Male coccids likewise live for a maximum of a few dozen hours, but their early development takes several months.

The imago of most insects lives only a few days or weeks and seldom for several years. If a species forms more than one generation, the length of the imagos' lives in the individual generations is not necessarily the same. This applies particularly to hibernating generations; the lives of such individuals are longer, but this is not active life, since most of it is spent hibernating.

On an average, many lepidopteran, coleopteran, hymenopteran and dipteran imagos live for three to five weeks, but their pre-imaginal life is substantially longer. An adult Cockchafer lives for four to five weeks, but its development takes three to four years, while the adult Stag Beetle, which lives roughly the same length of time, takes three to five years, and often longer, to develop. In insects which develop during the season of vegetation growth, however, often in several generations, the duration of the imago's active life can be the same as that of its pre-imaginal development. In other cases, the imago may live much longer than it took to develop; the ground beetle *Calosoma sycophanta,* known as the Searcher or Caterpillar Hunter, develops in only a few months, but the imago lives for up to three years. Many weevils likewise live for much longer than they take to develop.

Ants appear to live the longest. The workers of the widespread species *Formica fusca* are said to live for eight years and those of the species *Camponotus ligniperda* for up to thirteen years. The queens of *Lasius niger,* one of the most common ant species, actually live for as long as fifteen years. Some termite queens are said to live for 50 years!

Life and habits

Social insects

The organisation of social insects is one of the most interesting aspects of insect life. The insects concerned co-exist in a colony, which is also called a state. Insect states are a specific characteristic of hymenopteran insects (bees, wasps, ants) and otherwise occur only among termites which are totally unrelated to hymenopterans. The size of the colonies, the manner in which the nests are built and the way in which the inmates live all differ, but they do have one thing in common: the state is headed by a single female (mother, queen) whose presence is of primary importance to the whole colony.

In addition to the mother who 'runs' the state and is the only fertilised female, the state mainly comprises workers (undeveloped females) and, in a given phase of its existence, males. The female, males and workers differ in regard to their form, size and colouring. These three types are to be found in the Honeybee and in bumblebees and wasps. In some species of ants, however, and especially among termites, the heteromorphism of the inhabitants of a single state is even greater. In such states we frequently find individuals with a large head equipped with huge mandibles or some other awesome device; these are known as 'soldiers', although the definition is not altogether exact.

In a great many cases the queen is the mother of all the members of the state. In some ant species, however, where the nest contains more than one queen, the organisation of the state is rather more complex.

The wasp state can be used as an example for a concise demonstration of how such a state is built, how it lives and how it becomes extinct. A wasp community, like a bumblebee community, stays together for a single season, whereas Honeybee and ant communities persist for years. After successfully surviving the winter, the young wasp queen looks for a suitable place to start building a nest in the spring. One of the easiest wasps to observe at work is the Tree Wasp (*Dolichovespula*), since it likes to nest in attics, wooden outhouses and garages, etc. The queen finds a piece of old wood, grates it up with her mandibles and mixes it with her saliva, forming a paper bead with which she begins to build the stalk of the nest. In the same way she sticks together a few cells of the first comb and builds part of the protective envelope round them. The cells are regularly hexagonal and in each of them the female places one egg. Up to this point the queen has had only herself to look after, but now she has new duties, since she will soon have to feed the first larvae, which she must rear in order to have workers to build and maintain the nest. The larvae grow quickly and pupate in their cells. After a few workers have appeared in the nest, the mother-queen stops working and settles down to laying eggs. The workers enlarge and look after the nest, feed the larvae, regulate the temperature, remove waste matter and take care of security measures. The peak period of development of the nest is characterised by the hatching of the young queens and the males. The end of the state is now not very far away. One of the reasons for its destruction is that wasps do not know how to lay in stores for the winter. The end of the state is accompanied by the death of the workers, the males and the old queen; fertilised young females are the only survivors. A wasp kingdom can be regarded as a perfect example of a peaceful state. Unlike bees, which throw their males out of the nest and kill them, wasps allow their males to shelter in the nest until they die a natural death.

Some wasps, such as *Vespula austriaca*, lack the building instinct and do not build a nest. Having no nest and no workers, they provide for their offspring by 'hi-jacking' another wasp nest. This wasp enters a nest that has already been built and contains a sufficient number of workers. It often kills the queen and takes over the task of laying the eggs itself. It lays these in waiting cells and the workers then tend the larvae just as conscientiously as those of their own species. As the larvae of the intruder begin to preponderate, however, the number of the original larvae steadily dwindles. Eventually the original workers also die, but by then their services are no longer needed, since the offspring of the 'cuckoo' wasp are already adult. Before the winter sets in, the males of the 'cuckoo' usurper wasp die and the young females, after overwintering, try to assure the future of their offspring in the same way they themselves were reared. Bumblebees also play host to such guests – the parasitic members of the genus *Psithyrus* likewise let their larvae be reared by other bumblebees.

The way in which ants live, found their colonies and build their nests is different from that of wasps and bees. The nest is far from being as perfectly built as the nest of a wasp or a bee, but is rather more a system of chambers and connecting passages. The building material – conifer needles, fragments of twigs, soil and occasionally wood – is also totally different. Here again, a new colony is founded by a queen. In some species, she finds a suitable place herself, settles in, lays her eggs, rears the first workers and thus actually founds the colony. The females of many species are unable to do this, however, and enter existing nests of their own species, where they are usually adopted without fuss as additional queens. It is not uncommon for ant nests to contain several queens. Other species, however, 'set up house' in the same way as cuckoo wasps and bumblebees, by entering nests belonging to other species of ants. A female entering the nest of a different species must fight, as a rule, for the occupation of the nest. When she has disposed of the original queen, she begins to lay eggs and the original occupants of the nest feed the larvae of the intruder for a time, until they die themselves.

The offspring of this intruder are a little different, however, from those of cuckoo wasps and bumblebees, which consist only of males and females; the first ants to be born are workers and the males and females come later. One of the species most frequently attacked is the large, black slave ant, *Formica fusca*, whose nest is doomed to certain destruction by the arrival of a usurper. The Amazon Ant (*Polyergus rufescens*) does not know how to build a nest, feed its offspring or even itself, so the female usually founds a new colony in an existing slave ant colony. She invades the colony, kills the queen, takes over the nest and begins to lay eggs. For a time the original inhabitants look after the larvae, but eventually they die. The Amazon Ants then go raiding other slave ant nests, where they steal further pupae. The carnage is terrible, as the heads and bodies of the slave ants are crushed by the powerful mandibles of the Amazon Ants. The latters' nests usually contain several more slaves than slave drivers. When workers emerge from pupae they set to work to look after the Amazon Ants.

We cannot describe life in insect states without mentioning termites. Termites are in no way related to ants (as, distinct from ants, they develop by incomplete metamorphosis), although they are popularly known as 'white ants'. Termites have the biggest nests of all social insects and the number of their inhabitants is immense. The most perfect termite nest is described as 'concentric', because the living quarters are in the centre and are surrounded by protective layers. The most important part of the intricate termite nest is the royal chamber. As a rule there is only one such chamber in the colony and its only occupants are the queen and the king. The queen's body grows bulkier and bulkier as the size of her fat body and the number of eggs inside her increase. In the end, she is so huge that even if she wished she could not leave the chamber through any of the connecting passages used by the workers and all she can do is lie in the dark chamber and lay eggs. The workers carry the eggs away to convenient places and look after the newly hatched larvae.

Some termite nests are subterranean or tunnelled into timber. Other nests are built as towering mounds rising to a height of 4–6 m (13–20 ft); the builder-inhabitants themselves are only a few millimetres long. Let us compare their architectural achievements with those of twentieth-century man. Assuming that the average length of one termite is 1 cm ($\frac{3}{8}$ in) (we have made it just a little longer than it really is), the height of the average mound is 400–600 times greater. Since a human being is about 170 times longer than a termite, our tallest buildings would have to measure 1,000 m (3,280 ft) or more to compete. Despite the existence of skyscrapers, we shall have to wait a long time for buildings like that.

Care of offspring

The notion of the care of offspring is mainly associated with the care of children (in humans), kittens, puppies and other animals in which parental care is visible. It is also to be found in insects, however, though in a less obvious form. In some species (and even whole groups) it is actually highly developed. True, insect parents do not generally see the birth of the next generation, but sometimes the females do not die until after the appearance of the young imagos.

Care of the offspring is most highly developed in social insects, but other hymenopterans, as well as the social bees, wasps and ants, also display a high degree of parental care.

Some potter wasps are remarkably clever builders. Their creations are not random constructions, but are 'cells' destined for the rearing of larvae. Before laying an egg, the potter wasp (genus *Eumenes*) looks for a suitable site for the 'cell' – generally on a plant, but sometimes on a rock. The wasp bites up pieces of earth, mixes

them with saliva and flies to the chosen site with them. Here it sticks them together, piece by piece, until it has formed a receptacle resembling an ancient Greek water-pot. It gives this a narrow neck, makes a round opening, suspends an egg inside it and goes in search of small caterpillars. The wasp paralyses the caterpillars with its sting, but does not kill them; it then carries them back to the 'cell' and seals the opening. Cuckoo wasps (genus *Chrysis*) also need to assure the future of their offspring, but lack the building talents of potter wasps, and so while the latter are away hunting, they quickly lay their eggs in the neck of the still open 'cells' or 'pots'. The cuckoo wasp larva devours the food prepared for the potter wasp larva and it is therefore a cuckoo wasp that later emerges from the 'cell'.

Digger wasps (genus *Ammophila*) likewise provide for their offspring, but in a different manner. First of all they dig a nest in the ground and then fly in search of a suitable caterpillar as a source of food for the future larva. They stun their prey with their sting, but do not kill it, and then carry it back to the nest, crawl inside and slowly pull the caterpillar in after them. Once the caterpillar is inside, they place an egg on it and then seal and disguise the entrance to the nest. With this, their parental duties are at an end.

A few species of sand wasps (genus *Bembix*) belonging to the same family (Sphecidae) as the genus *Ammophila* carry care of their offspring still further. They also nest in the ground, but keep the larvae constantly supplied with fresh food.

Beetle wasps (family Scoliidae) do not do nearly so much for the future generation as digger wasps, but the manner of their care is nevertheless quite interesting. It consists primarily in the finding and stunning of suitable larvae on which their own larvae can feed. Beetle wasps have a fairly specialised choice of prey. *Scolia maculata* look for nice fat Rhinoceros Beetle (*Oryctes nasicornis*) grubs on which to lay eggs, but since the number of Rhinoceros Beetles is diminishing, this beetle wasp is also an endangered and dying species. *Scolia quadripunctata* is less particular in its choice of prey and is content with the larvae of various lamellicorn beetles belonging to the genera *Anoxia, Anomala, Anisoplia, Epicometis* and *Oxythyrea* and to the chafer genera *Cetonia* and *Liocola*. Many of these hosts are still abundant, so this species is not endangered.

Ichneumon flies, braconids, chalcids and many others provide the new generation with suitable conditions. With them also, the finding of a suitable host, its immobilisation and the laying of eggs are the sole features of parental care. After that they are on their own.

Among hymenopterans, the chief form of parental care is feeding the larvae. Beetles provide their offspring with food of both vegetable and animal origin. Parental care among beetles is also many-sided; it is manifested in assuring the safety of the eggs and larvae, guarding and feeding the larvae and (in exceptional cases) in the care of the entire development from the egg to the young beetle.

One of the simplest forms of care for the next generation is the choice of a suitable place where the larvae will find sufficient food. Examples of this are innumerable. Aphidivorous ladybirds lay their eggs where there are sufficient aphids, while bark beetles lay them in suitable wood.

The eggs may be covered with a protective film, or enclosed in a variety of sheaths made of native or exogenous material. Water scavenger beetles (superfamily Hydrophiloidea) form only protective egg capsules. The female of the species *Spercheus emarginatus* weaves a basket for her eggs, which she carries on the underside of her abdomen until the larvae are hatched. The basket is normally visible, but if disturbed the female can tuck it out of sight under her abdomen with her hindlegs. Other water scavenger beetles give themselves less trouble with the eggs. The female weaves a silken cocoon, lays the eggs in it, seals it with fluffy webbing and lets the cocoon float freely on the water.

One of the highest forms of care of the offspring is known among burying (sexton) beetles, although it was by no means easy to study. Burying beetles look for small animal carcases (mice, shrews, moles, etc.) and bury them in the ground. They knead the decomposing carcase into a ball and the female then lays her eggs underground, along the sides of a maternal passage near this unsavoury lump of food. When she has finished, she returns to the food ball, bites a hole in the tip and releases digestive juices into it. She

sucks up the resultant liquid (she feeds perorally) and when she is full she closes up the hole. Just before the larvae are hatched, the female runs repeatedly along the maternal passage and her odour enables the larvae to make their way to the carcase (she also removes from the passage any fragments on which the larvae might injure themselves). The hungry larvae collect on the carcase, the fronts of their bodies held erect, and try, one after the other, to obtain a drop of brown liquid from the female's mouth. After a few hours she stops feeding them, because by then they are able to feed themselves, but after moulting they will need to be fed again and are not completely independent until they are fully grown. They penetrate the carcase, where they lie close together, side by side, and secrete drops of digestive juice which decompose the carcase tissues. The action of a large number of drops released simultaneously hastens the decomposition and liquefaction of the carcase. After seven days of larval development they pupate.

Leaf-roller beetles (Attelabidae) have a very practical way of providing for their eggs and larvae. From one or a few leaves they form a beautifully made capsule and in this they lay the eggs. Some of these species are rare, but the Birch Leaf Roller (*Deporaus betulae*) is common everywhere. Its cases, which are to be found mainly on birches, are made by the female, but before she actually begins, she closely inspects the size and quality of the leaf. When she has made her choice, she bites an S-shaped curve from the edge of the leaf to the primary vein, where she stops, damages the vein and then cuts her way to the opposite side. When the leaf has withered a little, the beetle twists the lower and larger part into a cornet-shaped roll, in which she lays only two eggs. She does not place the eggs directly onto the leaf, but makes incisions in the cuticle and lays each egg in the resultant pockets. The eggs are protected on one side by the leaf tissues, from above by the cuticle, and in addition by the capsule. The curve made in the leaf is not always the same and depends on the length and width of the leaf; how the beetle manages to estimate its cuts accurately is more than remarkable. It would never be able to make a capsule from a badly cut leaf.

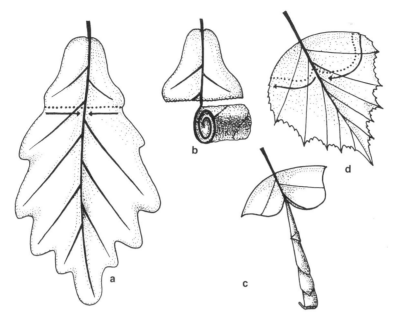

Construction of a leaf-capsule by different leaf rollers (family Attelabidae): a–b *Attelabus nitens*, c–d *Deporaus betulae*. Arrows indicate the direction in which the female cuts the leaf.

Other leaf-rollers do not cut the leaf, but make a capsule in other ways. The female Vine Leaf Roller (*Byctiscus betulae*) bites the petiole to impair the water circulation. A few hours later, when the blade has started to wither, the female twists in into a tubular roll, held together by secretion.

Weevils, which were classified until quite recently in the same family as leaf-rollers, are likewise endowed with the instinct of forming a shelter for the eggs and choosing a satisfactory environment for the larvae. They are not as skilful or inventive as leaf-rollers, however. The female *Furcipus rectirostris* bores a small canal in a young cherry, lays an egg in it and seals the opening with secretion. *Anthonomus rubi* has an entirely different method. It looks for a bud of a strawberry, raspberry, blackberry or some other rosaceous plant, lays a single egg in it, seals the puncture hole and then bites an incision in the stem. The bud containing the developing larva does not flower, but shrivels and drops to the ground, where the larva pupates inside it.

The parental care of dung beetles (genera *Geotrupes, Onthophagus*, etc.) is very varied, but is based on a single principle. The beetles excavate tunnels which they fill with mammals' excrement. Each tunnel has several chambers and the beetles lay one egg on the food store in each

chamber, sealing the entrance with earth or excrement. In the ground the eggs are safe and the larvae have more food than they can consume. Related species have truly exceptional

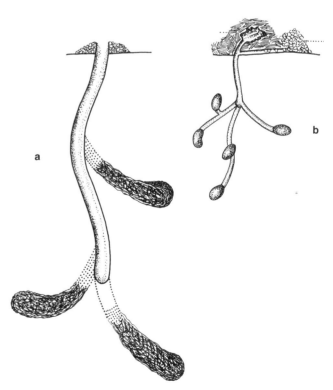

Scheme of subterranean nests of lamellicornian beetles: a – *Geotrupes stercorarius* (family Geotrupidae), b – *Onthophagus nuchicornis* (family Scarabaeidae)

parental care. These are the members of the genus *Copris,* which care for the new generation from the egg to the emergence of the young beetle. Unlike other scarabaeids, which excavate several nests, *Copris* species are content with just one, a small underground cavern in which the whole of their family life takes place. In the summer, the male, together with the female, brings dung to the nest and the female kneads this into several pear-shaped lumps. In the top of each lump she makes a small chamber in which she places an egg. The female remains on guard in the nest and looks after the larvae developing in the dung. She stays in the nest until the young beetles emerge and only leaves it when they do.

Earwigs are surrounded by a web of superstition, but little is known about their actual care of the eggs. The female lays them in an underground chamber, but does not abandon them. She stays near them, guards them from other hungry animals, licks them to rid them of fungal spores, removes any that may be dead and survives long enough not only to see the hatching of the larvae, but to clean and feed the offspring for quite a while.

Maternal care of offspring among bugs is the exception rather than the rule, but *Elasmucha ferrugata* tends both the eggs and the nymphs. The female lays eggs on a bilberry leaf or on the leaf of a birch or some other deciduous tree, and then literally sits on them. When the nymphs hatch, she still protects them with her body until they are independent and can crawl away.

One more group of insects is characterised by very practical care of their eggs. These are the scale insects. Females, which lead a sessile existence under a waxy and chitinous shell, also lay their eggs there – they actually have no choice, as they are legless and incapable of active movement (e.g. Diaspididae). The females of the family Coccidae are also sessile by the time they lay their eggs. Many of them lay the eggs beneath their bodies, which become increasingly convex and provide the eggs with a safe shelter. Ensign coccids (Ortheziidae) have developed the highest degree of care of their eggs. At the tip of their abdomens they form an ovisac (egg-sac) made of fine white waxy fibres and in this they carry the eggs about with them until the nymphs hatch.

Insects on plants

Insect life without plants is just as unimaginable as plant life without insects. Although immensely important, pollination is only one aspect of the relationship between insects and plants. (Pollinators will be discussed in detail on page 37.) Plants are a source of food for the imagos and young of many species; this applies chiefly to phytophagous insects, of course, but also to omnivorous species, and even, in individual cases, to carnivorous (predacious) insects. Some insects bite off pieces of plant tissue, others suck their juices. Some favour the leaves, others live on or in the roots, while for many the fruit, seeds, pollen or nectar are the important part. Many like their plant food fresh, but others prefer it dry or processed in some way. Sap flowing from a damaged trunk or branch can be a special delicacy and many insects will spend a long time at its source. Species which feed on the juices, pollen or tissues of a plant are not the only visitors, however. Many insects come to catch phytophagous insects and to lay their eggs. Ladybirds and their larvae, neuropterans, soldier beetles, searcher beetles and many others hunt aphids, scale insects and caterpillars on plants, while crickets, mantids and many hymenopterans and dipterans lie in wait on plants for other insects.

If we look below the bark or inside the wood of coniferous and deciduous trees, we find that they are also full of life and that the insect-plant and insect-versus-insect relationship applies here, in the dark, just as much as in the light of day. Small imagos, which live on fine wood debris and on destructive fungi beneath the bark, are, in turn, often the prey of species which prefer animal tissues. The space between the bark and the wood is occupied by a rich selection of the larvae of longhorn beetles, metallic woodborers, bark beetles and weevils and a great many small dipteran larvae living on wood debris. Many of them leave clearly discernible traces of their activity and the patterns made by their tunnels are often a clue to their identity. Hunters are also to be found here, the most frequent being the pink grubs of the Ant Beetle (*Thanasimus formicarius*), the flat larvae of cardinal beetles (Pyrochroidae) and snakefly and rove beetle larvae, together with many others. The larvae of some insects live for a time beneath the bark and later invade the wood (longhorn beetles), or live deeper in the wood (horntails, stag beetles, etc.).

Many insects specialise in fungi and various kinds of rotting organic matter, where they spend the whole or part of their lives, or simply visit to look for food. Many beetle and fly larvae are closely associated with fungi and even hymenopterans have manifold relationships to them. Some larvae have a preference for tree fungi. These often swarm with hundreds of tiny beetle larvae belonging to the fungus-eating family Cisidae, but may also contain other beetle larvae (Staphylinidae, Melandryidae, Scaphidiidae, etc.). Other species live in the soft fruit bodies of mushrooms. The minute legless, worm-like larvae of the fungus gnats (Mycetophilidae family) can reduce various kinds of fungi practically to a liquid mess. The soft fungal tissues often contain large numbers of rove beetles, many of which devour the hyphae (the fungal fibres), but others then come for the consumers of the fibres! Puffballs have their own characteristic inhabitants. The members of the Endomychidae family are now rare, but *Pocadius ferrugineus,* which belongs to the sap-beetle family (Nitidulidae), is still quite common.

The relationship of insects to fungi is sometimes concealed from sight. The females of some insects whose larvae live in wood lay their eggs with the spores of fungi which then proliferate in the passages excavated by the larvae. Being unable to digest cellulose, the larvae live on the mycelium of the fungi. This fungus-insect relationship is known in *Hylecoetus dermestoides,* in some bark beetles (Scolytidae) and in big wood wasps *(Sirex juvencus).* Some ants also have a hidden, but strong relationship to fungi, which they cultivate in their nests as a delicacy.

At given times, various tumours, outgrowths, bulges and swellings appear on many plants. They are particularly conspicuous on oaks and briars. These structures, known as galls, are produced by the plant itself, but their formation is stimulated by an insect. The main agents are gall wasps, gall-midges and gall-forming aphids, but they are not the only ones.

The gall is a neoplasm which begins to develop when the eggs hatch. Very often this is on the blade of a leaf, bud, petiole, stalk or root. The plant's tissues, injured and irritated by the presence of the egg, begin to proliferate; the cells rapidly multiply and the gall gradually acquires its definitive shape. Meanwhile, the larva hatches inside it and devours its tissue. The larva moults, grows and pupates in the gall, which is eventually abandoned by the imago. The gall wasp, *Diastrophus rubi,* whose striking galls are formed on the axis (less often on the petioles) of raspberry canes and brambles, develops in this simple manner. The gall, which can measure 8 cm (3 in) or more, contains a large number of chambers, in each of which a larva develops. The development of many gall wasps is very complicated, however. Those which live on oaks develop by metagenesis, i.e. by the regular alternation of non-sexual (agamous or only female) generations with sexual generations. In some gall wasp species each generation develops on a different part of the same host plant (e.g. one on the leaves and the next on the flowers, etc.). With other gall wasps, each generation develops on a different host plant.

In addition to oak galls, spindle-shaped galls are to be found on beech trees almost everywhere. These are green and red and there are generally several on one leaf; they house the larvae of the tiny gall-midge *Mikiola fagi* (family Cecidomyiidae).

Many aphids also form galls, some of which are large and striking.

Beetles also form striking galls. The larva of the longhorn beetle, *Saperda populnea,* which lives in a young poplar branch, irritates the tissue until it proliferates and forms a swelling. The amount of tissue formed is sometimes so great that the larva is unable to eat it all and is crushed to death.

Communication between insects

Insects can communicate with each other. We do not know exactly how this is done, how they hear it, but research has discovered that they can communicate by sound, dance, contact, the secretion of pheromones (specific odours) and by light signals.

The sounds emitted by insects are familiar to everybody. Insects can drum, hum, stridulate and squeak and some of their sounds are so typical and loud that even our own imperfect hearing can distinguish them.

Stridulation is produced by two parts of the body being rubbed together. Quite often it is only the males that stridulate, but sometimes the females and even the larvae are able to do so. Stridulation is often used by the male to entice the female, or by the female to summon the larvae (sexton beetles).

Crickets and grasshoppers are particularly famous for their stridulation. They never seem to tire and without their concerts the whole of the Mediterranean region would lose its character. The crickets have special stridulation organs at the base of their front wings and the two parts move against each other like scissors cutting in the horizontal plane. Locusts and short-horned grasshoppers make sounds by rubbing the teeth along the inner surface of their tibiae against prominent veins on their front wings. Bugs, beetles, hymenopterans and others are also able to stridulate. The 'song' of cicadas is produced by the vibration of membranes stretched over the underside of their first abdominal segment; it can be compared to the result of rapid repeated pressure on the bottom of a tin can.

It is vitally essential for social insects to be able to distinguish the members of their own colony from enemies. For this they need pheromones, odours specific to each nest. The ability to communicate is most highly developed in the Honeybee. Bees returning to the hive from the fields perform a dance to inform their companions that they have found a good supply of food. The type of dance tells the other bees how far and in which direction they have to fly. Bees have a very complex language. In addition to dances they have various signals which relate to the situation in the hive. In the event of danger, the guards emit short signals and the inhabitants of the hive prepare against an attack. When the danger has passed, they emit a different tone and the excitement subsides. This series of events can be compared to an air-raid warning followed by an all-clear signal.

Ants communicate partly by means of their antennae, but chiefly by means of the secretions of their scent glands, i.e. pheromones. Worker ants which have found prey too big for them to carry away themselves mark the way to it by short-acting pheromones, and other workers come hurrying along to help to drag the precious burden back to the nest.

The ability to emit light is yet another means of communication. In Europe there are only a few luminescent species, such as the glow-worm and the firefly; the majority live in the tropics. The remarkable feature of insect light signals is that all the energy is converted to light and not to heat.

In principle, all insects have the possibility of communicating in some way with their own kind; we have succeeded in deciphering a few words and phrases from their language, but there is still much that we do not know.

Insects' faculties

During the past few decades we have gained a new and unprecedented insight into the insect world and have come to realise just how efficiently insect life is organised. Insects are able to care for their offspring, lay in food reserves (honey, fungi) and produce wax, shellac, dyes and silken threads. Insects are also the oldest paper manufacturers. Wasps and hornets chew up old wood, mix it with saliva and stick it together to make a nest which is one of the most remarkable insect creations. Wood concrete, another insect invention, is used by termites when building their nests. Insects can also make mortar without having to use cement; they moisten pieces of earth with their saliva and stick them together in the form of a pot or tubular extension.

Insects were the first to practise anaesthesia. As we have already seen in the example of digger wasps, various hymenopterans place insect larvae, imagos and even spiders in their nests as food for their larvae. They cannot simply dump them in the nest, however, because they would be able to escape. The wasp therefore gives its prey an 'injection', in a dose which makes any active movement impossible. The paralysed larvae do not die, but remain fresh until they are eaten by the wasp larvae. In other words, they are temporarily preserved. Many other insects also paralyse their hosts, since this is the only way of keeping them fresh until the larvae need them.

Number of species and their distribution

We need only look at one or two books to see the variety of figures given by different authors for the number of insects in the world in general, and in local faunas in particular. The differences run into hundreds of thousands. Some authors put the world insect population at about one million species, others put the figure much higher. However, as many parts of the world have not yet been fully investigated, future research will certainly add to the existing number of known species. This applies especially to small insects like thrips, aphids, coccids, plant-hoppers, jumping plant lice, parasitic wasps and small flies. If we double the present estimate by adding the same number of hitherto undiscovered, but presumed species, we come to the result that our planet is inhabited by about two million different species of insects, and even this is too low a figure.

Regardless of which estimates are correct, insects are unquestionably numerically the largest class of animals and comprise over 80 per cent of all the known animal species.

On a worldwide scale, the numerically largest order is the beetles, with 350,000–400,000 species, followed by moths and butterflies, with about 150,000 species. The number of hymenopterans already exceeds 100,000, and dipterans, which are now being studied intensively all over the world, have already crossed the 85,000 mark. Heteroptera and Homoptera together number over 70,000 species and Orthoptera over 15,000 species. Conversely, some orders have very few species, such as Grylloblattodea (just over 10 species), snakeflies (150 species), web-spinners (about 200 species) and sucking lice, over 400 species of which are known today.

This number of species applies to the world in general, and not to smaller territorial units. The numbers of species given for central Europe will not be the same throughout the whole of that territory, since even a relatively small area like central Europe is composed of many different types of country. Similarly, the four biggest insect orders are the numerically largest in central Europe, but are in a different sequence than for the world as a whole. First come the hymenopterans, which have not been studied equally thoroughly everywhere, so that their number is put at roughly 11,000–14,000. Next come the dipterans which until recently have been studied very inadequately. New discoveries in recent years have raised the number of their species to 8,000. Beetles, which in the world in general stand in first place, must be content with third place in the central European insect fauna; they are reckoned to number about 7,000 species. The number of lepidopteran species (moths and butterflies) is over 3,000. Of the remaining orders, only Homoptera have over 2,000 species and Heteroptera almost 1,000 species. The other orders are represented by only a few single, a few dozen or a few hundred species. The order Mantodea is represented in central Europe by only one species – the Praying Mantis (*Mantis religiosa*) – and there are a few orders which have no representatives here, such as the webspinners (Embioptera), whose nearest species occur in the Balkans and the Mediterranean region.

Important zoogeographical regions

During their long evolution, insects have succeeded in colonising practically the whole of the globe. The majority of species, with the most splendid forms and colours and the biggest sizes, inhabit the tropics, where conditions for their development are exceptionally favourable. But insects have also penetrated far to the north and south, and a small number of species have even adapted themselves to the grim climate of the Arctic and Antarctic.

Some insects have managed to adapt themselves to the most diverse conditions and have therefore been able to spread over practically the whole of the globe. The majority of species, however, require a given type of country and climate and do not prosper elsewhere.

To give us a better idea of how animals are distributed, the earth has been divided into seven zoogeographical regions, each of which contains some typical species which do not occur anywhere else.

The biggest area is the Palaearctic region, which covers roughly the whole of Europe (as far as the North Pole), northern Africa, Asia Minor and the Middle East, the northern part of the Arabian peninsula, Soviet Asia, China, Korea and Japan. It is spread over the temperate and subtropical climatic belts and has four subregions. The Eurosiberian subregion occupies the northern part of Eurasia; the Mediterranean subregion is the part round the Mediterranean Sea; the Central Asia subregion comprises Soviet central Asia, Afghanistan, a large part of Iran, Mongolia, Tibet and north-western China; the East Palaearctic subregion lies over the territory of Japan, Korea, the basin of the River Amur, the Pacific coast of China and the southern slopes of the Himalayas. Although it does not possess any gigantic insects, the Palaearctic region is inhabited by many economically important species.

The Nearctic region covers North America and the adjacent islands to the north, including Greenland, and extends in the south to central

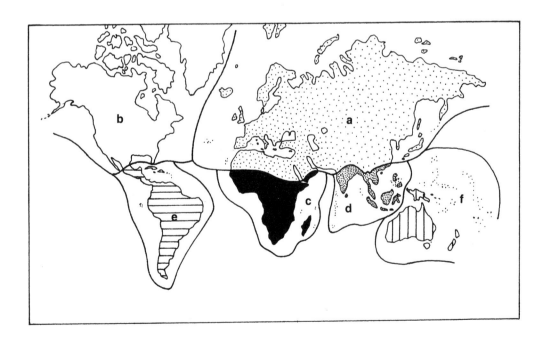

Map of the zoogeographical regions: a – Palaearctic; b – Nearctic; c – Ethiopian (Africa); d – Oriental; e – Neotropical; f – Australian

Mexico. Its fauna closely resembles the Palaearctic fauna and the two regions are often joined together in a single region known as the Holarctic region.

The Neotropical region spreads over South and Central America and the Greater and Lesser Antilles; in the north it extends into central Mexico, where it borders on the Nearctic region. It is a region of large insect species, including the biggest beetles in existence (*Dynastes hercules, Titanus giganteus, Macrodontia cervicornis*), and giant lepidopterans, among them *Thysania agrippina,* the biggest moth. It is the home of the handsome, brilliant blue or bluish-violet butterflies of the genus *Morpho*. There is still a great deal of work awaiting entomologists in this region.

The Australian region comprises the Australian continent, New Guinea, Tasmania, New Zealand, Oceania and also, perhaps, the Hawaiian Islands. With regard to its ancient and remarkable fauna, it is divided into several subregions. One of the typical inhabitants of Australia is the termite *Amitermes meridionalis,* which makes 'compass' nests.

The Oriental, or Indomalaysian region stretches from India across Malaysia and Indonesia. In the north it is bounded by the southern slopes of the Himalayas and in China by the tropic of Cancer. Despite its small extent, its insect fauna is unique and is characterised by large beetles belonging to families such as Lucanidae, Scarabaeidae and Buprestidae, and by gigantic, brightly coloured swallowtails and other butterflies.

The African or Ethiopian region covers the African continent south of the tropic of Cancer and the southern part of the Arabian peninsula. It is characterised by an exceptionally rich assortment of insects, including the remarkable Goliath beetles, swallowtail butterflies and longhorn beetles.

The Madagascar region is usually taken to be part of the Ethiopian region, but is coming to be increasingly regarded as a separate region.

The importance of insects

Insects have a far-reaching effect on people for they play a vital role in nature. However, they are not always properly understood by the public at large. Many people fail to see, or do not want to see, the complexity and extent of the natural cycle, in which everything has its appointed place, including insects.

According to tradition, insects are usually judged by their relationship to people and are thus described as useful, valuable, harmful or indifferent.

From time to time, insect activities have a detrimental effect in spheres which humans consider to be their own, from fields, forests and gardens, to nurseries, shops and even works of art. Insects appear here in the role of pests.

The extent of the damage done by insects is varied, but depends on the severity of our criteria. While many species really are dangerous pests which we would like to wipe out, there are very many other species which do a certain amount of damage, but not enough to justify the use of drastic poisons whose effects, in a roundabout way, often eventually recoil on us.

A great many species do damage in both the imaginal and the larval form. For instance, the larvae of bark beetles excavate passages in trees below the bark and the imagos nibble the young bark itself. The larvae and imagos of the Colorado beetle both live on the leaf tissues of potato plants. All stages of aphids, jumping plant lice, coccids, white flies and cicadas also suck plant tissues. Thrips are similar pests and their appearance on vegetables and flowers is always a danger signal.

Quite often, however, only the larvae are the guilty party and the imagos are either indifferent or actually useful. This is the case with some lepidopterans. Moth caterpillars are unpleasant and dreaded pests of textiles, flour and other foodstuffs in households (e.g. Tineidae and Pyralidae species), but the adult moths are indifferent. Adult death watch beetles are likewise harmless, but their larvae do irreparable damage to wooden floors and ceilings, furniture, picture frames, doorposts, valuable wooden carvings and old altars. A series of successive generations can turn the inside of a wooden structure into crumbling yellow sawdust. Cabbage White and other pierid caterpillars can be pests in some places, but the adult butterflies are useful pollinators.

Insects whose larvae are in general indifferent, but whose imagos do damage, form another, smaller group. As an example we can cite the Garden Chafer (*Phyllopertha horticola*), whose larvae live in the ground and feed on the rootlets of plants, while the imagos nibble plant tissues themselves, including the petals of flowers. This is particularly annoying for flower gardeners.

Insects pests are to be found practically everywhere and have accompanied human activities and culture since time immemorial. Many of them are prominent forest pests. Some are specialised and frequent only a given type of forest, or require trees of a particular age. The most dangerous are species which used to cause, and in some places still do, calamities. The chief culprits are the Gipsy Moth (*Lymantria dispar*) and the Engraver Beetle (*Ips typographus*). The Green Oak Tortrix Moth (*Tortrix viridana*), certain sawflies (Tenthredinidae) and beetles (other bark beetles, weevils and perhaps occasionally longhorn beetles) and homopterans (chiefly aphids) are less serious and more local pests. The fight against them is costly and difficult and with chemical weapons there is always the danger that useful insects will also be affected.

Fields are an artificial habitat and their pests are therefore more or less specialised for a given type of crop. Cornfields, beet fields, rape fields and other cultures each have their own pests. The best known of these are locusts and the Colorado beetle, which infests potato fields. Aphids are also very serious crop pests, for they cause diseases as well as simply taking sap.

Gardens and parks, which are artificial habitats, have a wider range of pests. Today, orchards are frequently infested by *Tortrix* species and other small moths and by aphids, jumping plant lice, some weevils (*Anthonomus, Fur-*

cipus), sawflies and a few species of dipterans (e.g. *Rhagoletis cerasi*). The main pests of kitchen gardens are aphids, thrips, pierid caterpillars, small weevils and a few dipterans, while in flower gardens the commonest pests are aphids; most to suffer are roses, but other plants are not exempt. Roses are also attacked by sawflies, and bulbous plants are frequently plagued by thrips.

Insect pests also affect households, where they find a sufficient amount of all kinds of food, warmth and damp. The commonest are the larvae of small moths (clothes moths, flour moths) and various small beetles and their larvae; even cockroaches are still to be seen occasionally. Many species are omnivorous and have no difficulty in finding food. Modern housing estates often provide satisfactory conditions for Pharaoh ants (*Monomorium pharaonis*). Many of the pests which annoy us at home are also to be found in foodstores, mills, bakeries and hotels.

Personally vexatious insects deserve a mention too. They are generally found among the two-winged insects. In the summer we are plagued by mosquitoes. They seem to be everywhere. The female settles on our skin, stabs it with her proboscis, drinks the blood and can completely spoil our day, especially if we are in forests or beside water. The males ignore us and merely sip nectar from the flowers, while the larvae live in water and are a welcome titbit for aquatic animals, especially fish; in this way, the larvae are useful and even important. Horse-flies are another scourge of both people and animals. Being considerably larger than mosquitoes, they have a correspondingly larger consumption of blood. They approach their victims almost inaudibly and are particularly greedy just before a thunderstorm. As with mosquitoes, it is only the females which suck blood. Black-flies and stable-flies are likewise unpleasant insects.

From tormentors to parasites is only a small step. The latter are always to be found in contact with humans and although there are immeasurably fewer of them than the tormentors, they have a very long and colourful history. Our main parasites are lice, bugs and fleas. Some species are more or less specialised for a particular host, others display a fine impartiality. Fleas, which jump and are able to go for long periods without nourishment, suck blood. When they stab a victim with their proboscis, toxic substances are released into the person's blood stream, causing itching and a red swelling at the site of the stab. Fleas can transmit various diseases and rat fleas were formerly noted for the spread of *Pasteurella pestis,* the causative agent of plague. Bugs, such as bedbugs, are also blood-suckers. They live together with people and possess a number of properties which enable them to survive under unfavourable conditions. Lice are limited in their movements. They hang on to a hair by a claw, lacerate the skin and suck their host's blood. Various pathogens enter the host through the wound, so that lice have also earned themselves a bad name in the history of human disease.

Many insects can be classified as useful, however. Their usefulness takes diverse forms, but pollinators and certain predators can be regarded as useful species.

In nature, nothing can take the place of pollinators. Insects are attracted by the scent and sweet juices of flowers and by the colour of their petals. They visit the flowers, not to pollinate them, but to satisfy their hunger and thirst with pollen and nectar. As they fly from flower to flower, they carry pollen from the anthers of one flower to the stigma of another. In this way the insects eat their fill and the plant can be sure of bearing fruit. Some insects drink only as much nectar and take only as many grains of pollen as they need for their immediate requirements, but social insects – such as bees – lay in stores for a rainy day and as food for their offspring. There are many insect pollinators, but the majority are hymenopterans. The originally biting mouthparts of these insects have been variously adapted for sucking nectar and there are hairs on the body to which the pollen grains can adhere. Among hymenopterans, the Honeybee, many hundreds of solitary bees and bumblebees have the most highly developed mouthparts. Bumblebees have the longest proboscis and are important pollinators of long, trumpet-shaped flowers for which the Honeybee's proboscis is too short. Pollinators are also to be found in other insect orders, in particular butterflies, two-winged flies and beetles. The long, narrow proboscis of but-

terflies is ideal for collecting nectar and their hairy thorax ensures the transfer of pollen.

The best known pollinators among dipterans are hover-flies, which number several hundred species and appear on flowers and in inflorescences from the spring until very late in the autumn. They chiefly favour composite and umbelliferous plants and at the height of spring and summer several will be found on a single head or umbel. Further fly pollinators include bee-flies, thick-headed flies and March-flies. Several beetles pollinate flowers, including longhorns, many species of which have a small, narrow head making it easy for them to drink nectar and gather pollen. Many rove beetles are also pollinators, as are chafers and numerous related lamellicorn species. Many other insects, which settle on flowers without drinking nectar or collecting pollen, but merely in search of prey, also occasionally act as pollinators.

Another group of insects of great importance in nature are the predators, such as dragonflies, bush crickets, mantids, beetles, hymenopterans, neuropterans and some dipterans. Since they often live entirely on insects which are troublesome to people, they are highly valued. Aphids are frequently the prey of predacious insects, in particular ladybirds and their larvae, soldier beetles, lacewings and hover-fly larvae. These allies of humans do not wipe out the aphids completely, but they do noticeably reduce their numbers. In years in which aphids overmultiply, there is a similar increase in the number of predacious insects. Big ground beetles, caterpillar hunters, large rove beetles, wasps and dragonflies require larger prey; big ground beetles hunt in fields, woods and gardens on the ground and caterpillar hunters climb trees in search of prey. The Fourspot Carrion Beetle (*Xylodrepa quadripunctata*) also hunts caterpillars on trees and shrubs. Big rove beetles run about in debris and old leaves and lurk on decaying vegetable matter and animal organisms. Dragonflies also hunt above water and in forest clearings and wasps seize their prey (mainly flies and mosquitoes) in the air. Some robber-flies lie in wait for prey on felled timber or on tree stumps. Others lurk in flowers or catch their prey on the wing. Typical behaviour is for them to sit in wait and then dart out to catch other insects in mid-air. Some predacious insects do not eat the prey themselves, but use it for rearing the future generation.

We can also include among the useful insects a great many species which help to decompose the bodies of animals and plants. For instance, dung beetles not only live on excrement, but knead it into lumps of food for their larvae. The larvae of hister beetles, carrion beetles and other beetles and the larvae of many flies live in carcases and help to break them down. Sexton beetles look for the carcases of small animals, bury them and convert them to a lump of food to provide nourishment for their larvae. In reference to their activities, these remarkable insects have been nicknamed 'health police'.

The big red ants of the genus *Formica* are extremely important insects in nature. There are several species and all are very similar. They are exceptionally rapacious and snap up any insect, imago or larva within a wide radius around their nest. Since pests form the greater part of their prey, these ants are given every protection, are replaced in localities from which they have disappeared, or are used to colonise completely new localities.

The whole list of useful insects is unquestionably headed by the Honeybee (*Apis mellifera*). Our relationship to the bee has been known for several thousand years. We have tried, and still try, to turn this bee into a 'domestic animal', but when the swarm, together with its queen, leaves the comfort of its manmade hive, we can see that they have kept their independence. The Honeybee provides us with many useful products. Honey is a highly nutritious substance which the bees prepare from nectar, gradually dehydrate and place in the cells of the comb, which they seal with wax, itself another useful bee product. The bees secrete wax for the construction of their combs and people use it in cosmetics and dentistry. Propolis (bee cement) is a mixture of wax and the resin from buds of various trees. It has bactericidal properties and is used in medicine. There is also a demand for bee poison and royal jelly and the pollen collected by bees is processed as a source of vitamins and several other biologically valuable substances.

The Silkworm Moth (*Bombyx mori*) also has a relationship with people going back several thousand years. It is one of the species whose caterpillars secrete silky fibres which they wrap round their bodies to form a cocoon in which they pupate. Silkworms have been bred since about 3000 BC; they were kept in China, where their breeding was a strictly guarded secret. Despite this, some eggs were smuggled out and brought to Europe, where silkworm breeding flourished first in ancient Byzantium and, much later, in France. The caterpillars of saturnid moths also make themselves large cocoons. The two best known species are *Antheraea pernyi* from China and *Antheraea yamamai* from Japan, which also does well in southern Europe.

Honeybees and bumblebees are not the only insects that secrete wax. It is secreted by a great many others, but most significantly by the lac insect, *Ericerus pela*, which lives in China. The male nymph of this coccid secretes a lump of wax the size of a hen's egg. There are usually a large number of nymphs on the host plant and the individual lumps of wax run together to form a thick layer. The wax is used for the production of homemade candles and also in medicine.

The shellac-producing coccids of the family Lacciferidae are likewise useful insects. The majority live in India, others in Africa, Australia and Central America. The thickness of the shellac layer on their bodies varies with the species. Shellac is used for the production of varnishes and insulating materials.

Many insects produce pigments, but the best known group in this respect are coccids. The coccid *Dactylopius coccus*, which lives on cacti in Mexico, is famous as the producer of cochineal.

Very few people in northerly latitudes know that many insects have a place on the bill of fare in the tropics. In places inhabited by termites, the native peoples wait for them to swarm and then catch and roast them. Others eat plump beetle grubs, locusts and caterpillars. Some insects are served as a delicacy.

In the twentieth century human beings have put themselves in the ridiculous situation of being obliged to protect nature and the creatures that co-inhabit the world against our own activities. Human supremacy over nature, so proudly proclaimed until quite recently, has proved to be disastrous for nature and hence for us ourselves.

It is the duty of every civilised country to protect nature, including the insects which are an inseparable part of nature. That is the only way of saving what it is still possible to save. Much has already been destroyed beyond recall. Not so long ago insects were still able to defend themselves successfully against all kinds of enemies, but they are not a match for the greatest enemy of all – people. With modern technology and chemistry, we have often made senseless and dangerous inroads into the balance of nature.

The animate inhabitants of the earth, 80 per cent of which are insect species, represent immense cultural wealth for mankind. That is why scientists catalogue them and keep an account of their incidence and distribution. Records of the numbers of native species are published in the majority of European countries.

In insect protection, attention should be paid primarily to rare, dying and endangered species. Many of these are already protected in theory, but mere protection of a species *per se* is not enough; its habitat and its ecosystem as a whole must also be preserved. Many species are very sensitive to changes in their environment and do not survive them.

The level of insect protection in Europe is not the same everywhere. In some countries it is based on the results of serious scientific study (for instance, in Germany); in others it receives less, or minimal attention. Insect protection requires immediate measures, for we are now watching the disappearance of once common species. Thousands of species are in danger.

Development of zoological nomenclature

Efforts to name and depict insects go back many centuries. The Honeybee was one of the first insects to arouse our interest. Stylised images are known from the fourteenth to thirteenth centuries BC and can be seen on a Persian sword fashioned in the twelfth or eleventh century BC. There is abundant evidence showing that the ancient Egyptians were also well acquainted with the Honeybee. Alongside the bee, on the pylons of their temples and in their tombs, we also find many pictures of the sacred Scarab Beetle, which the Egyptians saw as the symbol of new life.

In Ancient Greece and Rome, the Honeybee inspired poets like Homer and Virgil and prompted Aristoteles (384–322 BC) to make a detailed study of them. His results are still admired today. He ranked the bee among the insects *(entoma),* distinguished six legs and the wings, and knew of the collecting apparatus on the legs. Leonardo da Vinci was also an admirer of the bee which is also beautifully illustrated in Cesi's book *Apiarium.*

People have long paid attention to insects which are either useful or troublesome to them. One such insect is the silkworm moth, whose his-

tory goes back to the third millenium BC. Pests likewise have a long history. For instance, in the twelfth century AD, Hildegard von Bechelheim, the Abbess of Bingen Convent in Germany, wrote a treatise on fleas and lice.

It was not until the eighteenth century that foundations for the serious study of insects were laid. Réaumur wrote *Mémoires pour servir l'Histoire des Insectes* (1734–42), which contains innumerable data on insects, but is not very reliable with regard to their names. At roughly the same time, the Swedish naturalist Linnaeus began to publish his findings, which culminated in the tenth edition of his memorable *Systema Naturae* (1758). This edition proved to be a turning-point in zoological terminology. In it, Linnaeus included all the species of animals known up to that time and named other, previously unknown, species. All the names were in Latin and earlier names lost their validity. For species, Linnaeus introduced dual names, i.e. names composed of two words – the first to denote the genus and the second the species.

The name of a species is followed by the abbreviated (or whole) name of the worker who first invented it and described the genus or species. The best known abbreviation is L., which stands for Linnaeus. The next commonest is F. for Fabricius, another author who named a great many insects.

Where several species belong to one genus, their specific names are always different, while their generic name is the same. Ground beetles (genus *Carabus*) comprise many large and well known species, such as *Carabus coriaceus* L., *Carabus violaceus* L., *Carabus auratus* L. and *Carabus hortensis* L., etc. The generic name *Carabus* is repeated every time. In the same way, in the family Silphidae there is the genus *Nicrophorus*, which includes *Nicrophorus germanicus* L., *Nicrophorus vespillo* L., *Nicrophorus vespilloides* Herbst and others.

With the passage of time, the way in which species are named has become stabilised. The number of species has increased (and is still increasing), however, and so has knowledge of the interrelationship of species, while the number of genera was found to be too small and new genera had to be created. New findings made it necessary to 'shift' many species to other genera. As nomenclature developed, some species were moved about repeatedly from one genus to another and even today the views of research workers on the classification of certain species are not unanimous.

The species is not a constant unit. It develops and often breaks up into smaller units termed subspecies or geographical races. This is also reflected in the nomenclature. The name of the subspecies consists of three words, the third word being the actual name of the subspecies. Tendencies to the formation of geographical races are common among lepidopterans and beetles, but are also present in other orders. As an example we can take the Moorland Clouded Yellow butterfly (*Colias palaeno* L.). Linnaeus described it in northern Europe, but it later transpired that the individuals of this species occurring in central Europe differed from those in the north. The central European population was therefore given the name *Colias palaeno europome* Esp. and the north European race was named *Colias palaeno palaeno* L.. Among beetles, ground beetles of the genus *Carabus* incline particularly to the forma-

tion of geographical races; *Carabus auronitens* F. forms several. The subspecies *Carabus auronitens auronitens* F. occurs in central Europe (without the eastern Alps); *Carabus auronitens kraussi* Lapouge inhabits the eastern Alps and the Vienna forest; while *Carabus auronitens escheri* Palliardi is a Carpathian species.

Many insects are characterised by a very pronounced colour variability, which is sometimes so great that it would be hard to find two individuals exactly alike. Colour variability is also common among beetles, especially spotted species. This is not a case of geographical races, however, but of individual differences. In the earlier literature these deviations used to be termed aberrations (ab.) or varieties (var.), but modern taxonomy has abandoned the use of these terms.

In the history of nomenclature it often happened (and still happens today) that different workers gave the same species different names. According to the law of priority, the name that was published first, i.e. the oldest name, is the valid one and the other names are synonyms.

Alongside scientific names, every language has its own vernacular names. These are more or less selective, however, and are mostly given only to species which are widespread, familiar and economically important. There would be no point in giving names to the tens of thousands of insect species which inhabit a small continent like Europe, for nobody would remember them. In any case, no one who is seriously interested in entomology can dispense with scientific names, which are often easier to remember than the vernacular names (of which there are frequently more than one).

In the creation of generic and specific names, the name should express a particular property of the insect in question, or its habits or colouring. The names are in Latin, but they often come from the Greek and have been Latinised. The specific name is frequently very informative. For instance, *subterraneus* means that the species lives underground, while *niger, luteus, purpureus* and *griseus*, etc., stand for black, yellow, purple or grey. The name may also describe the colouring of a given part of the body, e.g. *nigritarsus* (black-footed) or *erythrocephala* (redheaded), etc. Names like *bipunctatus, septempunctata* and *vigintiduopunctata,* tell us that the species is marked with two, seven or 22 spots. Sometimes the names of famous entomologists or collectors appear in specific names, e.g. *obenbergeri, klapperichi* and *schmuttereri* (with a small initial letter); other names tell where the species was found, such as *germanicus* (in Germany), *britannicus* (in Great Britain) or *bohemicus* (in Bohemia). Even Greek and Roman mythology have not been forgotten, as seen from the names *Parnassius apollo, Dynastes hercules, Sisyphus schaefferi* and others.

Up to this point the reasons for the choice of specific names have been perfectly clear. There are exceptions, however, in which the names are the result of seemingly random and inexplicable combinations, such as the beetle genera *Nacerda* and *Sphindus,* or the specific name *opeticus.*

Entomological nomenclature is not just a self-objective list of names. The international name makes it possible for scientists speaking the most diverse languages to understand one another more easily. Nomenclature is significant in popular literature and in the translation of technical texts; without its existence the translation of names into different languages would be quite impossible.

The insect system

Entomologists are still trying to discover and elucidate the insects' phylogenetic relationships so that they can classify them in higher systematic categories. In consequence, the insect system is constantly undergoing new changes. Only recently there was a basic change in the highest categories, when the former insect orders Protura, Collembola and Diplura were raised to the status of independent classes. The names of orders which are dealt with and illustrated in this book are set *in bold type*. These orders include families whose representatives are depicted in the pictorial section. *The real number of families is naturally much higher*. The contemporary insect system is therefore as follows (though it must be pointed out that not all entomologists agree on it).

Superclass: Hexapoda
Classes: (Protura)
        (Collembola)
        (Diplura)
        Insecta
Subclass: Thysanura ('Apterygota')
Orders: Archaeognatha
        Zygentoma: Lepismatidae
Subclass: Pterygota (winged insects)
Orders: **Ephemeroptera** (mayflies): Baetidae, Ephemeridae
    Odonata (dragonflies and damselflies): Calopterygidae, Lestidae, Agrionidae, Coenagrionidae, Aeshnidae, Gomphidae, Cordulegasteridae, Corduliidae, Libellulidae
    Plecoptera (stoneflies): Nemouridae
    Embioptera (web-spinners)
    Grylloblattodea
    Dermaptera (earwigs): Labiidae, Forficulidae, Labiduridae
    Mantodea (praying mantids): Mantidae
    Blattodea (cockroaches): Blattidae
    Isoptera (termites or white ants): Rhinotermitidae
    Zoraptera
    Phasmatodea (stick- and leaf-insects, spectre-insects): Bacillidae, Lonchodidae
    Ensifera (crickets and bush-crickets): Tettigoniidae, Phaneropteridae, Ephippigeridae, Rhaphidophoridae, Gryllidae, Gryllotalpidae
    Caelifera: (locusts, grasshoppers): Tetrigidae, Catantopidae, Acrididae
    Psocoptera (psocids, book lice): Trogiidae
    Mallophaga (bird lice, biting lice): Trichodectidae
    Anoplura (sucking lice): Pediculidae Rhynchophthirina
    Thysanoptera (thrips): Thripidae
    Heteroptera (true bugs): Cydnidae, Pentatomidae, Acanthosomidae, Coreidae, Rhopalidae, Lygaeidae, Pyrrhocoridae, Aradidae, Tingidae, Reduviidae, Nabidae, Anthocoridae, Cimicidae, Miridae, Hydrometridae, Gerridae, Saldidae, Notonectidae, Corixidae, Naucoridae, Nepidae
    Homoptera (recently divided into three orders) (cicadas, leaf-hoppers, aphids, white flies, scale-bugs): Cixiidae, Cicadidae, Cercopidae, Membracidae, Cicadellidae, Callaphididae, Aphididae, Ortheziidae, Coccidae, Diaspididae, Aleyrodidae, Psyllidae
    Megaloptera (alder flies): Sialidae
    Raphidioptera (snakeflies): Raphidiidae
    Neuroptera (Planipennia) (lacewing flies): Osmylidae, Chrysopidae, Hemerobiidae, Nemopteridae, Ascalaphidae, Myrmeleontidae
    Coleoptera (beetles): Cicindelidae, Carabidae, Haliplidae, Dytiscidae, Gyrinidae, Hydraenidae, Hydrophilidae, Histeridae, Catopidae, Silphidae, Scaphidiidae, Staphylinidae, Pselaphidae, Lucanidae, Geotrupidae, Scarabaeidae, Helodidae, Byrrhidae, Heteroceridae, Dryopidae, Buprestidae, Elateridae, Lampyridae, Lycidae, Cantharidae,

Dermestidae, Anobiidae, Ptinidae, Bostrychidae, Lyctidae, Cleridae, Korynetidae, Dasytidae, Malachiidae, Lymexylonidae, Nitidulidae, Rhizophagidae, Cucujidae, Byturidae, Erotylidae, Phalacridae, Coccinellidae, Endomychidae, Mycetophagidae, Cisidae, Colydiidae, Tenebrionidae, Lagriidae, Salphingidae, Pythidae, Pyrochroidae, Mordellidae, Meloidae, Oedemeridae, Cerambycidae, Bruchidae, Chrysomelidae, Anthribidae, Attelabidae, Apionidae, Curculionidae, Scolytidae

Strepsiptera (twisted-winged insects, stylopids): Stylopidae

Hymenoptera (bees, wasps, ants): Pamphiliidae, Siricidae, Xiphydriidae, Argidae, Cimbicidae, Diprionidae, Tenthredinidae, Ichneumonidae, Braconidae, Cynipidae, Scoliidae, Chrysididae, Mutillidae, Formicidae, Myrmicidae, Pompilidae, Eumenidae, Vespidae, Sphecidae, Colletidae, Andrenidae, Halictidae, Melittidae, Megachilidae, Anthophoridae, Apidae

Trichoptera (caddis flies): Philopotamidae, Phryganeidae, Limnephilidae

Lepidoptera (moths, butterflies): Hepialidae, Adelidae, Tineidae, Psychidae, Gracillariidae, Yponomeutidae, Coleophoridae, Oecophoridae, Sesiidae, Tortricidae, Zygaenidae, Pterophoridae, Cossidae, Lasiocampidae, Sphingidae, Saturniidae, Syssphingidae, Hesperiidae, Papilionidae, Pieridae, Lycaenidae, Nymphalidae, Satyridae, Pyralidae, Crambidae, Drepanidae, Thyatiridae, Geometridae, Notodontidae, Lymantriidae, Ctenuchidae, Arctiidae, Noctuidae

Mecoptera (scorpion flies): Panorpidae, Boreidae

Diptera (true, i.e. two-winged, flies): Tipulidae, Culicidae, Chironomidae, Cecidomyidae, Bibionidae, Rhagionidae, Stratiomyidae, Tabanidae, Asilidae, Therevidae, Bombyliidae, Empididae, Syrphidae, Conopidae, Tephritidae, Drosophilidae, Scatophagidae, Anthomyidae, Muscidae, Hippoboscidae, Calliphoridae, Tachinidae, Hypodermatidae

Siphonaptera (fleas): Pulicidae, Ctenopsyllidae

Pictorial Section

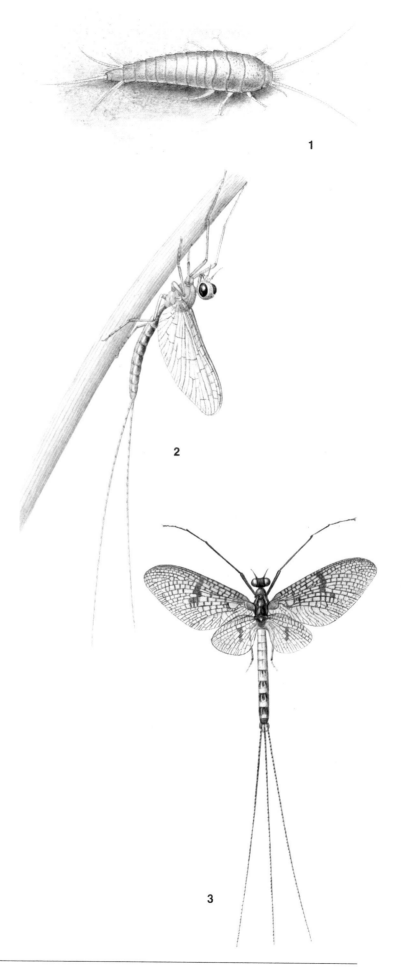

1 *Lepisma saccharina* L.   Lepismatidae
Silverfish

2 *Cloeon dipterum* L.   Baetidae

3 *Ephemera danica* Müll.   Ephemeridae

Several groups of wingless animals classified until quite recently as insects are no longer counted among them. The best known of these creatures are springtails (Collembola). A few originally wingless forms which do not fit traditional conceptions were left among the insects, however. The Silverfish (*Lepisma saccharina*) is a characteristic and common representative of wingless insects. It lives in a close association with people (i.e. it is a synanthropic species), whose homes provide it with ideal conditions. At night it prowls about bathrooms, lavatories and kitchens looking for organic debris and substances containing the cellulose which forms its staple food. If a light is suddenly switched on, it makes for a dark corner. Its development takes three years.

Mayflies, most of which fly above or near water, usually have four wings, but there are exceptions, such as *Cloeon dipterum,* which has only two wings. This species produces two generations a year – one in May and June and the other in August and September. The nymphs develop in stagnant water in lowlands and uplands.

Ephemera danica is a representative of the typical mayflies. It is a common species and is to be seen in the greatest numbers in June, when the imagos frequent damp localities near sources of water. Like other mayflies, the adult insect is very short-lived and takes no food during the 24 hours of its brief life. The nymphs spend two years in the water of sandy streams and rivers, where they live on algae and organic detritus. The full-grown nymph is first of all transformed to a semi-adult (subimago) closely resembling the adult mayfly, but its body, including all appendages, is wrapped in a fine membrane. In a very short time the imago emerges from its protective covering.

1. *Lepisma saccharina:* 7—10 mm ($\frac{5}{16}$—$\frac{3}{8}$ in). Over the entire globe.
2. *Cloeon dipterum:* ♂ 6—7 mm + bristles 13—17 mm; ♀ 7—8 mm + bristles 8—10 mm (♂ $\frac{5}{16}$ in + bristles $\frac{1}{2}$—$\frac{11}{16}$ in; ♀ $\frac{5}{16}$ in + bristles $\frac{5}{16}$—$\frac{3}{8}$ in). The temperate belt of Eurasia.
3. *Ephemera danica:* ♂ 15—18 mm + bristles 30—40 mm; ♀ 18—24 mm + bristles 14—25 mm (♂ $\frac{5}{8}$—$\frac{11}{16}$ in + bristles $1\frac{3}{16}$—$1\frac{9}{16}$ in; ♀ $\frac{3}{4}$—$\frac{15}{16}$ in + bristles $\frac{9}{10}$—1 in). The whole of Europe.

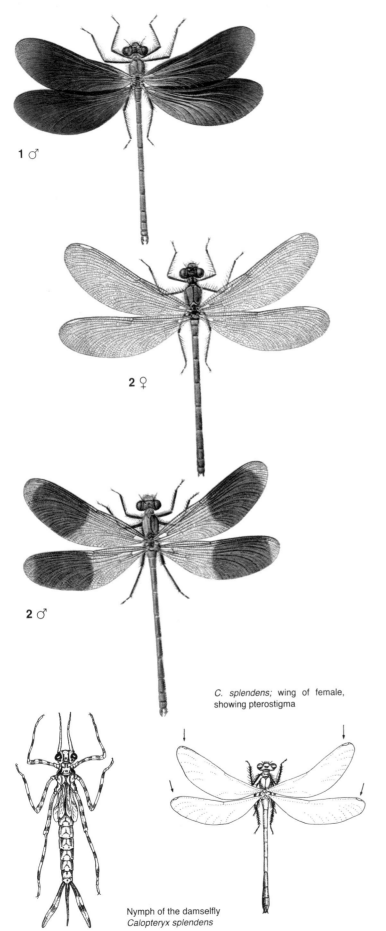

1 ♂

2 ♀

2 ♂

C. splendens; wing of female, showing pterostigma

Nymph of the damselfly
Calopteryx splendens

1 *Calopteryx virgo* L. Calopterygidae
Beautiful Demoiselle

2 *Calopteryx splendens* Harr.
Banded Demoiselle

Demoiselle flies flutter above the vegetation beside rivers and streams. When the insects are at rest the wings are held pressed together. The sexes are differently coloured and only the females have a white 'blaze' on the anterior edge of their wings.

The Beautiful Demoiselle *(Calopteryx virgo)* appears from the end of April to the beginning of September. It likes fast-flowing water with an abundance of vegetation and is to be found quite high up in the mountains. The females mostly sit on plants; the males fly about, but never far from water. They often spend the night together, clinging to plants. This is a predacious species which catches mosquitoes and other small arthropods. The fertilised female lays eggs in aquatic plants; she usually sits on the plant above the surface, curving her abdomen below the surface in a semicircle, although sometimes she herself is also submerged. The eggs may also be laid in parts of the plant above the surface, if these are wet enough; they are laid during the daytime, preferably when it is sunny and warm. The laying female is not accompanied by the male. Sometimes several females lay their eggs in close proximity. The nymph is long-legged and the first two segments of its antennae are exceptionally long. It lives in quiet places on the bed, under banks and stones, etc., and is predacious. After two winters it leaves the water. The imagos emerge on dry land.

In the Banded Demoiselle *(Calopteryx splendens)*, the sexes are much easier to distinguish by their colouring, since the males have a large dark spot on each of their wings. The imagos fly from the spring to the autumn, but, as distinct from the Beautiful Demoiselle, they occur beside lowland streams and rivers. The imagos of both species are very short-lived. The way in which they catch prey and reproduce, their nuptial flight, egg-laying and the course of their nymphal stages are likewise similar.

1. *Calopteryx virgo:* 50 mm, wing span 70 mm (2 in, wing span 2¾ in). The temperate belt of Eurasia, in Europe up to the Arctic Circle.
2. *Calopteryx splendens:* 50 mm, wing span 70 mm (2 in, wing span 2¾ in). The temperate belt of Eurasia, Asia Minor, northern Africa.

1 *Lestes sponsa* Hansem.   Lestidae
Emerald Damselfly

2 *Lestes viridis* v.d.L.

3 *Pyrrhosoma nymphula* Sulzer   Agrionidae
Large Red Damselfly

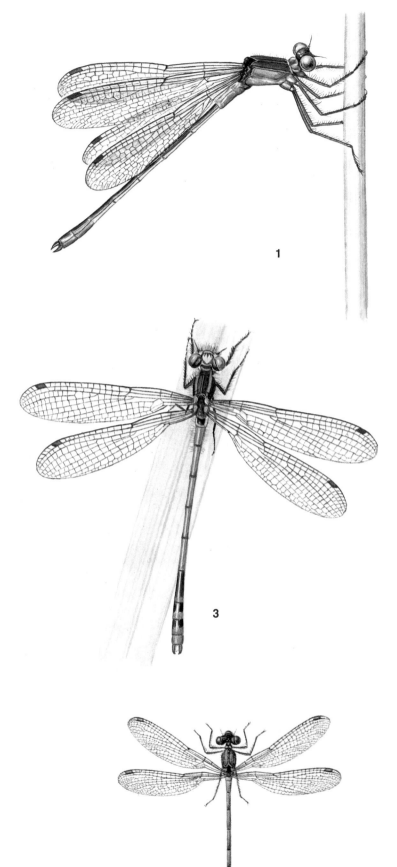

The slender body and transparent wings of members of the genus *Lestes* make them almost invisible when they settle after a short flight on aquatic plants and shrubs. They sit on the vegetation with their wings half-spread and sometimes fly quite a long way away from water. The Emerald Damselfly *(Lestes sponsa)* is the most common species. The imagos fly from the spring to the autumn and they frequent ponds, pools and any stagnant water with an adequate supply of aquatic plants. The fertilised female lays her eggs in aquatic herbaceous plants, such as soft-rush, club-rush, water-soldier, irises and reedmace, and is accompanied by the male. The male grips her thorax with his anal claspers, holding his abdomen slightly curved. The eggs are laid above the water-line, but the female sometimes submerges, together with the male. The position of the eggs is betrayed by a vertical row of small punctures on the plant. The nymphs, which hatch the following spring, develop quickly; in about eight weeks they leave the water and the imago emerges onto dry land.

The female *Lestes viridis* lays her eggs in the branches of various shrubs bordering reservoirs and is likewise accompanied by the male; gall-like structures are formed at the puncture sites. One female lays about 200 eggs.

The Large Red Damselfly (*Pyrrhosoma nymphula*) has a conspicuously red abdomen. It flies from April to the beginning of August in the vicinity of ponds, pools and slow-flowing water. The eggs are laid in various aquatic plants, such as water forget-me-not, marsh-grass, pondweed and hornwort. The male grips the female's thorax with his anal claspers and sometimes submerges with her. The nymphs live among aquatic plants, spend the winter on the bottom, leave the water in the spring and are then transformed to imagos.

1. *Lestes sponsa:* 35 mm, wing span 45 mm ($1\frac{3}{8}$ in, wing span $1\frac{3}{4}$ in). Central and northern Europe, northern Asia as far as Japan.
2. *Lestes viridis:* 45 mm, wing span 60 mm ($1\frac{3}{4}$ in, wing span $2\frac{3}{8}$ in). Europe (except the north), northern Africa, Middle East, Asia Minor.
3. *Pyrrhosoma nymphula:* 35 mm, wing span 45 mm ($1\frac{3}{8}$ in, wing span $1\frac{3}{4}$ in). The whole of Europe except the extreme north and south, Asia Minor.

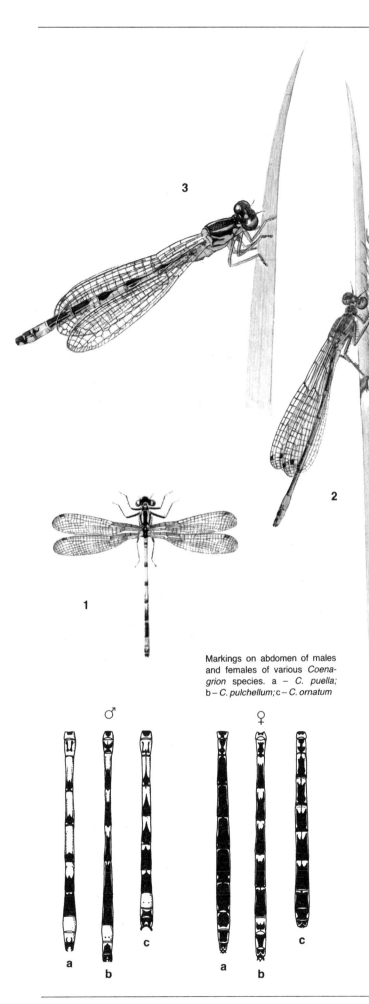

1 *Coenagrion puella* L.   Coenagrionidae
Azure Damselfly
2 *Coenagrion pulchellum* v.d.L.
Variable Damselfly
3 *Coenagrion ornatum* Selys

When we see bright blue damselflies flying over still water and settling on aquatic plants, they are usually males of the genus *Coenagrion;* the females are coloured differently. The sexes are distinguished from each other by dark markings on the abdomen, which are altogether different in the male and the female.

The males of the Azure Damselfly (*Coenagrion puella*) are blue, while the females are green to yellowish-green and only seldom blue. This damselfly inhabits pools, fishponds and slow-flowing water. The imagos fly from May to the end of September. The males often spend the night grouped together on plants. The female lays her eggs in the petioles or leaves of small aquatic plants, including various kinds of pondweed, water milfoil, frogbit and arrowhead, for example; she is accompanied by the male, who stands perched on her thorax, with his legs drawn up to his body. The nymphs, which are hatched in two weeks or more, live in water, where they spend the winter; development to the imago is completed the following spring on dry land.

Variable Damselfly (*Coenagrion pulchellum*) males have an exceptionally thin, slender abdomen. The females of this damselfly occur in two shades, and are predominantly blue or green. The markings on the abdomen vary greatly. This species inhabits stagnant water. The female, with the male standing on her body, lays the eggs on the underside of the leaves of plants such as water-lilies, bog arum, frogbit, pondweed and duckweed. While doing so she may be completely submerged.

The females of the species *Coenagrion ornatum* can also appear in two colour variants – blue like the male, or green. This damselfly is much rarer than the two preceding species. It inhabits peat-bogs and muddy streams and is to be seen mainly in June.

Markings on abdomen of males and females of various *Coenagrion* species. a – *C. puella;* b – *C. pulchellum;* c – *C. ornatum*

1. *Coenagrion puella:* 35 mm, wing span 40—50 mm ($1\frac{3}{8}$ in, wing span $1\frac{9}{16}$—2 in). Europe (in the north to the south of Sweden), Near East, north-west Africa.
2. *Coenagrion pulchellum:* 35 mm, wing span 40—50 mm ($1\frac{3}{8}$ in, wing span $1\frac{9}{16}$—2 in). Europe (except the extreme north), Near East.
3. *Coenagrion ornatum:* 30 mm, wing span 35—40 mm ($1\frac{3}{16}$ in, wing span $1\frac{3}{8}$—$1\frac{9}{16}$ in). Central, western and southern Europe, Near East.

1 *Aeshna juncea*
Common Hawker

Aeshnidae

2 *Aeshna cyanea* Müll.
Southern Hawker

The males of the large dragonflies of the genus *Aeshna* can be easily distinguished from the females by their colouring and the shape of their hindwings, which are pointed at the base in the males. The males also have 'auricles' (lobes) on their second abdominal segment. These are the largest species in the order Odonata.

The Common Hawker (*Aeshna juncea*) lives in the lowlands in the north, but at higher altitudes further south. It commonly inhabits grassy salt-marshes and peatbogs. It is to be found near water, but also occurs at the edge of forests and in clearings. The imagos fly from June until late in the autumn (often to the end of October). They are predacious and, like all the big dragonflies, catch flying insects. To rest they hang from a twig with their abdomens held vertically and their wings spread. The eggs are laid in July and August, mainly in the evening, in various plants – horsetails, bog-moss, bur-reed and sedge. The female may dip her abdomen into water up to its base, but does not submerge completely; while laying, she is not accompanied by the male. Development from egg to dragonfly takes four years.

The Southern Hawker (*Aeshna cyanea*) is to be seen near pools, fishponds and occasionally reservoirs. The first individuals appear in the middle of June and the last do not disappear until November. This dragonfly will also visit small garden ponds in towns and has a predilection for country railway embankments. The imagos like to fly after dusk, when the mosquitoes are swarming. The female lays her eggs mainly in August and September, on mossy stones, in the old leaves of aquatic plants and in dead branches, etc., generally a few centimetres above the surface of water. The nymphs are hatched the following year; they live in the water and zealously catch almost anything they can find, in particular mosquito larvae. The nymph overwinters; a year later it climbs out of the water and attaches itself firmly to a plant, where it finally moults to become the adult insect.

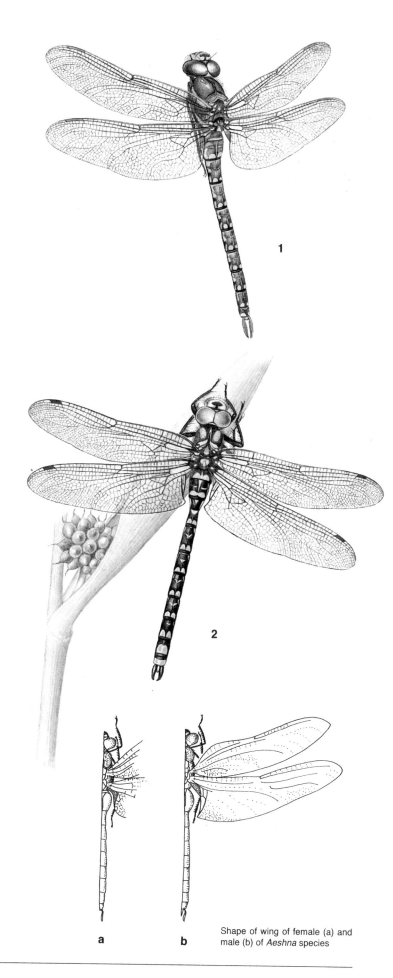

1

2

a   b

Shape of wing of female (a) and male (b) of *Aeshna* species

1. *Aeshna juncea*: 70—80 mm, wing span 90—105 mm ($2\frac{3}{4}$—$3\frac{1}{8}$ in, wing span $3\frac{9}{16}$—$4\frac{1}{8}$ in). The temperate belt of Eurasia.
2. *Aeshna cyanea*: 65—80 mm, wing span 95—110 mm $2\frac{9}{16}$—$3\frac{1}{8}$ in, wing span $3\frac{3}{4}$—$4\frac{3}{8}$ in). The whole of Europe to the north of Sweden, Asia Minor, northern Africa.

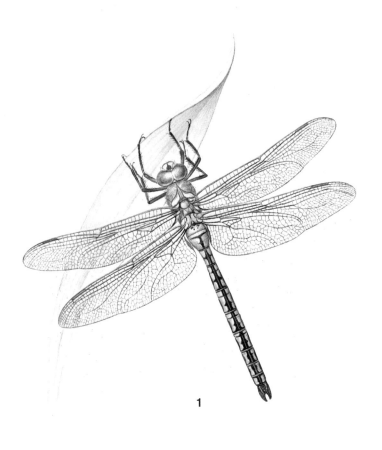

1

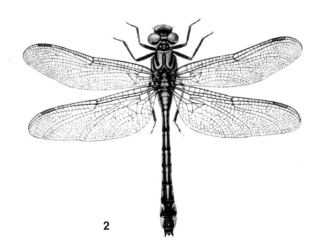

2

As it sails tirelessly over the countryside on warm, sunny days, the huge, handsome Emperor Dragonfly *(Anax imperator),* with its gorgeous colouring, elegant flight and delicate wings, does full justice to its name. The male has a sky-blue abdomen with dark markings, the female a bluish-green abdomen with reddish-brown markings. The Emperor Dragonfly occurs near still water such as fishponds, small pools and artificial garden ponds with vegetation, but it also flies far away from water. It is essentially a lowland species and is rarely found at higher altitudes or in mountains. Its swift flight and outstanding vision enable it to catch prey with perfect ease. It lives mainly on small insects, in particular dipterans, but is not afraid to tackle butterflies and smaller dragonflies. The eggs are laid in various aquatic plants, such as water milfoil, Canadian pondweed and curled pondweed. Considering its size, this dragonfly develops very quickly, since the eggs are laid at the end of July or the beginning of August and the nymphs hatch in two to four weeks. Although at first very small, and not at all like dragonflies, they soon acquire the form of nymphs of other species. They overwinter in water, but in June they leave the water for good and sometimes climb high up into the trees, where the imago leaves its larval skin.

A whole series of dragonflies have a black, yellow-spotted abdomen. The Club-tailed Dragonfly is one of these. It flies in the vicinity of clean streams and rivers, but also wanders quite far afield. The imagos appear from the middle of June to the end of September. Their eggs are laid in a different manner from those of the preceding species. The female flies about 20–30 cm (8–12 in) above the surface of the water and from time to time dips the end of her abdomen into the water, each time releasing some of the eggs (up to 500 altogether). The nymphs, which are hatched on the bed, overwinter three to four times in the water.

1. *Anax imperator:* 70—80 mm, wing span 100—110 mm $2\frac{3}{4}$—$3\frac{1}{8}$ in, wing span $3\frac{15}{16}$—$4\frac{3}{8}$ in). Europe (in the north as far as the south of England and Sweden), a large part of Africa and Asia.
2. *Gomphus vulgatissimus:* 45—50 mm, wing span 60—70 mm ($1\frac{3}{4}$—2 in, wing span $2\frac{3}{8}$—$2\frac{3}{4}$ in). A large part of Europe, Asia Minor.

1 *Cordulegaster boltoni* Donov.
Gold-ringed Dragonfly

Cordulegasteridae

2 *Cordulia aenea* L.
Downy Emerald Dragonfly

Corduliidae

From time to time, near clear mountain streams, you may catch a glimpse of the beautiful Gold-ringed Dragonfly (*Cordulegaster boltoni*), although it does not fly as well or as enduringly as other large dragonflies. The imagos often remain suspended from a dry branch or a plant just above the river bank, with their wings spread straight out. They seldom move away from the water, except to chase prey or move to a new site. They fly from June to the end of August. The eggs are laid in a rather unusual manner. The female flies just above the surface of shallow water, suddenly plunges the lower half of her abdomen into it and, with a thrust of her long ovipositor, lays an egg in the sandy or muddy bed. She quickly repeats the process many times in the same spot, flies a little further away and starts all over again. The nymphs live in shallow water. In hot, dry summers, if the water threatens to dry up, they instinctively move to more satisfactory quarters. The robust nymph has a large facial mask and, at the other end of its body, three sharp stylets. It lies in wait for its prey (mayfly, alder fly and midge larvae), which it catches with great accuracy. After overwintering several times on the bed of the stream, it climbs out of the water, attaches itself to a plant and, a little later, the imago emerges from the cracked skin.

The Downy Emerald Dragonfly (*Cordulia aenea*), can be seen from the beginning of May to the end of August, hovering on bright sunny days over different types of water or even far away from water. It is an excellent flier and, like other dragonflies, a predator. It is primarily a lowland species, but is often to be found at higher altitudes. To lay the eggs, the female flies just above the surface of the water, occasionally plunging her abdomen into it and releasing a few eggs. The nymphs live in water and overwinter several times; they live on the larvae of aquatic insects and on other small animals. Finally, they climb out of the water, attach themselves to a plant, the larval skin splits and the imago emerges.

1. *Cordulegaster boltoni:* 70—85 mm, wing span 90—105 mm ($2\frac{3}{4}$—$3\frac{3}{8}$ in, wing span $3\frac{9}{16}$—$3\frac{15}{16}$ in). A large part of Europe.
2. *Cordulia aenea:* 50—55 mm, wing span 65—75 mm (2—$2\frac{1}{8}$ in, wing span $2\frac{9}{16}$—$2\frac{15}{16}$ in). Eurasia.

Nymph of the dragonfly *Cordulia aenea*

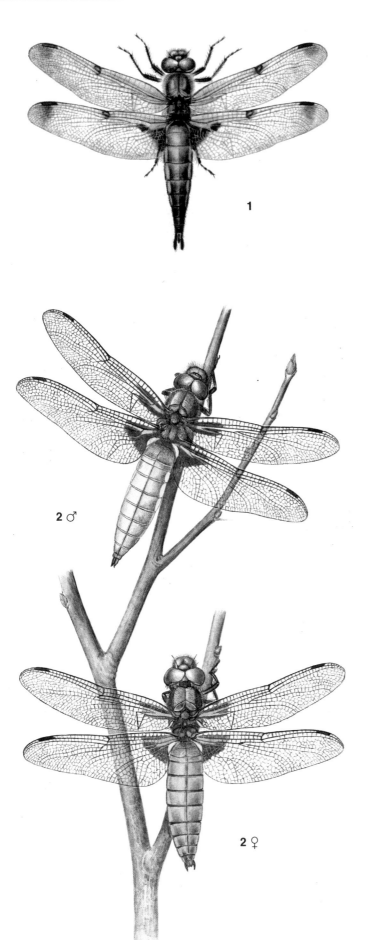

1 *Libellula quadrimaculata* L. Libellulidae
Four-spotted Chaser

2 *Libellula depressa* L.
Broad-bodied Chaser

Quite often, scientific names (and sometimes vernacular names) express some characteristic feature or property of the genus or species to which they were given. Such is the case with the Four-spotted Chaser (*Libellula quadrimaculata*, from the Latin *quatuor* – four – and *macula* – spot), which actually has four spots on its wings. The imagos appear in the morning and can be seen from the beginning of May to the middle of August. They inhabit stagnant water and peaty ponds. When laying the eggs, the female flies over the surface of the water, usually in places with an adequate number of aquatic plants below the surface. The eggs, which are always released a few at a time, are wrapped in a sticky substance for protection. As they sink, they are caught on the plants. The nymphs, which are hatched a few weeks later, are very active and run about on the bottom of the pond or swim. After two winters in the water, they climb out onto the bank and attach themselves to a plant some 20–40 cm (8–16 in) above the ground. In the early morning the larval skin begins to split and the imago emerges.

The Broad-bodied Chaser (*Libellula depressa*) has a strikingly flat abdomen and there are colour differences between the male and the female and between young and old specimens. The young dragonflies have an olive-brown abdomen, older males a blue abdomen, while females are olive-brown. All, however, have yellow crescent-shaped spots on their sides. This species frequents stagnant water (chiefly small pools). It flies very fast and is to be seen mainly in May and June. The nymphs live at the bottom of small pools, where they hide away from their enemies in the mud. If the pool dries up, they usually leave it to look for a better place and, if necessary, they can spend the whole day on dry land. Sometimes, however, they bury themselves in the mud and 'go to sleep' until conditions have returned to normal. Their development takes one or two years, depending on conditions.

1. *Libellula quadrimaculata:* 40—50 mm, wing span 70—85 mm (1$\frac{9}{16}$—2 in, wing span 2$\frac{3}{4}$—3$\frac{3}{8}$ in). The temperate zone of Eurasia, North America.
2. *Libellula depressa:* 40—45 mm, wing span 70—80 mm (1$\frac{9}{16}$—1$\frac{3}{4}$ in, wing span 2$\frac{3}{4}$—3$\frac{1}{8}$ in). Europe, Near East.

1 *Sympetrum flaveolum* L. Libellulidae
Yellow-winged Darter

2 *Sympetrum sanguineum* Müll.
Ruddy Darter

3 *Nemoura cinerea* Retz. Nemouridae

Among the *Sympetrum* species, which are very similar and almost the same size, the Yellow-winged Darter (*Sympetrum flaveolum*) can be identified from the yellow spots at the base of its wings. It occurs in both the lowlands and the mountains from the end of June to the end of September, usually far away from any water. After copulation, the female lays the eggs, usually with the participation of the male, which holds her in a firm grip and appears to supervise the process, although it is sometimes done without his presence. Wet meadows round ponds and lakes and even the surface of water are the best terrain for laying. The eggs are not wrapped in any sticky substance. If they are laid early enough, the nymphs are hatched the same year; later eggs overwinter and develop the following spring. Development is relatively rapid; the nymphs live in stagnant water among aquatic plants and devour the larvae of various aquatic insects (e.g. mayflies) and other small animals. On completing its development, the nymph leaves the water and the imago emerges from the larval skin.

The Ruddy Darter (*Sympetrum sanguineum*) lives in a similar way to *Sympetrum flaveolum,* but is a lowland species. The male has a bright red abdomen, the female a yellowish-red to russet abdomen.

Some stoneflies, especially large species, are fairly easy to identify, but you are more likely to encounter small species, which in some places abound in the vicinity of water. They are all very similar and thus difficult to identify. *Nemoura cinerea,* one of the smaller stoneflies, is common on plants round various types of water from the spring to the autumn. As in several other members of the same family, part of the venation of the forewings forms a letter X. The nymphs, which live in both flowing or stagnant, clean or polluted water, overwinter once.

1. *Sympetrum flaveolum:* 35 mm, wing span 50—60 mm. ($1\frac{3}{8}$ in, wing span 2—$2\frac{3}{8}$ in). Europe, Near East and northern Asia.
2. *Sympetrum sanguineum:* 35—40 mm, wing span 50—60 mm ($1\frac{3}{8}$—$1\frac{9}{16}$ in, wing span 2—$2\frac{3}{8}$ in). Europe, Near East.
3. *Nemoura cinerea:* 5.5—7 mm ($\frac{3}{16}$—$\frac{1}{4}$ in). The whole of Europe.

Forewing of the stonefly *Nemoura cinerea,* showing venation in the form of a letter X

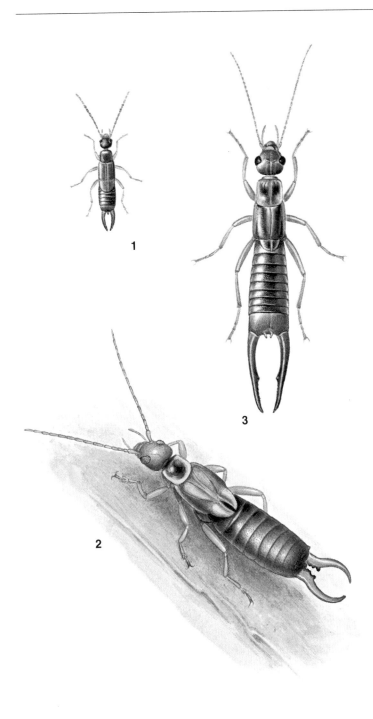

1 *Labia minor* L. Labiidae

2 *Forficula auricularia* L. Forficulidae
Common Earwig

3 *Labidura riparia* Pall. Labiduridae

The superstition that earwigs can crawl into one's ear and bite a hole in the eardrum dates from ancient times. While it can happen, it is highly unlikely to do so today and must have been much more common in olden days when people slept on straw. Earwigs creep into all kinds of nooks and crannies: under stones and wooden logs, in cracks in rocks and in old rags, as long as they are suitably damp. The number of earwig species is not very large, but in climatically favourable years there are plenty of earwigs almost everywhere. With their short wing-cases and the large pincers at the end of their abdomens they are very easy to identify. There is no need to be afraid of them, since earwigs do not 'bite'. They are all nocturnal insects, but our smallest species, *Labia minor,* also flies by day.

The development of earwigs has been very thoroughly studied. The female first hollows out a chamber in the ground and then lays a few dozen eggs in it. That is not very many, but the female then guards the eggs, so subsequent losses are small. She moves the eggs about, throwing out defective ones, and licks them to keep them free of debris and fungi spores; she also drives away predacious larvae and other robbers and remains in the chamber after the nymphs have hatched for the second time.

Views differ as to whether earwigs are useful or harmful, but they apply only to the Common Earwig (*Forficula auricularia*), which can be considered a pest when it settles in households. On the other hand, it does devour aphids and in this respect it can be said to be useful.

Labidura riparia, the largest earwig, is rare. It occurs in damp places from May to November and lives beside water, where it makes tubular capsules for itself.

Appendages ('pincers') on the abdomen of the earwig *Forficula auricularia;* a – male; b – female

Appendages on the abdomen of the earwig *Labia minor*

1. *Labia minor:* 5—9 mm ($\frac{3}{16}$—$\frac{3}{8}$ in). A large part of Europe; other continents also.
2. *Forficula auricularia:* 14—23 mm ($\frac{9}{16}$—$\frac{15}{16}$ in). Over the whole globe.
3. *Labidura riparia:* 13—30 mm ($\frac{9}{16}$—1$\frac{3}{16}$ in). Over practically the whole globe.

1 *Mantis religiosa* L.
Praying Mantis

Mantidae

2 *Empusa pennata* Thunb.

Mantids are typical representatives of tropical insects. Some are very large and their bizarre forms are unique among insects. They like considerable warmth and as one goes northwards their numbers rapidly diminish, so that in central Europe we find only a single species – the Praying Mantis (*Mantis religiosa*), which is green or brown and, like all mantids, has raptorial forelimbs adapted for seizing prey. The imago appears in grassy places from August until late autumn. It sits motionless for hours in the same place and follows any movements in its vicinity with a watchful eye, holding its forelegs folded as if in prayer, but with quite different intentions. As soon as a suitable prey comes within reach, the mantis seizes it like lightning and holds it between the femur and tibia of its first pair of legs. The legs are armed with spines, which penetrate the victim's body and make escape impossible; in any case, the prey (usually insect imagos and larvae) is quickly devoured. At egg-laying time the female secretes a substance from special abdominal glands, which hardens on contact with the air and is used to form capsules (oothecae) which contain 100–300 eggs. The capsule protects the eggs from inclement weather and from cold and heat; it is about 40 mm (1 $\frac{9}{16}$ in) long and is attached to a stone or a branch. One female makes several capsules. The eggs overwinter once and the young pronymphs, which bear no resemblance to the imago, are hatched in the spring. In fact, they are worm-like when they hatch, but they throw off a skin almost immediately and then are clearly mantis nymphs. The Praying Mantis is also known for its cannibalism. As a rule, the female devours the male after copulation, or even during it. This is an endangered species and is now legally protected in six countries, though not everywhere in Europe. It can now be found only in pockets in central Europe.

The mantid fauna of southern Europe is richer, but likewise comprises only a few species. One of the best known is *Empusa pennata*, which appears much earlier than the Praying Mantis. The imagos emerge in May and live up to the end of July. The relatively small ootheca is made longer by a kind of stalk. The nymphs overwinter and can sometimes be seen on fine winter days.

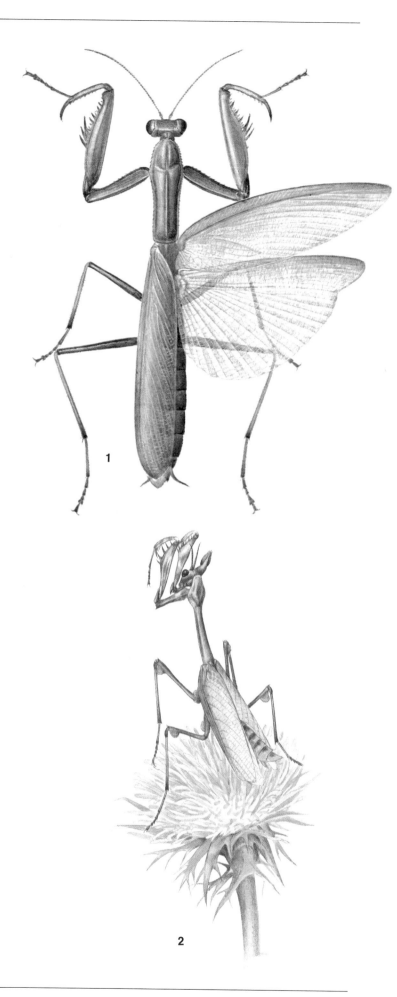

1

2

1. *Mantis religiosa*: ♂ 40—61 mm, ♀ 48—80 mm (♂ $\frac{9}{16}$—2$\frac{3}{8}$ in, ♀ 1$\frac{7}{8}$—3$\frac{3}{16}$ in). Southern and central Europe, the warm parts of Asia, Africa and Australia; carried to North America.
2. *Empusa pennata*: ♂ 47—60 mm, ♀ 54—67 mm (♂ 1$\frac{7}{8}$—2$\frac{3}{8}$ in, ♀ 2$\frac{3}{16}$—2$\frac{11}{16}$ in). Southern Europe, south-east Asia, northern Africa.

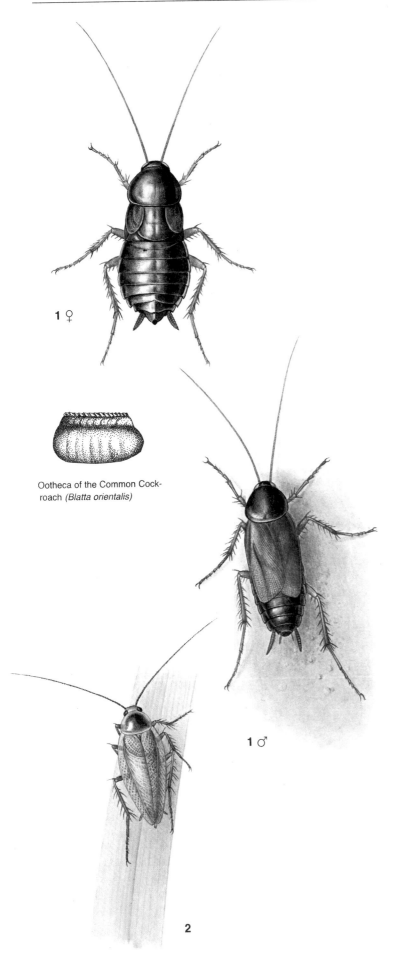

1 *Blatta orientalis* L.
Common Cockroach or Blackbeetle

2 *Ectobius lapponicus* L.
Dusky Cockroach

Nobody knows just how long the Common Cockroach (*Blatta orientalis*) has lived in human company, but written records go back to the seventeenth century. Its numbers have recently diminished and in many places, thanks to better hygiene, it has disappeared completely. Here and there, however, it is still a common and widespread synanthropic species. It likes warmth and is therefore particularly abundant in bakeries, rural hospitals, hotels, houses, hostels and the like. In southern Europe, however, it also lives in the open.

The male is distinguished from the female by his long wings and a further pair of appendages at the end of his abdomen. The female also has very short, stumpy wings. The Common Cockroach is omnivorous and makes itself unpleasant by leaving its excrement lying around. It is a flightless species and its flattened body enables it to crawl out of sight into all kinds of crannies during the daytime. Its development is very protracted. The female lays her eggs in a capsule rather like a small purse, 7–12 mm ($\frac{1}{2}$ in) long and about 6 mm ($\frac{1}{4}$ in) wide. Development passes through six larval instars.

Some cockroaches do not care for human company, but prefer the open. One of these is the very common Dusky Cockroach (*Ectobius lapponicus*). The male and female of this typically forest-dwelling species are different in colour and their wings are different lengths. The slightly larger male has a dark, light-bordered scutum and dark legs, while the female's scutum and legs are light. The males can fly and mostly frequent shrubs and grasses. When disturbed, they immediately dive for shelter, the females preferring to hide under old leaves. The imagos appear in May or June, depending on the locality, and remain until August. Like other cockroaches, this one lays its eggs in a grooved capsule about 3 mm ($\frac{1}{8}$ in) long, the bulging surface of which is strewn with tiny teeth. The nymphs overwinter.

1 ♀

Ootheca of the Common Cockroach (*Blatta orientalis*)

1 ♂

2

1. *Blatta orientalis:* ♂ 20—25 mm, ♀ 18—30 mm (♂ $\frac{13}{16}$—1 in, ♀ $\frac{3}{4}$—1$\frac{5}{16}$ in). Over the entire globe.
2. *Ectobius lapponicus:* ♂ 9—10 mm, ♀ 8—9.5 mm (♂ $\frac{3}{8}$ in, ♀ $\frac{5}{16}$—$\frac{3}{8}$ in). A large part of Europe, western Asia.

1 *Reticulitermes flavipes* Koll. Rhinotermitidae
2 *Bacillus rossii* Lam. Bacillidae
3 *Carausius morosus* Brun. Watt. Lonchodidae
Laboratory Stick Insect

Apart from hymenopterans, termites are the only social, or state-forming insects. Their kingdom is likewise a matriarchate ruled by a single queen and inhabited by various castes, though termite colonies have a king as well. Their giant mounds are inseparably associated with tropical landscapes, although isolated species also inhabit the temperate belt. A termite discovered in greenhouses in Schönbrunn (Vienna) in 1837 was named *Reticulitermes flavipes*. A few years later it was found and described under another name in natural surroundings in America. Over 100 years later the termite reappeared in central Europe – in West Germany, France and Austria. In the USA it is kept in laboratories for testing various preparations. A similar species to *flavipes* is *R. lucifugus*. Both species are common around the Mediterranean, living on dead wood.

Some insects imitate leaves, others flowers or twigs. Stick insects look very much like thin twigs. *Bacillus rossii* lives on vegetation under natural conditions, while the Laboratory Stick Insect (*Carausius morosus*) is often bred in insectaria. When in danger, stick insects 'freeze' into immobility; they are also able to part with a maimed limb or with segments of their antennae. In young specimens which still have at least two moults ahead of them the lost parts regenerate. Laboratory Stick Insects are very easy to keep and their food requirements are modest, since they live on diverse leaves and in the winter can be given ivy or Bergenia. Stick insects can reproduce parthenogenetically, i.e. without fertilisation. Males are very rare and as a rule number just one to several hundred females. Laboratory breeds comprise nothing but females. The female lays several hundred eggs. The rate of development depends on temperature and humidity. An adult stick insect lives for about five to seven months.

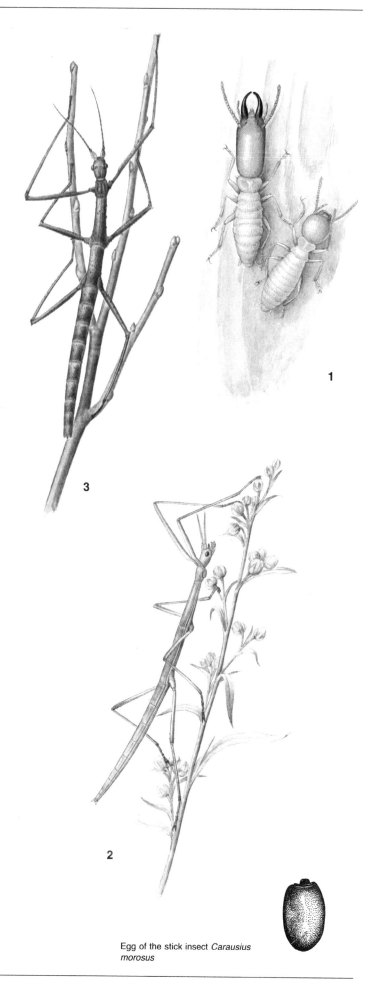

1

3

2

1. *Reticulitermes flavipes:* worker 4 mm, soldier 5 mm (worker $\frac{5}{32}$ in, soldier $\frac{3}{16}$ in). Nearctic region, introduced into central and western Europe.
2. *Bacillus rossii:* ♂ 58—62 mm, ♀ 80—105 mm (♂ $2\frac{5}{16}$—$2\frac{7}{16}$ in, ♀ $3\frac{1}{8}$—$4\frac{1}{8}$ in.) Mediterranean region.
3. *Carausius morosus:* ♂ 5—5.5 mm, ♀ up to 80 mm (♂ $\frac{3}{16}$ in, ♀ up to $3\frac{1}{8}$ in). Oriental region. Bred artificially in Europe.

Egg of the stick insect *Carausius morosus*

1 *Tettigonia viridissima* L. Tettigoniidae
Great Green Bush Cricket

2 *Tettigonia cantans* Fuess.

3 *Decticus verrucivorus* L.
Wart-biter

Male bush crickets are very easy to distinguish from the females, which have an ovipositor of variable length and thickness at the tip of their abdomens. The ovipositor of the Great Green Bush Cricket (*Tettigonia viridissima*) only just reaches the top of the wings when at rest, whereas in *Tettigonia cantans* it stretches far beyond its wings. Both species occur from July to October in meadows, fields and forests and are even not uncommon in gardens. They are predators and kill their prey (other bush crickets and grasshoppers being among the commonest victims as well as small caterpillars, moths and butterflies, two-winged flies and various larvae) with their powerful jaws. The males stridulate untiringly, mainly towards evening, but quite frequently during the day as well. The female lays her eggs in the soil and the nymphs are hatched the following spring.

The Wart-biter (*Decticus verrucivorus*), whose Latin name has the same meaning (*verruca* means 'wart' and *voro* 'devour'), was actually said to be used by Swedish peasants for the removal of warts. This bush cricket's colouring is very variable. The species inhabits lowlands, uplands and mountains and is to be seen from June to the end of September. It lives in both dry and damp meadows, in fields and sometimes on the outskirts of forests and even on heaths. It is both carnivorous and herbivorous, catches all kinds of caterpillars and beetle larvae, including the thick-bodied grubs of the Colorado Beetle, collects and eats dead insects and is very fond of the juicy leaves of certain plants, such as dandelions. The males stridulate very penetratingly in a somewhat lower key than the Great Green Bush Cricket. Like other bush crickets, the female lays her eggs in the ground, using her long ovipositor. The eggs are about 5 mm ($\frac{3}{16}$ in) long and the nymphs are hatched in the spring.

1. *Tettigonia viridissima*: 28—42 mm ($1\frac{1}{8}$—$1\frac{11}{16}$ in). Palaearctic region.
2. *Tettigonia cantans*: 23—38 mm ($\frac{15}{16}$—$1\frac{1}{2}$ in). Palaearctic region.
3. *Decticus verrucivorus*: 24—44 mm ($\frac{15}{16}$—$1\frac{3}{4}$ in). A Euro-siberian species.

1 *Isophya pyrenea* Serv.   Phaneropteridae
2 *Ephippiger ephippiger* Fieb.   Ephippigeridae
3 *Tachycines asynamorus*   Rhaphidophoridae
Adel.
Greenhouse Camel Cricket

Some crickets and grasshoppers have very short wing sheaths (tegmina). In the male *Isophya pyrenea* these are the same length as the scutum; in the female they are only half that length. The female has a striking, sabre-like, toothed ovipositor. From June to September this species frequents the vegetation at the edge of forests, forests paths and clearings with shrubs. It lives on leaves and relishes the flowers of grasses. The stridulation of the males, which begins after dusk, is soft and unobtrusive. The females lay eggs in the ground in groups of five or six.

Ephippiger ephippiger has short wing sheaths (tegmina). It likes warm, dry surroundings and is widely distributed in southern Europe. The imagos, which live from July to September, mainly frequent small trees and bushes, as they cannot fly and do not climb very high. The nymphs live more on bushes and low vegetation. The males and the females both stridulate. They live on plant tissues and small insects.

The Greenhouse Camel Cricket (*Tachycines asynamorus*) has exceptionally long antennae, measuring 75 mm (3 in) in the male and 80 mm ($3\frac{1}{8}$ in) in the female. Its powerfully developed hindlegs enable it to take leaps 1.5 m (5 ft) long and 40 cm (16 in) high. It is assumed that this species comes from central China. In Europe it appeared for the first time in Prague, towards the end of the nineteenth century, and then in Hamburg and other cities, where it settled in the greenhouses of botanical gardens and in nurseries. It is a completely wingless, nocturnal and basically carnivorous insect, which catches various insects injurious to greenhouse plants; it devours plant tissues itself only when it has insufficient water. The female lays several hundred eggs in the soil; the nymphs are hatched in two to three months and the imago lives for about one year.

1. *Isophya pyrenea:* 16—26 mm ($\frac{5}{8}$—$1\frac{1}{16}$ in). Southern and central Europe.
2. *Ephippiger ephippiger:* 22—30 mm ($\frac{7}{8}$—$1\frac{3}{16}$ in). Europe.
3. *Tachycines asynamorus:* 13—19 mm ($\frac{9}{16}$—$\frac{3}{4}$ in). China; introduced into Europe and North America.

1 *Gryllus campestris* L.   Gryllidae
Field Cricket

2 *Acheta domestica* L.
House Cricket

3 *Gryllotalpa gryllotalpa* L.   Gryllotalpidae
Common Mole Cricket

The Field Cricket is extremely rare in Britain and an endangered species. Its males stridulate incessantly from morning to evening. Field Crickets settle in warm surroundings, where they dig burrows for themselves. They live on grassy verges, on sandy slopes and in pinewoods. The Field Cricket is flightless and extremely timid and as soon as it feels itself to be in danger, it dives into hiding. It is omnivorous. The female lays her eggs from May to July. At first, the nymphs live all together in underground chambers and under stones, but later they scatter and in the autumn they dig their own burrows and spend the winter in them.

The House Cricket (*Acheta domestica*) has quite different habits. It also likes warmth, but has attached itself to people. It colonises houses, bakeries, cellars and hospitals, where it stridulates untiringly; in the summer it also ventures into the open. The House Cricket flies well and, being nocturnally active, remains in hiding during the daytime and then goes hunting at night. It has very modest requirements and is content with human food remains, bread, flour, carrots and dead insects. The female lays about 200–300 eggs.

The Common Mole Cricket (*Gryllotalpa gryllotalpa*) is well adapted for an underground existence. Its curiously formed forelegs are useful tools for digging burrows. It can go both forwards and backwards and is also able to fly. It lives in damp soil in meadows, gardens and peat-bogs and can even swim. In water, air bubbles adhere to the hairs on its body and give this a silvery appearance. The Common Mole Cricket is carnivorous and catches various kinds of larvae. When excavating burrows it may bite through the roots of cultivated plants which bar its progress, but it cannot be said to be a serious pest. The Common Mole Cricket is very rare in Britain and is an endangered species.

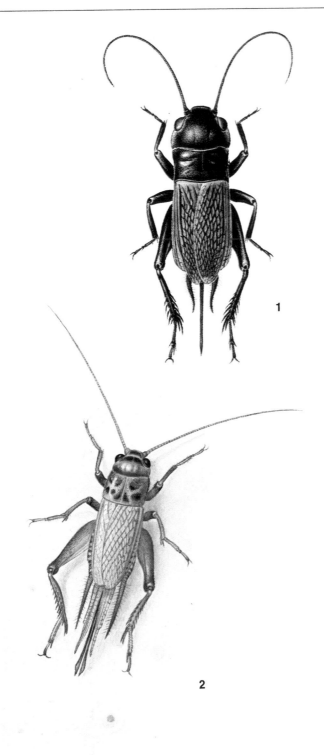

2

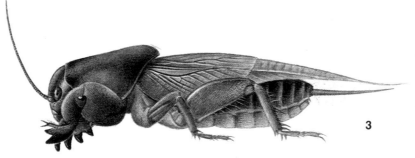

3

1. *Gryllus campestris:* 20—26 mm ($\frac{13}{16}$—$1\frac{1}{16}$ in). Central and southern Europe, western Asia, northern Africa.
2. *Acheta domestica:* 16—21 mm ($\frac{5}{8}$—$\frac{13}{16}$ in). Europe, western Asia, northern Africa, North America (introduced).
3. *Gryllotalpa gryllotalpa:* 35—50 mm ($1\frac{3}{8}$—2 in). Europe, western Asia, northern Africa.

1 *Tetrix subulata* L.
Slender Groundhopper

Tetrigidae

2 *Calliptamus italicus* L.

Catantopidae

3 *Psophus stridulus* L.

Acrididae

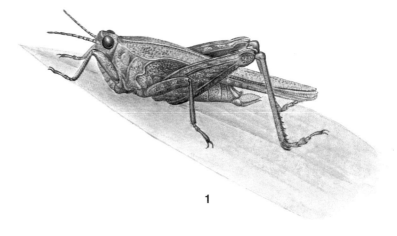

1

Some Caelifera have very strict environmental requirements; others are less choosy. The latter species include the Slender Groundhopper (*Tetrix subulata*), which prefers damp meadows and the banks of rivers and ponds, but also frequents dry heaths and open woods. It is common, flies well and is able to swim. It overwinters either as a nymph or as an imago; in the former case the imagos appear in the spring and can be seen until June, while a new generation imagos fly from August until October. Both imagos and nymphs live mostly on mosses and leaves.

Calliptamus italicus has a marked preference for dry and warm surroundings. It inhabits grassy places such as dry meadows and fallow land, where it occurs from July until October. On a stone or in vegetation it is virtually invisible, but when it flies its pink hindwings can be seen. In dry, hot summers, when it tends to population explosions, it can be destructive to crops. It was once thought that this species was silent, or that it produced sounds by rubbing its hind femurs against its wing sheaths, but it was recently found that it stridulates with its mandibles. It is not found in Britain.

Psophus stridulus, a particularly thermophilic species, inhabits mountain meadows, dry, sunny slopes, clearings in mountain forests, moors and the outskirts of woods, where it occurs from August to October. The female sits in the vegetation, or hops and softly stridulates, while the flying male is conspicuous for its red hindwings and its unusually loud, penetrating stridulation. The sexes can be differentiated by the length of their tegmina, which are longer than the body in the male and shorter in the female. Like other Caelifera, this is a herbivorous species.

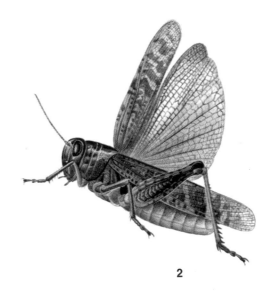

2

1. *Tetrix subulata:* 7—10 mm ($\frac{1}{4}$—$\frac{3}{8}$ in). Europe, Siberia, northern Africa.
2. *Calliptamus italicus:* 15—34 mm ($\frac{5}{8}$—$1\frac{3}{8}$ in). Palaearctic region.
3. *Psophus stridulus:* 23—32 mm ($\frac{15}{16}$—$1\frac{1}{4}$ in). Europe, Siberia.

3

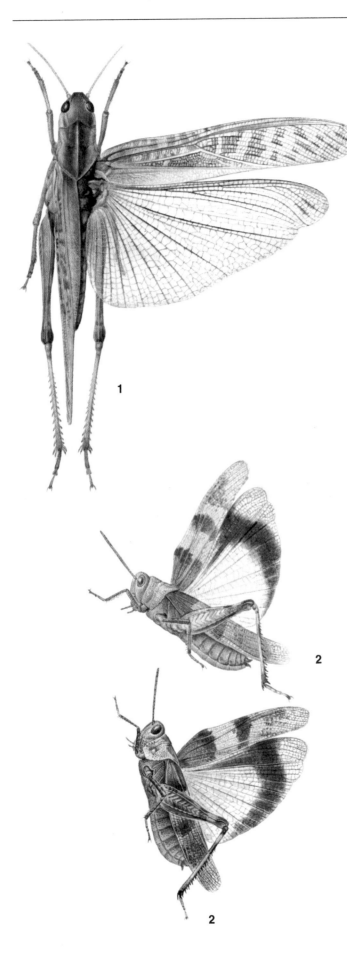

1

2

2

1 *Locusta migratoria* L. Acrididae
Migratory Locust

2 *Oedipoda coerulescens* L.

The variably coloured Migratory Locust (*Locusta migratoria*), an occasional visitor to Britain, is one of the biggest European members of the family. It is also one of the most dreaded species. The calamities which it once caused in central Europe are now a thing of the past, but in the tropical and subtropical belt Migratory Locusts still do untold damage. Normally the locust occurs in the sedentary phase (*sedentaria*), when it is more or less harmless, but in given circumstances, brought about by its overmultiplication and a consequent lack of food, the sedentary phase begins to change to the migratory phase (*gregaria*) and then the locusts invade new regions. Once the impulse is given, the huge swarm rises into the air like a cloud and then settles on new territory, where it devours everything down to the last blade of grass and leaves behind a trail of complete destruction. The danger is so great that the migrating locusts are sprayed with insecticides from the air.

When at rest, *Oedipoda coerulescens* is almost indistinguishable from its background, but when it soars into the air it shows its coloured hindwings, which are usually blue, with a dark border, but are occasionally yellow or pink. This species favours warm, dry places with scanty vegetation. It therefore mainly inhabits grassy places, abandoned quarries, sand-dunes and the outskirts of open woods. The imagos appear from July to September, but the first frosts can kill them. They mostly remain on the ground and make short flights only when disturbed, as they soon tire. *Oedipoda coerulescens* lives mostly on grasses, which it finds in abundance in its chosen localities. In captivity, however, it also devours the remains of dead locusts. Like other grasshoppers, the female lays her eggs in the ground and dies soon after.

1. *Locusta migratoria:* 30—60 mm ($1\frac{3}{16}$—$2\frac{3}{8}$ in). Southern and central Europe, Near East, Africa, Madagascar.
2. *Oedipoda coerulescens:* 15—28 mm ($\frac{5}{8}$—$1\frac{1}{8}$ in). Europe, Asia Minor and the Near East, northern Africa.

1 *Oedipoda germanica* Latr.   Acrididae

2 *Stenobothrus lineatus* Panz.
Stripe-winged Grasshopper

3 *Chorthippus biguttulus* L.

Oedipoda germanica has very definite environmental requirements. It needs dry and warm surroundings and inhabits stony grasslands with a limestone base and the edge of open woods and vineyards and heaths. It is fast becoming rare in central Europe. It closely resembles *Oedipoda coerulescens,* but has red hind-wings (a few individuals have yellow or dull blue wings). As with *Oedipoda coerulescens,* its general colouring matches its surroundings.

Red, blue, or yellow hindwings are unusual among grasshoppers. Most hindwings are more or less transparent, or possibly brown-tipped, as in *Stenobothrus lineatus.* The imagos of this common (and in some places abundant) species occur from July until September in dry meadows, in forests on footpaths and in clearings and on heaths from lowlands to mountains. Its general colouring is very variable and it stridulates sweetly and not very loudly.

The stridulation of *Chorthippus biguttulus* is so unique that this species has been nicknamed the 'nightingale locust'. It inhabits dry woods, meadows and open fields. The imagos appear in abundance from June to October; they are most numerous in lowlands and their numbers decrease with an increase in the altitude. In the autumn the female lays her eggs in a brown ootheca on or just below the ground; the nymphs are hatched in the spring.

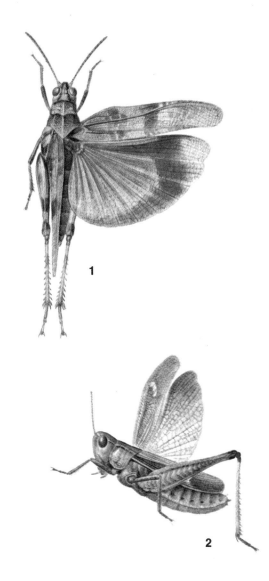

1

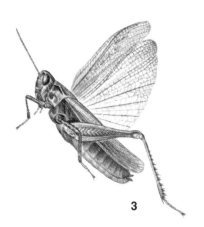

2

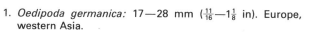

3

1. *Oedipoda germanica:* 17—28 mm ($\frac{11}{16}$—$1\frac{1}{8}$ in). Europe, western Asia.
2. *Stenobothrus lineatus:* 16—25 mm ($\frac{5}{8}$—1 in). Europe, western Asia (Siberia).
3. *Chorthippus biguttulus:* 13—22 m ($\frac{9}{16}$—$\frac{7}{8}$ in). Europe, Siberia, northern Africa.

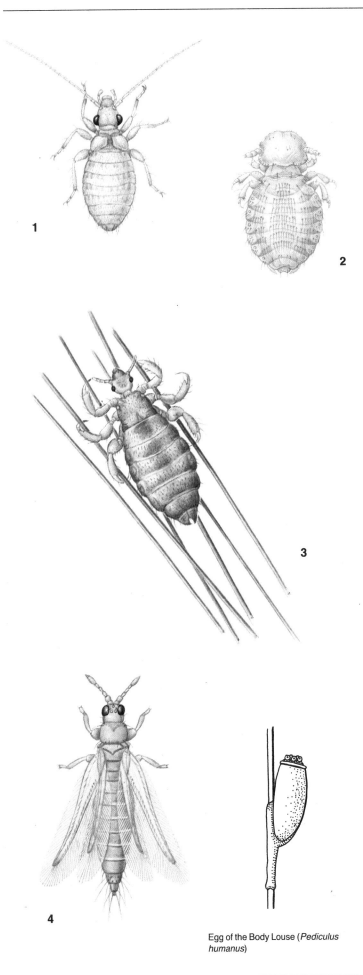

1 *Trogium pulsatorium* L. Trogiidae
2 *Trichodectes canis* Deg. Trichodectidae
Dog-louse
3 *Pediculus humanus* L. Pediculidae
Body Louse, Clothes Louse
4 *Frankliniella intonsa* Trybom Thripidae

Many Trogiidae species live in the vicinity of people, in their homes, cellars and storehouses. *Trogium pulsatorium* is found most frequently in damp dwellings, storerooms, mills and warehouses, as well as in beehives and birds' nests. It has very short wings. It is omnivorous and if it overmultiplies it can do considerable damage. The females make weak sounds by beating their abdomens on the underlying support.

The life of animal lice is very closely associated with a particular host. The Dog-louse (*Trichodectes canis*) is a common parasite of dogs. It probably affects long-haired dogs most and usually clings to the hairs on the neck and head. The louse lays its eggs in the host's coat, where the rest of their development takes place.

People and animals have been plagued with lice since time immemorial. The dreaded and unpleasant Body or Clothes Louse (*Pediculus humanus*) appears in two forms, living in human hair and on the body. The lice and their nymphs live on blood. Their bite injects saliva into the wound and causes persistent itching. The eggs are familiar as nits. The female of the form infesting the head attaches her eggs to the hairs, while the body form usually lays them in clothing. As well as being a nuisance, lice can transmit the pathogens of dangerous diseases, resulting in serious epidemics. This happens most often during or after a war or in times of famine. Through the ages lice have been responsible for the deaths of millions of human beings.

The majority of thrips occur on plants, where they suck the tissues; their wings are finely fringed. *Frankliniella intonsa* is one of the most common.

Egg of the Body Louse (*Pediculus humanus*)

1. *Trogium pulsatorium:* 1.5—2 mm ($\frac{1}{32}$—$\frac{3}{32}$ in). Over the entire globe.
2. *Trichodectes canis:* 1.4—2 mm ($\frac{1}{32}$—$\frac{3}{32}$ in). Over the entire globe.
3. *Pediculus humanus:* 2.4—4.2 mm ($\frac{1}{16}$—$\frac{5}{32}$ in). Over the entire globe.
4. *Frankliniella intonsa:* 0.8—1 mm ($\frac{1}{32}$ in). The Palaearctic region.

1 *Tritomegas bicolor* L. Cydnidae

2 *Thyreocoris scarabaeoides* L.
Negro Bug

3 *Graphosoma lineatum* L. Pentatomidae
Striped Bug

Many plant bugs have a very varied diet, but others are restricted to a few plants or even only one. *Tritomegas bicolor,* whose host plant is the White Deadnettle, is one of the latter species, although it can also be found on certain shrubs on which it settles during its spring migration. The imagos generally spend the winter in moss – sometimes together with many others of their kind. They pair from about the middle of April to the beginning of July. This species looks after its offspring. The female makes a small depression in dry soil, lays 40–45 minute eggs in it and remains alongside them, moving them about with her proboscis. The young nymphs crawl about over the host plant and, after five larval instars, develop into imagos in about six weeks.

The tiny Negro Bug (*Thyreocoris scarabaeoides*) is a warmth-loving species living in dry localities such as sand-dunes or grassy places on a limestone base. Both the sexes stridulate. The female lays her eggs in May or in June; the nymphs overwinter.

Flowering umbelliferous plants act as hosts for the most diverse insects all through the summer. One of their regular visitors in warm localities is the Striped Bug (*Graphosoma lineatum*), which immediately strikes the eye because of its colouring and its large scutum, which stretches to the tip of its body. This species inhabits dry meadows, grass verges and the outskirts of woods. It is polyphagous. The imagos appear from the early summer until the autumn. The nymphs resemble the adult bugs, but lack the black stripes and are uniformly orange-red. The imagos hibernate.

1. *Tritomegas bicolor:* 5—7 mm ($\frac{3}{16}$—$\frac{1}{4}$ in). Palaearctic region.
2. *Thyreocoris scarabaeoides:* 3—4 mm ($\frac{1}{8}$—$\frac{3}{16}$ in). Europe, Asia Minor, northern Africa.
3. *Graphosoma lineatum:* 9—11 mm ($\frac{3}{8}$—$\frac{7}{16}$ in). Central and southern Europe, Asia Minor, Middle East.

1 *Aelia acuminata* L.   Pentatomidae
Bishop's Mitre

2 *Palomena viridissima* Poda

3 *Dolycoris baccarum* L.
Sloe Bug

The Bishop's Mitre (*Aelia acuminata*) needs grass and cereals for its life and development and is therefore to be found beside footpaths, on heaths and sand-dunes and sometimes in cornfields. The imagos hibernate and do not leave their winter quarters until the end of April or the beginning of May. Pairing takes place at the end of May or the beginning of June. During June the female lays her eggs in two parallel rows on blades of grass. The new generation of bugs, which matures in about six or seven weeks, remains until October, when the imagos retire underground. The European fauna comprises several related species.

Palomena viridissima and the Green Shield Bug (*P. prasina*) are two species which have a similar form and colour. For a reliable differentiation it is necessary to evaluate the length ratio of the second and third antennal segment and the shape of the scutum. Both species are commonly found on cultivated and wild herbaceous and ligneous plants. After overwintering, the imagos reappear very late in the spring. The females lay eggs during the summer on various herbaceous plants and the nymphs develop until September, when the new generation of imagos begins to make its appearance.

The Sloe Bug (*Dolycoris baccarum*) is a very common and striking representative of the European bug. It occurs in forests, clearings, fields and gardens and is primarily herbivorous. The nymphs and the imagos suck the juices of flowers and sometimes the fruits of wild and cultivated plants; it is particularly common on bilberries. Wherever it feeds, it leaves a disagreeable odour from a secretion from its scent glands. It sucks potato and sugar beet plants, cereals and even aphids' and beetles' eggs. The imagos hibernate and pair in June. The female lays groups of eggs on leaves. The young bugs complete their development during August.

Part of the antennae of the bugs *Palomena viridissima* (a) and *P. prasina* (b)

1. *Aelia acuminata:* 7—10 mm ($\frac{1}{4}$—$\frac{3}{8}$ in). A large part of the Palaearctic region.
2. *Palomena viridissima:* 12—14 mm ($\frac{1}{2}$—$\frac{9}{16}$ in). A large part of Europe.
3. *Dolycoris baccarum:* 10—12 mm ($\frac{3}{8}$—$\frac{1}{2}$ in). The Palaearctic, Neotropical and Oriental regions.

1 *Eurydema dominulus* Scop. Pentatomidae

2 *Eurydema oleracea* L.
Cabbage Bug, Brassica Bug

3 *Pentatoma rufipes* L.
Red-legged Stink Bug, Forest Bug

Cultivated and wild cruciferous plants act as hosts to many bugs, including the two well-known and widespread species *Eurydema dominulus* and *E. oleracea*. These are immediately distinguishable from each other by their colouring. Compared with *E. dominulus, E. oleracea* is somewhat variably coloured. The markings on its scutum and wing sheaths are sometimes predominantly red and sometimes yellow and whitish. However, both species overwinter in the imago stage and lay their eggs in double rows on the leaves of their host plants in the spring. In central and northern Europe both species produce one generation a year.

The Forest Bug (*Pentatoma rufipes*) is one of the largest of the many species of the Pentatomidae family. It lives chiefly in deciduous and mixed woods, most commonly on oaks and alders, but also on other deciduous trees, such as birches and hazels. It also occurs in gardens and orchards on apple, pear and cherry trees. With its long, thin proboscis it sucks the juices of plants, dead insects and caterpillars. The imagos appear on the plants in about the middle of July and pair at the end of July and the beginning of August. The female then lays the eggs on leaves; they are smooth and yellow and have a red spot. The females live longer than the males and can sometimes still be encountered at the beginning of November. The yellow, dark-streaked nymphs are hatched in April and September. Part of their development takes place in the autumn. They then overwinter and leave their winter retreat in spring to continue their development. (This usually happens in April, but can be earlier.) Their development is complete in July.

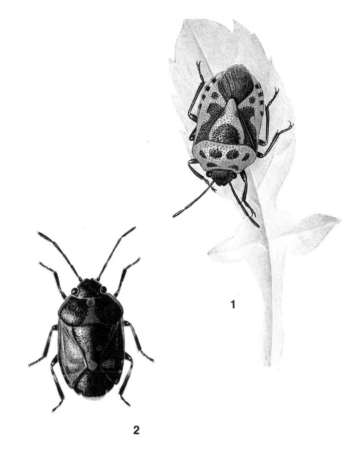

1

2

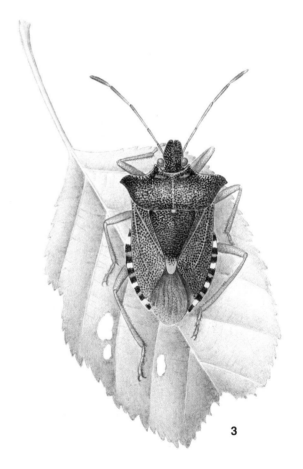

1. *Eurydema dominulus:* 6—8.5 mm ($\frac{1}{4}$—$\frac{11}{32}$ in). Europe, Transcaucasia, Siberia.
2. *Eurydema oleracea:* 5—7 mm ($\frac{3}{16}$—$\frac{1}{4}$ in). Palaearctic region.
3. *Pentatoma rufipes:* 12—16 mm ($\frac{1}{2}$—$\frac{5}{8}$ in). Europe, northern Asia.

3

1 **Elasmucha ferrugata** F.   Acanthosomatidae

2 **Mesocerus marginatus** L.   Coreidae

3 **Corizus hyoscyami** L.   Rhopalidae

Care of the offspring is not normally found among bugs in the perfect form in which it is known in beetles and hymenopterans. There are some notable exceptions, however, such as *Elasmucha ferrugata*. The female lays approximately 35 eggs, from the end of May, on the underside of bilberry leaves and then stays with them; she also protects the newly hatched nymphs. The nymphs do not leave the parental colony until the second instar, when they disperse all over the plant. This forest species is most common on bilberry plants, but is also to be found on brambles. The secretions of its scent glands spoil the flavour of the berries. The imagos hibernate.

The European fauna comprises many squash bugs (Coreidae), but in the tropics there are far more and their colours are more splendid. One of the most widespread European species is *Mesocerus marginatus*, which inhabits the outskirts of forests and fields, clearings and rubble, wherever it can find a suitable host plant (usually some type of sorrel). The imagos hibernate and the female lays her large brown eggs on sorrel leaves from the end of May. During July the adult bugs die and the development of the new generation is complete in August. The bugs then live on plants until the middle of October, when they hibernate.

A few species of bugs closely resemble one another because of their black and red colouring. One of these is the scentless *Corizus hyoscyami* which can be found in some places on sunny hillsides, as well as in dry meadows and limestone localities. It favours Compositae to live on, but the range of its food plants is much wider. The imagos hibernate.

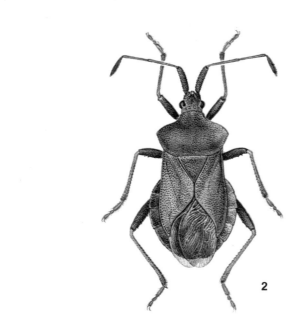

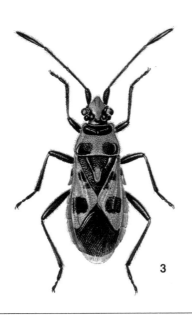

1. *Elasmucha ferrugata:* 7.5—9 mm ($\frac{5}{16}$—$\frac{3}{8}$ in). Central and western Europe (absent from Scandinavia). Rare in the British Isles.
2. *Mesocerus marginatus:* 12—14 mm ($\frac{1}{2}$—$\frac{9}{16}$ in). Europe (north to 65° latitude), Siberia.
3. *Corizus hyoscyami:* 8—10 mm ($\frac{5}{16}$—$\frac{3}{8}$ in). Palaearctic region.

1 *Lygaeus saxatilis* Scop.   Lygaeidae
2 *Pyrrhocoris apterus* L.   Pyrrhocoridae
Firebug
3 *Aradus depressus* F.   Aradidae

Most bugs are easily distinguished by their colour and form. Other species are more difficult to identify. An example of this is the ground bug *Lygaeus saxatilis* which closely resembles *L. equestris,* but lacks the light spot on the membraneous part of the hemielytra. The adult *L. saxatilis* and its developmental stages suck various plants, but display a special predilection for umbelliferous and composite plants. They live mainly in warm localities at the edge of fields, on grass verges and in meadows and sometimes occur in masses. The imagos hibernate.

With the first warm days of spring, the Firebug (*Pyrrhocoris apterus*) leaves its winter shelter and the imagos collect at the foot of old trees (mainly limes). They are not common in Britain, being found only in Devon. Elsewhere, though, they crawl about on footpaths and walls, suck the fruit capsules of old lime-trees and feed on all kinds of seeds. They also have a liking for dead insects and other animals and in times of a dearth of food they have been known to indulge in cannibalism. Firebugs pair early in the spring and the female lays 50—60 eggs on damp ground, under old leaves. The first nymphal stages appear in May and the first adult insects with the advent of winter, when they feed, but do not reproduce.

Their extremely flattened body enables some bugs to live beneath bark. The flatbug *Aradus depressus* is to be found chiefly below the bark of beeches, oaks, birches and other trees, where it looks for and sucks the mycelium of fungi. The female lays eggs over a large part of the vegetation season. The adult bugs sometimes occur in groups, together with the nymphs.

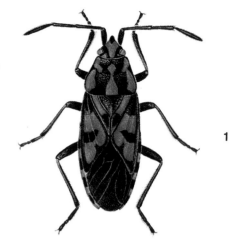

1

2

3

1. *Lygaeus saxatilis:* 10—12 mm ($\frac{3}{8}$—$\frac{1}{2}$ in). A large part of Europe, Asia Minor and the Near East, northern Africa.
2. *Pyrrhocoris apterus:* 7—12 mm ($\frac{1}{4}$—$\frac{1}{2}$ in). Europe (absent from the north of Scandinavia, present locally in the British Isles).
3. *Aradus depressus:* 5—6.5 mm ($\frac{3}{16}$—$\frac{9}{32}$ in). Europe, the temperate bellt in Asia.

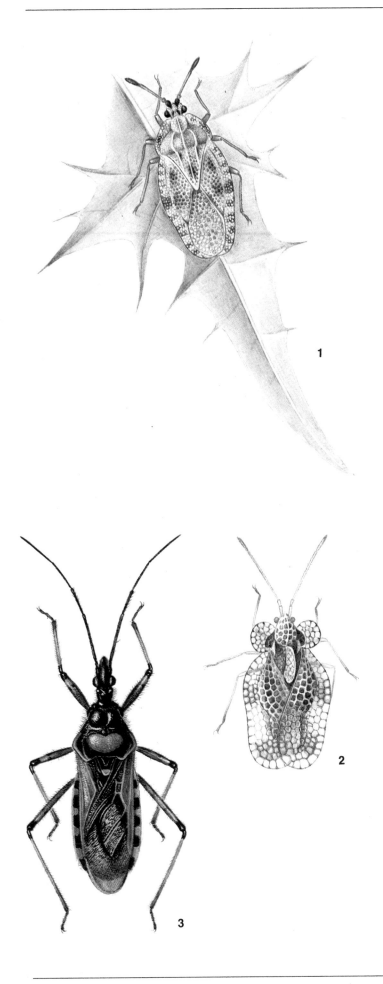

1 ***Tingis cardui*** L. Tingidae
Spear Thistle Lace Bug

2 ***Stephanitis pyri*** F.

3 ***Rhinocoris iracundus*** Poda Reduviidae
Red Assassin Bug

There is one family of bugs whose members are all characterised by very fine sculpturing on their scutum and hemielytra. These are the lace bugs, which occur on both herbaceous and ligneous plants. They are very tiny, and have to be searched for carefully. The Spear Thistle Lace Bug (*Tingis cardui*) generally abounds on thistles and sucks their juices. The imagos spend the winter in old leaves and debris on the ground. The females lay their eggs in thistle leaves during the summer and the young bugs appear from the end of July.

One of the prettiest lace bugs, with very fine sculpturing reminiscent of oriental filigree, is *Stephanitis pyri,* which is common in gardens with an adequate choice of host plants, including pear, apple, cherry and walnut trees. It is also to be found on hawthorn and whitebeam. It occurs on the leaves and small twigs, where it sucks the juices. The imagos hibernate. They hide under leaves – in gardens under the leaves on strawberry beds. The female lays her eggs on the underside of the host plants.

The strikingly coloured, long-legged Red Assassin Bug (*Rhinocoris iracundus*) is one of the biggest land bugs. It inhabits sunny localities with scrubby vegetation, where it prefers the taller plants. Both the nymphs and the adult bugs are predators. They lie in wait on plants for a variety of insects, including caterpillars and other larvae. When they have caught one, they thrust their long, curved proboscis into its body and suck it dry. This bug produces one generation a year. The nymphs overwinter and the imagos, which hatch in the spring, can be seen until the autumn.

1. *Tingis cardui:* 3.5—4 mm ($\frac{5}{32}$—$\frac{7}{32}$ in). A large portion of Europe (including all parts of the British Isles), Asia Minor, northern Africa.
2. *Stephanitis pyri:* 3—3.5 mm ($\frac{1}{8}$ in). A large part of Europe, the Middle East, central Asia, northern Africa.
3. *Rhinocoris iracundus:* 13—18 mm ($\frac{9}{16}$—$\frac{3}{4}$ in). Practically the whole of Europe, Asia Minor, the Near East.

1 *Himacerus apterus* F.   Nabidae
Tree Damsel Bug

2 *Anthocoris nemorum* L.   Anthocoridae
Common Flower Bug

3 *Cimex lectularius* L.   Cimicidae
True Bed-bug

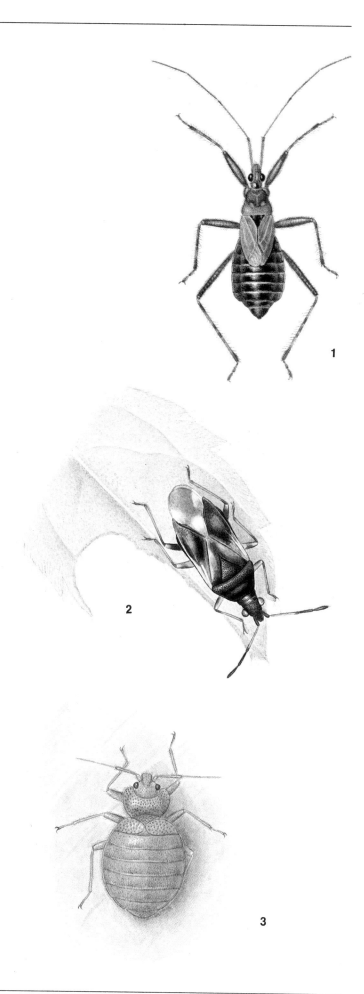

The Tree Damsel Bug (*Himacerus apterus*) lives on trees. It mainly frequents deciduous trees and their undergrowth and is less often to be found on conifers. The imagos generally have short wings reaching to their third or fourth abdominal segment, but occasionally, especially in females, to the tip of their abdomen. They are predacious and live on various small arthropods, such as mites, small bugs and aphids. The imagos are most numerous in August and survive until late autumn. During September the female lays the eggs on the host plants, in young wood.

The Common Flower Bug (*Anthocoris nemorum*) is found throughout most of the year. The imagos begin to leave their winter hiding-places early in the spring and appear first of all on flowering willows and then on oaks, fruit trees and various shrubs and herbaceous plants. They almost always inhabit growths of stinging nettles. Both the imagos and the nymphs are predacious; they catch small arthropods, chiefly aphids, but also jumping plant lice and mites. The female lays her tiny white eggs on the underside of a leaf. There are usually two generations in a year. Before the advent of winter, the imagos crawl under the bark of a tree or into a clump of old grass or old leaves to hibernate.

Like fleas and lice, bugs have long roused fear and aversion in people. In the greater part of Europe their mass incidence is now a thing of the past, but many parts of the world are still infested by them. The True Bed-bug (*Cimex lectularius*) is a nocturnal bug that inhabits human dwellings. It hides behind pictures, in beds and in cracks in the floorboards. If disturbed, it immediately scuttles into hiding. Both the imagos and the nymphs suck human blood, but if food is scarce they will also attack domestic animals. Their bite is painful and a red spot is formed at its site. If the temperature of a dwelling does not fall below 13 °C (55 °F), the bugs' development continues uninterrupted; at lower temperatures it stops.

1. *Himacerus apterus:* 8—10 mm ($\frac{5}{16}$—$\frac{3}{8}$ in). A large part of Europe.
2. *Anthocoris nemorum:* 3—4.5 mm ($\frac{1}{8}$ in). Europe, Asia Minor, northern Asia, northern Africa.
3. *Cimex lectularius:* 3.5—8 mm ($\frac{3}{32}$—$\frac{5}{16}$ in). Everywhere.

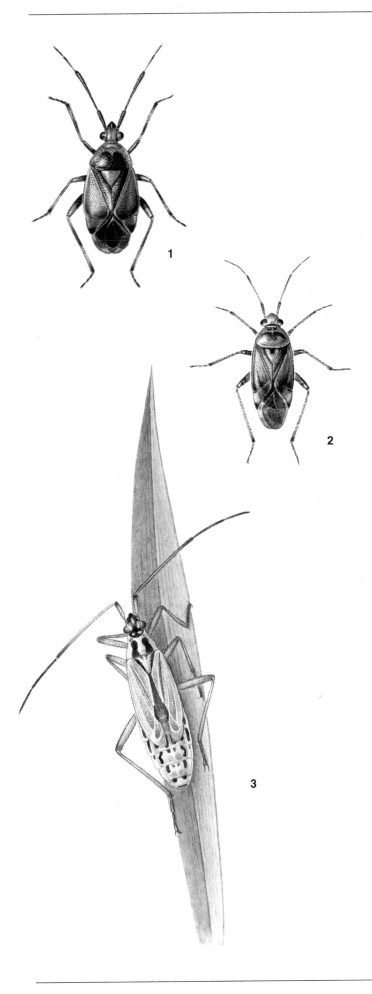

1 *Deraeocoris ruber* L.　　Miridae
Leaf Bug

2 *Lygus pratensis* L.

3 *Leptoterna dolobrata* L.
Meadow Plant Bug

The gaily coloured Leaf Bug *(Deraeocoris ruber)* is most common from July to September, when it appears on a diversity of deciduous shrubs and trees and on herbaceous plants. It is very variably coloured and a number of colour forms have been described. As a predator, it catches different kinds of insects (mostly aphids and small larvae) and is thus a useful bug. The female lays her eggs in August and September and the first larvae hatch the following May.

The imagos of the very common and widespread *Lygus pratensis* are to be seen from July onwards on various herbaceous plants and deciduous trees; they also occur on heather. The adult bugs overwinter and can then be encountered on conifers.

The brownish-yellow Meadow Plant Bug *(Leptoterna dolobrata)* is notable for its variable colouring and the different lengths of its wings. The males have fully developed wings, but only some of the females are fully winged; the majority have very short wings (the brachypterous form) and intermediate forms also exist. Even winged forms do not fly very far away from their fixed habitat. The imagos abound (sometimes in masses) in grassy localities, such as meadows, grass verges and grassy slopes. They are most numerous at the end of June and in July, but can still be seen in August or even September. They usually frequent grasses, such as timothy grass, meadow foxtail and cock's-foot, and they sometimes appear on cereals. The eggs, which are laid in the late summer, change colour during the winter; the nymphs hatch in about the middle of May.

1. *Deraeocoris ruber:* 6.5—7 mm ($\frac{9}{32}$—$\frac{1}{4}$ in). The whole of Europe.
2. *Lygus pratensis:* 6—7.3 mm ($\frac{1}{4}$—$\frac{9}{32}$ in). The Palaearctic region.
3. *Leptoterna dolobrata:* 7—10 mm ($\frac{1}{4}$—$\frac{3}{8}$ in). The Palaearctic and Nearctic region.

1 *Hydrometra stagnorum* L. Hydrometridae

2 *Gerris gibbifer* Schumm. Gerridae

3 *Saldula saltatoria* L. Saldidae

Shore Bug

The banks of rivers, streams, ponds and pools are regularly inhabited by slim-bodied bugs with long, thin legs, which crawl over the plants or on the surface of the water near the bank. As a rule they are water-measurers. *Hydrometra stagnorum* is a predacious bug which hunts mosquito larvae and other small arthropods on the surface of the water and gathers drowning insects. It stabs prey with its proboscis and usually sucks its contents on the bank. The eggs of this species, which are laid on plants above the water, have a very ornamentally sculptured surface.

Pond skaters can be seen on the surface of pools, ponds and slow streams or rivers almost everywhere, skating over them without getting themselves wet. Their forelegs are adapted for catching prey and their middle legs and hindlegs for locomotion. The family comprises many similar species. *Gerris gibbifer* prefers acidulous shallow water. It frequently occurs in peat-bog pools and in artificial reservoirs, is predacious and hunts other aquatic animals. It produces two generations in a year; the first reaches adulthood in July and the second in September. The imagos of the second generation overwinter; sometimes, if the weather is warm, they appear on the water in January, but usually not until April or May.

The tiny Shore Bug (*Saldula saltatoria*) is almost always found in large numbers at the edge of ditches, ponds, garden pools and slow-flowing water. It is very rapacious and constantly searches the mud for prey, which it stabs and overcomes without the aid of its fore limbs. The imagos hibernate, often in a clump of grass, but the first spring sunshine brings them out. Pairing takes place from the end of April and the eggs are laid in the mud and in various kinds of small holes.

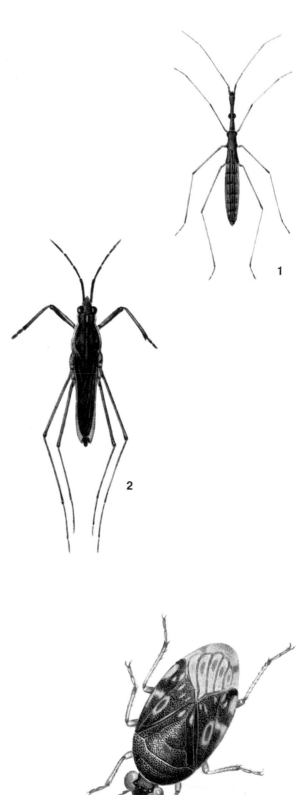

1. *Hydrometra stagnorum:* 9—12 mm ($\frac{3}{8}$—$\frac{1}{2}$ in). Europe, Middle East, northern Africa.
2. *Gerris gibbifer:* 10—13 mm ($\frac{3}{8}$—$\frac{9}{16}$ in). Europe (diminishing towards the north), northern Africa.
3. *Saldula saltatoria:* 3.5—4 mm ($\frac{5}{32}$—$\frac{7}{32}$ in). The Palaearctic and Nearctic regions.

1 *Notonecta glauca* L. — Notonectidae
2 *Corixa punctata* Ill. — Corixidae
Water-boatman
3 *Ilyocoris cimicoides* Stal.
Saucer Bug

1

If you were to stand still for a while and observe the surface of a pool or a pond, before long you would see a whole series of small and larger insects which come up for air and then disappear again. *Notonecta glauca,* one of the back-swimmers, is the commonest and most familiar water bug, with several more related species in Europe. It swims expertly with its long, hairy hind limbs. It likes water with rich vegetation and occurs in pools and ponds and near the banks of gently flowing streams and rivers. It has a short, but very strong proboscis for sucking its prey, which consists of various aquatic animals from tiny mosquito larvae to the larvae of big predacious diving beetles, tadpoles and small fish. Anybody who has handled a back-swimmer carelessly has felt the strength of its proboscis and the smarting pain caused by the poisons released as it stabs – the burning sensation continues long afterwards. Male back-swimmers have a stridulation apparatus and both sexes have an auditory organ. The imagos copulate during the winter and in February the female begins to lay her eggs. The young back-swimmers appear from August onwards.

The Water-boatman (*Corixa punctata*) inhabits both still and gently flowing water, but if the temperature rises too high it migrates. The imagos pair during the winter and the new generation needs three to four months to develop, so that the young Water-boatmen appear in July.

The Saucer Bug (*Ilyocoris cimicoides*) is a predacious bug. It reproduces during the winter. Poorly developed muscles prevent it from flying, but it is a very fast runner.

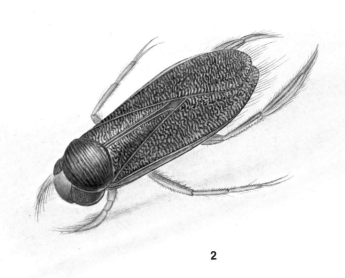

2

3

1. *Notonecta glauca:* 14—16 mm ($\frac{9}{16}$ — $\frac{5}{8}$ in). Eurasia, north-western Africa.
2. *Corixa punctata:* 13—15 mm ($\frac{9}{16}$ — $\frac{5}{8}$ in). Europe, Asia Minor, northern Africa, India.
3. *Ilyocoris cimicoides:* 12—16 mm ($\frac{1}{2}$ — $\frac{5}{8}$ in). Most of Europe, the Caucasus.

1 *Ranatra linearis* L.
Water Stick Insect

2 *Nepa cinerea* L.
Water Scorpion

Nepidae

The two Nepidae species illustrated here are obviously different, but they nevertheless do share a few features, in particular the shape and function of their raptorial first pair of legs, the tube at the end of their abdomen (through which they obtain air) and their short, three-jointed antennae and stabbing proboscis.

Already very long to start with, the Water Stick Insect (*Ranatra linearis*) is made even longer by its breathing tube, which is roughly the same length as its body. With a life span of two years, this is a long-lived species. The Water Stick Insect frequents different types of water and is to be found chiefly on the muddy river bed or in vegetation, lying in wait for prey, which it seizes with its forelegs; it is also able to swim. When moving to new surroundings it flies. The female lays her eggs in the stems of aquatic plants in the spring. The eggs are relatively large and are equipped with two filaments, which protrude from the plant and betray the position of the eggs. The imagos overwinter. The Water Stick Insect has now disappeared from many localities where not so long ago it was still quite common.

The Water Scorpion (*Nepa cinerea*) also used to be much more abundant than it is today, owing to the progressive destruction of its natural habitats, including small muddy pools, ponds and slow-flowing water with muddy banks. It is predacious. The older nymphs and the imagos lie in wait for prey (mainly various aquatic insects and other small animals) in the mud; the young nymphs also catch small creatures which happen to fall onto the water. This species produces one generation a year. The imagos sometimes overwinter on the bank. Pairing takes place in the spring and the females then lay eggs in aquatic plants. After five larval instars, the new generation of imagos appears in August.

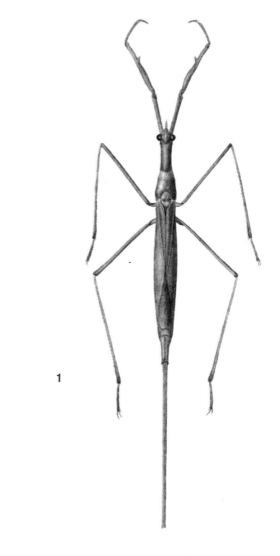

1

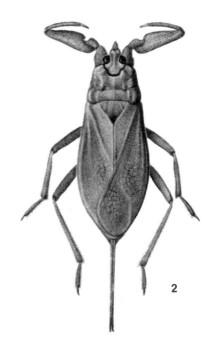

2

1. *Ranatra linearis:* 30—40 mm ($1\frac{3}{16}$—$1\frac{9}{16}$ in). A large part of the Palaearctic region.
2. *Nepa cinerea:* ♂ 15—18 mm, ♀ 20—23 mm (♂ $\frac{5}{8}$—$\frac{3}{4}$ in, ♀ $\frac{13}{16}$—$\frac{15}{16}$ in). Much of the Palaearctic region.

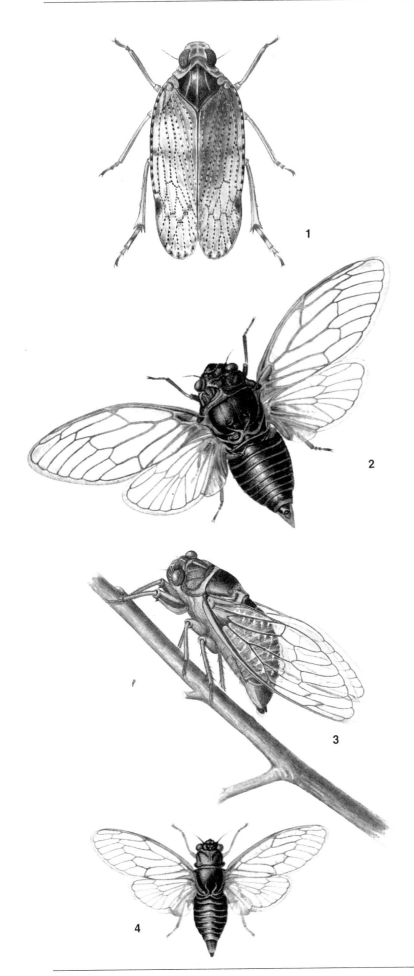

1 *Cixius nervosus* L. Cixiidae
2 *Tibicen haematodes* Scop. Cicadidae
3 *Cicada plebeja* Scop.
4 *Cicadetta montana* Scop.
Mountain Cicada

Cixius nervosus is a planthopper. The imagos of this species are common from June into the autumn on goat-willows, ash trees and other trees. The nymphs, which live on the roots of various grasses and under stones, secrete waxy fibres from their abdominal segments.

Cicadas are sap-sucking bugs found mainly on trees and bushes. Three members of the family Cicadidae are illustrated here – *Tibicen haematodes, Cicada plebeja* and *Cicadetta montana*. A cursory glance shows them all to be very much alike; their bionomics and reproduction are also similar. The males make shrill, chirping sounds which are an essential component of the sounds of the Mediterranean region and the warmer parts of central and southern Europe; the females are soundless. Cicadas are also able to receive sounds via a special auditory apparatus. Their 'singing' aids their detection and an expert can differentiate among them by their chirping. All three species are highly thermophilic and in consequence their territory frequently coincides with vineyard regions. *Cicadetta montana* is one of the most common species. It is smaller than the other two and its song is much quieter: it sounds somewhat like the buzzing of large hover-flies. The female lays her eggs in branches, but the young nymphs leave the host plant and develop in the ground, where they live on grass roots; their forelegs are specially adapted for digging. The fully grown nymph leaves the soil, climbs up a plant and takes a firm hold on it; the larval skin then splits and the young cicada leaves it soon afterwards.

1. *Cixius nervosus:* 6.5—8.5 mm ($\frac{9}{32}$ — $\frac{11}{32}$ in). A large part of the Palaearctic region.
2. *Tibicen haematodes:* 26—38 mm (1$\frac{1}{16}$ — 1$\frac{1}{2}$ in). Mediterranean. Occurs in warm parts of central Europe, e.g. vine-growing regions on the Main and Neckar, etc, in southern Moravia and in southern Slovakia.
3. *Cicada plebeja:* 30—36 mm, wing span up to 100 mm (1$\frac{3}{16}$ — 1$\frac{7}{16}$ in, wing span up to 3$\frac{15}{16}$ in). Mediterranean. Known near Vienna and formerly in southern Germany.
4. *Cicadetta montana:* 16—27 mm ($\frac{5}{8}$ — 1$\frac{1}{16}$ in). A large part of the Palaearctic region.

1 *Aphrophora alni* Fall.
2 *Cercopis vulnerata* Illig.
3 *Philaenus spumarius* L.
Spittle-bug

Cercopidae

On the leaves of many plants, especially in grassy clearings in woods and in gardens, you may come across clusters of white froth just above the ground, sometimes in large numbers over a small area. The froth encloses an inconspicuous little creature resembling a cicada. This creature is the nymph of a spittle-bug, which secretes this layer of froth around itself for protection and undergoes the whole of its development inside it.

The species *Aphrophora alni,* one of the commonest spittle-bugs, inhabits clearings, the margins of woods and gardens. The imagos settle on the young twigs of deciduous trees (birches, willows, poplars, alders and others) and suck their juices. If disturbed, they hop a little way off. Their colouring often blends with their surroundings. The female lays her eggs in various herbaceous plants, such as ribwort, hawkweed, wild strawberries and mint, and in young tree shoots.

Cercopis vulnerata, a red spittle-bug common in clearings in upland and foothill woods and on bushy hillsides, differs from the Blood-red Spittle-bug (*C. sanguinolenta*) by the characteristic red markings on its wings. It sucks the juices of grasses, deciduous trees and shrubs. The nymphs develop on the roots of various herbaceous plants in a protective layer of hardened froth.

The Spittle-bug *(Philaenus spumarius)* is characterised by its large numbers and great colour variability. It frequents meadows, fields and gardens, where it sucks the juices of various herbaceous plants. The female lays her eggs in diverse shelters for protection. The nymphs, which are likewise wrapped in a layer of froth, are hatched the following year. These insects are also called froghoppers.

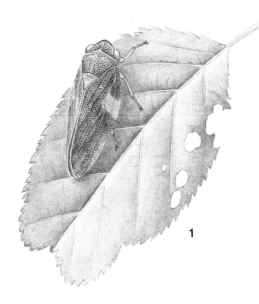

1. *Aphrophora alni:* 8—11 mm ($\frac{5}{16}$—$\frac{7}{16}$ in). Europe, eastern Asia.
2. *Cercopis vulnerata:* 9—11 mm ($\frac{3}{8}$—$\frac{7}{16}$ in). Most of Europe.
3. *Philaenus spumarius:* 5—6 mm ($\frac{3}{16}$—$\frac{1}{4}$ in). The Palaearctic and Nearctic regions; in Europe from the south to north of the continent.

Eggs of the Spittle-bug (*Philaenus spumarius*)

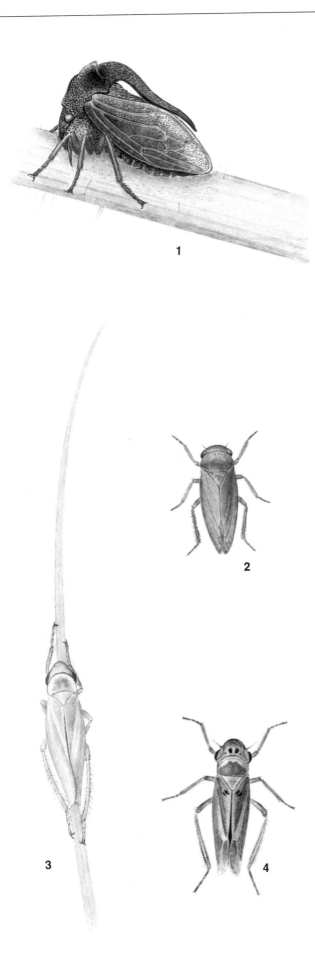

1 *Centrotus cornutus* L. — Membracidae

2 *Iassus lanio* L. — Cicadellidae

3 *Dicraneura variata* Hardy

4 *Cicadella viridis* L.

In warm, sunny places in deciduous woods you may come across a strange-looking bug sitting on herbaceous plants and on the branches of birches, hazels, poplars and willows. Its scutum is developed sideways to horns and posteriorly to a long keel above its abdomen; the best view is obtained from the side. The bug is the tree-hopper *Centrotus cornutus*, a representative of the family Membracidae, whose members live mostly in the tropics. The nymphs of this species hibernate.

Iassus lanio, a leafhopper whose colouring varies from green to brown, is a summer inhabitant of oakwoods and in some places is quite common.

If you sit for a while in the grass of forest undergrowth and look carefully around, you will soon see a great many tiny animals crawling or hopping about. Some of them will no doubt belong to the leafhopper species *Dicraneura variata*, which occurs until late in the autumn – sometimes as late as November.

Like many other plant bugs, *Cicadella viridis* is characterised by considerable colour variability. It is mostly bright green, but some specimens are predominantly bluish-black. Being fond of moisture, the bug is found regularly in wet meadows, beside water, in marshes and around small puddles and ditches in the woods. It occurs in the greatest numbers from June to August, but can often be seen much later. Its favourite host plants, are soft rush, club-rush and sedge.

1. *Centrotus cornutus:* 7—9 mm ($\frac{1}{4}$—$\frac{3}{8}$ in). Most of Europe except the north.
2. *Iassus lanio:* 7—8.5 mm ($\frac{1}{4}$—$\frac{11}{32}$ in). Europe.
3. *Dicraneura variata:* 3—4 mm ($\frac{1}{8}$—$\frac{3}{16}$ in). The Palaearctic region.
4. *Cicadella viridis:* 7—9 mm ($\frac{1}{4}$—$\frac{3}{8}$ in). The Palaearctic and Nearctic regions.

1 *Phyllaphis fagi* L. Callaphididae

2 *Brevicoryne brassicae* L. Aphididae
Cabbage Aphid

3 *Myzus cerasi* L.
Black Cherry Aphid

4 *Sacchiphantes viridis* Ratz. Adelgidae
Yellow Fir Gall-louse

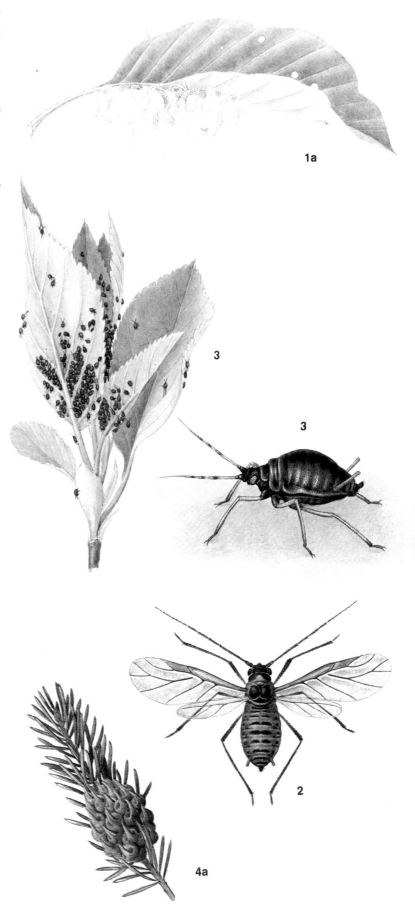

1a

3

3

2

4a

In the spring, bunches of striking long, whitish-blue, wax threads, looking rather like cotton-wool (1a) appear on young beech twigs and the undersides of young, light green leaves. They are secreted from the wax glands of the spring generation of *Phyllaphis fagi*, which produces several generations a year. Morphologically different individuals are formed during the year, but, distinct from many other aphids, they do not change their host plant and remain the whole time on beeches. Hibernation takes place in the egg stage (the eggs are laid in a crack in a branch). This species is common on beech trees everywhere.

Together with other insects, the Cabbage Aphid (*Brevicoryne brassicae*) is a pest of cruciferous plants. It settles chiefly on the upper surfaces of the leaves and the stalks. It appears in the spring and produces up to sixteen generations in a year. It is a particularly noxious pest, which damages the plant both by sucking its nutrient juices and by secreting sticky honeydew all over it; it also causes the leaves to become deformed.

The Black Cherry Aphid (*Myzus cerasi*) is an unpleasant pest of sweet and morello cherries, and often sucks the leaves of these trees in huge numbers. In summer it migrates to other plants, such as bedstraw, eyebright and woodruff, but in the autumn it returns to the cherry trees, where it lays its eggs on the wood. The eggs overwinter.

Many aphids, such as the Yellow Fir Gall-louse (*Sacchiphantes viridis*) form galls (4a) on spruce trees. The nymph develops and hibernates in the gall, leaves it the following summer and is transformed to the imago on its surface.

1. *Phyllaphis fagi:* ♂ 1.3 mm, ♀ 3 mm (♂ $\frac{1}{32}$ in, ♀ $\frac{1}{8}$ in). Europe, Near East, North America.
2. *Brevicoryne brassicae:* 2—2.4 mm ($\frac{1}{8}$ in). Over the entire globe.
3. *Myzus cerasi:* 1.7—2 mm ($\frac{3}{32}$ in). Over the entire globe.
4. *Sacchiphantes viridis:* 1.7—2 mm ($\frac{3}{32}$ in). Europe, the temperate belt in Asia, North America.

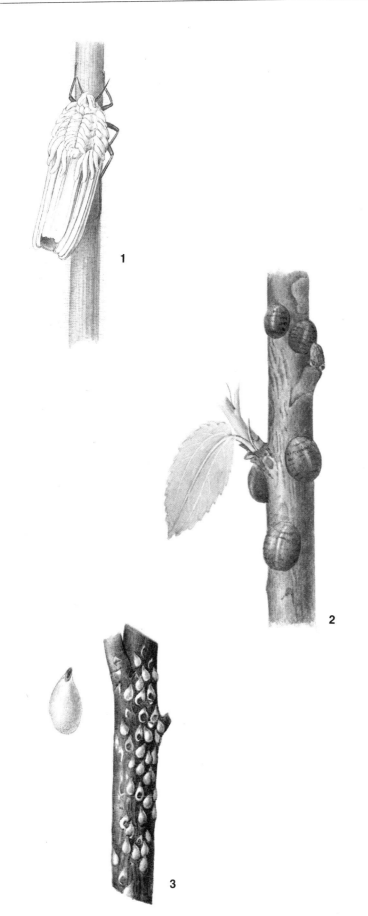

1 *Orthezia urticae* L. Ortheziidae

2 *Parthenolecanium corni* Bouché Coccidae
European Fruit Lecanium

3 *Chionaspis salicis* L. Diaspididae

Few insects show such marked differences between the male and the female as coccids. The males have two wings and eyes (sometimes compound), but rudimentary mouthparts. The females are always wingless, are blind or have only simple eyes, and have a strongly developed proboscis for their mouthpart. The two sexes also develop differently. *Orthezia urticae,* one of the phylogenetically oldest coccids, lives along the edge of water, roads and forests. The female and the nymphs, covered with plates of white wax, spend their lives on the stems or leaves of plants. In the breeding season, the female forms a long pouch (ovisac) for the eggs at the end of her body, to make sure that the eggs are well protected. The older nymphs hibernate.

The branches of plum trees, false acacias and many other trees are often strewn with slightly bulging, firm, hard structures. These are the dead bodies of females of the European Fruit Lecanium (*Parthenolecanium corni*), which in some places is still a common coccid pest. The males are seldom seen, but the females can be seen in abundance. This is a polyphagous species. The young females are flat on death, but their bodies soon bulge and turn into strong cases protecting the minute eggs beneath them. The nymphs hibernate.

Small white spots, often clustering close together, frequently appear on the trunks of young rowan trees, alders and limes and on bilberry plants and berries. Under a magnifying glass they are seen to be the delicate wax and chitin shields of *Chionaspis salicis*. Either males or females develop underneath them. If they are males, the shields are elongate; if they are females they are scale-like. The females, which are blind and completely immobile, lay their eggs under the shield during the summer and die when they have finished. The eggs overwinter in their shelter and their development continues the following spring.

1. *Orthezia urticae:* ♀ 3—3.5 mm, with ovisac up to 10 mm (♀ $\frac{5}{32}$ in, with ovisac up to $\frac{3}{8}$ in). A large part of the Palaearctic region.
2. *Parthenolecanium corni:* ♀ 2.5—6 mm (♀ $\frac{3}{32}$—$\frac{1}{4}$ in). Over most of the globe.
3. *Chionaspis salicis:* shield of ♂ 0.8 mm, of ♀ 2.2 mm (shield of ♂ $\frac{1}{32}$ in, of ♀ $\frac{3}{32}$ in). The whole of the Palaearctic region.

1 *Aleurochiton aceris* Mod.   Aleyrodidae

2 *Trialeurodes vaporariorum*
Greenhouse White-fly

3 *Psylla mali* Schm.   Psyllidae
Apple-sucker

In the spring and summer, the tiny white imagos of *Aleurochiton aceris,* which look like small flies, cling to the undersides of maple leaves. However, wherever maples grow we are much more likely to find their last developmental (winter) instar, the puparium. It is firmly attached to the underside of a leaf, drops to the ground with the leaf in the autumn and overwinters on it. The development of this species is complicated. Two generations, whose developmental stages differ in appearance, are formed during the year. In spring the puparium, which overwinters, gives rise to the summer generation, whose stages are short and, unlike the conspicuous, thick winter puparia, form thin, transparent puparia. Winter puparia appear on the leaves from the end of July.

The Greenhouse White-fly (*Trialeurodes vaporariorum*) is a frequent, and in places troublesome, pest of greenhouse plants. Its puparia occur together with the imagos and nymphs on the undersides of the leaves of the host plants, which include ornamental plants, tomatoes, cucumbers and tobacco.

The Apple-sucker (*Psylla mali*) is a serious pest of apple trees. It forms a single, very large generation. The eggs overwinter and the nymphs (3a), which hatch in the spring, disperse over the flowers and leaf buds. They secrete large amounts of honeydew over the buds, so that they do not open and the leaves are deformed. When fully grown, the nymphs crawl onto the undersides of the apple leaves and are transformed to imagos; the empty skins (exuviae) remain behind on the leaves. The imagos (3), fly away, but return to the apple tree in the autumn to lay their eggs.

1. *Aleurochiton aceris:* puparium 1.9 mm ($\frac{1}{16}$ in). A large part of Europe.
2. *Trialeurodes vaporariorum:* puparium 0.7 mm ($\frac{1}{32}$ in). Over the entire globe.
3. *Psylla mali:* 2.6—3 mm ($\frac{3}{32}$—$\frac{1}{8}$ in). Over most of the globe.

81

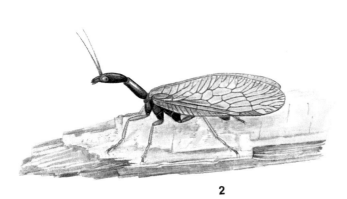

1

2

1 *Sialis lutaria* L.　　　　Sialidae
Common Alder Fly

2 *Raphidia notata* F.　　　Raphidiidae
Snakefly

3 *Osmylus fulvicephalus* Scop.　Osmylidae

Together with many other animals, the Common Alder Fly (*Sialis lutaria*) frequents the sides of ponds and pools. From April to June the imagos sit on the vegetation with their wings folded roof-wise over their bodies. The female lays the eggs on land in large batches on plants' veins and leaves. The larvae crawl into the water unaided and develop there, but eventually return to the land to pupate. The imago is predacious and seizes prey with its powerful mandibles.

Snakeflies are a small, but clearly defined order. They have a long, slender prothorax, a flat-topped, elongated head and four wings with marked venation, which are held folded roof-wise over the body. The Snakefly lives in different types of woods – deciduous and coniferous – crawls over branches and stones and hunts small arthropods; it also flies very well. The female lays the eggs under bark. The flat-bodied larvae likewise live below bark, where they hunt the larvae of bark beetles. The larvae grow slowly and overwinter twice before pupating below the bark. The pupa is capable of active movement and goes in search of a suitable spot below the bark where it can complete its metamorphosis to the imago.

From May to August you may come across a rare net-winged insect in the shade of thick vegetation on the banks of a stream. *Osmylus fulvicephalus* flies during the night; in the daytime it only flutters short distances. The larva develops by the waterside; in the water it can submerge, but is not able to swim. It is predacious. After overwintering, it pupates in the spring on dry land. Owing to the destruction of its natural habitats, this is a disappearing species.

3

1. *Sialis lutaria:* 15 mm, wing span 23—33 mm ($\frac{5}{8}$ in, wing span $\frac{15}{16}$—$1\frac{5}{16}$ in). Europe, the temperate belt in Asia. Absent from the north of Finland and Scandinavia.
2. *Raphidia notata:* 10 mm, wing span 19—31 mm ($\frac{3}{8}$ in, wing span $\frac{3}{4}$—$1\frac{1}{4}$ in). The temperate part of Europe (missing in the south, the Balkans and the Iberian peninsula).
3. *Osmylus fulvicephalus:* 25 mm, wing span 37—52 mm (1 in, wing span $1\frac{7}{16}$—$2\frac{1}{16}$ in). The greater part of Europe (to the south of Sweden in the north).

1 *Chrysopa perla* L. Chrysopidae
2 *Hemerobius humulinus* L. Hemerobiidae
Brown Lacewing
3 *Nemoptera sinuata* A. Ol. Nemopteridae

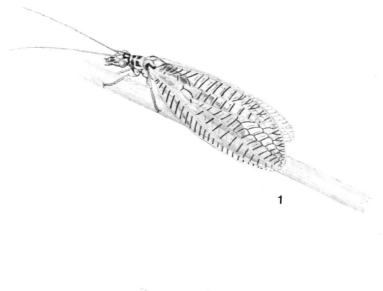

The species of the families Chrysopidae and Hemerobiidae look very much alike and it is therefore not surprising that they are often confused with one another. Under a magnifying glass, however, they can easily be differentiated by the character of the short transverse veins along the edge of their forewings; in the family Chrysopidae the veins are simple, while in Hemerobiidae they are branched at the tip. *Chrysopa perla* is a very familiar and widespread green lacewing (family Chrysopidae) with dark X-shaped markings on its frons between the antennae. Like other green lacewings, in particular the very common and widespread Golden-eye (*Chrysoperla carnea*), it is a useful insect. From May until September it flies through forest meadows and clearings and settles on shrubs and low vegetation. The female lays the eggs on thin pedicels in places frequented by aphids, which are the staple diet of both the larvae and the adult lacewings. Like *Chrysopa carnea* this species is very useful; it flies into houses and very often overwinters there in the company of various ladybird species.

The Brown Lacewing (*Hemerobius humulinus*) occurs in two generations from spring to late autumn. It is found on the outskirts of deciduous woods, on bushy hillsides and at the edge of clearings. It is not very active (it is evidently not a very keen flier) and prefers merely to crawl over the plants. The larvae develop quickly and pupate in only two to three weeks. The larvae and imagos are both predacious; they live mainly on aphids, coccids and mites.

Nemopteridae, which inhabit the warmer parts of the world, have greatly modified hindwings. This also applies to the south European species *Nemoptera sinuata*. The larvae, which have an unusually long neck, live in sand.

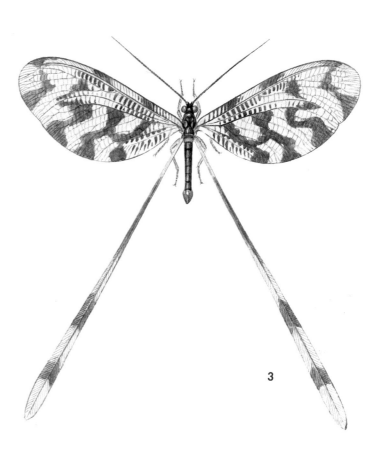

1. *Chrysopa perla:* forewing span 25—30 mm (1—1$\frac{3}{16}$ in). Europe, the temperate belt in Asia.
2. *Hemerobius humulinus:* wing span 13—18 mm ($\frac{9}{16}$—$\frac{3}{4}$ in). The Palaearctic and Nearctic regions.
3. *Nemoptera sinuata:* forewing span 55 mm (2$\frac{3}{16}$ in). Southern Europe.

1 *Libelloides coccajus* Schaef. Ascalaphidae
2 *Myrmeleon formicarius* L. Myrmeleontidae
Ant Lion Fly

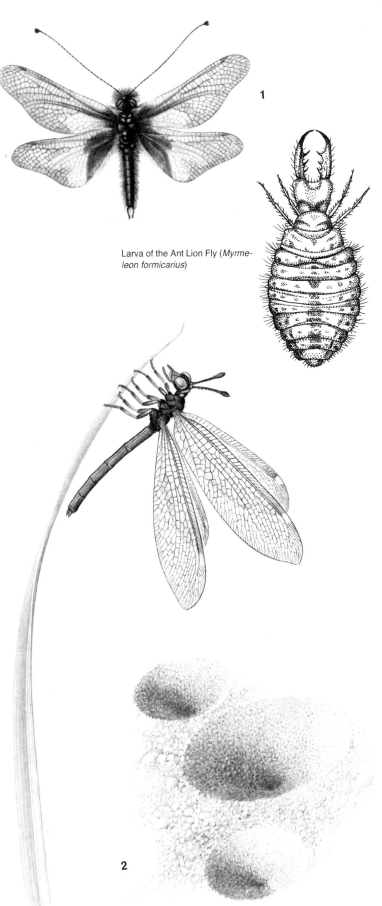

Larva of the Ant Lion Fly (*Myrmeleon formicarius*)

When at rest, *Libelloides coccajus* holds its wings folded roof-wise over its body. In flight the imago looks a little like a dragonfly, but its antennae are a different shape and length and end in a club tip. This is an explicitly warmth-loving species which flies from May to July in grassy places. The eggs have a pedicel and are laid on plants. The larva resembles the larva of the Ant Lion Fly except that it lives among plants and in cracks in the soil. It is predacious and over-winters twice. This species is sensitive to changes in its habitat and the pollution of the environment and its numbers are steadily decreasing.

Not everybody is fortunate enough to see the fluttering imago of the Ant Lion Fly (*Myrmeleon formicarius*), which usually flies after dark. The larvae, which have remarkable habits, live in small to largish pits in sandy soil. The newly hatched tiny larva digs a small pit for itself in the sand, makes itself comfortable at the bottom and waits for any small insects to come crawling along and fall into the trap. At first it is satisfied with small, soft-bodied aphids, but later, when the pit is deeper and wider, it catches larger insects, mostly ants. The unwitting ant suddenly finds the ground cut away from under its feet, falls to the bottom of the pit, is snapped up by the large, sharp mandibles of the larva and is soon sucked dry. The larva injects poison and digestive juices into its prey to liquefy the tissues. Sometimes the ant does not fall all the way to the bottom of the pit and tries to scramble out. In that case the larva throws sand over it and frequently succeeds in forcing it down again. The larva's development takes two to three years. Before the advent of winter it makes itself a burrow in the sand. When its development is complete, it wraps itself in a sandy cocoon and pupates. Several other species of the family live in the same manner, but some ant lion larvae merely live in or on the ground without making pits.

1. *Libelloides coccajus:* wing span 40—50 mm ($1\frac{9}{16}$—2 in). Central and southern Europe.
2. *Myrmeleon formicarius:* wing span 65—75 mm ($2\frac{9}{16}$—3 in). Europe.

1 *Cicindela campestris* L.
Green Tiger Beetle

2 *Cicindela silvatica* L.
Wood Tiger Beetle

3 *Cicindela hybrida* L.

Cicindelidae

On sunny days from early spring, the Green Tiger Beetle (*Cicindela campestris*) can be seen at the edges of forests and on heathland running about in search of food; it can also fly. This rapacious tiger beetle has strong, sharp, toothed mandibles; it lives on various insect larvae and small imagos, but also catches spiders. The female lays eggs just below the surface of sandy soil. The tiny larvae dig a vertical shaft and lie in wait for prey at the opening; like the adult beetles they catch insect larvae and small imagos. Their flat heads close the entrance to the shaft like a trap-door. The larva drags prey into the shaft and digests it there. It grows fast and pupates in the autumn on the floor of the shaft. The beetle also emerges in the autumn, but does not leave its shelter until the following spring. The imagos and the larvae are useful, but they are sensitive to the increasing use of chemicals in agriculture and nowadays far fewer of them are to be seen on field paths.

The Wood Tiger Beetle (*Cicindela silvatica*) is a no less useful tiger beetle whose rapacity makes it a good ally in the natural fight against forest pests. It lives on forest paths, in sandy clearings and on heaths, where it catches various insects and where its larvae also develop. This tiger beetle can easily be distinguished from others by its black labrum (upper lip).

Cicindela hybrida closely resembles the preceding species, but has a light-coloured labrum. It is to be seen from April, mainly on soft drift sand, field paths and sandy river terraces from the lowlands to the mountains. The beetles occur from spring until late in the autumn. The larvae likewise excavate underground shafts, often close together.

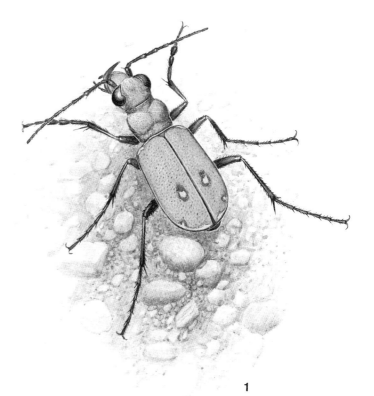

1

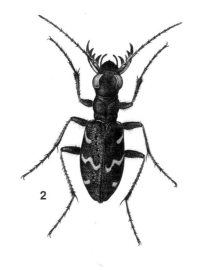

2

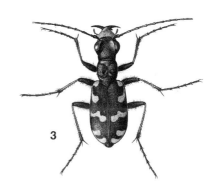

3

1. *Cicindela campestris:* 10.5—14.5 mm ($\frac{7}{16}$ — $\frac{9}{16}$ in). The whole Palaearctic region.
2. *Cicindela silvatica:* 14—20 mm ($\frac{9}{16}$ — $\frac{13}{16}$ in). Europe; rarer towards the south.
3. *Cicindela hybrida:* 11.5—15.5 mm ($\frac{13}{32}$ — $\frac{5}{8}$ in). Europe, Asia Minor, the Caucasus.

1 *Calosoma sycophanta* L. Carabidae
Searcher or Caterpillar Hunter

2 *Calosoma inquisitor* L.

Few big ground beetles are as popular as the handsome Searcher or Caterpillar Hunter (*Calosoma sycophanta*). This is a rare visitor to Britain and is most common in southeastern Europe. Its form and metallic colouring are so typical that it cannot be mistaken for any other beetle. It inhabits deciduous and conifer woods from lowlands to the mountain zone. The beetles are active and nimble and are able to crawl quickly up trees and along branches. They also fly well. Since they have a life span of two to four years they belong to the long-lived species. The Searcher or Caterpillar Hunter is a very rapacious and useful beetle, which hunts the caterpillars and pupae of forest lepidopterans, including large and hairy caterpillars. During the vegetation season it consumes about 400. Its dark-coloured larva, which lives on the caterpillars and pupae of various forest pests, is no less rapacious. It is interesting that, in its choice of pupae, it gives precedence to female pupae – a habit which makes it particularly useful. The female lays eggs singly in the ground – fewer in its first year than in the others. The larva develops in about two to three weeks; it then retires underground, excavates a chamber for itself and pupates in it. The imago emerges late in the summer, but remains underground and hibernates; in August the beetles of the previous year also go into hibernation. The importance of the Searcher in forestry is borne out by the fact that it was introduced into the USA during the first decade of the present century to help combat lepidopterans brought into the country from outside.

The brown-coloured *Calosoma inquisitor* is the second best known species of this genus. It lives primarily in deciduous woods, but can also be found in gardens on fruit trees. It hunts geometer and tortrix caterpillars on trees and on footpaths in the woods and as soon as the caterpillars have disappeared it goes into hibernation. It lives for two to three years. During one season the female lays about 50 eggs singly in the soil. This species was also introduced into the USA to help the fight against harmful caterpillars.

1. *Calosoma sycophanta:* 20—30 mm ($\frac{13}{16}$—$1\frac{3}{16}$ in). The Palaearctic region; introduced into North America and Java.
2. *Calosoma inquisitor:* 13.5—20 mm ($\frac{9}{16}$—$\frac{13}{16}$ in). Europe, the temperate belt in Asia, introduced into North America.

1 *Procerus gigas* Creutz.
2 *Carabus coriaceus* L.

Carabidae

The ground beetle family includes a few dozen explicitly large species, headed by *Procerus gigas*. This large, robust beetle is a forest species inhabiting hilly country and mountain forests. Its imagos, which have a life span of more than three years, are active from May to September. In the daytime they hide under leaves, logs or stones, but occasionally they go reconnoitring; they are slow crawlers. They are active mainly in the evening. They catch live snails, but also devour cadavers. After decomposing their food extra-intestinally with digestive juices, they suck the resultant liquid. Practically all ground beetles feed in this way.

The biggest *Carabus* species in central Europe is the stout-bodied *Carabus coriaceus,* which inhabits open woods (mainly beech woods) in lowlands and foothills, as well as wet meadows, fields and, occasionally, gardens. It likes plenty of moisture. It hides in leaves, moss and various kinds of holes and under stones and fallen leaves. The imagos occur all year, but aestivate from May to the beginning of July. When they reappear, they are active again, both by day and in the evening. Their food consists of various small invertebrates such as snails, slugs and insect imagos and larvae, but cadavers also attract them. *C. coriaceus* lives for two to three years. The female lays her eggs in the ground, often at the foot of a tree, but sometimes under a stone or in moss. The predacious larvae catch snails and caterpillars and are not averse to cadavers. They pupate in an underground chamber. The beetles (at all ages) and the larvae hibernate.

1

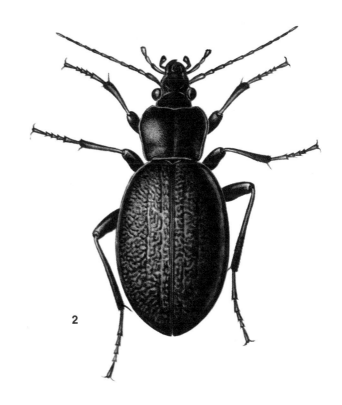

2

1. *Procerus gigas:* 40—60 mm ($1\frac{9}{16}$—$2\frac{3}{8}$ in). South-eastern Europe, Carinthia, Styria. Absent from the British Isles.
2. *Carabus coriaceus:* 30—40 mm ($1\frac{3}{16}$—$1\frac{9}{16}$ in). Europe except the north and south; absent from the British Isles.

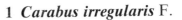

1 *Carabus irregularis* F.

2 *Carabus violaceus* L.
Violet Ground Beetle

Carabus irregularis is characterised by a flat body and a large head with powerful mandibles, the left one of which has a bulging outer edge. In addition, it has irregularly distributed green to copper-red dimples on its elytra. The imagos inhabit foothill and mountain regions; they live chiefly in beech woods or mixed (beech and fir) woods and are active from June into the autumn. They spend most of the day hidden under the bark of tree stumps, under stones and in leaves and moss. They are predacious and catch small insects attracted to the sap escaping from damaged trees; they ignore carcases. The larvae, which live in old, crumbling stumps are also predacious. The new imago generation appears in the autumn. Before the advent of winter, the beetles retire to their hideouts and several individuals hibernate together.

The large Violet Ground Beetle (*Carabus violaceus*), whose pronotum and finely sculptured elytra have a reddish-violet, bluish-green or blue border along the sides, is frequently to be encountered in damp woods, gardens and fields from low to high altitudes, where it is active from spring to autumn. In the daytime it is most likely to be found under a stone, in moss, at the foot of a tree or in a tree stump, but at night it goes hunting. It is distinctly rapacious and catches snails, earthworms and various larvae as well as having a liking for carrion and forest fungi. It pairs early in the spring and the eggs are laid at the beginning of summer. The predacious larvae catch the imagos and larvae of other insects; they develop in three to four weeks (during which they moult twice) and then pupate. Some imagos emerge the same autumn; they, and some of the larvae, hibernate in the stumps of deciduous trees and conifers.

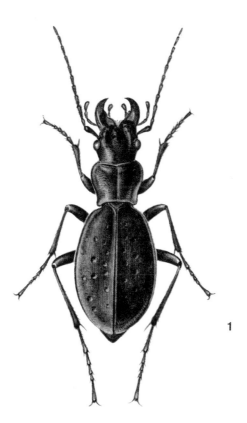

1

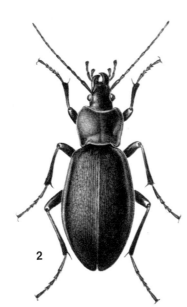

2

1. *Carabus irregularis:* 19—30 mm ($\frac{3}{4}$—$1\frac{3}{16}$ in). The mountains of central Europe. Absent from the British Isles.
2. *Carabus violaceus:* 22—35 mm ($\frac{7}{8}$—$1\frac{3}{8}$ in). Much of Europe (to beyond the Arctic Circle). Common in Britain.

1 *Carabus intricatus* L.

Carabidae

Blue Ground Beetle

2 *Carabus auronitens* F.

The Blue Ground Beetle (*Carabus intricatus*), another large ground beetle, mainly lives in deciduous woods, but is sometimes found in conifer forests and among the fauna of gardens, where it can occur in force. It appears in several colour forms; south European forms are known for their splendid metallic colouring. Early in the spring the beetles are tempted out of their winter shelters by the warmer weather. On sunny days they tend to hide in leaves, under felled timber, stones and in rotting wood. They hunt mainly in the evening. The Blue Ground Beetles are basically predators and account for a great many insects; they particularly like to catch live insects attracted by escaping sap, and are not interested in carcases. In addition, they are fond of the fruit bodies of fungi. The beetles aestivate, but when they reawaken they resume their normal activities. The imagos of the new generation appear in the autumn and sometimes even pair before the winter. In October they go into hibernation, often in the ground, in moss, leaves, or old, damp wood, where several dozen may be found together.

Carabus auronitens is another typical forest-dweller. It prefers spruce forests or deciduous woods in hilly and mountainous country. It does not occur in pinewoods. The beetles, which leave their winter shelters in April or May, are predacious; they catch snails, caterpillars, earthworms and other invertebrates, including insects. They pair early in the summer. The larvae develop quickly and then retire underground to pupate in a small chamber. The pupae give rise to the new imago generation in the same autumn. Before winter comes (in August in mountainous countries), the beetles look for somewhere to hibernate. They generally pick the damp wood of an old tree stump, but sometimes choose to hibernate in the ground or under a blanket of moss.

1

2

1. *Carabus intricatus:* 24—36 mm ($\frac{15}{16}$—1$\frac{7}{16}$ in). A large part of Europe. Very rare in Britain.
2. *Carabus auronitens:* 18—34 mm ($\frac{3}{4}$—1$\frac{3}{8}$ in). Chiefly central and western Europe. Absent from Britain.

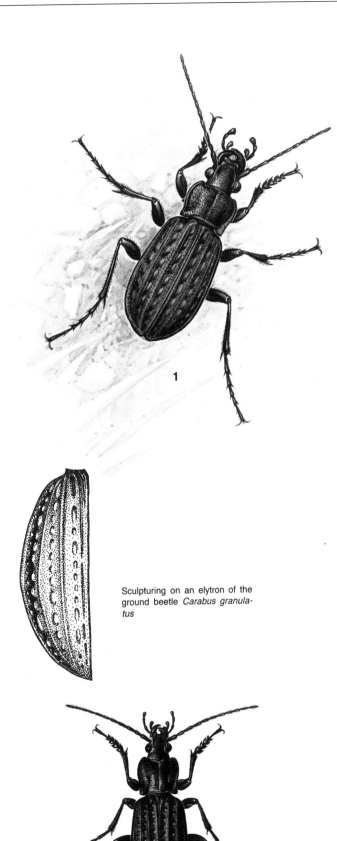

1 *Carabus granulatus* L.
2 *Carabus clathratus* L.

The elytra of many ground beetles are characterised by intricate sculpturing and ornaments. Some are pitted by dimples, others have fine grooves. A few species have longitudinal ribs alternating with chains on their elytra. The elytra of *Carabus granulatus, C. cancellatus* and *C. ullrichi* are decorated in this way. *C. granulatus* lives mainly in fields, meadows and gardens from lowlands to mountains. Its general colouring is somewhat variable; usually it is bronze or coppery-red, but can be greenish-black. The beetle likes damp and hides under stones and in leaves and moss. However, it will venture out on fine sunny days. Some specimens, especially in lowlands, have membraneous hindwings – an exceptional phenomenon among large ground beetles, most of which have no hindwings. The beetles have been seen to fly, but this is very rare. They are explicitly predacious and their menu includes earthworms, various developmental stages of insects, rotting fruit and dead animals; the Colorado Beetle is an important item of their diet. The female lays a total of about 40 eggs in individual holes in the ground; the larvae pupate in underground chambers. The imagos emerge in July and August. The beetles overwinter together in old tree stumps, under the bark of old trees and under moss.

All big ground beetles like moisture, but in *Carabus clathratus* this penchant is exceptionally strong. *C. clathratus* lives right at the water's edge in peat-bogs and reed-beds. It can even submerge for short periods, carrying its supply of air under its elytra. It can swim and hunt in the water, although the tissues of dead animals seem to be its main food. While it can fly, not all individuals have properly developed membraneous wings. Today this species is rapidly disappearing, since its natural habitats are being destroyed by land recovery projects.

Sculpturing on an elytron of the ground beetle *Carabus granulatus*

1. *Carabus granulatus:* 17—23 mm ($\frac{11}{16}$ — $\frac{15}{16}$ in). Europe (including the British Isles), the temperate belt in Asia.
2. *Carabus clathratus:* 20—38 mm ($\frac{13}{16}$ — $1\frac{1}{2}$ in). A large part of Europe, the Caucasus, Siberia, Japan. Local in Britain.

1 *Carabus cancellatus* Illig.   Carabidae
2 *Carabus auratus* L.

Carabus cancellatus is an occasional visitor to Britain and is an important species in the insect fauna of fields and the outskirts of woods. Its general colour is variable and bronze, brassy-green, coppery and even black individuals can be found. This species forms geographical races in its area of incidence. It is diurnal, and thus something of an exception among the large ground beetles. From the early spring the beetles prowl in search of food and consume more than their own weight each day. In addition to carrion, they live on various kinds of insects; in potato fields they wreak havoc among the larvae, pupae and imagos of the Colorado Beetle. From May to July the female lays about 45 single eggs in depressions in the ground. The egg, which is relatively large and over 5 mm ($\frac{3}{16}$ in) long, is at first cylindrical, but later kidney-shaped. The predacious larvae hunt prey on the ground, but can also burrow quickly into the soil, where they complete their development. The imagos emerge in the autumn, overwinter and live until August the following year.

Carabus auratus, is a handsome ground beetle with a metallic sheen. It occurs in the fauna of fields, vineyards, gardens and the edge of damp meadows. Like *Carabus cancellatus* it is a diurnal species and is thus something of an exception among the large ground beetles. It is active during the day, but in the evening it goes into hiding under stones. It is able to climb plants, including tree trunks. It has a very varied diet including dead animals, various insects and mushrooms. The larvae are predacious and, unlike the beetles, they are nocturnal. The imago emerges in an underground chamber in autumn and either remains there until the spring, or comes out for a short time before retiring underground, or into moss or an old tree stump, to hibernate. Some females manage to lay a second batch of eggs in the next year, but die after doing so.

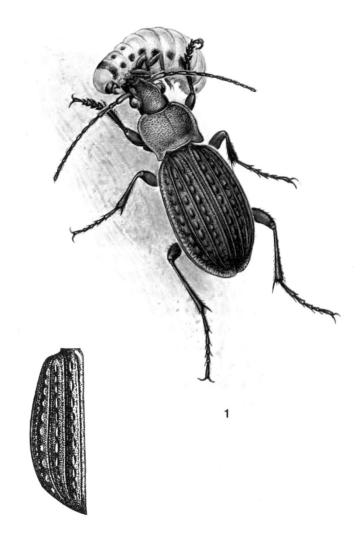

1

Sculpturing on an elytron of the ground beetle *Carabus cancellatus*

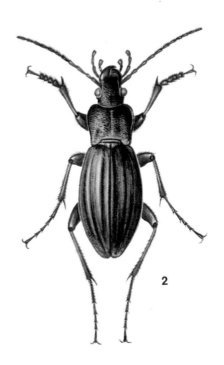

2

1. *Carabus cancellatus:* 17—32 mm ($\frac{11}{16}$—$1\frac{1}{4}$ in). Europe, the temperate belt in Asia; carried to the British Isles.
2. *Carabus auratus:* 17—30 mm ($\frac{11}{16}$—$1\frac{3}{16}$ in). Central and western Europe; carried to the British Isles, introduced into North America.

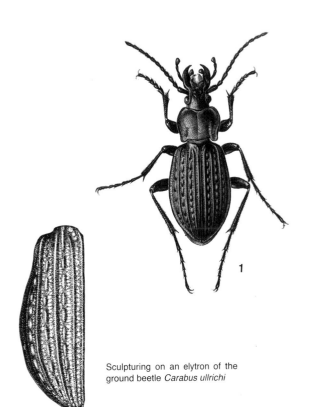

Sculpturing on an elytron of the ground beetle *Carabus ullrichi*

1 *Carabus ullrichi* Germ.

Carabidae

2 *Carabus arvensis* Herbst

3 *Carabus monilis* F.

Carabus ullrichi is another large ground beetle which can be found living in fields, orchards and vineyards, but not woods. It closely resembles *Carabus cancellatus,* but is larger and more robust and has only a small notch at the tip of its elytra. It likes warmth and occurs on heavy soils in lowlands and hilly country, where it hides under stones, clods of earth, or leaves. It is active during the daytime. It is no less rapacious than other big ground beetles and hunts insect larvae and other small invertebrates. The imagos occur mainly from June to August. The female lays about 20 eggs, which develop in the same way as those of related species.

Carabus arvensis is one of the ground beetles that are active from the spring to the autumn. It is not closely associated with a particular type of habitat and can be encountered in forests, meadows and gardens from lowlands to mountains, where it ascends above the forest limit. It hides under stones, in moss, under old leaves or felled timber, but often runs about during the daytime. Its main food includes snails and animal cadavers. The young beetles mature in the autumn and overwinter in old tree stumps and moss.

Carabus monilis is a pretty ground beetle which also lives in meadows, fields and gardens. Its general colouring varies greatly, but it is most often bronze, green or blue. The sculpturing on its elytra also varies. This species occurs in both lowlands and mountains, up to altitudes of over 2,500 m (8,200 ft). It shelters under stones, clods of earth or, sometimes, clumps of grass; at hay-making time it has even been found under piles of hay. It is sometimes seen during the daytime. It lives on insect larvae, various kinds of worms and dead insects. The female lays her eggs singly during the night in shallow depressions which she makes in the ground.

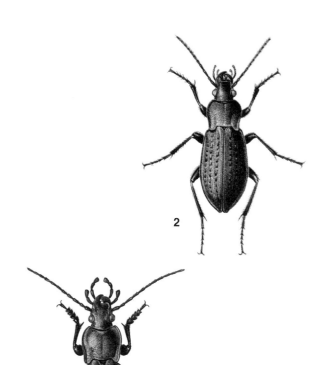

1. *Carabus ullrichi:* 22—34 mm ($\frac{7}{8}$—$1\frac{3}{8}$ in). Central, southern and eastern Europe; absent in the north.
2. *Carabus arvensis:* 16—22 mm ($\frac{5}{8}$—$\frac{7}{8}$ in). Europe, the temperate part of Asia.
3. *Carabus monilis:* 17—32 mm ($\frac{11}{16}$—$1\frac{1}{4}$ in). Western, central and northern Europe (including the British Isles).

1 *Carabus nemoralis* O. Müll. Carabidae
2 *Carabus hortensis* L.

Carabus nemoralis can be one of the most useful large ground beetles in the garden, because in some places it is one of the commonest. It can also be found in damp woods and in fields, from flat country to low altitudes in mountains. Like the preceding species, it hides under stones or moss, in leaves or under clods of earth. It is not fussy in its choice of food and hunts snails, earthworms and caterpillars and finds over-ripe fruit irresistible. Since it digests its food extra-intestinally, it often spends a long time over its prey. In the spring the female lays eggs singly in the ground, where they develop quickly. The predacious larvae often drag their prey underground. The imagos sometimes emerge in July and hibernate; at other times the larvae or the pupae hibernate and the beetles emerge in the spring. Imagos which overwinter reappear early in the spring and aestivate in July; after aestivating they do not recover their energy and die.

From its name, one would assume that *Carabus hortensis* (from *hortus,* the Latin for garden) is a garden species. In fact, it is not particularly interested in gardens, in which, as in fields, it is more of an accidental visitor. It lives mostly in and at the edge of woods, irrespective of their type, and it hides under bark or in leaves or moss. After dark it comes out and goes in search of prey (dead animals and insects). It also looks for escaping sap on woody plants, because this attracts insects and makes it easier for the beetle to catch them. *Carabus hortensis* is still a common species in woods, especially in hilly country, where it may be the chief large forest beetle. It can also be encountered, though less often, at altitudes of up to 2,000 m (6,560 ft) and over. The imagos like to hibernate in old, damp tree stumps, or crawl under moss.

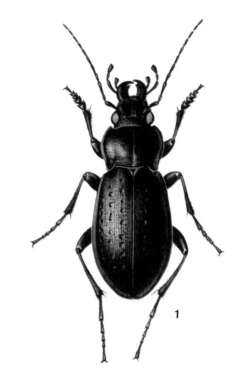

1

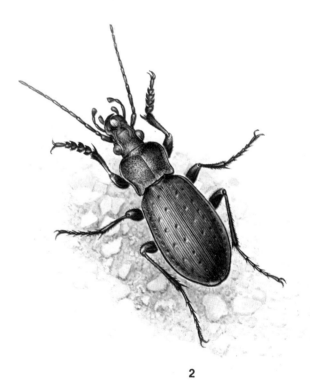

2

1. *Carabus nemoralis:* 18—28 mm ($\frac{3}{4}$—1$\frac{1}{8}$ in). Europe (including the British Isles); introduced into North America.
2. *Carabus hortensis:* 22—30 mm ($\frac{7}{8}$—1$\frac{3}{16}$ in). Chiefly central and northern Europe (minus the British Isles).

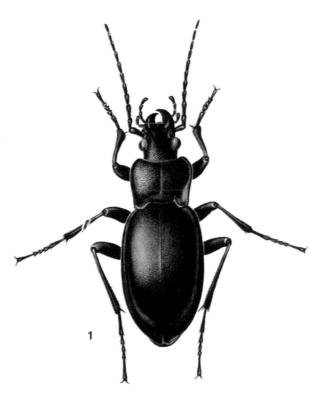

1

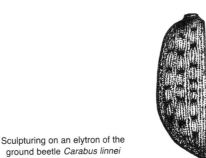

Sculpturing on an elytron of the
ground beetle *Carabus linnei*

1 *Carabus glabratus* Payk.
2 *Carabus linnei* Panz.

Carabidae

Carabus glabratus is a relatively common inhabitant of beech, spruce and pinewoods in lowlands and hilly country and on mountainsides at altitudes of up to about 2,500 m (8,200 ft). Like other big ground beetles, it shelters under stones, moss, leaves or felled trees. It also hunts during the daytime, especially after rain or during damp weather, and frequents forest paths or the banks of forest streams. It catches earthworms, insects and snails and has a liking for mushrooms. The imagos occur in large numbers from the late spring to the early autumn. Copulation takes place in the summer and the female lays her eggs singly in the ground. The larva, which is predacious like the adult beetle, leads a secretive existence, often under stones or leaves. The young beetles usually emerge in the autumn, but can wait until the next spring. They hibernate in damp tree stumps or under moss.

Some ground beetles are mountain-dwellers and are so thoroughly adapted to a montane climate that we do not come across them at low altitudes. *Carabus linnei* is one of these species. It forms geographical races in the damp forests and peat-bogs in the mountains of central Europe and the Carpathians. It is a very dainty, slender, copper-coloured beetle, which sometimes has a greenish sheen. In the daytime it remains below the bark of tree trunks or stumps, under wood or stones and in moss and other hiding-places, but at night it goes hunting. Like practically all ground beetles, it digests its prey extra-intestinally. It grips the prey with its mandibles, releases digestive juices over it until it is decomposed and then sucks the liquid into its mouth. Before the winter sets in the beetles look for damp stumps in which to overwinter; several individuals generally hibernate together.

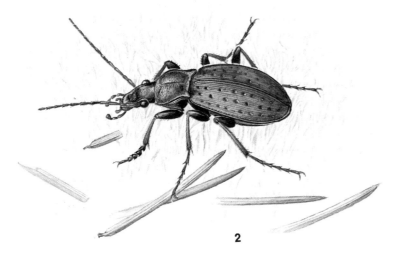

2

1. *Carabus glabratus:* 22—34 mm ($\frac{7}{8}$—1$\frac{3}{8}$ in). Europe.
2. *Carabus linnei:* 16—22 mm ($\frac{5}{8}$—$\frac{7}{8}$ in). The mountains of central Europe.

1 *Carabus silvestris* Panz.   Carabidae
2 *Cychrus caraboides*

Together with *Carabus linnei*, *Carabus silvestris* is the most widespread mountain ground beetle. It inhabits mountain forests and damp meadows from altitudes of about 550 to 2,500 m (1,148 to 8,200 ft) and forms several geographical races with a very limited incidence. Its colouring is very variable, but brassy or coppery green-tinged specimens are the commonest and black or bluish individuals are rare. The beetles, which like plenty of moisture, hide during the daytime under stones, in moss and leaves or below the bark of felled timber or old tree stumps. Their diet is similar to that of other large ground beetles. The female lays her eggs in the ground at the beginning of summer and the larvae appear in July or August, according to the weather. Eventually they dig themselves an underground chamber and pupate in it. The young beetles start to appear at the end of July. They overwinter in damp spruce stumps, usually in the company of several of their family.

Compared with other large ground beetles, *Cychrus caraboides* has a markedly tapering head. It inhabits both coniferous and deciduous woods with adequate moisture. Occasionally it ventures out of the wood into fields and meadows. In lowlands it is rather rare, but in foothills and mountains it can still be found quite frequently. It hides under stones, leaves and old wood and appears from spring to autumn. It is predacious and lives largely on slugs and snails; with the latter, it pushes its long head into the shell, releases digestive juices inside it and then sucks the contents – a process which sometimes takes quite a long time. It is not affected by the slime secreted by the mollusc in self-defence. Its elytra curve downwards at the sides and protect the spiracles (respiratory orifices) from becoming clogged with slime. Air is pumped towards the spiracles by the movements of the tip of the abdomen. The beetles generally hibernate in old tree stumps and under bark.

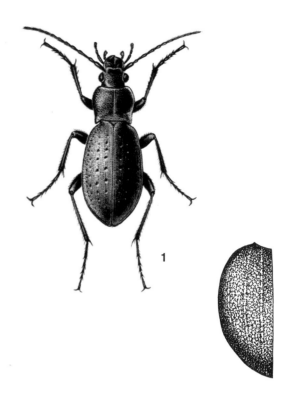

1

Sculpturing on an elytron of *Cychrus caraboides*

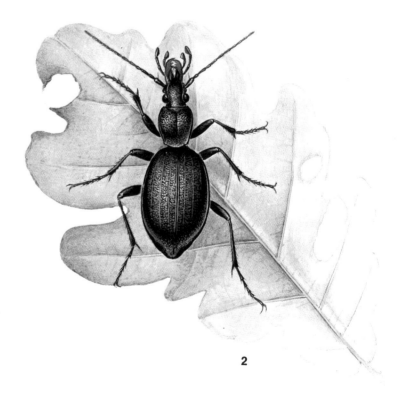

2

1. *Carabus silvestris:* 17—27 mm ($\frac{11}{16}$—1$\frac{1}{16}$ in). The mountains of central Europe.
2. *Cychrus caraboides:* 12.5—20 mm ($\frac{1}{2}$—$\frac{13}{16}$ in). Europe (up to 68 ° latitude north). Local in Britain.

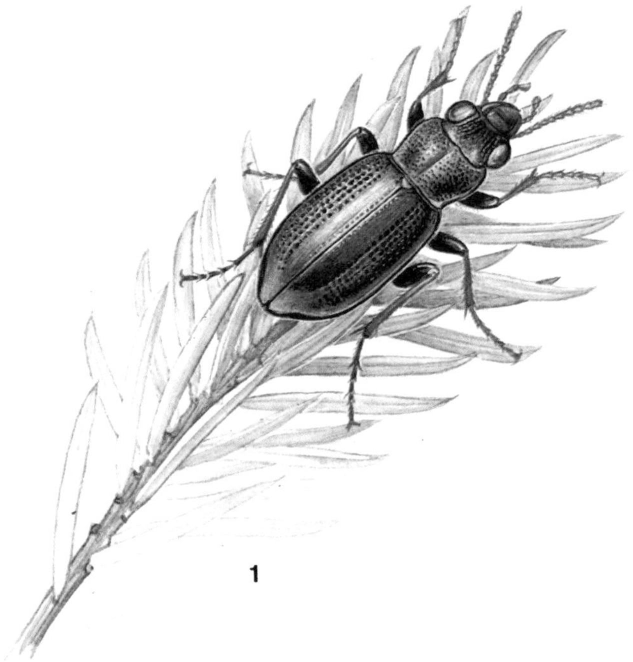

1

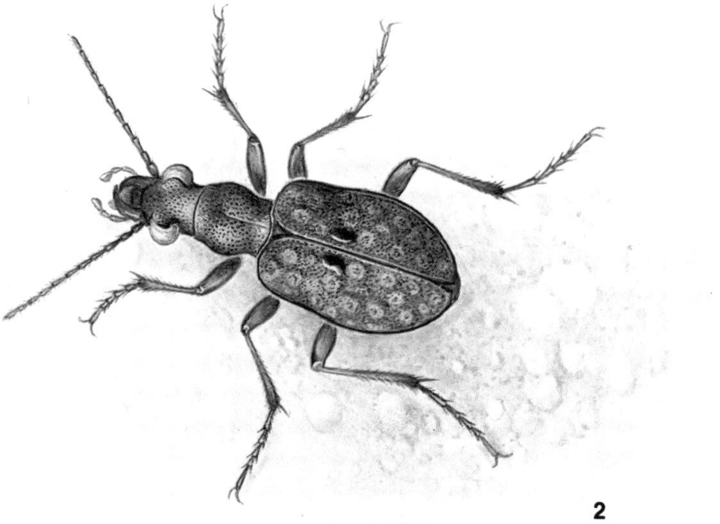

2

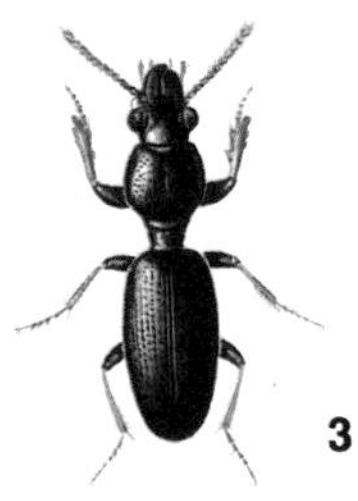

3

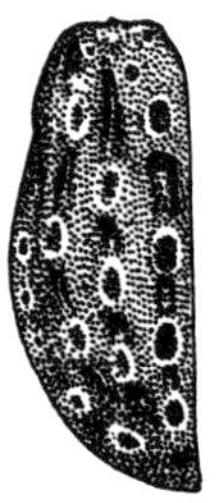

Sculpturing on an elytron of *Elaphrus riparius*

1 *Notiophilus biguttatus* F. — Carabidae
2 *Elaphrus riparius* L.
3 *Clivina fossor* L.

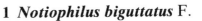

Notiophilus biguttatus is a tiny, nimble ground beetle with a coppery lustre, which can be seen running about in sunny spaces in coniferous and deciduous woods and beside water. It occurs at both low and high altitudes. It generally appears on sunny days and otherwise rests in moss or dry needles, or under stones. The larvae develop and pupate in tree stumps. This is one of the most common small ground beetles. Several other similar species live in Europe.

The small ground beetles of the genus *Elaphrus* have strikingly large and prominent eyes and richly sculptured elytra. The most common European species is *Elaphrus riparius,* which chiefly inhabits lowlands and hills. Being particularly fond of moisture, it lives beside water with sparse rather than rich vegetation, in marshy meadows, and on the muddy bed of emptied ponds or half-dry pools. The imagos run very quickly; they often come out in the daytime and their colours blend with their environment. When resting, they hide under stones and leaves. They feed on small insects and their larvae. The larvae of this pretty beetle live in the same places as the adult insects. The young generation is developed by the autumn.

The forelegs of some adult ground beetles and their larvae are variously adapted for digging. In *Clivina fossor,* which is one of these species, the tibiae of the forelegs are wide and are equipped with a few spiny processes. Since it lives in damp surroundings, the beetle has no difficulty in digging a burrow for itself, in which it hides and hibernates. It is predacious and catches insect larvae and imagos. The larva spends the summer in a tunnel in the ground, where it eventually pupates.

1. *Notiophilus biguttatus:* 3.5—5.5 mm ($\frac{5}{32}$—$\frac{1}{4}$ in). The whole of Europe.
2. *Elaphrus riparius:* 5.5—7 mm ($\frac{1}{4}$—$\frac{5}{16}$ in). Europe, the Caucasus, Asia Minor, Turkestan.
3. *Clivina fossor:* 5.5.—6.5 mm ($\frac{1}{4}$—$\frac{9}{32}$ in). The Palaearctic and Nearctic regions.

1 *Broscus cephalotes* L.   Carabidae
2 *Bembidion tetracolum* Say
3 *Asaphidion flavipes* L.
4 *Patrobus atrorufus* Stroem

Broscus cephalotes is a nocturnal predator that inhabits sandy soil in fields, vineyards, gardens and woods which provide sufficient warmth and not too much vegetation. It is found mostly on the coast in Britain. It also occurs in lowlands and in hilly country. During the daytime the beetle hides in a slanting burrow which it excavates itself to a depth of about 15 cm (6 in). It lies in wait for prey at the mouth of the burrow, then seizes it, drags it down inside the burrow and digests it at the bottom. When in danger it raises the front of its body in a warning posture. The larvae, which develop from August, are predacious and devour carrion; after overwintering, they pupate the following spring. The imagos live from the spring to the autumn.

Bembidion is a numerically large genus; over 100 species live in central Europe alone. Their differential characteristics are often so slight that only an expert can identify them reliably. Some, however, are distinctively coloured, such as *Bembidion tetracolum*, which mostly occurs in waterside vegetation, damp meadows, fields and sometimes gardens, from spring to autumn.

Asaphidion flavipes is a striking and common ground beetle with large eyes. It has no special environmental requirements and lives in fields and meadows and on the outskirts of woods. Sometimes it is active during the daytime. The larvae develop in a burrow in the ground.

Patrobus atrorufus is a small ground beetle of riparian woods. It occurs from spring to autumn beside water and in damp meadows. The imagos hide under stones, in damp leaves, moss and debris and below the bark of trees. The larvae hibernate and pupate in the spring.

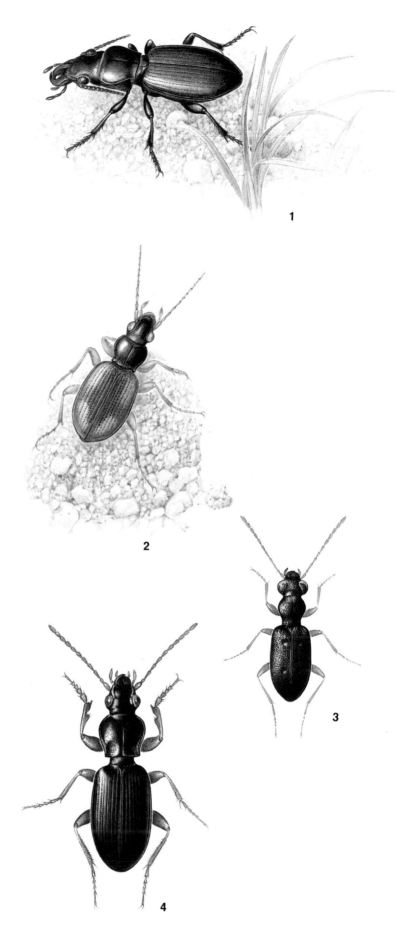

1. *Broscus cephalotes:* 17—22 ($\frac{11}{16}$—$\frac{7}{8}$ in). Europe, the Caucasus, western Siberia.
2. *Bembidion tetracolum:* 5—6.3 mm ($\frac{3}{16}$—$\frac{1}{4}$ in). Europe, the Caucasus, Asia Minor, Siberia, North America.
3. *Asaphidion flavipes:* 4—5.3 mm ($\frac{5}{32}$—$\frac{7}{32}$ in). The Palaearctic region.
4. *Patrobus atrorufus:* 7—9.5 mm ($\frac{5}{16}$—$\frac{3}{8}$ in). Northern, western and central Europe, the Caucasus, Siberia.

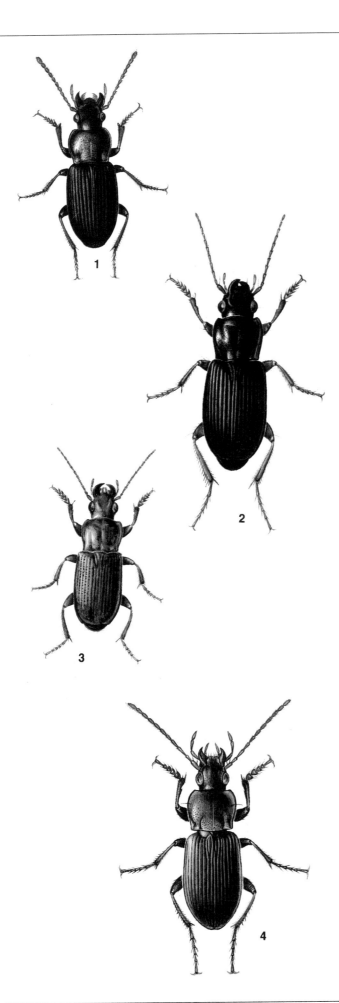

1 *Anisodactylus binotatus* F.   Carabidae
Black Ground Beetle

2 *Harpalus rufipes* De Geer

3 *Harpalus aeneus* F.

4 *Poecilus cupreus* L.

The Black Ground Beetle (*Anisodactylus binotatus*) is often very difficult to distinguish from the many other black members of the same family. It lives in damp places at low to moderately high altitudes and from spring to autumn is quite commonly found in woods, meadows, fields, peatbogs and marshes.

The two *Harpalus* species – *H. rufipes* and *H. aeneus* – are very similar in form, but are differently coloured. *Harpalus rufipes* (once known as *H. pubescens* from its hairy elytra) likes clay soils. It lives in lowlands and at low mountain altitudes, beside water (including the seashore), in clearings and in fields; it hides under stones and clods of earth. It hunts snails, insects and worms, but supplements this diet with seeds and soft fruits, such as strawberries. The beetles occur from spring to autumn; the larvae hibernate.

Harpalus aeneus (often also called *H. affinis*) is abundant almost everywhere from spring to late autumn. It is to be found in clay fields, meadows and gardens, at the margin of woods and beside water. In addition to animals it also eats plant food (the seeds of conifers and deciduous trees).

There is often considerable colour variability among beetles with metallic colouring, such as *Poecilus cupreus*. This can sometimes be a gleaming green or blue and sometimes like brass or bronze. This species occurs at both low and high altitudes and inhabits damp meadows, woods and the banks of streams, where it hides under stones, in leaves and under old wood.

1. *Anisodactylus binotatus:* 9—13 mm ($\frac{3}{8}$—$\frac{9}{16}$ in). The Palaearctic region.
2. *Harpalus rufipes:* 11—16 mm ($\frac{7}{16}$—$\frac{5}{8}$ in). The Palaearctic region.
3. *Harpalus aeneus:* 9—12 mm ($\frac{3}{8}$—$\frac{1}{2}$ in). The Palaearctic region.
4. *Poecilus cupreus:* 9—13 mm ($\frac{3}{8}$—$\frac{9}{16}$ in). The temperate belt in Eurasia.

1 *Pterostichus metallicus* F.
Carabidae
2 *Pterostichus niger* Schall.
3 *Abax parallelopipedus* Pill. et Mitterp.

When the snows melt in the mountains and the first surviving beetles appear after their winter sleep, *Pterostichus metallicus,* a striking, moderately large, glossy ground beetle, with distinct rows of fine dots down its copper-coloured, greenish-gold or bluish-violet elytra, may be seen among them. It is a forest species closely associated with mountain forests and can be found at altitudes of about 2,500 m (8,200 ft). It generally hides under stones, in moss and leaves and under the bark of tree stumps, but sometimes it runs about over conifer needles during the daytime, looking for prey.

The larger *Pterostichus niger* is another member of this genus. As its scientific name (*niger*) tells us, it is black. It occurs in lowlands and mountains (up to about 2,000 m [6,560 ft]) and likes damp places in forests and fields, beside stagnant and flowing water and in swamps, wherever it can find adequate shelter. It is usually found under stones, in moss and leaves, under felled trees or below the bark on the stumps. It hunts various small invertebrates. The larvae generally develop between May and July. It is mostly the young beetles that hibernate, but quite often one may come across hibernating larvae.

The large, black ground beetle *Abax parallelopipedus* used to be called *Abax ater,* which is more in keeping with its colour (in Latin, *ater* means black or dark). It inhabits damp deciduous woods and conifer forests, but prefers beechwoods. Sometimes it strays into damp fields adjoining the wood. It is known in low-lying country, but is more common in foothills and mountains. It occurs from spring to autumn. During the daytime the imago hides under a stone, a piece of old wood or a felled tree, and at night it goes hunting. The predacious larvae live under stones and in rotting wood.

1. *Pterostichus metallicus:* 12—15 mm ($\frac{1}{2}$—$\frac{5}{8}$ in). Central Europe, stretching to the Balkans in the south; absent from the north and the British Isles.
2. *Pterostichus niger:* 15—21 mm ($\frac{5}{8}$—$\frac{13}{16}$ in). Europe, Siberia, Iran, Turkestan.
3. *Abax parallelopipedus:* 16—21 mm ($\frac{5}{8}$—$\frac{13}{16}$ in). Europe.

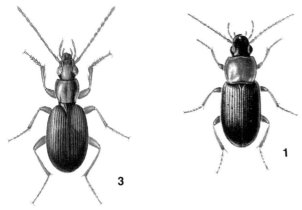

1 **Calathus melanocephalus** L. Carabidae

2 **Agonum sexpunctatum** L.

3 **Platynus dorsalis** Pont.

4 **Platynus assimilis** Payk.

Among the small ground beetles, *Calathus melanocephalus* attracts attention because of its orange-red pronotum and its toothed claws. It lives in woods, meadows, pastures and fields, on heaths and beside water from lowlands to high up in the mountains, where it can be found from spring until late autumn. It hides under stones, in leaves and moss, below bark and in debris. If it leaves its shelter, it sometimes climbs up grasses and flowering plants. Although predacious, it is known to visit mushrooms. The predacious larva hibernates, but the beetle has also been found hibernating.

It would be hard to find another ground beetle looking like *Agonum sexpunctatum*. According to the scientific definition, this species ought to have six spots on its elytra and the first specimen to be described probably had that number. In fact, they sometimes have only four or as many as eight spots. This species is not bound to a particular type of habitat and it lives in woods and fields, on grass verges and footpaths and in meadows. It is active from early spring and can sometimes be seen on sunny days.

Platynus dorsalis, one of the strikingly coloured small ground beetles, can be found hiding, together with others of its kind, under stones or leaves in woods, sunny fields, hillsides, meadows and gardens.

Platynus assimilis could be described as ubiquitous; it is certainly one of the most common ground beetles. It inhabits damp and rather cool places in woods, but also lives on heaths and in fields and is an essential inhabitant of gardens. The beetles are active from early spring until late autumn. They are nocturnal insects and spend the day under stones or leaves, or beneath bark. The imagos often hibernate together under bark and in old tree stumps.

1. *Calathus melanocephalus:* 6—9 mm ($\frac{1}{4}$—$\frac{3}{8}$ in). The Palae-arctic region.
2. *Agonum sexpunctatum:* 7—9.5 mm ($\frac{5}{16}$—$\frac{3}{8}$ in). Europe (rare in Great Britain), the Caucasus, Siberia.
3. *Platynus dorsalis:* 5.8—7.5 mm ($\frac{1}{4}$—$\frac{5}{16}$ in). A large part of Europe.
4. *Platynus assimilis:* 10—12 mm ($\frac{3}{8}$—$\frac{1}{2}$ in). Europe, the Caucasus, Siberia.

1 *Amara aenea* De Geer
2 *Chlaenius vestitus* Paykull
3 *Dromius quadrimaculatus* L.
4 *Brachinus explodens* Duftschm.
Bombardier Beetle

Carabidae

The tiny *Amara aenea* is most commonly found in fields, dry meadows, footpaths or grassy verges. It runs and flies on sunny days and lives on both animal and plant food, including the seeds of various grasses. Several dozen similar relatives of this widespread species live in Europe.

Chlaenius vestitus is one of the prettiest small ground beetles. It likes plenty of moisture and can therefore be found in damp meadows, beside running and stagnant water and on marshy ground in lowlands and hills. It hides under stones, in leaves and in plant debris. It produces one generation a year; the beetles emerge in the autumn and then hibernate.

Dromius quadrimaculatus is a small ground beetle which can always be found beneath the bark of pines, spruces, other conifers and deciduous trees. With its dorsally flattened body it can live under bark and hunt the larvae and pupae of bark beetles in their passages. Sometimes, however, it may appear under a stone or in moss. Its larvae live beneath bark.

A few ground beetles have a gift for pyrotechnics. When in danger, the Bombardier Beetle (*Brachinus explodens*) releases substances into a small bladder from glands in its abdomen. It then squirts this into the air where it 'explodes' in a cloud of blue smoke. In the ensuing confusion the beetle escapes. These beetles are fond of warmth. They live gregariously under stones, on footpaths in fields, on chalky ground, in hedgerows and sometimes in open woods.

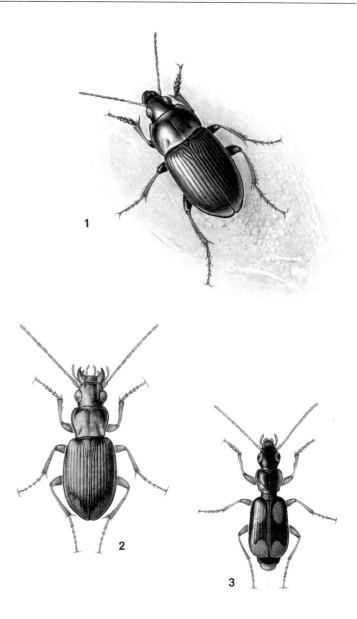

1. *Amara aenea:* 6.5—8.5 mm ($\frac{9}{32}$—$\frac{11}{32}$ in). The Palaearctic region.
2. *Chlaenius vestitus:* 8.5—11 mm ($\frac{11}{32}$—$\frac{7}{16}$ in). The Palaearctic region.
3. *Dromius quadrimaculatus:* 4.7—6 mm ($\frac{3}{16}$—$\frac{1}{4}$ in). Europe.
4. *Brachinus explodens:* 4.9—7.5 mm ($\frac{3}{16}$—$\frac{5}{16}$ in). Central and southern Europe, western Asia.

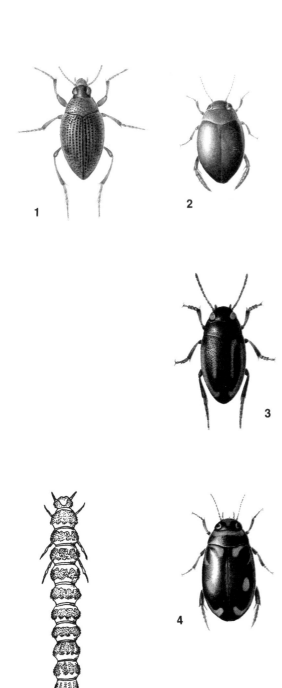

Larva of *Haliplus ruficollis*

1 ***Haliplus ruficollis*** De Geer   Haliplidae

2 ***Hyphydrus ovatus*** L.   Dytiscidae

3 ***Graptodytes granularis*** L.

4 ***Platambus maculatus*** L.

Small pools, meadow ditches, streams and slow-flowing rivers with clean water and abundant vegetation usually teem with aquatic beetles, such as *Haliplus ruficollis*. Although this is a water beetle, its movements in the water are somewhat clumsy when compared with predacious diving beetles. It flies very well, however, and thus has no difficulty in changing its abode. It breathes oxygen from the air which it takes up at the surface. It lives mostly on algae which it sucks. It can live for over two years. The phytophagous larva also lives in water until it is fully grown, when it crawls out to make itself a chamber in the ground to pupate in.

The best known predacious diving beetles (Dytiscidae) are the large and moderately large species. They do include many smaller species, however, which tend to abound in clean pools with abundant vegetation.

Hyphydrus ovatus has a strikingly thick, convex body and inhabits stagnant water. *Graptodytes granularis*, whose elytra and pronotum have orange markings, is most common in small pools, backwaters, ponds and ditches, but sometimes occurs in slow-flowing water.

Platambus maculatus is more commonly found in running water such as rivers and streams. The larvae live among the vegetation or on the river bed and hunt small aquatic animals, but pupate on dry land like other water beetles. Both larvae and beetles have been found hibernating; the latter hibernate either in the water, under stones or in turf on the bank.

1. *Haliplus ruficollis:* 2.5—2.8 mm ($\frac{3}{32}$—$\frac{1}{8}$ in). Europe, western Siberia, Asia Minor, Kazakhstan, North America.
2. *Hyphydrus ovatus:* 4—5 mm ($\frac{5}{32}$—$\frac{3}{16}$ in). Europe, the temperate belt in Asia.
3. *Graptodytes granularis:* 2.0—2.3 mm ($\frac{1}{8}$ in). A large part of Europe.
4. *Platambus maculatus:* 7—8.5 mm ($\frac{5}{16}$—$\frac{11}{32}$ in). Europe (right to the north), the Caucasus, Transcaucasia, Siberia, Mongolia.

1 *Agabus bipustulatus* L.　　Dytiscidae

2 *Ilybius fuliginosus* F.

3 *Rhantus exsoletus* Forst.

4 *Colymbetes fuscus* L.

The members of the genus *Agabus* are all very similar and suitable optical equipment is needed to be able to indentify them. Inter-species differences concern the microscopic sculpture of the elytra. Most of the beetles are dark brown, but some have orange-red or brown spots, such as *Agabus bipustulatus*. This species occurs mostly in stagnant water, in small forest pools and in open country and, though less often, in running water. The beetles and the larvae are both predacious and hunt small animals. The eggs are laid on aquatic plants or their remains.

Ilybius fuliginosus resembles the preceding species, but the claws on its hind limbs are of unequal lengths. It mainly inhabits gently running water, but also lives in drainage canals, ponds and pools in peat-bogs. It is equally common in lowlands and in mountains.

Rhantus exsoletus is a common species in permanent reservoirs, backwaters and slow-flowing rivers from low to mountain altitudes. It frequents aquatic vegetation in which the predacious larva also hunts.

Colymbetes fuscus is a moderately large diving beetle. It lives mainly in stagnant water, where it catches large insects, crustaceans or fish fry, and is even tempted by dead animals.

The female lays her eggs, a few at a time, on aquatic plants. She is very prolific and it has been estimated that she can lay up to 1,000 eggs altogether. The young larva devours small crustaceans, while the older larva feeds on larger aquatic animals and mosquito larvae. The beetle overwinters in the water, but during the winter crawls out occasionally onto the land.

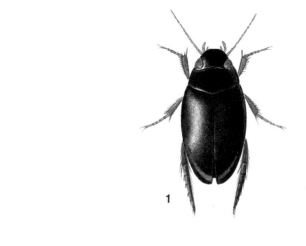

1

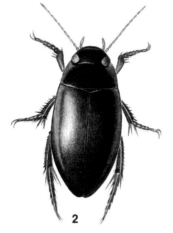

2

3

4

1. *Agabus bipustulatus:* 8—11 mm ($\frac{5}{16}$—$\frac{7}{16}$ in). The Palaearctic region.
2. *Ilybius fuliginosus:* 10—11 mm ($\frac{3}{8}$—$\frac{7}{16}$ in). The Palaearctic region, North America.
3. *Rhantus exsoletus:* 9.5—11 mm ($\frac{3}{8}$—$\frac{7}{16}$ in). A large portion of the temperate part of Eurasia.
4. *Colymbetes fuscus:* 16—18 mm ($\frac{5}{8}$—$\frac{3}{4}$ in). A large part of Europe, Asia Minor, Transcaucasia, North Africa.

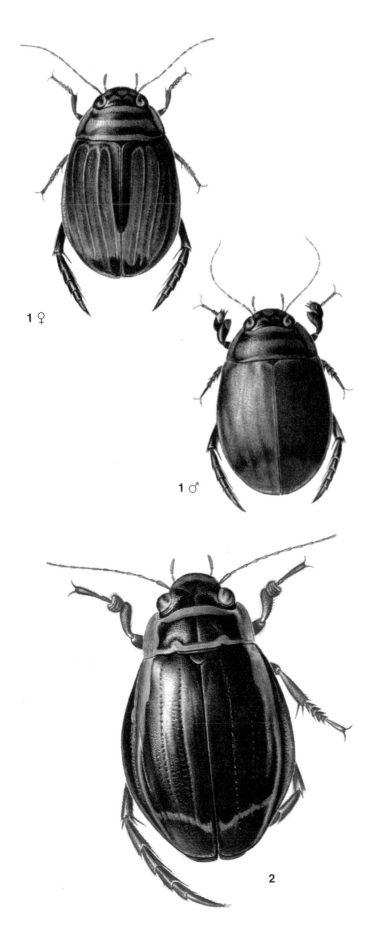

1 ♀

1 ♂

2

1 *Acilius sulcatus* L.

2 *Dytiscus latissimus* L.

Dytiscidae

The male and female *Acilius sulcatus* are very different from each other. The male has a smooth back, while the female has grooved elytra. This is one of the commonest large predacious diving beetles. It inhabits various types of water – small meadow pools and lakes, flooded quarries, fishponds, puddles on forest paths and running water. It is an excellent swimmer and, in common with most beetles, breathes by means of tracheae, so that from time to time it has to surface to take in a fresh supply of air. As a predator it catches diverse aquatic animals and even keeps a look-out for dead individuals. The female lays the eggs above the surface of the water in cracks in rotting floating logs, wet moss and damp soil on the bank; they are laid 30–50 at a time, but the total number is about 500. The aquatic larvae catch small crustaceans; when fully grown they leave the water and pupate in wet soil on the bank or in rotting wood.

The biggest members of most beetle families live in the tropics and those in the temperate belt are often small by comparison. That does not apply to water beetles, however, whose biggest representatives live only in the temperate belt. *Dytiscus latissimus*, the biggest predacious diving beetle with the widest body, needs large ponds, lakes or rivers with adequate vegetation and food, but can be found in small pools. As it can fly very well it can change its abode if it is necessary. The beetles hunt various aquatic animals, from fishes and tadpoles to water bugs and their larvae, caddis-worms, and even carcases. The female starts laying in April. She thrusts her ovipositor into the tissues of aquatic plants and lays about a hundred eggs. Water pollution and the addition of fertiliser to fishponds have turned this beetle into a rare species and in many places it has actually disappeared.

1. *Acilius sulcatus:* 16—18 mm ($\frac{5}{8}$—$\frac{3}{4}$ in). A large part of Europe, western Siberia, Asia Minor, northern Africa.
2. *Dytiscus latissimus:* 36—44 mm ($1\frac{7}{16}$—$1\frac{3}{4}$ in). Most of Europe except the south, western Siberia. Absent from Britain.

1 *Dytiscus marginalis* L.   Dytiscidae
Great Diving Beetle

2 *Gyrinus substriatus* Steph.   Gyrinidae

Among the few big predacious diving beetles, the
Great Diving Beetle (*Dytiscus marginalis*) is the most
common. Male and female beetles display considerable differences. The male, unlike the female, has
suction discs on its fore and middle pair of legs. The
male also has smooth elytra, while the female usually
has longitudinally grooved elytra (although some females have smooth elytra like the males). The Great
Diving Beetle inhabits ponds and pools. It swims
and flies very well, but is clumsy on its feet. Since it
breathes aerial oxygen, it must constantly renew its
supply of air. Every few minutes it rises to the surface,
where it adopts a typical position. It pushes its abdomen out of the water, spreads its hindlegs wide apart
and when it has collected sufficient air in the space
below its elytra, it 'rows' down to the bottom. The
beetle and the larva are both predacious. The beetle
likes to rise with its prey and grind it to smaller pieces
with its mandibles at the surface, but the larva sucks
its prey dry by means of a canal on the inner surface of
its mandibles. Like the larvae of other diving beetles,
the fully grown larva crawls out onto dry land and
pupates in the ground.

Whirligig beetles trace circles on the surface of the
water with incredible speed and accuracy. As a rule,
members of several related and similar species pursue
these activities together. *Gyrinus substriatus,* like the
other whirligigs, is wonderfully adapted for life on the
surface of water. Its middle and hindlegs are like flip-
pers and its eyes are divided into an upper and a lower
part. Rapid zigzag movements save the beetles from
birds and other enemies. If the danger is particularly
great, they secrete an evil-smelling substance, or submerge and swim below the surface. On land they are
clumsy, but they are able to fly. They catch insects
which live on the surface of the water or have happened to fall into it. The eggs are laid on aquatic
plants. The larvae live in the water and, as distinct
from other water beetles, they breathe by means of
tracheal gills growing along the sides of their abdomen. They pupate on dry land.

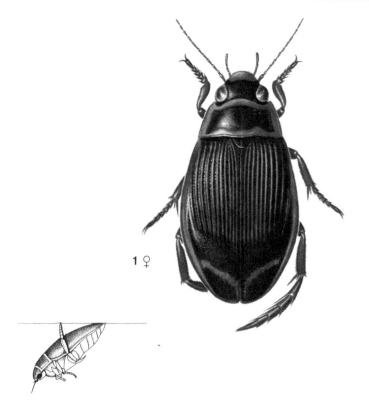

1 ♀

Predacious diving beetle collecting air at the surface

Larva of the Great Diving Beetle
(*Dytiscus marginalis*)

1. *Dytiscus marginalis:* 27—35 mm (1$\frac{1}{16}$—1$\frac{3}{8}$ in). Almost the
   whole of Europe, the Caucasus, Siberia, Japan, North
   America.
2. *Gyrinus substriatus:* 5—7 m ($\frac{3}{16}$—$\frac{5}{16}$ in). Europe, Asia Minor, western Asia, northern Africa.

1 ♂

2

105

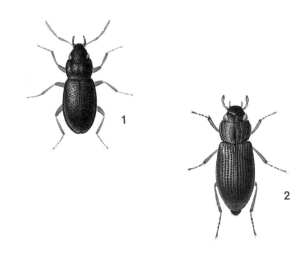

1 *Hydraena gracilis* Germ. Hydraenidae

2 *Helophorus flavipes* F. Hydrophilidae

3 *Sphaeridium scarabaeoides* L.

4 *Hydrobius fuscipes* L.

The stones and moss in clear mountain and submontane streams provide shelter for a great many beetles, including some of the many members of the genus *Hydraena*, all of which resemble one another. *Hydraena gracilis* is a common species.

The water scavenger beetle family (Hydrophilidae) comprises both minute species and one of the largest water beetles there is. The beetles differ in their size, and also show differences in habits, nutrition and reproduction. *Helophorus flavipes*, one of the smallest species, is very common at all altitudes.

Most of the members of the family Hydrophilidae live in water, but there are some which live on land and feed on rotting plants and decaying animal organisms; some actually live in excrement. *Sphaeridium scarabaeoides* settles in fresh cow dung or horse manure in pastures and on footpaths in forests and fields frequented by cattle or horses. If the supply of dung is not large enough, it settles in rotting plant tissues. The female makes provision for the offspring, although her care takes a somewhat simpler form than that of the females of larger species. The eggs are laid in small batches, each of which is wrapped in a protective cocoon, and are then left in the substrate in which the female lived herself. The larvae are thus hatched in an environment in which they are well supplied with food.

Hydrobius fuscipes, which is rather hard to distinguish from related and similar species, often rises to the surface of stagnant water when the sun is shining on it. It appears relatively often in garden water tanks and water-butts.

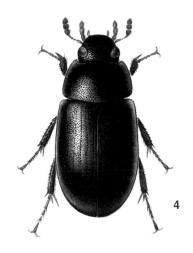

1. *Hydraena gracilis:* 2—2.2 mm ($\frac{1}{16}$ in). Central and northern Europe to beyond the Arctic Circle.
2. *Helophorus flavipes:* 3—4.2 mm ($\frac{1}{8}$ — $\frac{3}{16}$ in). Europe.
3. *Sphaeridium scarabaeoides:* 4—7 mm ($\frac{3}{16}$ — $\frac{5}{16}$ in). The Palaearctic region (in northernmost Europe, Lapland).
4. *Hydrobius fuscipes:* 6—9 mm ($\frac{1}{4}$ — $\frac{3}{8}$ in). The Palaearctic region, North America.

1 *Hydrochara caraboides* L.   Hydrophilidae
2 *Hydrophilus piceus* L.
Great Silver Water Beetle

Hydrochara caraboides inhabits the backwaters of rivers, pools, large puddles and ponds with rich vegetation. It occurs chiefly in lowlands and foothills and only occasionally at higher altitudes. The female is endowed with the same maternal instinct as other water scavenger beetles. When ready to lay eggs, she looks for a leaf (preferably twisted) floating on the surface. She packs the eggs, in an egg cocoon, inside the leaf and then lets it drift away.

In addition to the great Silver Water Beetle (*Hydrophilus piceus*), another, very similar black species (*Hydrophilus aterrimus*) lives in central Europe. The main difference between them is the shape of their abdominal segments; in *H. piceus* the segments are ridged, while in *H. aterrimus* they are rounded. *H. piceus* is the biggest water beetle in Europe. It inhabits stagnant and slow-flowing water with sufficient vegetation (it is phytophagous). It breathes by means of tracheae, like predacious diving beetles, but collects the air by means of its club-tipped antennae and comes up head-first like all other members of its family. On the underside of its body there is a sharp spine whose stab can be very painful. The female lays her eggs on a leaf floating on the surface of the water. She forms a mesh on its underside from fibres spun by her palps from a substance secreted by special glands at the end of her abdomen and then, round her own abdomen, spins a hollow case in which she lays about 50 eggs. Wrapped in their white capsule, the eggs, fixed to the leaf, float freely away. The larvae live in the water. Unlike the beetle, they are predacious, but do not pounce on their prey like the larvae of diving beetles; they generally crawl over the bed, looking for water snails. When fully grown, they climb out onto dry land, make themselves a hole in the ground and pupate in it. Today, the Great Silver Water Beetle is very rare and in some countries it is protected by law.

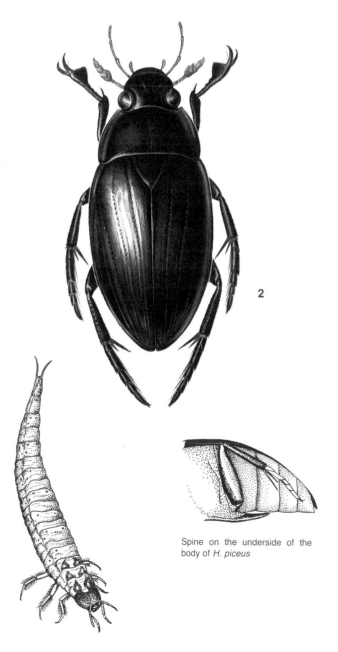

Ootheca of *Hydrochara caraboides*

Spine on the underside of the body of *H. piceus*

Larva of *Hydrophilus piceus*

1. *Hydrochara caraboides:* 14—19 mm ($\frac{9}{16}$—$\frac{3}{4}$ in). The Palaearctic region.
2. *Hydrophilus piceus:* 34—50 mm (1$\frac{3}{8}$—2 in). The Palaearctic region; in northern Europe only the south of Finland and Scandinavia.

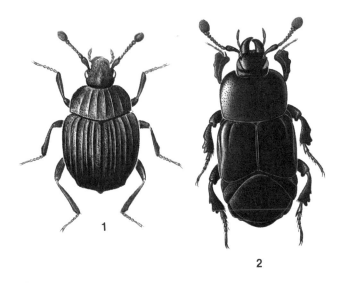

1 **_Onthophilus striatus_** Forst.

2 **_Hololepta plana_** Sulzer

3 **_Hister cadaverinus_** Hoffm.

4 **_Hister quadrinotatus_** Scr.

The members of the family Histeridae, to which all four species illustrated here belong, are very similar to one another. They are small, but stout, and their elytra do not cover the tips of their abdomens. Very often they are black and glossy. They frequent rotting vegetation, decaying animal organisms and excrement and they occur beneath bark, in birds' and mammals' nests and in caves. They are predacious.

Onthophilus striatus is one of the species with longitudinally grooved elytra. It lives in fields and on the outskirts of woods under rotting plants, in excrement, in birds' nests and on escaping sap.

Its very flat body enables _Hololepta plana_ to live below bark; it is mostly to be found on poplars, but sometimes on willows, beeches or false acacias. The predacious beetles and larvae hunt the larvae of various insects living under bark. The beetles and the larvae both hibernate.

One of the best known – and probably the most common – hister beetles is _Hister cadaverinus_ (also known under the names _H. impressus_ and _H. brunneus_). It inhabits open sandy terrains where animal cadavers and excrement are to be found. It also occurs in jackdaws', kestrels' and other birds' nests. The female lays the eggs singly, close to a carcase or excreta. The predacious larvae mostly catch larvae of the hover-fly genus _Eristalis_, large numbers of which live in excrement. The imagos hibernate.

Some hister beetles (e.g. _Hister quadrinotatus_) have red spots on their elytra. This species lives in dung, carrion and rotting plants. The imagos hibernate.

1. _Onthophilus striatus:_ 1.7—2.5 mm ($\frac{1}{16}$—$\frac{3}{32}$ in). A large part of Europe, including the Mediterranean region, the Caucasus.
2. _Hololepta plana:_ 8—9 mm ($\frac{5}{16}$—$\frac{3}{8}$ in). A large part of the Palaearctic region.
3. _Hister cadaverinus:_ 6—8.5 mm ($\frac{1}{4}$—$\frac{1}{3}$ in). The temperate belt in Eurasia (in Europe up to the Arctic Circle); introduced into North America.
4. _Hister quadrinotatus:_ 6—8 mm ($\frac{1}{4}$—$\frac{5}{16}$ in). Central and southern Europe (but not the north), the Caucasus, Transcaucasia, the Near East.

1 *Catops chrysomeloides* Panz.   Catopidae
2 *Thanatophilus sinuatus* F.   Silphidae
3 *Xylodrepa quadripunctata* L.
syn. ***Dendroxena quadrimaculata***
Four-spot Carrion Beetle

Dead animals and decaying plants provide nourishment for a great many insects, which live either on the decaying matter itself, or on larvae which develop in it. *Catops chrysomeloides*, which lives on carrion and in rotting mushrooms (and sometimes in birds' nests), is one of the former type. The beetles are to be seen until late in the autumn and occasionally on fine days in December. The imagos hibernate.

Thanatophilus sinuatus, like many other members of the Silphidae family, frequents carcases. This species is most common in open country, where it forms three generations between the spring and late autumn.

The Four-spot Carrion Beetle (*Xylodrepa quadripunctata*) has somewhat different habits and colouring from other members of the family. It lives mainly in oak and beech woods at low altitudes, because the spruce monocultures characteristic of higher altitudes would not provide it with sufficient food. Hibernating beetles appear in April and remain on trees or shrubs until June. Unlike most other carrion beetles, this one does not live on decaying organic matter, but hunts living prey, in particular caterpillars, sawfly larvae and small aphids; it has a special predilection for the caterpillars of the Green Oak Tortrix Moth (*Tortrix viridana*), European Processionary Moth (*Thaumetopoea processionea*) and Gipsy Moth (*Lymantria dispar*) and is thus a very important predator in deciduous woods. The female lays her eggs in the ground. The larvae are black and their body segments are produced sideways. They live on the ground and are predacious, but sometimes also eat dead insects. They pupate in the ground. The imago emerges in the autumn and hibernates.

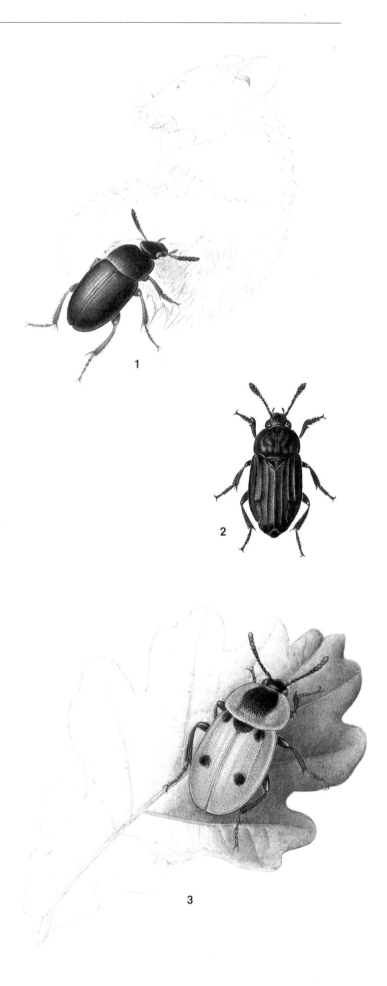

1. *Catops chrysomeloides:* 3.5—5.5 mm ($\frac{5}{32}$—$\frac{1}{4}$ in). Europe, the Caucasus.
2. *Thanatophilus sinuatus:* 9—12 mm ($\frac{3}{8}$—$\frac{1}{2}$ in). Western part of Palaearctic region.
3. *Xylodrepa quadripunctata:* 12—14 mm ($\frac{1}{2}$—$\frac{9}{16}$ in). A large part of Europe.

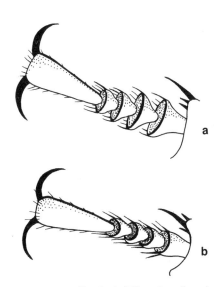

1 *Oiceoptoma thoracicum* L.   Silphidae
2 *Aclypea opaca* L.

To the carrion beetle *Oiceoptoma thoracicum*, the smell of a ripe stinkhorn, some other fungus or the body of a dead animal, is very tempting. The beetle could hardly be mistaken for any other species. The male can be distinguished from the female by the wider tarsi of its forelegs. This carrion beetle is a common and usually abundant forest species, which can be encountered in favourable localities from the spring to the autumn. Very often, several specimens can be found on large cadavers and stinkhorn fruit bodies. The beetles also frequent fermenting sap on deciduous trees, excrement and food remains. The female lays her eggs beneath a carcase; the larvae do not burrow in the ground.

Aclypea opaca belongs to a group of carrion beetles which eat plant tissues; their daily consumption is about 4–5 sq cm ($\frac{1}{2} - \frac{3}{4}$ sq in). The beetles overwinter in warm places under a thin layer of debris, at the foot of a tree or in the remains of plants. In April they come out and can be seen on footpaths and in fields and pastures. They live on goosefoot plants (including sugar beet), cruciferous plants, potatoes and peas. They nibble the leaves from the edge inwards, at the same time releasing from their mouths a blackish-green slime which forms a dark border round the blade of the leaf and helps to decompose the tissue. The female lays about a hundred spherical to slightly ovoid white eggs 1–2 mm ($\frac{1}{16}$ in) long in a pre-excavated depression in the ground. The larvae, which hatch a few days later, develop rapidly. Like the beetles, they are polyphagous. They do not secrete green slime while feeding, so that there is no dark border on the leaf. They are very timid and if in danger they hide on the undersides of leaves or feign death. They are entirely black, except for the yellow outgrowths on their sides. Their development is completed in two to three weeks; they then burrow in the ground, take a short rest and pupate. The largest numbers of young imagos appear from July onwards. In some regions this beetle is listed as a pest of crops.

Fore tarsi of *Oiceoptoma thoracicum:* a – male; b – female

1. *Oiceoptoma thoracicum:* 12—16 mm ($\frac{1}{2}$—$\frac{5}{8}$ in). The temperature belt in Eurasia (as far as the Arctic Circle).
2. *Aclypea opaca:* 9—12 mm ($\frac{3}{8}$—$\frac{1}{2}$ in). Europe (in the north to northernmost Finland and Scandinavia), northern and central Asia, North America.

1 *Silpha obscura* L.

2 *Silpha atrata* L.
Black Carrion Beetle

3 *Necrodes littoralis* L.

Silphidae

The genus *Silpha* includes a few dark species closely resembling one another. They are all flat-bodied and the differences relate to the character of the ribs and spots on their elytra and the shape and length of some of the antennal segments. *Silpha obscura* is one of the commonest of these species. It lives in woods and fields, where it hides during the daytime under stones, in leaves or in clumps of grass. It is very abundant at low altitudes; in the Alps it ascends to about 1,500 m (4,920 ft). It lives on various insects, worms, the cadavers of small vertebrates and plant tissues. The beetles appear, in a single generation, from April to November.

The Black Carrion Beetle (*Silpha atrata*) is immediately conspicuous by its long head. It is abundant throughout practically the whole of the vegetation season, hiding beneath damp, rotting bark on felled trees and old stumps or under stones during the daytime and going out hunting, mostly for slugs and snails, at night. It tracks its prey down by the trails left on the ground. Its long head is very useful for delving into snail shells and sucking out the contents.

Necrodes littoralis is one of the biggest carrion beetles. It is entirely black except for the three red terminal segments of its clavate antennae. The male and female are easy to tell apart; the male has very thick hind femurs and the tarsi of its first and middle pairs of legs are wider than the female's. This large carrion beetle occurs mainly in damp woods. It is explicitly necrophagous, but settles only on large cadavers, where it encounters various other carrion beetles and members of other beetle families. The female lays her eggs beneath a cadaver.

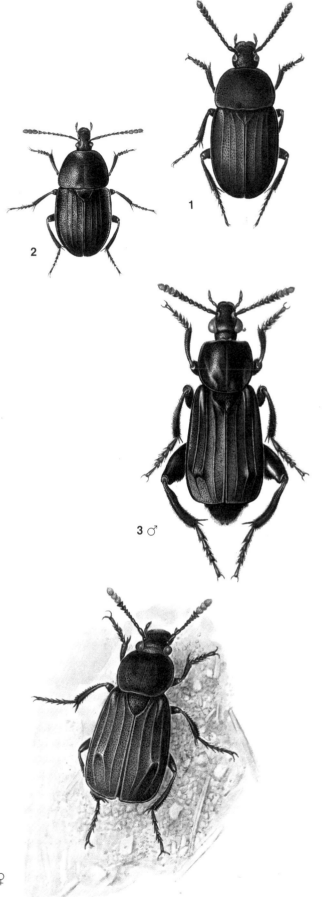

1

2

3 ♂

3 ♀

1. *Silpha obscura:* 14—17 mm ($\frac{9}{16}$—$\frac{11}{16}$ in). The temperate belt in Eurasia.
2. *Silpha atrata:* 10—16 mm ($\frac{3}{8}$—$\frac{5}{8}$ in). Most of Europe (to beyond the Arctic Circle), the Caucasus, Siberia, Japan.
3. *Necrodes littoralis:* 16—25 mm ($\frac{5}{8}$—1 in). Europe, the Caucasus, Siberia, Japan.

1

2

3

4

1 *Nicrophorus vespillo* L.
Silphidae
Common Sexton or Burying Beetle

2 *Nicrophorus vespilloides* Herbst

3 *Nicrophorus humator* Goeze

4 *Scaphidium*
Scaphidiidae
quadrimaculatum Oliv.
Shining Fungus Beetle

Burying beetles are known chiefly for their habits of burying carcases. The adult beetles are predacious and hunt different larvae on cadavers and rotting plants; in the breeding season, however, they are necrophagous. From distances of up to 1 km ($\frac{1}{2}$ mi) and over they gather on some small animal cadaver and try to bury it. At first, several beetles compete for the cadaver, but eventually one couple is successful. They bury the prize, strip it clean of fur or feathers and knead it into a ball, round which they build a smooth-walled chamber connected to the maternal burrow. With most species only the female then remains underground, to lay a few eggs in the maternal burrow. Before the larvae are hatched, she keeps returning to the food lump to feed herself, each time releasing digestive juices into it to hasten its decomposition. After about five days, just before the larvae hatch, she makes a hole in the tip of the lump. The larvae find their way into the chamber, where at first the female feeds them, even after their first moult. When they are older they feed themselves, sometimes plunging their heads deep into the putrid mass. The female tries to keep the lump in the proper shape and protects the larvae from enemies. The larvae pupate in the ground.

The two commonest species are the Common Sexton Beetle (*N. vespillo*) and *N. vespilloides*. They resemble each other but are easily differentiated by the colour of the club tip of their antennae, which is black in *N. vespillo* and red in *N. vespilloides*. As a rule, the male *N. vespilloides* remains in the chamber with the female and even helps to feed the larvae.

N. humator is black and, like the two preceding species, it forms two generations.

Many beetles live on tree fungi. One such species is the Shining Fungus Beetle (*Scaphidium quadrimaculatum*) which inhabits deciduous woods.

---

1. *Nicrophorus vespillo:* 10—24 mm ($\frac{3}{8}$—$\frac{15}{16}$ in). The Palaearctic region, North America.
2. *Nicrophorus vespilloides:* 10—18 mm ($\frac{3}{8}$—$\frac{3}{4}$ in). The temperate belt in Eurasia.
3. *Nicrophorus humator:* 18—28 mm ($\frac{3}{4}$—$1\frac{1}{8}$ in). The Palaearctic region.
4. *Scaphidium quadrimaculatum:* 4.5—6.6 mm ($\frac{3}{16}$—$\frac{9}{32}$ in). Most of Europe, Asia Minor, northern Africa.

1 *Siagonium quadricorne* Kirby   Staphylinidae
2 *Proteinus brachypterus* F.
3 *Anthophagus caraboides* L.

Large rove beetles are quite easily distinguishable from other beetles, but small species might be confused with members of the family Pselaphidae (although the latter are rarer than rove beetles). Rove beetles mostly have very short elytra covering only a few of their abdominal segments. They have membraneous wings folded below the elytra; they are thus able to fly and on sunny days many of them fly very actively. The majority are predacious. They occur in the most diverse habitats and since they dispose of the remains of plants and animals, they play an important role as scavengers.

The male of the species *Siagonium quadricorne* is unique among the rove beetles. It has a horn, pointing straight forwards, in front of each eye and a curved horn on each mandible. It hides below the bark of freshly felled beeches and elms, where it finds sufficient moisture. It is not particularly abundant, but in suitable localities it often occurs together with other small beetles living below bark. Both the beetles and the larvae are evidently saprophagous.

Proteinus brachypterus, a small rove beetle, can be seen from early in the spring to late in the autumn at both low and high altitudes. It lacks the typical rove beetle form, since it is tubby and not elongate. It abounds in old fungi, on felled timber, in moss, in rotting higher plants and in carrion.

Anthophagus caraboides is already to be found in damp localities at high altitudes early in the spring. It appears in large numbers, first of all on flowering blackthorn and later on hawthorn, rowan trees and other trees and shrubs. It can be seen until September.

1

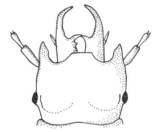

'Horns' on the head of the rove beetle *Siagonium quadricorne*

2

3

---

1. *Siagonium quadricorne:* 4.5—5.5 mm ($\frac{5}{32}$—$\frac{1}{4}$ in). Central and western Europe (but not the north).
2. *Proteinus brachypterus:* 1.6—1.9 mm ($\frac{1}{16}$ in). The Palaearctic region.
3. *Anthophagus caraboides:* 4.5—5.5 mm ($\frac{5}{32}$—$\frac{1}{4}$ in). Mainly central and northern Europe (up to the northern limit of the continent).

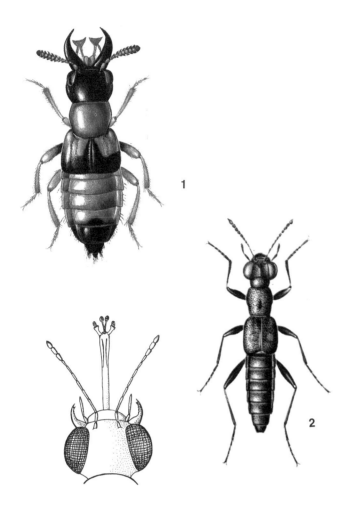

1 *Oxyporus rufus* L. Staphylinidae

2 *Stenus biguttatus* L.

3 *Stenus similis* Herbst

Oxyporus rufus is a typical mushroom rove beetle distributed in both lowlands and mountains. The imago crawls through the cap of a mushroom, biting out a passage approximately the same width as its own body. It evidently consumes some of the mushroom tissue thus removed, but it also catches the larvae of other insects living in mushrooms; its larvae are mycetophagous, however. The beetles appear in the greatest numbers in July and August, but are often to be seen in May and late in the autumn. The very similar, robust *Oxyporus maxillosus,* which is roughly the same size, has yellowish elytra and only its outer posterior corners are black; this species is also somewhat rarer.

The members of the genus *Stenus* are slender, with a big head and large eyes making the head appear larger still. Their pronotum is long and narrow. Their retractable lower lip is used for catching prey and in this respect could perhaps be compared with the mask of dragonfly nymphs. These beetles can be difficult to identify; there are over a hundred species in central Europe alone. It is usually necessary to examine the copulatory organs of the males. Only some species have such unequivocal morphological characteristics that they can be identified with a high degree of probability. One of these is *Stenus biguttatus,* which has two red spots on its elytra (it is not the only species with spots, however). It abounds on muddy banks with sparse vegetation from the spring to the autumn. *Stenus similis,* another common species, inhabits damp meadows, swamps, damp moss and the edge of water and ditches. It is to be found from lowlands to mountains and often appears quite early in the spring.

Device for catching prey on the head of the rove beetle *Stenus similis*

1. *Oxyporus rufus:* 7—12 mm ($\frac{5}{16}$—$\frac{1}{2}$ in). The Palaearctic region.
2. *Stenus biguttatus:* 4.5—5 mm ($\frac{5}{32}$—$\frac{3}{16}$ in). The Palaearctic region (in the north as far as the Arctic Circle).
3. *Stenus similis:* 5—5.5 mm ($\frac{3}{16}$—$\frac{1}{4}$ in). The Palaearctic region.

1 *Paederus riparius* L.   Staphylinidae
2 *Lathrobium fulvipenne* Grav.
3 *Atrecus affinis* Payk.

With their partly metallic colouring, the rove beetles of the genus *Paederus* are some of the prettiest of the entire family. Their metallic-blue elytra contrast sharply with their yellowish-red pronotum and bi-coloured abdomen. *Paederus riparius* is one of the most common among the approximately ten central European *Paederus* species. It is abundant mainly in lowlands, although it sometimes occurs in mountain valleys, although this is rare. It is to be found in the greatest numbers in the spring and autumn. It chiefly inhabits marshes, damp forest outskirts and the sides of small lakes and pools, where it runs about in the mud or stays on the vegetation. It also hides in old, damp leaves; here it occasionally encounters the related *P. fuscipes*. Early in the evening it moves to new sites and settles there on the vegetation. It is a predacious beetle which catches various small animals. The imagos often hibernate together.

The slender, long-bodied rove beetle *Lathrobium fulvipenne* can be found chiefly in the spring, from February to May, and again from October to December. It frequents damp meadows, fields and woods and has even been found on beaches. It hides under stones and the remains of plants. It occurs at both low and high altitudes and ascends the Alps up to 2,000 m (6,560 ft).

Atrecus affinis is one of the smaller forest rove beetles. It is to be seen mainly in the spring and in late summer and autumn; the larvae develop during the summer. This is another beetle that likes the damp. It hides under damp bark on old spruce and pine stumps or on long-felled trees, and if there are any fungi on the trees it is to be found on those as well. It also crawls into rotting wood, but only if it has the right degree of dampness, and it has been found below damp beech bark. It is predacious and hunts various dipteran larvae occurring beneath bark.

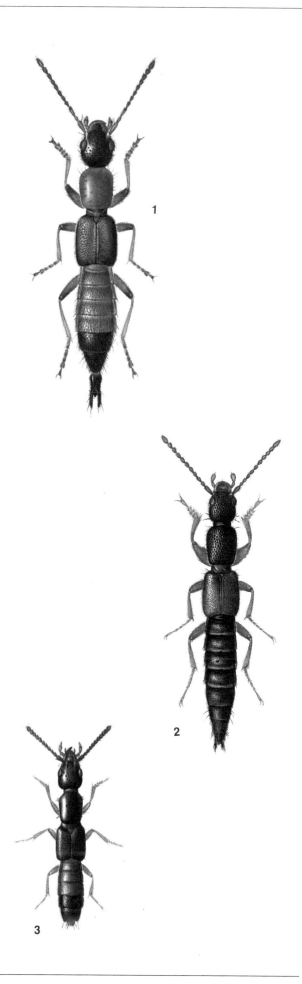

1. *Paederus riparius:* 7.5—8 mm ($\frac{5}{16}$ in). A large part of the Palaearctic region.
2. *Lathrobium fulvipenne:* 7.2—8.7 mm ($\frac{5}{16}$—$\frac{3}{8}$ in). The Palaearctic region, far to the north.
3. *Atrecus affinis:* 6—8 mm ($\frac{1}{4}$—$\frac{5}{16}$ in). The temperate belt in Eurasia (up to 66 ° latitude north).

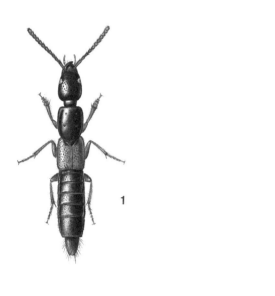

2

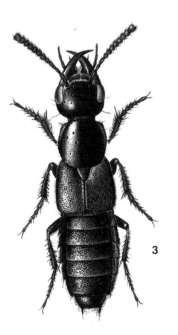

3

1

1 *Othius punctulatus* Goeze   Staphylinidae

2 *Cafius xantholoma* Gravenhorst

3 *Philonthus politus* L.

The long, slim rove beetle *Othius punctulatus* closely resembles many others of the same and related genera. It inhabits deciduous and conifer woods, where it hides in rotting leaves, leaf litter and moss on old tree stumps and under stones; it has also been found in dung and on forest mushrooms. The imagos occur mainly in the autumn and, after overwintering, in the spring; the summer is the time when the larvae develop. The larvae are hatched in eight to ten days and develop during June and July (about seven weeks); the pupal stage lasts just under two weeks. There is thus one generation per year.

Rove beetles even have a typical representative on the seashore. *Cafius xantholoma* is abundant from the early spring (March) until late in the autumn. It is differentiated from other rove beetles by the eight deep dimples in its pronotum and the patches of hair on its abdomen. It is a halophilic species, i.e. it likes a salty environment. It lives under rotting seaweed and the remains of other plants and hides under old wood or stones.

Philonthus politus, whose elytra have a bronze lustre, lives in lowland and mountain fields and forests and occurs up to an altitude of about 2,000 m (6,560 ft). It is to be found on dung, on old mushrooms, on carrion and on sap escaping from deciduous trees, but neither dung nor carrion form part of its diet. A great many dipteran and other insect larvae develop in this environment, and it is in these that the beetle is interested. Its large mandibles leave no doubt as to its rapacity and it can also cope with other small invertebrates. The larvae are likewise predacious.

1. *Othius punctulatus:* 10—14 mm ($\frac{3}{8}$—$\frac{9}{16}$ in). The Palaearctic region.
2. *Cafius xantholoma:* 6—9 mm ($\frac{3}{8}$—$\frac{9}{16}$ in). The coast of Europe and northern Africa, the Black Sea coast, Iceland.
3. *Philonthus politus:* 10.5—14 mm ($\frac{7}{16}$—$\frac{9}{16}$ in). The Palaearctic, Nearctic and Australian regions.

1 *Staphylinus erythropterus* L.   Staphylinidae
2 *Staphylinus caesareus* Ced.
3 *Parabemus fossor* Scop.

A few large rove beetles are characterised by brown-ish-red elytra and some of their abdominal segments have yellow spots formed from yellow hairs (tomentum). They are all rather similar, but are not difficult to identify. *Staphylinus erythropterus* can be recognised from its yellow-haired scutellum and the yellow spots on its fourth to sixth segments. The closely related *Staphylinus caesareus* has a dark scutellum and tomentum spots on its first abdominal segments. *S. erythropterus* chiefly inhabits the damp parts of woods, where it is to be found in leaf litter, in moss, under stones or running about on paths and tracks; it is less common in open country. It is likewise to be seen hunting prey on excrement and decaying plants, since it is predacious and lives on various insect larvae and other invertebrates; in forests it hunts the larvae of click beetles. It avoids dry localities. The beige-coloured eggs, which are about 3 mm ($\frac{1}{8}$ in) long, are laid in May and June. The predacious larvae live in the same places as the beetles, are fully grown by August and then pupate.

Staphylinus caesareus prefers open country, meadows, uncultivated land and the outskirts of woods. It runs about on paths, hides under stones and also appears on rotting animal and plant matter, hunting prey.

Parabemus fossor is a xerophilic species. The yellow-haired posterior half of its elytra makes it easy to identify. It inhabits lowlands and uplands and occurs in mountains up to the forest limit. It is active in bright sunlight, when it runs over paths and tracks in open, dry woods, on fallow land or on heaths. To rest it hides under stones, in moss and below bark.

1. *Staphylinus erythropterus:* 14—18 mm ($\frac{9}{16}$—$\frac{3}{4}$ in). Central and northern Europe, some of the northern part of southern Europe.
2. *Staphylinus caesareus:* 17—25 mm ($\frac{11}{16}$—1 in). Europe including the Mediterranean region, Transcaucasia, Asia Minor, the Near East, North America.
3. *Parabemus fossor:* 15—20 mm ($\frac{5}{8}$—$\frac{13}{16}$ in). Central and western Europe, the mountainous parts of southern Europe.

1 *Staphylinus olens* Müll. Staphylinidae
Devil's Coach-horse

2 *Creophilus maxillosus* L.

3 *Ontholestes tessellatus* Fourcroy

In Europe, the biggest staphylinid beetles are black and are represented primarily by two species – *Staphylinus olens* and *S. tenebricosus* – which closely resemble each other and are the same size. *Staphylinus olens* occurs in lowlands and at submontane altitudes in valleys, but not any higher. It loves damp localities in deciduous woods and at the margins of forests and is rarely to be seen in open country, e.g. in fields, meadows or pastures, but is common in gardens. It appears mainly in the autumn. During the daytime it hides under stones, in damp leaves or moss or in decaying wood. The beetle is well equipped for its highly predacious mode of life and the bite of its large mandibles can be quite painful. It mostly hunts invertebrate animals living in the soil.

The genus *Creophilus* has only one species, *C. maxillosus,* which can be distinguished from other rove beetles by the greyish-white patches formed on its elytra and abdomen by tufts of fine hairs. Its altitude distribution ranges from lowlands to the subalpine zone (about 1,300 m [4,264 ft]). It frequents the cadavers of large animals, excrement, manure heaps and decaying forest mushrooms, where it mostly catches the larvae and puparia of two-winged insects.

Ontholestes tessellatus is the commonest of three similar species occurring in Europe. It has a variety of habitats and can be found in woods, fields, meadows and gardens. It settles on rotting plants (and on old mushrooms in woods), cadavers and excrement and is normally to be found in compost. The beetles often gather together in quite large numbers. Their prey consists of insect larvae developing in excrement, carrion and decaying vegetation.

1. *Staphylinus olens:* 22—32 mm ($\frac{7}{8}$—$1\frac{1}{4}$ in). Central, western and southern Europe, the southern part of northern Europe, northern Africa, the Canary Islands.
2. *Creophilus maxillosus:* 15—23 mm ($\frac{5}{8}$—$\frac{15}{16}$ in). The Palaearctic, Nearctic and Oriental regions; carried to the Hawaiian Islands.
3. *Ontholestes tessellatus:* 14—19 mm ($\frac{9}{16}$—$\frac{3}{4}$ in). The northern parts of the Palaearctic region, absent from the Mediterranean region.

1 *Lordithon lunulatus* L.   Staphylinidae
2 *Tachyporus chrysomelinus* L.
3 *Tachyporus hypnorum* F.
4 *Bolitochara pulchra* Grav.

Many insects occur on forest fungi. *Lordithon lunulatus* lives on the fruit bodies of a whole series of mushrooms and has occasionally also been found on dead animals. The imagos run over the mushrooms, hunting the many dipteran larvae which live in them. They drag the larvae out of the pores, release drops of digestive juice to hasten their decomposition, and then devour them in comfort. The beetles occur mainly in the autumn, in the mushroom season, and again in the spring up to May.

The genus *Tachyporus* comprises a number of very similar species with a sharp-pointed abdomen and yellowish-red and black colouring. Some of them are counted among the most numerous rove beetles. *Tachyporus chrysomelinus* and *T. hypnorum*, illustrated here, occur in damp localities practically the whole year round, in moss, damp leaves and decaying matter. *T. chrysomelinus* has a higher altitude range than *T. hypnorum*.

Bolitochara pulchra is a common mycetophilic rove beetle with catholic tastes, since its menu includes *Boletus*, *Amanita*, *Lactarius* and *Hypholoma* species, other mushrooms and toadstools and tree fungi of the genus *Polyporus*, although it will also make do with an old, rotting tree stump overgrown with various fungi, or a few layers of old, mouldy beech leaves. The beetles are most numerous between August and November. They are to be found mostly at low altitudes, but can ascend to altitudes of about 1,000 m (3,280 ft).

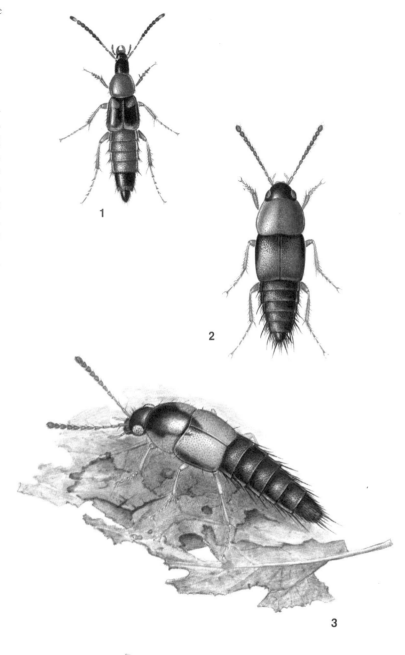

1. *Lordithon lunulatus:* 5—7 mm ($\frac{3}{16}$—$\frac{5}{16}$ in). The Palaearctic region.
2. *Tachyporus chrysomelinus:* 3.5—4 mm ($\frac{5}{32}$—$\frac{3}{16}$ in). The temperate belt in Eurasia, North America.
3. *Tachyporus hypnorum:* 3—4 mm ($\frac{1}{8}$—$\frac{3}{16}$ in). The Palaearctic region.
4. *Bolitochara pulchra:* 3.5—4.5 mm ($\frac{5}{32}$—$\frac{3}{16}$ in). The Palaearctic region.

119

1

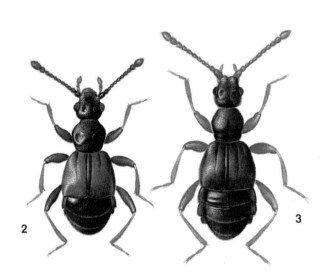

2

3

4

1 *Zyras humeralis* Grav. Staphylinidae

2 *Trissemus antennatus* Aubé Pselaphidae

3 *Tyrus mucronatus* Panz.

4 *Claviger testaceus* Preyssler

While some rove beetles live in close association with forest fungi, others are regular guests of ants, with which they have very complex relationships. *Zyras humeralis*, which is one of the most common, lives mainly with *Lasius fuliginosus*, but also with other ants of the same genus and the big ants of the genus *Formica*. It is likewise to be found under stones over a wide radius round ant colonies. The beetles occur from the spring to the autumn, but are most numerous in the spring.

Pselaphids (Pselaphidae) are small to very small beetles whose elytra cover only part of their abdomen; many of them have strongly developed palps. *Trissemus antennatus*, one of the moderately large species, lives in damp localities – in meadows, swamps and moss growing on the banks of streams, or near waterfalls. In suitable localities the imagos can also be found during the winter. The somewhat larger *Tyrus mucronatus* inhabits crumbling wood in hollow trees, moss growing on old logs and old tree stumps, where it prefers the inner surface of the bark. If often occurs in the company of various ants belonging to the genera *Lasius* and *Formica*.

Claviger testaceus, which is sometimes placed in a separate family, Clavigeridae, and sometimes in the family Pselaphidae, is specifically adapted for a life among ants. It is eyeless and secretes a fluid from pits on its abdomen, which the ants love to lick. For this reason they take very good care of the beetle. *C. testaceus* lives under stones in the nests of the yellow ant *Lasius flavus*. Since it is a light yellowish-brown colour itself, it is invisible among the ants.

1. *Zyras humeralis:* 5.5—6.5 mm ($\frac{1}{4}$—$\frac{9}{32}$ in). The temperate belt in Eurasia, far to the north in Europe.
2. *Trissemus antennatus:* 1.7—1.9 mm ($\frac{1}{16}$ in). Southern Europe, the south of central Europe.
3. *Tyrus mucronatus:* 2.2—2.4 mm ($\frac{1}{8}$ in). Most of Europe, the Caucasus.
4. *Claviger testaceus:* 2.1—2.3 mm ($\frac{1}{8}$ in). Chiefly central Europe and the southern part of northern Europe.

1 *Lucanus cervus* L.

Lucanidae

Stag Beetle

The male Stag Beetle (*Lucanus cervus*) is very different from the female in form and size. It is the largest beetle in Europe. The difference in the size of the sexes is due mainly to the large head and powerful mandibles of the male. The female is smaller and stouter, her head is narrower than her pronotum and she has relatively small mandibles. Sometimes we may find small males with poorly developed mandibles; they are described as the form *capreolus* and are the outcome of development of the larvae under unfavourable nutritional conditions. The Stag Beetle inhabits old oak woods, but owing to intensive exploitation these are rapidly disappearing and so is this handsome beetle. In many countries it is now a protected species and its collection is prohibited, but the only way in which protection can be effective is to protect its original habitats, since only there can it find the proper conditions for its development. The beetles appear in June and July. During the daytime they remain in hiding and do not show signs of increased activity until early in the evening. They fly to trees with escaping sap – their only nourishment – which they lick without having to use their huge mandibles. The main purpose of the mandibles is to act as a weapon in fights between males for a female. Quite often, the weaker rival is maimed by them, lifted into the air and thrown down from a branch to the ground.

The female uses her mandibles to burrow her way into old wood to lay her eggs. The beetle's development takes three to five years, depending on the conditions. The larva lives in rotten wood in old oak trunks and stumps and sometimes in a beech, a willow or a fruit tree. It is blind, yellowish-white and grows steadily fatter; when fully grown it is up to 10 cm (4 in) long. When ready to pupate, it leaves the crumbling wood and buries itself about 20 cm (8 in) deep in the ground, where it forms a hard case, the size of a fist, round itself and pupates inside that. If you were to open a case you could easily tell from the size of the mandibles whether the beetle developing inside it was a male or a female. The imago emerges in the autumn, but overwinters in the pupal case.

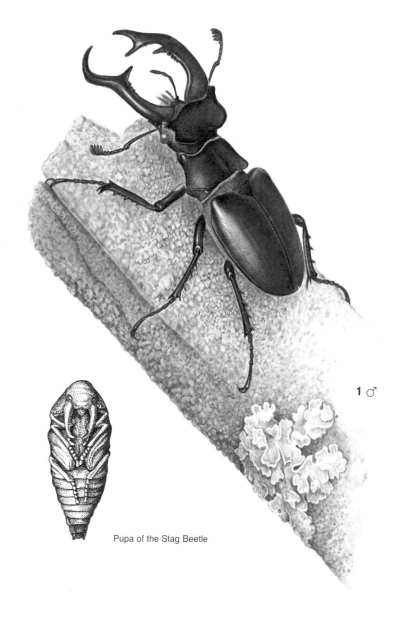

1 ♂

Pupa of the Stag Beetle

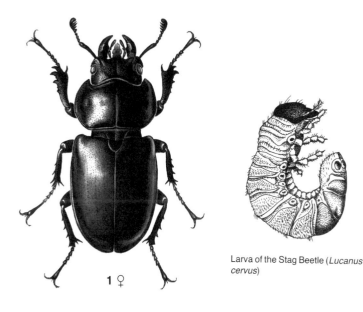

1 ♀

Larva of the Stag Beetle (*Lucanus cervus*)

---

1. *Lucanus cervus:* ♂ 35—75 mm, ♀ 30—45 mm (1⅜— 3 in, ♀ 1 3/16—1¼ in). Central, southern and western Europe, Asia Minor, the Near East (Syria).

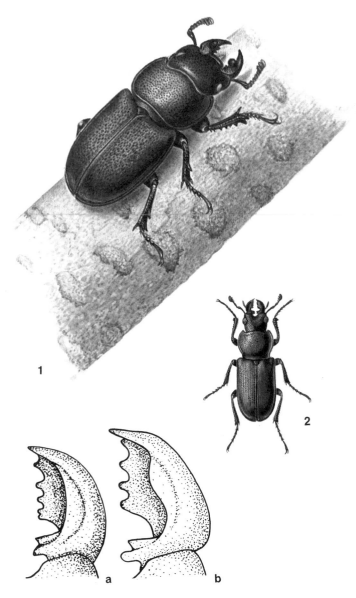

1 ***Dorcus parallelopipedus*** L.   Lucanidae
Lesser Stag Beetle

2 ***Platycerus caraboides*** L.

3 ***Sinodendron cylindricum*** L.

In addition to the Stag Beetle, the fauna of Europe includes a few smaller species belonging to the same family. The male and female of the Lesser Stag Beetle (*Dorcus parallelopipedus*) are not strikingly different from each other. The beetles live from June to August in deciduous woods in lowlands and hilly country. They generally lie hidden under bark or crawl slowly over the trunks or stumps of deciduous trees (chiefly oaks), in which their larvae also develop. In the evening they are sometimes attracted to lights. The fully grown larva measures only about 25 mm (1 in). The beetle's development usually takes three years.

Of the two members of the family with metallic bluish-green colouring, *Platycerus caraboides* is the more abundant; it differs from *P. caprea* by the curving outer edge of its mandibles. It inhabits deciduous woods at low altitudes, while *P. caprea* is a mainly mountain species. The adult beetles begin to make their appearance at the end of spring. As they fly, they keep a look-out for injured deciduous trees with sap oozing from them. The only difference between the male and the female is in the size of the teeth on their mandibles. The larvae develop for three to four years in rotting wood in oaks, beeches, birches and other deciduous trees.

The round-bodied *Sinodendron cylindricum* is a typical small stag beetle which can be encountered quite frequently in old beech woods. The male is clearly distinguishable from the female by the horn on its frons and the deep depression in its pronotum, both of which are visible to the naked eye. The imago spends most of its time below the bark of old beech and oak trunks and stumps in lowland and mountain regions with natural beech woods. The larvae live mainly in old, crumbling beech trunks and stumps; their development takes three years (a year longer in mountain regions).

Mandibles of *Platycerus caraboides* (a) and *P. caprea* (b)

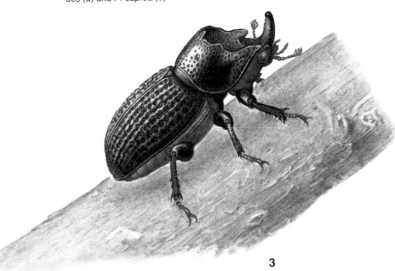

1. *Dorcus parallelopipedus:* 20—32 mm ($\frac{13}{16}$—$1\frac{1}{4}$ in). Europe, Asia Minor, northern Africa.
2. *Platycerus caraboides:* 9—13 mm ($\frac{3}{8}$—$\frac{9}{16}$ in). Central Europe, the north of southern Europe.
3. *Sinodendron cylindricum:* 12—16 mm ($\frac{1}{2}$—$\frac{5}{8}$ in). Europe, western Siberia.

1 *Geotrupes stercorosus* Scr.   Geotrupidae
2 *Geotrupes stercorarius* L.
3 *Geotrupes vernalis* L.

All dor beetles (Geotrupidae) are characterised by very strongly developed care of their offspring. One of the most common is *Geotrupes stercorosus,* which is most frequently to be found along the edge of forest tracks and footpaths. It lives on dung, which it buries in the ground, but it also licks oozing sap. It is an ungainly flier. It starts to build a nest at the beginning of the breeding season. The male and the female dig a burrow below a pile of dung, or in its immediate vicinity, with three or four side passages, to a depth of about 50 cm (20 in). At the end of each passage they place dung, kneaded into a lump, on which the female lays a single egg before sealing the passage. The larva slowly consumes the dung, overwinters in the nest and pupates in the spring. The beetles emerge the same year, but do not attain sexual maturity until after they have hibernated.

Geotrupes stercorarius is the largest central European member of the genus. It occurs in the same type of localities as *G. stercorosus,* from which it can be distinguished by the three cross ridges on its hind tibiae. Its development is likewise similar. The nest lies below fresh horse dung and resembles the nest of *G. stercorosus.* The beetles build several nests during the vegetation season. This is a rapidly disappearing species.

Geotrupes vernalis, conspicuous for its smooth and highly glossy elytra, is fairly common on sandy hillsides and in woods. It lives on horse and cattle dung. When building the nest, the beetles first dig a funnel-shaped hole about 50 mm (2 in) deep, with several horizontal passages leading from the bottom. They place a supply of dung in each of these passages and then dig a vertical shaft from the bottom of the funnel which terminates in a chamber containing a lump of food with an egg in it. They sprinkle sand over the lump and fill the shaft with dung, so that the young beetle is assured of an adequate food supply.

1. *Geotrupes stercorosus:* 12—19 mm ($\frac{1}{2}$—$\frac{3}{4}$ in). Europe (up to 67 ° latitude north), the Caucasus, western Siberia.
2. *Geotrupes stercorarius:* 16—25 mm ($\frac{5}{8}$—1 in). The temperate belt in Eurasia, Canada.
3. *Geotrupes vernalis:* 12—20 mm ($\frac{1}{2}$—$\frac{13}{16}$ in). Europe, Asia Minor, Iran.

Cross ridges on the hind tibia of *Geotrupes stercorosus* (a) and *G. stercorarius* (b)

123

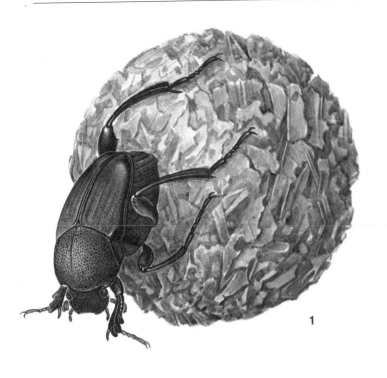

1 *Sisyphus schaefferi* L.   Scarabaeidae
2 *Onthophagus ovatus* L.
3 *Onthophagus nuchicornis* L.

Sisyphus schaefferi likes plenty of warmth. The hibernating imagos come out of hiding in the spring, eat to make good their winter losses and then breed. Together, the male and female form dung into a ball as food for the future larva; they prefer sheep dung and resort to substitutes only when it is not available. The beetles dig a hole and roll the dung towards it by means of their long, curved hindlegs. When the dung is in the hole, the female fashions it into a pear-shaped lump and lays an egg in it. The beetles then proceed to dig another hole. In addition to the pear-shaped lumps for their offspring, each beetle makes and buries a lump of dung for its own consumption.

The life of the small, stout-bodied dung beetles of the genus *Onthophagus* is associated with dung, on which both the imagos and the larvae live. These beetles likewise make provision for their offspring. The larvae develop in underground nests filled with dung. The unicoloured *Onthophagus ovatus* uses sheep and goat dung, but also lives in manure and rotting mushrooms. It is to be found mainly on sunny pastures and less often in woods. *Onthophagus nuchicornis*, which is more interestingly coloured, lives chiefly in cow dung and is common from spring to autumn. The beetles also live in other excrement, on rotting plants and on small carcases, but do not use them as food for the larvae. As in other species, the nest is built chiefly by the female, aided by the male. It is situated mainly on sandy tracks with little vegetation. It consists of a main passage, usually with two side passages and about five to eight chambers, in each of which a single larva develops and eventually pupates.

2

3

1. *Sisyphus schaefferi:* 8—10 mm ($\frac{5}{16}$—$\frac{3}{8}$ in). The central and southern part of the Palaearctic region.
2. *Onthophagus ovatus:* 4—6 mm ($\frac{3}{16}$—$\frac{1}{4}$ in). Europe, Asia Minor, Near East.
3. *Onthophagus nuchicornis:* 6—9 mm ($\frac{1}{4}$—$\frac{3}{8}$ in). Europe, Asia Minor, Siberia, northern Africa, North America.

1 *Aphodius prodromus* Brahm   Scarabaeidae
2 *Aphodius fimetarius* L.
3 *Aphodius rufipes* L.
4 *Serica brunnea* L.

The small beetles of the genus *Aphodius* appear early in the spring. Guided by their sense of smell, they seek out the faeces of various animals (mostly mammals) as food for themselves and their future offspring. There are many species, all differently coloured. The three basic types illustrated here – with yellow, red and black elytra – are very common species. *Aphodius prodromus* prefers cow, horse and sheep dung and also likes human excrement. It flies from early spring until June and again from the middle of August until late autumn. *Aphodius fimetarius* is one of the most frequent species; it appears on warm March days, flying over fields in search of dung. It is polyphagous and although it evidently prefers horse and cow dung it also frequents rotting vegetable matter (compost) and carcases. The female lays 20–25 eggs in dung at a given stage of decomposition suitable for growth of the larvae; its choice of dung forms part of its care of the offspring. When fully grown, the larvae crawl below the dung and pupate in the ground. The dark-coloured *Aphodius rufipes* prefers cow dung, but is also to be found in other types; it flies from the spring to the autumn.

Serica brunnea hides during the daytime under bark, a stone, old wood, moss or a cluster of leaves. In the evening and at night it comes out and swarms; quite often it is attracted to lights. It occurs in the greatest numbers from June to August. The female lays the eggs in the ground at a depth of just a few centimetres. The larvae live in the soil and nibble the rootlets off various plants, particularly grasses. The last larval instar grows to a length of about 20 mm ($\frac{13}{16}$ in) and then pupates.

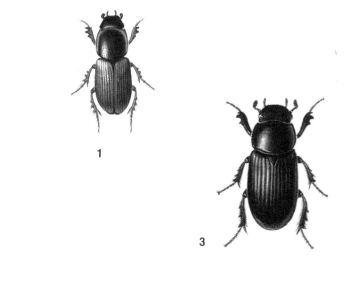

1

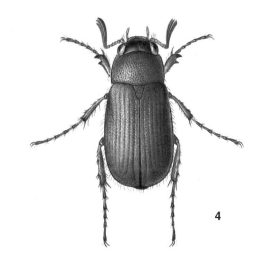

3

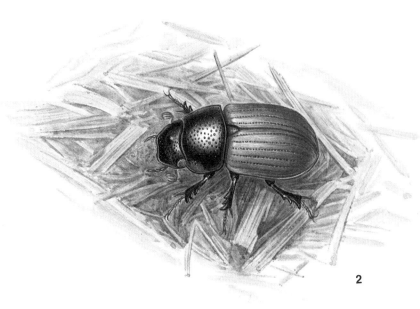

2

4

1. *Aphodius prodromus:* 4—7 mm ($\frac{5}{32}$—$\frac{9}{32}$ in). Europe, central and northern Asia, North America.
2. *Aphodius fimetarius:* 5—8 mm ($\frac{3}{16}$—$\frac{5}{16}$ in). The Palaearctic region, North America.
3. *Aphodius rufipes:* 10—13 mm ($\frac{3}{8}$—$\frac{9}{16}$ in). The Palaearctic and Nearctic regions, southern Africa, South America.
4. *Serica brunnea:* 8—10 mm ($\frac{5}{16}$—$\frac{3}{8}$ in). Europe (minus the Mediterranean region), Siberia, Korea, Japan.

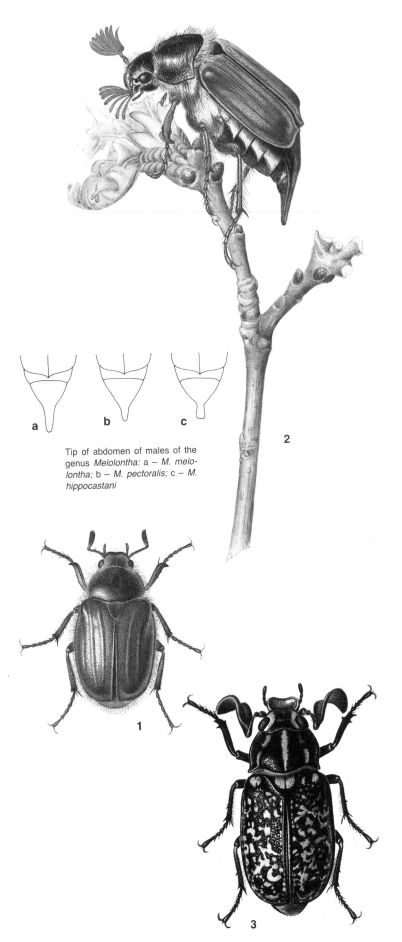

Tip of abdomen of males of the genus *Melolontha*: a – *M. melolontha*; b – *M. pectoralis*; c – *M. hippocastani*

1 *Amphimallon solstitialis* L. Scarabaeidae
Summer Chafer

2 *Melolontha melolontha* L.
Common Cockchafer, Maybug

3 *Polyphylla fullo* L.

On warm summer evenings sometimes as early as the end of June, the Summer Chafer (*Amphimallon solstitialis*) swarms round trees and above meadows. It flies in gardens, in tree-bordered lanes, in parks and on the outskirts of woods. The beetles begin to swarm suddenly and stop equally suddenly after about three-quarters of an hour. It is mostly the males that fly; the females dangle from twigs or squat in the grass. When they have finished swarming, the beetles settle on leaves or rest underground until it is time to swarm again. Their development takes two years. The beetles mate at swarming time. The female lays eggs singly in the ground. The larvae live on the rootlets of various plants and hibernate twice; when fully grown they measue about 20 mm ($\frac{13}{16}$ in) and weigh about 1 g.

The Common Cockchafer (*Melolontha melolontha*) is the most common member of its group. It lives mainly in low-lying country, or in uplands, and is to be found in woods, fields and orchards. The imagos swarm in the evening. The females lay the eggs in fields, digging to depths of about 20–30 cm (8–12 in) to do so. The grubs live on the rootlets of diverse plants. The development cycle of this species usually takes three years, but sometimes four.

Polyphylla fullo, the largest chafer in central Europe, inhabits pinewoods on sandy soil. The male has large flabellate antennae with seven segments; the female's antennae have only five short segments. The female lays her eggs on open ground with abundant vegetation at the edge of forests, where the larvae can find sufficient food in the form of the rootlets of different plants. The development cycle takes three years. The beetles live about four weeks, roughly from the end of June to the end of July. During the daytime they sit on branches, but in the evening, after sunset, they swarm round trees.

1. *Amphimallon solstitialis:* 14—18 mm ($\frac{9}{16}$—$\frac{3}{4}$ in). The Palaearctic region.
2. *Melolontha melolontha:* 20—30 mm ($\frac{13}{16}$—1$\frac{3}{16}$ in). Europe (including the British Isles but minus the Iberian peninsula and southern Italy).
3. *Polyphylla fullo:* 24—40 mm (1—1$\frac{9}{16}$ in). Europe, the Caucasus, northern Africa.

1 *Euchlora dubia* Scop.   Scarabaeidae

2 *Phyllopertha horticola* L.
Garden Chafer

3 *Hoplia farinosa* L.

4 *Hoplia philanthus* Fuess.

Small lamellicorn beetles are often characterised by considerable colour variability. This is particularly evident in *Euchlora dubia,* which is known to have several dozen colour variants, from blackish-blue and black individuals to green and yellow. Beetles with a green pronotum and yellowish-brown elytra are very frequent. The imagos swarm mainly on sunny days in June and July, but they sometimes fly as early as May and as late as August. They require a sandy terrain. The female lays her eggs in a shallow layer of sandy soil; the larvae hibernate and the new generation appears late the following spring.

Briar roses are often visited by the Garden Chafer (*Phyllopertha horticola*). On sunny days in May and June the beetles can be seen flying at the edge of woods and in meadows and gardens. They nibble the flowers and leaves of various trees such as hazels, birches, willows and oaks. The female lays eggs singly in small chambers in the ground. The larvae nibble the rootlets of grasses and other plants. The larvae overwinter and pupate the following year.

Hoplia farinosa and *H. philanthus* have several features in common. Both have scales on their elytra and both are active during the daytime; they swarm in the morning. *H. philanthus* is to be found on the leaves of bushes and trees, such as willows, alders, young fruit trees and the branches of young pine trees, whereas *H. farinosa* frequents the flowers of various shrubs and herbaceous plants (e.g. elder, hawthorn, dogrose, dogwood, spiraea and ox-eye daisies). The larvae of both species live in the soil and pupate there in a small chamber.

1. *Euchlora dubia:* 12—15 mm ($\frac{1}{2}$—$\frac{5}{8}$ in). A large part of Europe.
2. *Phyllopertha horticola:* 8.5—11 mm ($\frac{11}{32}$—$\frac{7}{16}$ in). The temperate belt in Eurasia.
3. *Hoplia farinosa:* 9—11 mm ($\frac{3}{8}$—$\frac{7}{16}$ in). Southern, western and central Europe.
4. *Hoplia philanthus:* 8—9 mm ($\frac{5}{16}$—$\frac{3}{8}$ in). Central and western Europe.

1 *Oryctes nasicornis* L.
European Rhinoceros Beetle

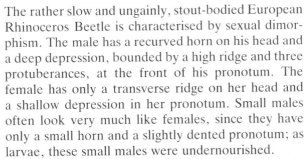

1 ♂

1 ♀

The rather slow and ungainly, stout-bodied European Rhinoceros Beetle is characterised by sexual dimorphism. The male has a recurved horn on his head and a deep depression, bounded by a high ridge and three protuberances, at the front of his pronotum. The female has only a transverse ridge on her head and a shallow depression in her pronotum. Small males often look very much like females, since they have only a small horn and a slightly dented pronotum; as larvae, these small males were undernourished.

The European Rhinoceros Beetle originally inhabited old oak woods and in some places is still to be found in them today. In the seventeenth century (as far as we can judge from contemporary reports) it began to appear in oak bark in tanneries and later in compost heaps containing tan-bark. With increasing construction of sawmills, the beetle began to settle in rotting wood waste, whose composition corresponded to the crumbling wood on which the larvae originally fed. In time, the Rhinoceros Beetle became a synanthropic species living in the vicinity of people. Today it is not exceptional for the beetles to fly about in the evening in big cities. The imagos are nocturnal insects; they fly noisily and not very fast. In the daytime they retire underground or into decaying wood. The adult beetles probably take no food. The female lays about 30 eggs, singly, in compost or sawdust. The grub is blind and lives on cellulose, which it digests by means of gut micro-organisms. When resting it curls up, often so tightly that its head touches its abdomen. For locomotion it uses its legs and its mandibles. It moults twice during its development. When fully grown it is very thick-bodied and measures 10–12 cm (4–4½ in). It finally works its way deeper into the ground, wraps itself in a large cocoon, which it sticks together, smoothing the inner wall, and pupates inside this. The sex of the future beetle can be determined from the outgrowths on the head of the pupa. When it first emerges, the beetle is soft; it must therefore remain some time in the cocoon until its cuticle has hardened and will not be damaged when it bites its way out. The development of this species takes two years and sometimes longer.

1. *Oryctes nasicornis:* 25—40 mm (1—1$\frac{9}{16}$ in). The Palaearctic region.

1 *Epicometis hirta* Poda   Scarabaeidae
2 *Oxythyrea funesta* Poda
3 *Cetonia aurata* L.
Rose Chafer
4 *Liocola lugubris* Herbst

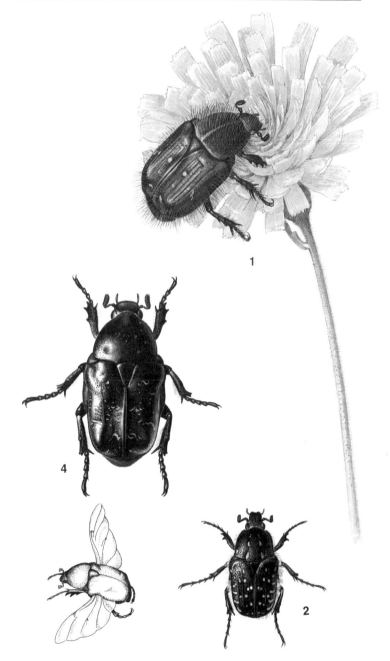

The small, black and extremely hairy rose chafer *Epicometis hirta* is a regular guest on a wide assortment of flowers. It prefers composite and cruciferous plants, but also patronises flowering fruit trees (including citrus fruits), rose bushes and cereal plants. It likes sweet juices. The female lays about twenty eggs singly in humus; the larva lives on decaying plant matter. The imago overwinters in the ground.

Oxythyrea funesta visits flowers in bright sunlight on warm spring and summer days to drink nectar and eat pollen; on cold days it remains in the ground. The female lays her relatively few eggs singly in the soil. They and the larvae develop fast, so that the imagos emerge at the end of the summer. They fly on fine days, but the first signs of autumn send them underground into hibernation.

The Rose Chafer (*Cetonia aurata*) is the best known member of the rose chafer subfamily. It likes any kind of flower, but prefers roses. It drinks nectar and collects pollen, flying noisily from flower to flower with closed elytra. In the spring the female lays about 40 eggs. The larvae often live in compost and in wood mould in old trees; the third larval instar hibernates. When fully grown, the larva pupates in a cocoon with a smooth, glossy inner surface. The imago, which emerges the same year, sometimes flies on fine autumn days, but as a rule it remains in the ground and hibernates.

Liocola lugubris develops and lives similarly to the Rose Chafer. It is a forest species and sucks nectar from flowers, but it also relishes sap escaping from felled deciduous trees.

Rose Chafer in flight (with closed elytra)

1. *Epicometis hirta:* 8—11 mm ($\frac{5}{16}$—$\frac{7}{16}$ in). A large part of Eurasia, northern Africa, North America.
2. *Oxythyrea funesta:* 8—10 mm ($\frac{5}{16}$—$\frac{3}{8}$ in). Europe, Transcaucasia, northern Africa.
3. *Cetonia aurata:* 15—20 mm ($\frac{5}{8}$—$\frac{13}{16}$ in). Europe, the temperate belt in Asia.
4. *Liocola lugubris:* 19—25 mm ($\frac{3}{4}$—1 in). Europe, eastern Siberia.

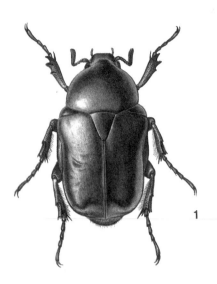

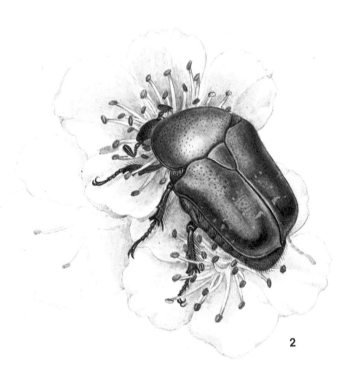

1 *Potosia aeruginosa* Drury

2 Potosia cuprea F.

3 *Valgus hemipterus* L.

In warm, sunny localities, untouched or only slightly altered by human activities, you may occasionally come across the large, handsome green-gold rose chafer *Potosia aeruginosa*. It frequents tree-tops (especially oaks), sits on young growths and licks sap oozing from damaged trunks. Its taste for sweet juices extends to over-ripe fruit, such as cherries and mulberries, and flowering bushes. The imagos live from May to July and sometimes longer. The female lays her eggs in a rotten trunk or the branch of an old oak, in which the larva develops for three years. When the larva measures about 65 mm ($2\frac{9}{16}$ in), it sticks wood slivers and debris together to make a very strong cocoon, in which it pupates.

Hollows and holes in the mounds of big forest ants (usually belonging to the genus *Formica*) are a sign that somebody has broken into the anthill in search of prey. In fact, fat chafer grubs (*Potosia cuprea*) can be caught there, as well as ants, and the Green Woodpecker loves to rake them out. The anthill is an excellent environment for the development of the larvae. It contains sufficient remnants of plants for them to eat, has the right temperature and the ants tolerate their presence; the larvae can also develop outside, however. The beetles fly mainly from May to July and sometimes still in August. They sit on roses, onion flowers and flowering shrubs and are to be found on escaping sap and, in the summer, on over-ripe fruit.

Valgus hemipterus is a small, dark chafer which can be found from autumn to spring, hibernating in decaying wood in the trunks and stumps of various deciduous trees, such as beeches, willows and fruit trees. In May and June the beetles sit on flowering herbaceous plants – most often umbelliferous plants, flowering hawthorn, roses, dogwood and spiraea. The larvae develop in rotten wood in old dead or dying trees; they pupate in a cocoon. The beetles occur in lowlands and hills.

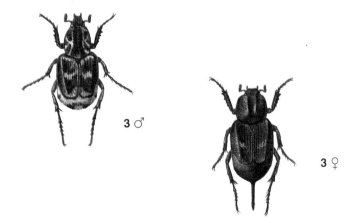

1. *Potosia aeruginosa:* 22—28 mm ($\frac{7}{8}$—$1\frac{1}{8}$ in). Southern and central Europe, sporadically in the north; Asia Minor.
2. *Potosia cuprea:* 14—23 mm ($\frac{9}{16}$—$\frac{15}{16}$ in). A large part of Eurasia.
3. *Valgus hemipterus:* 6—10 mm ($\frac{1}{4}$—$\frac{3}{8}$ in). Central and southern Europe, the Caucasus, southern Siberia, Iran, northern Africa.

1 *Osmoderma eremita* Scop.
Hermit Beetle

Scarabaeidae

2 *Gnorimus nobilis* L.

3 *Trichius fasciatus* L.
Bee Beetle

Some butterflies, bugs and beetles emit a characteristic odour. The smell of the Hermit Beetle (*Osmoderma eremita*) is said to resemble Russian leather. The beetles are active in the evening; they spend the day hiding in rotten wood on old deciduous trees or sitting on flowers. They occur from June to August and sometimes into September. The female lays her eggs in rotting hollows in the wood in the trunks and thick branches of deciduous trees – usually oaks, but also willows, limes, beeches and fruit trees – where the larvae develop over several years. The larva grows to a length of 60 mm ($2\frac{3}{8}$ in) or more; when fully grown it makes itself an egg-shaped cocoon with a smooth inner wall and pupates inside it.

Gnorimus nobilis favours beech woods but tends to occur in places unspoilt by people. On fine days the beetles bask in the sun on the light-coloured flowers of spiraea, elder, meadow-sweet, dogwood, dogrose and umbelliferous plants at the edges of woods and in open spaces in forests. They live from May until July or August. The larvae develop in dead wood on deciduous trees.

Variability of the number and size of the spots can usually be observed in beetles with spotted elytra. The Bee Beetle (*Trichius fasciatus*) and related species also have a number of colour variants. In some individuals the yellow colouring is suppressed by the black, in others the situation is reversed. On sunny days, mainly in June and July, the beetles fly over grassy clearings and the outskirts of woods and settle on the flowers of all kinds of herbaceous plants and shrubs. The larvae develop in dead and rotting wood on deciduous trees.

1. *Osmoderma eremita*: 24—30 mm ($\frac{15}{16}$—$1\frac{3}{16}$ in). A large part of Europe.
2. *Gnorimus nobilis*: 15—19 mm ($\frac{5}{8}$—$\frac{3}{4}$ in). Europe (except the north), Asia Minor.
3. *Trichius fasciatus*: 9—12 mm ($\frac{3}{8}$—$\frac{1}{2}$ in). Europe (to the north of the continent), the temperate belt in Asia (the Caucasus, Siberia, Japan).

Variability of the spots on the elytra
of *Trichius fasciatus*

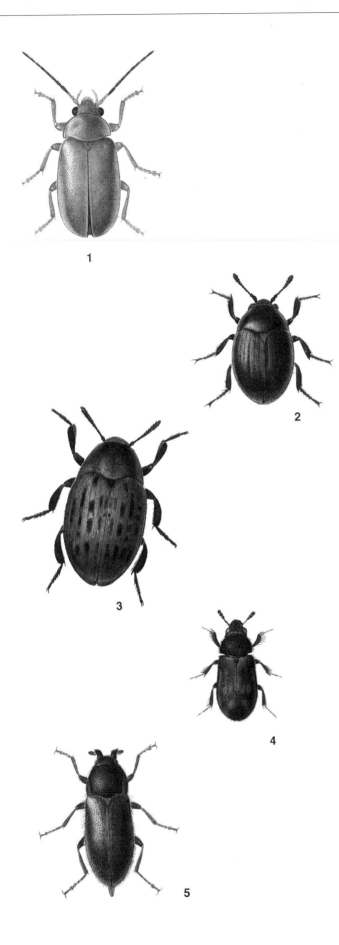

1 **Microcara testacea** L.   Scirtidae

2 **Cytilus sericeus** Forst.   Byrrhidae

3 **Byrrhus pilula** L.

4 **Heterocerus fenestratus** Thunb. Heteroceridae

5 **Dryops similaris** Bollow   Dryopidae

Microcara testacea and other species of the family Scirtidae like a damp environment. They occur near water and in marshy meadows on various plants.

Some species of the family Byrrhidae have a metallic colour. One of these is *Cytilus sericeus*, a generally common beetle found in moss in damp grassy spaces in woods from spring to summer. It lives in both lowlands and mountains. Its larva is the only byrrhid larva to crawl about in the open. The most specialised representatives of the family are notable for the way they defend themselves. When in danger they tuck their head and legs under their body and turn themselves into a little ball. *Byrrhus pilula* and other species are masters at the art. When it has assured itself that the danger is past, the beetle continues on its way. *Byrrhus pilula* often crawls along forest paths, from lowlands to high up in the mountains. The larvae live in the ground and nibble the rhizoids of mosses.

The species of the family Heteroceridae are all small and as a rule they have yellow-spotted elytra. *Heterocerus fenestratus* and related species live in tubular capsules in clay and sandy soil on the banks of flowing and stagnant water. Their identification is problematical and requires examination of the underside of the body or the male's copulatory apparatus.

Dryops similaris and a few similar species live in marshy pools, fishponds, backwaters and the banks of running water. The imagos and the larvae are both phytophagous; they live in water, but pupate on the land.

1. *Microcara testacea:* 3.2—6 mm ($\frac{1}{8}$—$\frac{1}{4}$ in). A large part of Europe.
2. *Cytilus sericeus:* 4.5—5.5 mm ($\frac{3}{16}$—$\frac{1}{4}$ in). Europe, the temperate belt in Asia.
3. *Byrrhus pilula:* 6.7—9.3 mm ($\frac{9}{32}$—$\frac{3}{8}$ in). Europe, the temperate belt in Asia.
4. *Heterocerus fenestratus:* 3—4.5 mm ($\frac{1}{8}$—$\frac{3}{16}$ in). Europe, the temperate belt in Asia.
5. *Dryops similaris:* 4.2—5.4 mm ($\frac{5}{32}$—$\frac{1}{4}$ in). Europe, the Caucasus, Asia Minor.

1 *Chalcophora mariana* L.
Pine-borer

Buprestidae

2 *Buprestis rustica* L.
Common Wood-borer

3 *Buprestis octoguttata* L.

The Pine-borer (*Chalcophora mariana*) is the largest metallic wood-borer in Europe. It flies in old pine-woods from May until August. On sunny days it is especially active along paths and in sunny clearings. It settles on tree stumps, felled timber and shrubs, its body glowing like copper in the rays of the sun. The larvae develop in the dead wood of old pines, mainly in stumps.

The Common Wood-borer (*Buprestis rustica*) is another metallic wood-borer inhabiting conifer forests, but chiefly spruce. When it sits on a branch, a trunk or a stone, its colouring blends with its surroundings. Its elytra and pronotum are sometimes greenish, bluish or violet and sometimes have a reddish-green or blackish tinge. The beetle flies on hot summer days from June to August, mostly in the middle of the day. It likes to settle on felled timber and stumps warmed by the midday sun. The larvae live in dead wood in felled conifers and their stumps (mainly spruce and pine, but also fir and larch). They tunnel below the bark. They hibernate twice before pupating.

The scientific name of *Buprestis octoguttata* tells us that the beetle has eight (*octo*) spots (*guttae*). The spots are bright yellow on a bluish background, which may be tinged faintly green. The beetles fly from May to August in pinewoods, in clearings and on steep sandy rocks overgrown with pines. They settle on the trees and their roots, on old stumps and on felled timber; they occur in lowlands, but in some places are found at fairly high altitudes. The larvae develop in dead pines, chiefly in the lower part of the trunk and the roots, or in pine stumps.

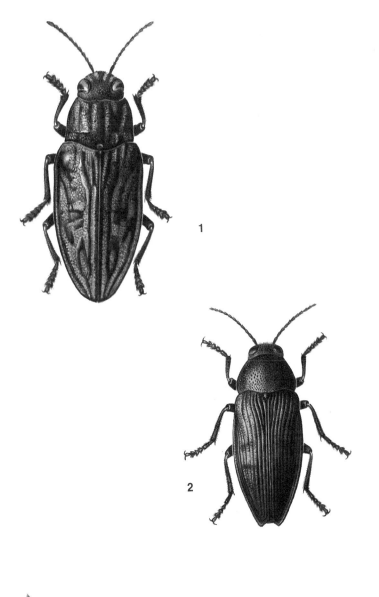

1

2

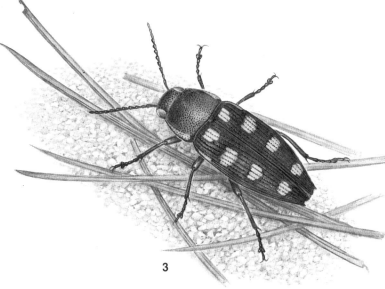

3

1. *Chalcophora mariana:* 25—33 mm (1—1$\frac{5}{16}$ in). Europe (especially the eastern part), the Caucasus, Siberia.
2. *Buprestis rustica:* 13—20 mm ($\frac{9}{16}$—$\frac{13}{16}$ in). Northern and central Europe (especially to the east), the Caucasus, western Siberia.
3. *Buprestis octoguttata:* 9—17 mm ($\frac{3}{8}$—$\frac{11}{16}$ in). Europe, the Caucasus, Siberia, northern Africa.

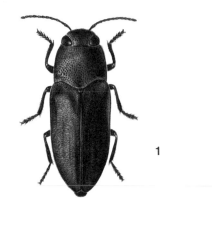

Phaenops cyanea inhabits pinewoods. It flies very actively from May to July, but is sometimes seen in August or even later in the mountains. It settles on trunks, stumps and stacked timber. On cloudy days it hides in cracks in the bark. The larva develops in or below the bark of freshly felled or diseased pines (only occasionally firs). Its development takes two years.

In June and July, the small inconspicuous *Anthaxia quadripunctata* is usually to be found in abundance in growths of hawkweed and dandelions; it also frequents other plants with yellow flowers, such as hawksbeard and buttercups. This species and *A. godeti* are so much alike that the identity of a single specimen is hard to determine. Such species are known as sibling species. In that case we must look for differences in the incidence and habits of the beetles, as well as in their appearance. *A. quadripunctata* lives more in foothills and develops in dying spruce, silver fir or larch branches and trunks, while *A. godeti* lives in lowlands and develops in pines.

The Metallic Wood-borer (*Anthaxia nitidula*) appears in May on sweet-briar, buttercups, ox-eye daisies and other flowers. Its colouring varies greatly. The males generally differ from the females, but colour differences also occur within the sexes. The beetles mainly live in lowlands or low-lying mountain valleys. The tiny larvae develop under the bark of fruit trees (in particular cherry and plum), but also on hawthorn and blackthorn.

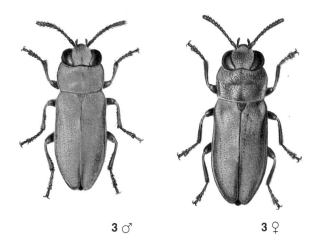

3 ♂   3 ♀

1. *Phaenops cyanea:* 7—12 mm ($\frac{5}{16}$—$\frac{1}{2}$ in). Most of Europe, seldom in the north-west.
2. *Anthaxia quadripunctata:* 4.5—8 mm ($\frac{3}{16}$—$\frac{5}{16}$ in). A large part of Europe, the Caucasus, Asia Minor, the Near East.
3. *Anthaxia nitidula:* 4.5—7.3 mm ($\frac{3}{16}$—$\frac{5}{16}$ in). Southern and central Europe, the Caucasus, Asia Minor, northern Africa.

1 *Chrysobothris affinis* F. Buprestidae

2 *Agrilus angustulus* Illig.

3 *Agrilus pannonicus* Piller et Mitt.
Two-spot Wood-borer

4 *Trachys minutus* L.

Characteristic of *Chrysobothris affinis* are the gold-gleaming spots and faint longitudinal ribs on its elytra. It inhabits deciduous woods (preferably oak-woods), where it flies very actively in bright sunlight from May to July. It settles on felled or stacked timber and on dry stumps, but does not visit flowers. The larvae develop underneath the bark on the trunks and thick branches of all kinds of deciduous trees, but mainly those of dying or freshly felled oaks and beeches.

The members of the large genus *Agrilus* are numerous and difficult to identify. In some species, identification of the female is particularly hard. The beetles often congregate on their host plants. *Agrilus angustulus* is a small species that occurs chiefly in oak woods; it is frequently found on young oaks and oak undergrowth. The larvae mainly develop in oaks, but can also do so in other deciduous trees. The beetles fly in July and August. The Two-spot Wood-borer (*Agrilus pannonicus*), one of the largest species of the genus, has two, easily recognisable, light streaks alongside the suture on the posterior half of its elytra. On fine days from May to July, the beetles, which are active fliers, settle on oak stumps and the leaves of oak undergrowth. The larvae develop underneath the bark (or in it, if the bark is thick) of drying oak branches and stumps.

The small, wide-bodied *Trachys minutus* frequents deciduous trees from the spring to the autumn. It is mostly seen on willows, but sometimes on roses or the flowers of umbelliferous plants. The female sticks her eggs to the upper surface of the downy leaves of various types of willows and other deciduous trees. The larvae develop in the leaves; the imagos hibernate.

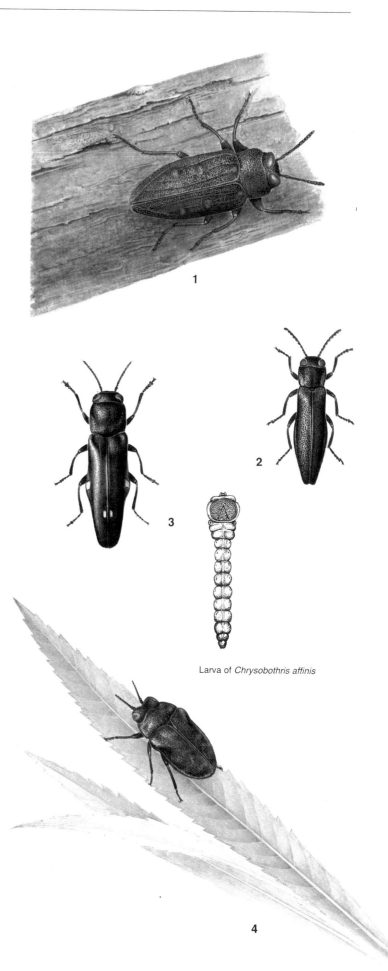

Larva of *Chrysobothris affinis*

1. *Chrysobothris affinis:* 10—16 mm ($\frac{3}{8}$—$\frac{5}{8}$ in). A large part of Europe, the Caucasus, Asia Minor, the Near East, Siberia, northern Africa.
2. *Agrilus angustulus:* 4.5—6.5 mm ($\frac{3}{16}$—$\frac{9}{32}$ in). Europe, the Caucasus, Siberia, northern Africa.
3. *Agrilus pannonicus:* 9—12 mm ($\frac{3}{8}$—$\frac{1}{2}$ in). A large part of Europe, the Caucasus, Asia Minor, the Near East, northern Africa.
4. *Trachys minutus:* 2.5—3.5 mm ($\frac{3}{32}$—$\frac{5}{32}$ in). Most of Europe, the Caucasus, Siberia, Asia Minor.

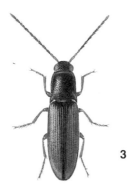

1

3

2

1 *Ampedus sanguineus* L.   Elateridae
Blood-red Click Beetle

2 *Ampedus balteatus* L.

3 *Dalopius marginatus* L.

Click beetles (family Elateridae) are characterised by an intricate spring device on the underside of the beetle's body, which enables it to shoot up into the air from a supine position, turn right over and land on its feet. (Jumping is not an isolated phenomenon among beetles; various others are also able to do it, but not in this way.) Click beetles also have characteristic larvae – the familiar 'wireworms' – which are long and thin, but have a thick cuticle. Many click beetles are plainly and inconspicuously coloured. They are often brown or blackish-brown, but some have a metallic lustre and others have red elytra or are red all over. The Blood-red Click Beetle (*Ampedus sanguineus*) has a black pronotum combined with red elytra. The imagos are more common at submontane altitudes, but also occur in lowlands. They settle on felled trees and stumps and sometimes visit flowers (especially Umbelliferae). The larvae often develop together under the bark and rotting wood of pine stumps and (though less often) of spruce stumps. The larvae of *Ampedus balteatus* also develop in rotting pine stumps. This species inhabits pinewoods and groups of pines growing in peat-bogs. Its development takes three years; the imagos hibernate.

The inconspicuous, variably coloured click beetle *Dalopius marginatus* appears on the vegetation in clearings and on the outskirts of forests from April to July. It lives in lowlands and hills and ascends mountains to altitudes of about 2,000 m (6,560 ft). It is an abundant to very abundant species. The larva, which grows to a length of about 15 mm ($\frac{5}{8}$ in), is a glossy brownish-yellow and lives in dry soil in conifer and deciduous woods. The larvae live in the soil, where they crawl about hunting the larvae and pupae of a great many forest insect pests, such as the pupae of the Pine Sawfly (*Diprion pini*) and the Bordered White Moth (*Bupalus piniarius*). The larva varies the composition of its diet by the addition of plant tissues.

1. *Ampedus sanguineus:* 13—18 mm ($\frac{9}{16}$—$\frac{3}{4}$ in). The Palaearctic region.
2. *Ampedus balteatus:* 7.5—10 mm ($\frac{5}{16}$—$\frac{3}{8}$ in). Central and northern Europe, the Caucasus, Siberia.
3. *Dalopius marginatus:* 6—8 mm ($\frac{1}{4}$—$\frac{5}{16}$ in). Europe, the temperate belt in Asia.

1 *Agriotes lineatus* L.
Wheat Wireworm

Elateridae

2 *Melanotus erythropus* Gmelin

3 *Agrypnus murinus* L.
Grey Click Beetle

Some click beetle larvae have the reputation of being serious pests. One is the Wheat Wireworm (the larva of *Agriotes lineatus*), but only if it lives in cultivated ground and nibbles the roots of crops (wheat, maize, tobacco, sugar-beet). In uncultivated soils it has no significance. At the age of four to five years it excavates a chamber and pupates in the ground. The beetles emerge in August, hibernate and the following year appear until July or August, so that they have an adult life span of about one year. They live in meadows and fields, but are rare in woods. They are common in lowlands and foothills and their numbers decrease with an increase in altitude. They are most abundant in May and June. They are active at night, when they sit on the leaves of grasses and vetches, nibbling the tissues; in the daytime they go into hiding. The female lays her eggs singly or in groups.

Melanotus erythropus is also mainly active at night. It visits the flowers of fruit trees and other plants and drinks the nectar. It occurs in gardens, at the edges of woods and in meadows and is most abundant from May to August. Sometimes it is held responsible for damaging the flowers of fruit trees and grapevines. The larva, which attains a length of up to 40 mm ($1\frac{9}{16}$ in), lives in damp, rotting wood in deciduous trees and conifers and lives primarily on insects. The imago overwinters in the pupal chamber and appears the following May.

The Grey Click Beetle (*Agrypnus murinus*) is one of the more common species. From April to autumn it is found in fields, meadows, woods and gardens. It settles on grasses and the flowers and leaves of woody plants, runs along paths and hides under stones; it flies late in the afternoon. The larva develops for several years in the soil before pupating; the young imago overwinters in the ground.

1. *Agriotes lineatus:* 7—10.5 mm ($\frac{5}{16}$—$\frac{7}{16}$ in). A large part of Europe, Asia Minor, the Near East, northern Africa, North and South America, New Zealand.
2. *Melanotus erythropus:* 12—20 mm ($\frac{1}{2}$—$\frac{13}{16}$ in). Europe, the Middle East, northern Africa, North America.
3. *Agrypnus murinus:* 12—17 mm ($\frac{1}{2}$—$\frac{11}{16}$ in). Europe, the Caucasus, Siberia, North America.

Larva of *Agrypnus murinus*

137

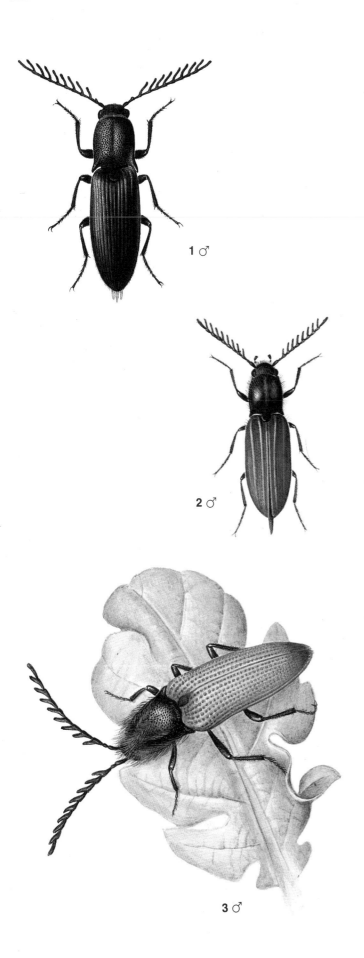

1 *Ctenicera pectinicornis* L.   Elateridae

2 *Anostirus purpureus* Poda

3 *Anostirus castaneus* L.

The antennae of the male click beetle *Ctenicera pectinicornis* (and of other click beetles) are markedly pectinate, while those of the female are dentate. *C. pectinicornis* occurs mainly in foothills and mountains, where it ascends above the forest limit; it lives in meadows and on the outskirts of woods. It flies in June and July, when it settles on leaves and flowers. The larva lives in the ground and when fully grown measures up to 28 mm ($1\frac{1}{8}$ in); it has a flattened, dark chestnut-brown body with a light yellow underside. *C. pectinicornis* closely resembles *C. cuprea;* the males can be differentiated by their antennae, but it is often difficult to distinguish between the females.

Anostirus purpureus lives typically at the damp edges of forests and near water in hills and mountains. From April to June (at higher altitudes until July) the beetles are to be found on oak, beech, birch, willow and hazel leaves, on grasses and on flowers. Their appearance is unmistakable. Their bodies are covered with fine ruddy-gold hairs. The larvae resemble those of other click beetles; they live in rotting roots (mainly of beeches). The elytra of the similar *Anostirus castaneus* are also covered with golden hairs. Like the preceding species, this one occurs singly. It lives in old beech woods in lowlands and at low altitudes on mountains. It appears very early in the spring and can be seen on the outskirts of forests, in meadows and in clearings, where it settles on shrubs, visits flowering hawthorn and hawkweed, and hides under stones. As a rule, the males die early. The beetles disappear at the beginning of June. The larva lives where it is warm, most often in rotting beech roots. The imagos already emerge in the autumn, but hibernate before coming out into the open.

1. *Ctenicera pectinicornis:* 14.5—18 mm ($\frac{9}{16}$—$\frac{3}{4}$ in). Central and northern Europe, Siberia.
2. *Anostirus purpureus:* 8.5—14 mm ($\frac{11}{32}$—$\frac{9}{16}$ in). Central Europe, the north of southern Europe, the south of northern Europe, the Caucasus, Transcaucasia, the Near East, the Himalayas.
3. *Anostirus castaneus:* 9—10.5 mm ($\frac{3}{8}$—$\frac{7}{16}$ in). Central and northern Europe, Siberia.

1 *Selatosomus aeneus* L.
2 *Denticollis linearis* L.
3 *Pseudathous hirtus* Herbst
4 *Athous subfuscus* Müll.

Elateridae

Selatosomus aeneus, one of the most familiar click beetles, is very variably coloured. It glows with every shade of metallic colour from green to violet and gleaming black. It lives in diverse habitats – in meadows, fields, woods, lowlands, foothills and mountains up to altitudes of 2,500 m (8,200 ft). From the early spring it can be seen on flowers and grasses, or hiding under bark or stones. It lays roughly 300 eggs in the ground; the larvae, which live in the soil, are probably omnivorous. The young imagos hibernate.

Denticollis linearis is an explicitly forest species which occurs in many colours. The beetles live in shady places on leaves and flowers during the late spring and summer. The larvae develop underneath old bark on coniferous and deciduous trees and in rotting wood. They are predacious and pupate below or actually in the bark, where they overwinter.

Pseudathous hirtus is common in meadows and at the margins of forests everywhere. In May and June it can be seen on leaves and flowers and it appears at alpine altitudes of about 2,500 m (8,200 ft). The larvae chiefly frequent rotting wood. *Athous subfuscus* lives in forests and on their outskirts, in clearings and in forest meadows. In May and June it is abundant everywhere on leaves and flowers, where it drinks nectar. The beetle is inconspicuously, but variably coloured. The larva is very glossy and about 18 mm ($\frac{3}{4}$ in) long. It lives in forests, in the ground or in crumbling wood and under the bark of stumps and rotting trunks. It is predacious and eats vegetable matter only if nothing else is available.

1. *Selatosomus aeneus:* 11—17 mm ($\frac{7}{16}$—$\frac{11}{16}$ in). Europe, the temperate belt in Asia.
2. *Denticollis linearis:* 9—12.5 mm ($\frac{3}{8}$—$\frac{15}{32}$ in). Europe (far to the north, in southern Europe only the northern part), Asia Minor, Siberia, Iran.
3. *Pseudathous hirtus:* 12—17 mm ($\frac{1}{2}$—$\frac{11}{16}$ in). Europe, the temperate belt in Asia.
4. *Athous subfuscus:* 7.8—10.5 mm ($\frac{5}{16}$—$\frac{7}{16}$ in). Most of Europe, Caucasus.

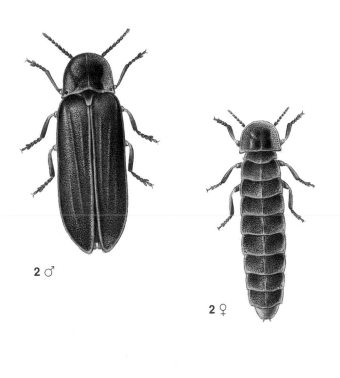

2 ♂

2 ♀

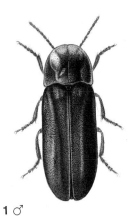

1 ♂

3 ♂

1 *Lamprohiza splendidula* L. Lampyridae
2 *Lampyris noctiluca* L.
Common Glowworm
3 *Phosphaenus hemipterus* Fourcr.

The highest incidence of glowworms (Lampyridae) is in the tropics, where we find the biggest species. European species are also worth noting. The imagos are not particularly conspicuous, but possess a faculty unique among beetles all over the world. At night, when they are active, they emit light by means of a special luminiscent organ on the underside of their bodies.

Glowworms live in damp localities, meadows and marshes and it is thus no wonder that they gave rise to tales of the elusive 'will-o'-the-wisp' or *ignis fatus* that enticed travellers to their death. The glowworm's light is the result of a very complex biochemical reaction and it is very economical; it is cold light unaccompanied by the release of heat (energy). Glowworms are characterised by very pronounced sexual dimorphism. The males generally have wings and are able to fly, while the females are wingless or have non-functioning wing stumps and crawl on the ground. The females light up to attract males flying overhead. *Lamprohiza splendidula* is one of the most common species, which can be encountered in parks, gardens, lowlands, hills and meadows, as well as beside streams and in forest clearings. The imagos do not seem to take any food, but the larvae are predacious and, like other glowworms, hunt various kinds of snails. The Common Glowworm (*Lampyris noctiluca*), which is larger, inhabits warmer localities. It appears early in the summer; the females crawl about in the undergrowth at the margins of forests and in meadows. The female of *Phosphaenus hemipterus*, another glowworm, is completely wingless and the male has greatly reduced wings. Unlike the above nocturnal species, this glowworm is active in the evening, after dusk, when the female's light attracts the wandering male. It tends to occur at somewhat higher altitudes; it crawls about in grass, or hides under stones or old wood. It is rarer than the other two species.

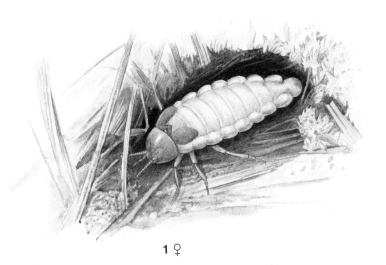

1 ♀

1. *Lamprohiza splendidula:* ♂ 8—9 mm, ♀ 9—11 mm (♂ $\frac{5}{16}$—$\frac{3}{8}$ in, ♀ $\frac{3}{8}$—$\frac{7}{16}$ in). Central and south-eastern Europe, the Caucasus.
2. *Lampyris noctiluca:* ♂ 10—12 mm, ♀ 15—20 mm (♂ $\frac{13}{32}$—$\frac{1}{2}$ in, ♀ $\frac{5}{8}$—$\frac{13}{16}$ in). The Palaearctic region.
3. *Phosphaenus hemipterus:* ♂ 6—8 mm, ♀ 8—10 mm (♂ $\frac{1}{4}$—$\frac{5}{16}$ in, ♀ $\frac{5}{16}$—$\frac{13}{32}$ in). Central and northern Europe.

1 *Dictyoptera aurora* Herbst
2 *Pyropterus nigroruber* De Geer
3 *Lygistopterus sanguineus* L.

Lycidae

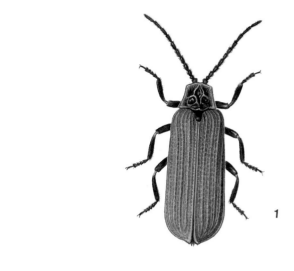

1

There are not many species of the Lycidae family in Europe, but those that exist are relatively easy to recognise. They have a soft, flat body, red or orange-red elytra and a (generally) black pronotum. The elytra are ribbed and there are usually a few deep depressions separated from one another by ridges on the pronotum. Tropical species are conspicuous for their gorgeous colours and varied forms and some of them display marked sexual dimorphism, which is not observed in European species.

Dictyoptera aurora is one of the largest European species. It inhabits old conifer forests from low to medium mountain altitudes. It occurs mainly at the edges of forests and in clearings from May to July. It settles on old, rotting or mossy stumps, on vegetation and sometimes the flowers of umbelliferous plants. The larvae live in rotting spruce and pine stumps; their development takes several years.

Pyropterus nigroruber occurs in damp clearings and beside paths and streams in conifer or mixed woods in low-lying and mountainous country. It lives mainly in July and August, but sometimes survives until September. It mostly frequents the leaves of various plants, and is often seen on ragwort, though it seldom appears on flowers. Its development takes several years; the mycetophagous larvae live in rotting wood.

Lygistopterus sanguineus differs from other members of the family by having a long, beak-like head, although this is often concealed below the pronotum. It inhabits deciduous or mixed woods, where it occurs from June to the end of August. Unlike other lycids, it has a marked preference for flowers and flies to flowering umbelliferous plants and elder flowers, where it picks out the grains of pollen. The larvae live several years in rotting deciduous tree stumps.

2

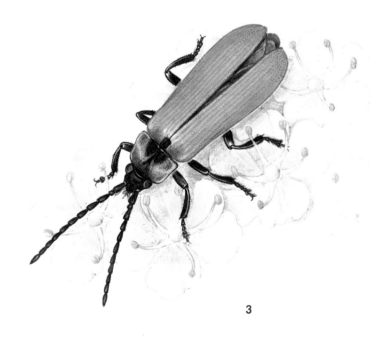

1. *Dictyoptera aurora:* 8—13 mm ($\frac{5}{16}$ — $\frac{9}{16}$ in). The Palaearctic region, North America.
2. *Pyropterus nigroruber:* 6.7—10 mm ($\frac{9}{32}$ — $\frac{13}{32}$ in). Europe, the temperate belt in Asia.
3. *Lygistopterus sanguineus:* 7—12 mm ($\frac{5}{16}$ — $\frac{1}{2}$ in). A large part of the Palaearctic region (in Europe far to the north).

3

141

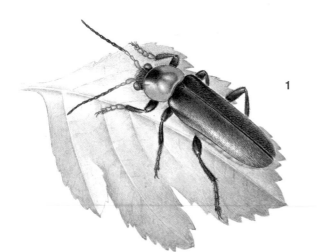

1 *Cantharis fusca* L.
2 *Cantharis obscura* L.
3 *Cantharis nigricans* Müll.

The greatest numbers of soldier beetles are to be seen in May and June. They fly in woods and meadows, parks and gardens, over grass verges and field and forest paths. They sit on the leaves of herbaceous and woody plants, where they mostly prey on aphids, flies, caterpillars and the pupae of lepidopteran pests, such as the Green Oak Tortrix Moth (*Tortrix viridana*); they are therefore useful. The imagos of some species often appear on flowers (especially hawthorn) and fruit trees and are abundant on umbelliferous flowers. Now and again, some species (e.g. *Cantharis obscura*) damage flowers, but the usefulness of soldier beetles as predators greatly outweighs any damage they may do. Soldier beetle larvae are velvety black; they often crawl along paths and roads and sometimes even appear in snow if driven out of their shelters by wind or sleet.

The colouring of many soldier beetles is a combination of black and red or yellowish-red. The species illustrated here have dark elytra and a red or yellow pronotum, which often (though not always) has a black spot on it. *Cantharis fusca* and *C. rustica* may have a completely red pronotum, but it is usually marked with a dark spot. In *C. fusca* the spot almost touches the anterior (and sometimes the posterior) edge of the pronotum, while in *C. rustica* it is some distance from the edge and is often heart-shaped. The other two species – *Cantharis obscura* and *C. nigricans* – have a yellow, or at least a yellow-edged, pronotum. In *C. nigricans* the pronotum may be completely yellow, but usually has a dark spot on it while *C. obscura* has a wide dark spot running down the whole of the pronotum.

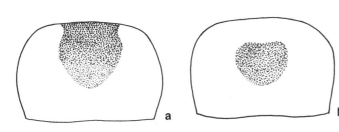

Scutum of two related species of soldier beetles:
a – *Cantharis fusca*, b – *Cantharis rustica*

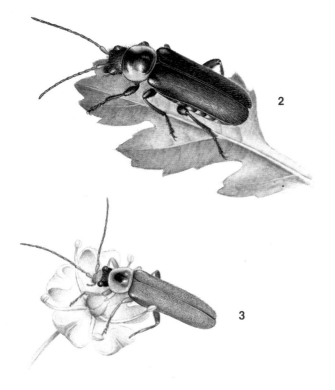

1. *Cantharis fusca:* 11—15 mm ($\frac{7}{16}$—$\frac{5}{8}$ in). Europe.
2. *Cantharis obscura:* 8.5—13 mm ($\frac{11}{32}$—$\frac{9}{16}$ in). Europe, western Asia.
3. *Cantharis nigricans:* 8—11 mm ($\frac{5}{16}$—$\frac{7}{16}$ in). Central and northern Europe, the Caucasus.

1 *Rhagonycha fulva* Scop.　　Cantharidae
2 *Malthinus biguttatus* L.
3 *Malthodes minimus* L.

Rhagonycha fulva is a summer beetle which can be encountered from May onwards. It occurs mainly in sunny places, at the edges of woods, in meadows, parks, gardens and grass verges. The imagos are very fond of flowers. They prefer umbelliferous plants in full bloom, but will settle on other flowers to catch small animals (often aphids) and eat pollen grains; several imagos are usually to be found on one umbel. The beetles also copulate on the flowers. The female lays the eggs in the topsoil. The larvae, which are velvety-brown, moult a few times, overwinter and pupate in the spring of the following year. Both the beetles and the larvae are useful predators and their usefulness in nature is enhanced by their large numbers.

A great many small soldier beetles, belonging chiefly to the genera *Malthinus* and *Malthodes*, have shortened elytra. The scientific name of *Malthinus biguttatus* is based on the two yellow spots at the tip of its elytra. This species occurs from lowlands to medium altitudes. The beetles are to be found in forest meadows, at the edges of woods and in open conifer forests, where they settle on the vegetation (at the edges of woods on oak leaves) or on grasses. They live in June and July.

Despite its name (*minimus* means smallest), *Malthodes minimus* is not the smallest species of its genus, but one of the most common. It mainly inhabits damp woods in lowlands and is seldom seen at higher altitudes. The imagos frequent forest vegetation from April to July, but are at their most numerous in June.

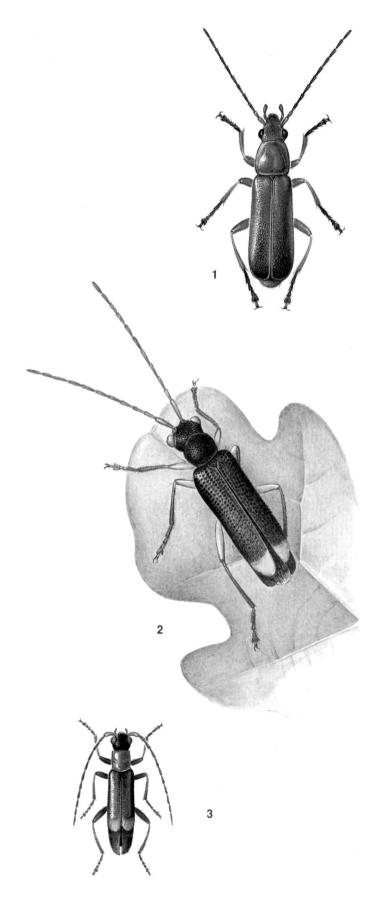

1. *Rhagonycha fulva:* 7—10 mm ($\frac{5}{16}$—$\frac{13}{32}$ in). A large part of Europe, the Caucasus, the Near East.
2. *Malthinus biguttatus:* 4.5—6 mm ($\frac{7}{32}$—$\frac{1}{4}$ in). Europe (minus the south), the Caucasus.
3. *Malthodes minimus:* 3.3—4 mm ($\frac{5}{32}$—$\frac{3}{16}$ in). Central and northern Europe.

1 **Dermestes lardarius** L.   Dermestidae
Larder Beetle

2 **Dermestes haemorrhoidalis** Küst.

3 **Attagenus pellio** L.
Fur Beetle

4 **Anthrenus scrophulariae** L.
Carpet Beetle

In the open, the Larder Beetle (*Dermestes lardarius*) occurs chiefly on drying small cadavers or in birds' nests, but it is far more common in warehouses and households. The female lays her minute eggs in little-frequented places. The highly voracious larvae are easily recognised by the long brown hairs on their bodies. They live on dried meat products (hence, the name of 'Larder' Beetles) as well as fur, woollen fabrics, feathers and stuffed animals. They pupate in a quiet spot, in felt, cork and even plastic, such as a polystyrene mat.

Dermestes haemorrhoidalis is increasingly found in households in large towns. Centrally-heated flats provide excellent conditions for its existence and for the development of its offspring. It also lives in warehouses. The full-grown larva is double the length of the beetle.

The imagos of some dermestids have a simple eye (ocellus) on their frons. This is a unique phenomenon among beetles. *Attagenus pellio* and *Anthrenus scrophulariae* have such an eye. *Attagenus pellio* lives freely in the open, but it is far more common in households and warehouses, where its larvae do damage to furs and textiles. *Anthrenus scrophulariae* also lives in the open and in households. Outdoors it appears on plants with white flowers from May to July; indoors it produces several generations. The larvae, called 'woolly bears', live mainly in woollen fabrics and are also a danger to entomological collections.

3

4

1. *Dermestes lardarius:* 7—9.5 mm ($\frac{9}{32}$—$\frac{3}{8}$ in). Over the whole globe.
2. *Dermestes haemorrhoidalis:* 6.1—8.7 mm ($\frac{1}{4}$—$\frac{11}{32}$ in). Over the whole globe.
3. *Attagenus pellio:* 3.5—6 mm ($\frac{5}{32}$—$\frac{1}{4}$ in). Over the whole globe.
4. *Anthrenus scrophulariae:* 3—4.5 mm ($\frac{1}{8}$—$\frac{7}{32}$ in). Over the whole globe.

1 *Ptilinus pectinicornis* L.   Anobiidae

2 *Stegobium paniceum* L.
  Biscuit Beetle

3 *Anobium punctatum* Deg.
  Woodworm, Furniture Beetle

4 *Anobium pertinax* L.

All the members of the Anobiidae family are similar small beetles. In the breeding season, the males attract the females by ticking sounds which they make by tapping their head and pronotum against the wall of their tunnels. Superstition once held that these sounds foreboded death. That, of course, is nonsense, but the damage done by the larvae in furniture, woodwork and wooden antiques is a serious reality.

Ptilinus pectinicornis, which lives in deciduous woods from May to July, is characterised by strikingly pectinate antennae in the males; the females have simple toothed antennae. The imagos settle on felled timber; the larvae tunnel in dead wood in standing and felled trunks, and in the branches of deciduous trees (mainly beeches and oaks) and have lately appeared with increasing frequency in furniture.

The Biscuit Beetle (*Stegobium paniceum*) has larvae that live in products made with flour (it is very fond of stale bread), but they also find enough to eat in chemist's shops (dried herbs, fish meal, cork, leather and paper). The insect is also called the Drugstore Beetle.

The Woodworm or Furniture Beetle (*Anobium punctatum*) is one of the most common members of the family. It occurs in the greatest numbers in June and July and it likes to crawl over white ceilings in houses. The female lays her eggs in the old wood of deciduous trees and conifers, where development may take two to three years. Articles attacked by this species are peppered with a quantity of small holes from which the adult has escaped. These holes enhance the impression of antiquity, but make the wood brittle and crumbly. *Anobium pertinax* is now a rare species.

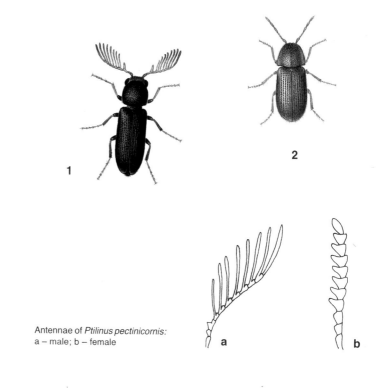

1

2

Antennae of *Ptilinus pectinicornis:*
a – male; b – female   **a**   **b**

3

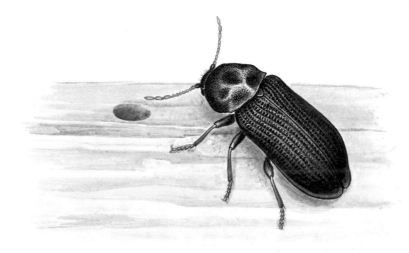

4

1. *Ptilinus pectinicornis:* 3.5—5.5 mm ($\frac{5}{32}$—$\frac{1}{4}$ in). Europe, the Caucasus, the Near East, Siberia, Central America.
2. *Stegobium paniceum:* 2—3 mm ($\frac{1}{16}$—$\frac{1}{8}$ in). Over practically the whole globe.
3. *Anobium punctatum:* 2.5—4 mm ($\frac{3}{32}$—$\frac{3}{16}$ in). The temperate belt in Eurasia, North America, Australia.
4. *Anobium pertinax:* 4.5—6 mm ($\frac{7}{32}$—$\frac{1}{4}$ in). Most of Europe (except the north).

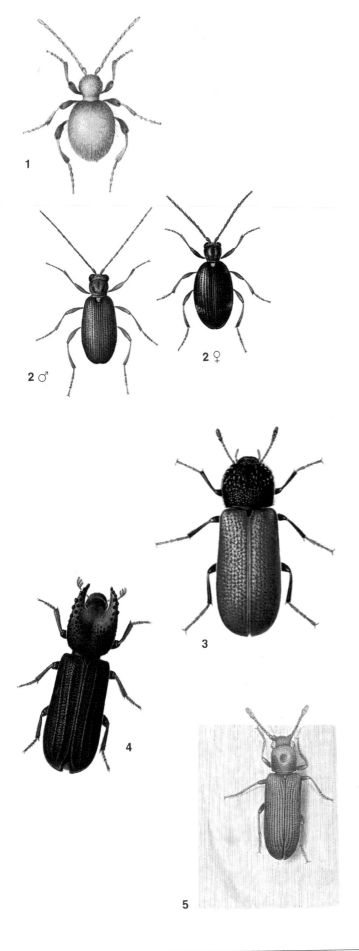

1 *Niptus hololeucus* Fald.   Ptinidae

2 *Ptinus fur* L.

3 *Bostrychus capucinus* L.   Bostrychidae

4 *Bostrychoplites cornutus* Oliv.

5 *Lyctus linearis* Goeze   Lyctidae

A whole series of beetles, especially those living in households and stores and in the vicinity of people in general, have been carried all over the world by trade and transport, so that nobody knows where they originally came from. *Niptus hololeucus*, one of these travellers, is a generally harmless species. In central Europe it forms two generations whose imagos appear from June to July and from October to November. *Ptinus fur*, an inconspicuous, slow spider beetle, is another synanthrophic species; it is also harmless. In households it is to be found mainly in bathrooms and lavatories. It also lives in the open, in old trees and birds' nests. It is mainly active at night, but can sometimes be found in the daytime.

The warmth-loving *Bostrychus capucinus* is a false powder-post beetle inhabiting woods and sometimes gardens. The larvae develop in the wood of oaks and fruit trees. The imagos occasionally appear in stores.

Bostrychoplites cornutus is a bizarre beetle occasionally brought to Europe from Africa with wooden folk carvings.

Powder-post beetles (Lyctidae) have gained their name from the very fine powder the larvae produce. They are a very small family with only a few species in Europe. *Lyctus linearis,* their best known member, inhabits deciduous woods, where the imagos appear in May and June. The larvae usually develop in oak. The beetles are sometimes to be found in timber yards, but although they were once regarded as serious pests, the damage they do today is negligible.

1. *Niptus hololeucus:* 2.6—4.6 mm ($\frac{3}{32}$—$\frac{7}{32}$ in). Over the whole globe.
2. *Ptinus fur:* 2.6—4.3 mm ($\frac{3}{32}$—$\frac{3}{16}$ in). The Palaearctic and Nearctic regions.
3. *Bostrychus capucinus:* 6—15 mm ($\frac{1}{4}$—$\frac{5}{8}$ in). The Palaearctic region (in Europe commoner in the south).
4. *Bostrychoplites cornutus:* 7—18 mm ($\frac{9}{32}$—$\frac{3}{4}$ in). Tropical Africa; occasionally carried to Europe.
5. *Lyctus linearis:* 2.5—5.5 mm ($\frac{3}{32}$—$\frac{1}{4}$ in). The Palaearctic region; carried to North America.

1 *Tillus elongatus* L.

2 *Opilo domesticus* Sturm

3 *Thanasimus formicarius* L.
  Ant Beetle

Cleridae

The male and female *Tillus elongatus* differ mainly as regards the colour of their pronotum, the male's being black and the female's red. The beetle is rather rare. It appears in May and June in old deciduous woods, where it settles on beech and oak trunks, dry birches and stacks of timber. It may be brought into the house with firewood and be seen crawling on the window-panes; it has also been found on flowering limes. If in danger, it drops to the ground. This predacious beetle hunts the larvae of various beetles that live in wood such as woodworms, wood-borers and long-horns. The larvae are also predacious.

Opilo domesticus lives up to its name (*domesticus*), since it is mostly found in houses and buildings. During the daytime it hides in nooks and crannies, but at night it goes out hunting. Both the beetle and the larvae live on woodworms. The beetles are particularly voracious and one beetle was observed to consume five woodworms within half an hour.

In size and appearance the Ant Beetle (*Thanasimus formicarius*) looks like a large ant – a fact which is reflected in both its scientific name (*formica* means ant) and its vernacular name. The beetle occurs in several colour forms. It mainly inhabits conifer forests from lowlands to mountains. The nimble, wary imagos run about on logs, but at the slightest disturbance they drop to the ground. They are predators and consume up to five bark beetles a day. The pink larvae, which at first live on debris, are later also predacious and live on various developmental stages of bark beetles; they pupate in a 'cradle' in the bark. The larva, pupa and beetle all hibernate.

1 ♂

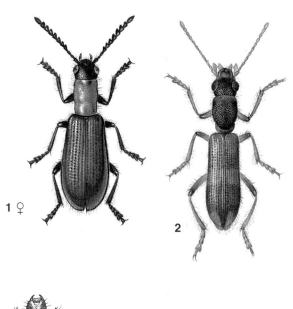

1 ♀   2

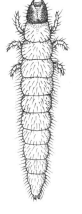

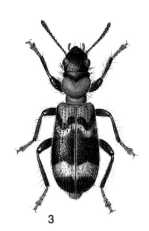

Larva of *Thanasimus formicarius*   3

---

1. *Tillus elongatus:* 6—10 mm ($\frac{1}{4}$—$\frac{3}{8}$ in). Europe, the Caucasus.
2. *Opilo domesticus:* 7—12 mm ($\frac{9}{32}$—$\frac{1}{2}$ in). Europe, the Caucasus, North and Central America.
3. *Thanasimus formicarius:* 7—11 mm ($\frac{9}{32}$—$\frac{7}{16}$ in). A large part of Europe, North America (introduced into the USA).

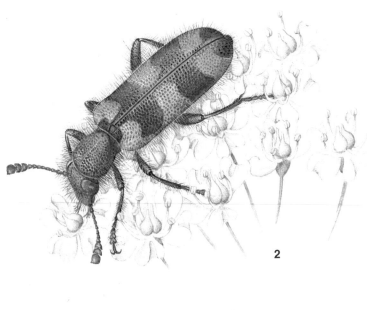

2

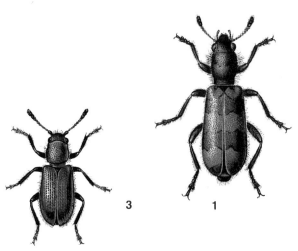

3   **1**

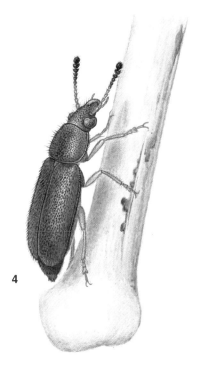

4

1 *Trichodes apiarius* L.   Cleridae
Bee-eating Beetle

2 *Trichodes favarius* Illig.

3 *Korynetes caeruleus* Deg.   Korynetidae

4 *Necrobia rufipes* Deg.

The handsome, strikingly coloured Bee-eating Beetle (*Trichodes apiarius*) is almost always seen in May and June on warm, sunny slopes that have sufficient flowers at both low and high altitudes. It is most abundant on flowering Compositae and Umbelliferae, where it eats pollen, but is interested mainly in the small insect larvae and imagos it finds in the flowers. The larvae, which are zoophagous, develop chiefly in the nests of solitary bees belonging to the genera *Osmia*, *Megachile* and *Anthophora;* descriptions of the damage they are supposed to do in beehives must be refuted. The similarly coloured *Trichodes favarius* also lives on flowers; it needs far more warmth and is rarer, however, and the most northerly limit of its distribution is central Europe.

Some entomologists classify the species of the genera *Korynetes, Necrobia* and others in a separate family, Korynetidae, while others are of the opinion that they all belong to the family Cleridae. *Korynetes caeruleus,* one of the most common, is sometimes a metallic blue colour and sometimes green. The beetles occur mostly in May and June, when they appear on wood, shrubs and flowers; the larvae develop in the wood of conifers, where they hunt bark beetles (Scolytidae) and woodworms (Anobiidae). The imagos are also predacious.

Necrobia rufipes is rarer in nature than related species, but its populations are reinforced by beetles brought over on ships. It lives in stores of plant and animal products and in rubbish dumps, where the predacious imagos and larvae prey on the larvae of other beetles, in particular dermestid species.

1. *Trichodes apiarius:* 10—18 mm ($\frac{13}{32}$—$\frac{3}{4}$ in). Central and southern Europe, the Caucasus, Asia Minor, northern Africa.
2. *Trichodes favarius:* 8—18 mm ($\frac{5}{16}$—$\frac{3}{4}$ in). The southeastern part of central Europe, the Caucasus, Asia Minor, the Near East.
3. *Korynetes caeruleus:* 3.5—7 mm ($\frac{5}{32}$—$\frac{9}{32}$ in). Over the entire globe.
4. *Necrobia rufipes:* 4—4.5 mm ($\frac{3}{16}$—$\frac{7}{32}$ in). Over the entire globe.

1 *Dasytes plumbeus* Müll.   Dasytidae

2 *Danacaea pallipes* Panz.

3 *Malachius aeneus* L.   Malachiidae

4 *Malachius bipustulatus* L.

The summer flowers on warm, sunny slopes would hardly be complete without the presence of some member of the genus *Dasytes*, whose many species live mainly in southern Europe. *Dasytes plumbeus*, one of the most common, usually appears from May to July. It can be found in lowlands and above the forest level in mountains, although here it is less abundant. The predacious larvae develop in old beech and elder wood and in the stems of clematis plants. *Danacaea pallipes* also occurs on flowers growing in warm, dry slopes at low and moderate altitudes. The imagos are the most abundant in June and July.

The beetles of the Malachiidae family have a curious characteristic. They have pouches along the sides of their thorax and abdomen which protrude when inflated and are retractable when deflated. In addition, the males of most species have 'excitors' on different parts of their body. These secrete a substance which attracts females and stimulates their pairing instinct. In *Malachius aeneus* and *M. bipustulatus* the excitors are in front of the antennae. The males of these two species are differently coloured and the second to fourth segments of their antennae are differently shaped. In *M. aeneus* only the second and third segments have a hook, but in *M. bipustulatus* the second, third and fourth segments are hooked. Both species occur chiefly in low-lying country and in some places are still quite common; they do not ascend to more than low montane altitudes. *M. bipustulatus* appears somewhat sooner than *M. aeneus*. Both visit flowering grasses and other herbaceous plants and flowering shrubs, where they gather pollen. The larvae develop below bark.

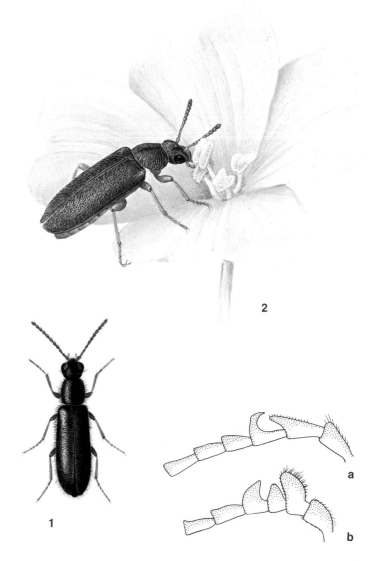

2

1

Part of antennae of the male *Malachius aeneus* (a) and *M. bipustulatus* (b)

a

b

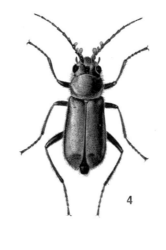

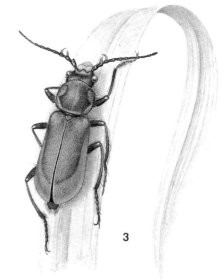

4

3

1. *Dasytes plumbeus:* 3.5—4.6 mm ($\frac{5}{32}$ — $\frac{7}{32}$ in). Europe (except the north), northern Africa.
2. *Danacaea pallipes:* 3.2—4.2 mm ($\frac{1}{8}$ — $\frac{3}{16}$ in). Central and southern Europe, the Caucasus, northern Africa.
3. *Malachius aeneus:* 6—7 mm ($\frac{1}{4}$ — $\frac{9}{32}$ in). Europe, the Caucasus, Asia Minor, the Near East, Siberia, North America.
4. *Malachius bipustulatus:* 5.5—6 mm ($\frac{1}{4}$ in). Europe, Asia Minor, Siberia.

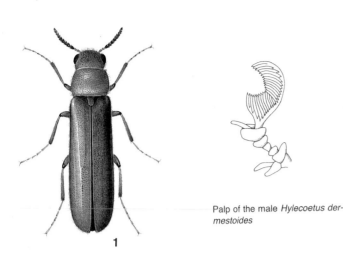

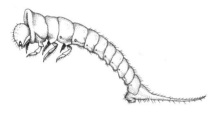

Palp of the male *Hylecoetus dermestoides*

Larva of *H. dermestoides*

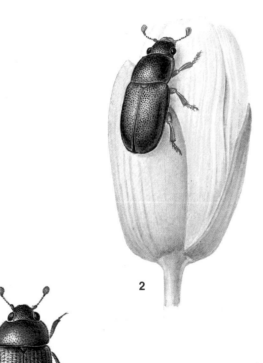

1 *Hylecoetus dermestoides* L.
Lymexylonidae

2 *Meligethes aeneus* F.
Pollen Beetle
Nitidulidae

3 *Pocadius ferrugineus* F.

Hylecoetus dermestoides is a long, slender beetle characterised by marked sexual dimorphism manifested primarily in the large, fan-shaped palps of the male. The female is yellowish-brown, but the male occurs in several colour forms, including a completely black form. This species inhabits deciduous and coniferous woods at low and medium altitudes. The imagos can be encountered from the beginning of April to June, but they live only a few days; they settle on stumps and sometimes on branches. The larvae usually develop in beech, oak or birch; they tunnel in the wood and live on the mycelium of fungi grown from spores sprinkled by the female over the eggs. After overwintering, the larvae make their way towards the surface of the wood and pupate there in a chamber.

The Pollen Beetle (*Meligethes aeneus*) is a familiar pest of oilseed rape and one of the very similar species found in all sorts of flowers. It appears in meadows and gardens early in the spring. It is particularly abundant on growths of colt's-foot or dandelions and on buttercups, where the imagos eat the pollen. When the rape plants begin to bud, the imagos migrate to the fields. They nibble the young leaves and flower buds and then work their way into the buds and destroy them by devouring their contents. When the rape is in full bloom they again eat pollen. The female lays the eggs in buds. When fully grown, the larva buries itself in the ground and pupates. The young beetles emerge during the same summer and at the end of the season retire into hibernation.

The entire life of *Pocadius ferrugineus* is bound up with fungi. Its host fungus is the puffball, but it may also occur on the drying fruit bodies of other fungi. One ripe puffball generally contains several beetles all at once.

1. *Hylecoetus dermestoides:* 6—18 mm ($\frac{1}{4}$—$\frac{3}{4}$ in). A large part of the Palaearctic region (to the limit of the continent in the north, rare in southern Europe).
2. *Meligethes aeneus:* 1.5—2.7 mm ($\frac{1}{16}$—$\frac{3}{32}$ in). The Palaearctic region, North America.
3. *Pocadius ferrugineus:* 2.6—4.6 mm ($\frac{3}{32}$—$\frac{7}{32}$ in). Europe (far to the north), the Caucasus.

1 *Glischrochilus quadripunctatus* L.   Nitidulidae
2 *Rhizophagus bipustulatus* F.   Rhizophagidae
3 *Uleiota planata* L.   Cucujidae
4 *Oryzaephilus surinamensis* L.
Saw-toothed Grain Beetle

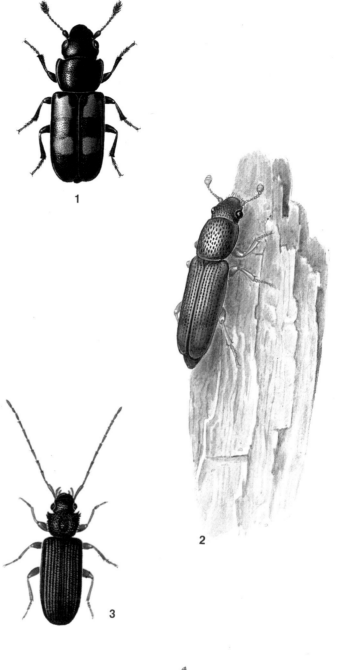

1

If you look underneath the bark of conifers and deciduous trees you can find beetles belonging to many different families. In some cases all the members of the family live in this way, in others only some of them, as in the family Nitidulidae, in which other species occur on flowers and elsewhere. *Glischrochilus quadripunctatus* is to be found from the early spring to the late autumn below the bark of conifers attacked by bark beetles (e.g. in the galleries of the genera *Blastophagus, Ips, Hylaster* and *Dendroctonus*) and seldom under the bark of deciduous trees. It occurs at both low and high altitudes. *Rhizophagus bipustulatus*, one of the most common members of its family, likewise lives below bark, mostly gregariously; it favours deciduous trees, but also frequents conifers. Its diet consists of the hyphae of fungi growing under old bark.

Uleiota planata, whose flat body fits it well for life under bark, lives – often gregariously – below dry, rather than damp bark. With its long antennae it looks slightly like a longhorn beetle. From the early spring until the autumn it can be found under the bark of dead deciduous trees (mainly oaks and beeches), in stumps and felled trunks and in stacked timber. Very occasionally it appears beneath the bark of conifers (particularly pines). The larvae also live below bark.

The Saw-toothed Grain Beetle (*Oryzaephilus surinamensis*), whose fine sculpturing needs a magnifying glass to be seen properly, is rarely seen in the open (e.g. in mouldy hay, in compost or under bark), but is quite common in grain stores and households. Despite its vernacular name, it is a basically zoophagous species; it hunts all kinds of insect larvae and only seldom turns its attention to damaged grain.

2

3

1. *Glischrochilus quadripunctatus:* 3—6.5 mm ($\frac{1}{8}$—$\frac{9}{32}$ in). Central and northern Europe.
2. *Rhizophagus bipustulatus:* 2.3—3.5 mm ($\frac{3}{32}$—$\frac{5}{32}$ in). Europe, the Caucasus, northern Africa.
3. *Uleiota planata:* 4.5—5.5 mm ($\frac{7}{32}$—$\frac{1}{4}$ in). The Palaearctic region.
4. *Oryzaephilus surinamensis:* 2.5—3.5 mm ($\frac{3}{32}$—$\frac{5}{32}$ in). Over the entire globe.

4

1

2

3

4

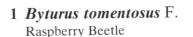

1 *Byturus tomentosus* F.   Byturidae
Raspberry Beetle

2 *Tritoma bipustulata* F.   Erotylidae

3 *Triplax russica* L.

4 *Olibrus millefolii* Payk.   Phalacridae

The Raspberry Beetle (*Byturus tomentosus*) occurs in two colour forms. When young, the beetle is light brown; when older it is greyish-brown. It lives mainly on raspberry canes and brambles, where it eats pollen and bites holes in the buds. The female lays eggs singly in the flowers and on the young fruits; the larvae are the familiar 'raspberry maggots'. When fully grown they leave the raspberry, fall to the ground and pupate in the soil. The beetles hibernate.

In addition to rove beetles (Staphylinidae), cisids (Cisidae), darkling beetles (Tenebrionidae) and other beetles, tree fungi are visited by members of the family Erotylidae, which are generally black, with red spots. In *Tritoma bipustulata* there is a red spot at the base of the elytra, while *Triplax russica* has a red pronotum. *Tritoma bipustulata* lives in fungi growing mainly on beeches and oaks, but also below mouldy bark on old tree stumps. The female lays the eggs, and the larvae develop, in fungi, but they eventually retire underground to pupate. *Triplax russica* lives in fungi growing on beeches, birches, maples and fruit trees and under mouldy bark.

In the summer, the small, convex beetles of the family Phalacridae are to be seen in large numbers on flowering camomile, dandelions and other plants. *Olibrus millefolii* has a predilection for milfoil (yarrow).

---

1. *Byturus tomentosus:* 3.2—4 mm ($\frac{1}{8}$—$\frac{3}{16}$ in). The Palaearctic region.
2. *Tritoma bipustulata:* 3.5—4 mm ($\frac{5}{32}$—$\frac{3}{16}$ in). Europe, the Caucasus, Siberia.
3. *Triplax russica:* 5—6.5 mm ($\frac{1}{4}$—$\frac{9}{32}$ in). Europe, the Caucasus, northern Africa.
4. *Olibrus millefolii:* 1.5—1.8 mm ($\frac{1}{32}$—$\frac{1}{16}$ in). A large part of Europe.

1 *Chilocorus renipustulatus* Scr. Coccinellidae

2 *Exochomus quadripustulatus* L.
Four-spot Ladybird

3 *Adonia variegata* Goeze

4 *Aphidecta obliterata* L.

Almost all ladybirds are very useful predators; the larvae and the imagos nearly all prey on aphids or coccids and are an important factor in the balance of nature as regulators of the number of pests.

Chilocorus renipustulatus, which has almost circular contours, frequents deciduous trees wherever it can find scale insects (*Chionaspis*), its staple food. The beetles overwinter in plant litter. The Four-spot Ladybird (*Exochomus quadripustulatus*) abounds on deciduous trees and conifers. It is not specialised in its choice of food and hunts aphids and various types of coccids. The beetles overwinter in moss, old leaves and leaf litter.

Like most ladybirds with spotted elytra, *Adonia variegata* shows marked variability of both the number and the size of the spots. This species lives in meadows, vegetable fields and gardens and at the margins of forests, where it catches many types of aphids on herbaceous plants. In the summer it is common on flowering milfoil. In the autumn the imagos crawl into dry leaves, where they hibernate together with other ladybird species.

Aphidecta obliterata, a typical forest species, also has variable markings. It occurs chiefly in spruce woods and less often in pine woods. The imagos and larvae crawl along the branches looking for gall-forming aphids (genus *Adelges*). This ladybird is thus an important predator, since it limits the number of aphids. It was actually introduced into the USA from Germany to help in the biological fight against aphids there. In the winter the imagos hibernate, often all together, under mossy bark on dry spruces and on felled timber.

1. *Chilocorus renipustulatus:* 4—5 mm ($\frac{5}{32}$—$\frac{3}{16}$ in). The Palaearctic region.
2. *Exochomus quadripustulatus:* 3—5 mm ($\frac{1}{8}$—$\frac{3}{16}$ in). The Palaearctic region.
3. *Adonia variegata:* 3—5.5 mm ($\frac{1}{8}$—$\frac{1}{4}$ in). The Palaearctic region, India.
4. *Aphidecta obliterata:* 3.5—5 mm ($\frac{5}{32}$—$\frac{3}{16}$ in). The Palaearctic region, North America.

153

1 **2**

3

Variability of the elytra of the Two-spot Ladybird (*Adalia bipunctata*)

1 *Tytthaspis sedecimpunctata* L. Coccinellidae
Sixteen-spot Ladybird

2 *Adalia decempunctata* L.
Ten-spot Ladybird

3 *Adalia bipunctata* L.
Two-spot Ladybird

The typical form of the Sixteen-spot Ladybird (*Tytthaspis sedecimpunctata*) has sixteen dark spots on its elytra. It is a variable species and it is not uncommon to find specimens with a row of four dark spots on both sides of the elytral suture and a dark stripe down the outer edge, which sometimes incorporates the shoulder spot and the apical spot. This ladybird appears early in the spring (often as early as March) in dry meadows, on sand-dunes and in cornfields. It lives on aphids. In the autumn the imagos collect in large numbers among dry plants and spend the winter there.

The Ten-spot Ladybird (*Adalia decempunctata*) is an exceptionally variable species. It lives at the edges of deciduous woods, in wooded parks with hornbeams and oaks and in lime tree avenues in towns. The beetles, which can be found from April to October, prey on aphids. A fairly reliable way to separate Ten-spot from Two-spot varieties is by leg colour. They are orange in Ten-spot Ladybirds and black in Two-spot Ladybirds.

Anybody who is not acquainted with the colour forms of ladybirds and tries to identify the individual species from their colour or the number of spots will probably not get far. Even the Two-spot Ladybird (*Adalia bipunctata*) appears in colour forms which a layman might automatically regard as separate species. One form has reddish-orange elytra with two dark spots, while another is black and has four to six red spots on its elytra – and these are only two of the possibilities. In favourable years this ladybird produces two generations. It is an outstanding predator and hunts different aphid species. It occurs in a variety of localities, including gardens, and is one of the most abundant ladybirds. It overwinters in cracks in tree trunks or below the bark, and in country cottages between the double glazing, where it regularly encounters *Synharmonia conglobata*, another ladybird winter refugee.

1. *Tytthaspis sedecimpunctata:* 2.5—3 mm ($\frac{3}{32}$—$\frac{1}{8}$ in). The Palaearctic region.
2. *Adalia decempunctata:* 3.5—5 mm ($\frac{5}{32}$—$\frac{3}{16}$ in). The Palaearctic region.
3. *Adalia bipunctata:* 3.5—5.5 mm ($\frac{5}{32}$—$\frac{1}{4}$ in). The temperate belt in Eurasia, the Nearctic region, central Africa.

1 *Coccinella septempunctata* L. Coccinellidae
Seven-spot Ladybird

2 *Coccinella quinquepunctata* L.
Five-spot Ladybird

3 *Synharmonia conglobata* L.

The familiar Seven-spot Ladybird (*Coccinella septempunctata*), which occurs practically everywhere, is much less variable than other ladybirds. The beetles leave their winter shelter in clumps of moss and grass, usually at the foot of trees, early in the spring. They appear in woods, meadows, gardens and fields at both low and high altitudes and in some years they are very abundant. The imagos and larvae (1a) are aphidophagous; they make no distinctions in their choice of species and each consumes several hundred aphids in the course of its lifetime. The female lays several hundred eggs in places frequented by aphids. The larva crawls about among them and pupates (1b) on the same plant. The young beetles emerge in the late summer; they are a deeper shade of orange than the parent generation. The modest food requirements of this beetle and the high frequency of its incidence add to its significance in nature as a natural regulator of the number of aphids.

The Five-spot Ladybird (*Coccinella quinquepunctata*) is likewise not fussy in its choice of aphids. It is abundant in dry and damp localities, in meadows, beside water and in gardens and is common on papillonaceous plants. In the autumn it retires into plant litter to hibernate.

Synharmonia conglobata occurs in two basic colour forms, one pink and one yellow. The black spots on the elytra are extremely variable. This ladybird inhabits mixed woods from lowlands to mountain altitudes. It mainly frequents deciduous trees, but occasionally can be found on pines. Since it lives more in the higher levels of the vegetation, it seems to be rarer than it is. The imagos and the larvae eat various kinds of aphids. *S. conglobata* overwinters, in the company of others of its kind, under the bark of deciduous trees and stumps and in the winter it can be found together with the Two-spot Ladybird (*Adalia bipunctata*) in houses, between the double glazing.

1a

1b

2

1

3

1. *Coccinella septempunctata:* 6—8 mm ($\frac{1}{4}$—$\frac{5}{16}$ in). The Palaearctic region; introduced into North America.
2. *Coccinella quinquepunctata:* 3—5 mm ($\frac{1}{8}$—$\frac{3}{16}$ in). The Palaearctic region.
3. *Synharmonia conglobata:* 3.5—5 mm ($\frac{5}{32}$—$\frac{3}{16}$ in). A large part of the Palaearctic region; in Europe does not extend right to the north.

Variability of the elytra of
Synharmonia conglobata

1 *Harmonia quadripunctata* Pontop.

2 *Calvia quatuordecimguttata* L.

3 *Propylaea quatuordecimpunctata* L.

Harmonia quadripunctata appears in pinewoods in lowlands and hills early in the spring. The spots on its elytra are very variable; the maximum number is sixteen, but they often run together until the dark colour almost preponderates over the light. The imagos and larvae prey on aphids on the genera *Pineus* and *Lachnus* living on pines. The beetles are easily attracted by lights. They hibernate below the bark of conifers and deciduous trees, often in the company of many others.

Calvia quatuordecimguttata is a typical ladybird of deciduous trees which inhabits the outskirts of woods and is also common in orchards. It occurs from lowlands to low montane altitudes. In addition to aphids, it eats jumping plant lice infesting deciduous trees. The imagos overwinter in leaf litter.

Propylaea quatuordecimpunctata is a very common ladybird characterised by great variability of the colouring of its pronotum and elytra. The square black spots on its elytra join together in different ways, forming different patterns. This ladybird occurs in meadows, fields, woods, gardens and parks in both dry and damp localities, from low-lying country to subalpine altitudes. It crawls over shrubs, trees and herbaceous plants and the imagos and larvae catch various kinds of aphids. The imagos are abundant throughout practically the whole of the vegetation season. Spring imagos are beetles which have hibernated and subsequently died, to be followed by their offspring; there is thus only one generation per year. The young beetles overwinter in forest litter, old leaves or clumps of old grass; some of them hibernate a second time. The females lay the eggs after they have come out of hibernation.

Variability of the elytra of *Propylaea quatuordecimpunctata*

1. *Harmonia quadripunctata:* 5.5—6 mm ($\frac{1}{4}$ in). A large part of Europe.
2. *Calvia quatuordecimguttata:* 4.5—6 mm ($\frac{7}{32}$—$\frac{1}{4}$ in). The Palaearctic and Nearctic regions.
3. *Propylaea quatuordecimpunctata:* 3.5—4.5 mm ($\frac{5}{32}$—$\frac{7}{32}$ in). The Palaearctic region.

1 *Neomysia oblongoguttata* L.   Coccinellidae
2 *Anatis ocellata* L.
Eyed Ladybird
3 *Thea vigintiduopunctata* L.

Neomysia oblongoguttata is a brown ladybird marked with yellow bars, which inhabits conifer forests from lowlands to the subalpine zone in mountains. The imagos and larvae live on various kinds of aphids. The beetles hibernate in leaf litter.

The Eyed Ladybird (*Anatis ocellata*) is one of the largest members of the family. It is also variably coloured. It has twenty black, yellow-ringed spots on its elytra, but the black may fade, leaving only yellow spots which may blend with the general colour of the elytra. This ladybird inhabits conifer forests (mainly spruce and silver fir) and occurs from the spring to the autumn. The beetles and their long-bodied larvae crawl over the branches looking mainly for forest aphids (e.g. Adelgidae), but also for sawfly (Tenthredinidae) larvae and the caterpillars of small moths. The Eyed Ladybird can catch sight of prey from a distance of 20–30 cm (8–12 in). Like other ladybirds, it produces only one generation per year, although some species can have two or three generations per year. The eggs are elongate and measure about 2 mm ($\frac{1}{16}$ in). The larva, which moults three times during its development, grows to a length of about 15 mm ($\frac{5}{8}$ in) and then pupates. The new generation emerges during the summer of the same year and hibernates in forest litter. This species is so large and so strikingly marked that it cannot be mistaken for any other.

Unlike other spotted ladybirds, *Thea vigintiduopunctata* is characterised by pronounced variability of its markings. As its Latin name tells us, it has 22 spots on its elytra (*viginti* = twenty, *duo* = two). It likes warm localities and is to be found at the margins of woods, in grass verges and in gardens, where it lives on the hyphae of fungi (family Erysiphaceae). It overwinters in litter or a clump of dry grass.

1

2

3

1. *Neomysia oblongoguttata:* 7—9 mm ($\frac{9}{32}$—$\frac{3}{8}$ in). Europe, the temperate belt in Asia, North America.
2. *Anatis ocellata:* 8—9 mm ($\frac{5}{16}$—$\frac{3}{8}$ in). Europe, the temperate belt in Asia.
3. *Thea vigintiduopunctata:* 3—4.5 mm ($\frac{1}{8}$—$\frac{7}{32}$ in). The Palaearctic region.

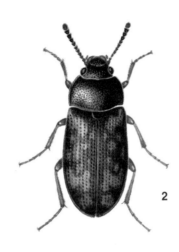

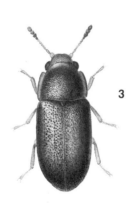

1 *Endomychus coccineus* L.   Endomychidae

2 *Mycetophagus atomarius* F.   Mycetophagidae

3 *Cis boleti* Scop.   Cisidae

4 *Bitoma crenata* F.   Colydiidae

Endomychus coccineus, which inhabits old deciduous woods, requires a damp environment. It lives mainly in mountains and foothills, but in some places is also known in lowlands. It thrives under mouldy bark on old beech, oak, poplar and other trunks lying on the ground, where it lives on the hyphae of fungi. It is equally at home underneath the bark of old stumps and colonises tree fungi, such as *Coriolus hirsutus*. The brightly coloured larvae develop in tree fungi. *Mycetophagus atomarius* (and related species) likewise lives under mouldy bark on deciduous trees and in tree fungi; this species is distributed from low to subalpine altitudes.

The family Cisidae comprises a quantity of small, inconspicuously coloured species that all resemble one another. *Cis boleti* is one of the largest. It inhabits tree fungi, its chief hosts being the species *Trametes gibbosus* and *Coriolus versicolor;* the imagos live inside the fungi and the larvae develop in them. The imagos and larvae riddle the fungus with their tunnels and transform it to fine debris which trickles out of the fruit body and is an obvious sign that the fungus is 'occupied'.

Bitoma crenata (sometimes spelt *Ditoma crenata*) is a small beetle living underneath bark, frequently gregariously. Its form and colouring are so distinctive that it cannot be confused with any other species. Its larvae also live under bark. They eat decaying substances, but are also predacious and even necrophagous.

1. *Endomychus coccineus:* 4—6 mm ($\frac{5}{32}$—$\frac{1}{4}$ in). Europe (very far to the north, in mountains in the south).
2. *Mycetophagus atomarius:* 4—5 mm ($\frac{5}{32}$—$\frac{3}{16}$ in). The whole of Europe.
3. *Cis boleti:* 3—4 mm ($\frac{1}{8}$—$\frac{5}{32}$ in). The Palaearctic region.
4. *Bitoma crenata:* 2.4—3.5 mm ($\frac{3}{32}$—$\frac{5}{32}$ in). The Palaearctic region.

1 *Blaps mortisaga* L.   Tenebrionidae
Cellar or Churchyard Beetle

2 *Opatrum sabulosum* L.

3 *Diaperis boleti* L.

The darkling beetle family (Tenebrionidae) comprises beetles curious both in their appearance and their habits. Quite often their form imitates that of other beetles, e.g. ground, carrion and leaf beetles. Many of them are completely or largely synanthropic and frequent homes, outbuildings and stores. The Cellar or Churchyard Beetle (*Blaps mortisaga*) is closely attached to people and lives in barns and old cellars. According to an ancient superstition, its presence is supposed to presage death (hence its scientific name – *mortisaga*). The beetle, however, is entirely innocent and lives under old boards in cellars, looking for decaying remains of plants to eat. If disturbed, it raises itself stiffly erect on its hindlegs. Like the beetle, the larva is also saprophagous.

In some parts of Europe, *Opatrum sabulosum* can be a pest of crops. It occurs mainly in April and May on dry and sandy ground, in cornfields, in grass, under stones and on footpaths. The female lays about a hundred eggs; the larvae live from May to July and feed on roots and so are thus pests. The young imagos emerge at the end of the summer or during the autumn, but as a rule they remain in the ground and do not come out until the following spring.

Diaperis boleti is a striking beetle inhabiting tree fungi. It mostly settles in fungi growing on deciduous trees and is sometimes to be found underneath the bark of old trees; it seldom occurs in fungi growing on conifers. It lives mainly in beech woods at low altitudes.

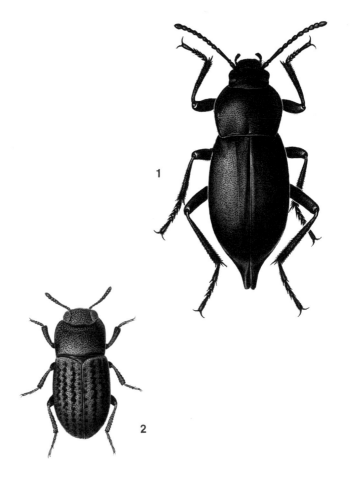

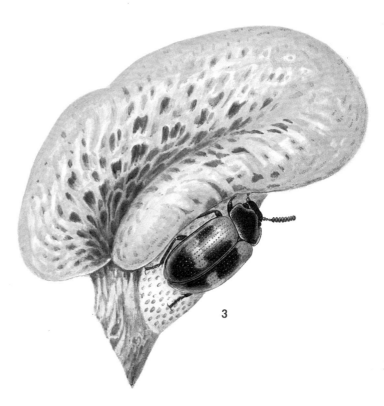

1. *Blaps mortisaga:* 22—24 mm ($\frac{7}{8}$—$\frac{15}{16}$ in). Central and eastern Europe, Asia Minor.
2. *Opatrum sabulosum:* 7—10 mm ($\frac{9}{32}$—$\frac{13}{32}$ in). Central and northern Europe, the Caucasus, Transcaucasia, Siberia.
3. *Diaperis boleti:* 6—8 mm ($\frac{1}{4}$—$\frac{5}{16}$ in). Europe, the Caucasus, the Near East, Siberia, northern Africa.

1

1 *Tenebrio molitor* L. Tenebrionidae
Darkling Beetle

2 *Scaphidema metallicum* F.

3 *Lagria hirta* L. Lagriidae

Breeders of exotic birds and reptiles, and anglers, are well acquainted with the 'meal-worm', which is actually the larva of the darkling beetle *Tenebrio molitor.* The larvae are quite easy to breed and they tolerate a dry environment. The imagos are most often to be found in human dwellings, where they develop in flour; they are also familiar in grain and flour stores. The beetles often fly into lighted houses. Occasionally, however, they live in the open; they hide under the bark of old trees and sometimes appear in birds' nests. The female lays several hundred tiny eggs with a sticky surface.

The gleaming *Scaphidema metallicum* appears from September to May underneath old bark on deciduous trees, in rotting wood and sometimes in tree fungi. The imagos often congregate together and they also live in rotting false acacia wood, which beetles otherwise tend to avoid. They live mainly in woods, but can sometimes be encountered in old parks and in gardens. The beetles come out of hiding in the evening and sit on the low vegetation.

Members of the family Lagriidae are to be found during the summer on various herbaceous and woody plants. *Lagria hirta,* one of the most common, occurs at the edges of deciduous woods and conifer forests, along forest footpaths, in damp meadows and beside streams at practically all altitudes. The phytophagous beetles nibble the tissues of young leaves. The larvae are likewise phytophagous, but eat the old, fallen leaves under which they live on the ground; they pupate in the topsoil. The similar, but rarer, *Lagria atripes* inhabits warm localities and lives mainly on oaks.

2

3

1. *Tenebrio molitor:* 12—18 mm ($\frac{1}{2}$—$\frac{3}{4}$ in). Over most of the globe.
2. *Scaphidema metallicum:* 4—5 mm ($\frac{5}{32}$—$\frac{3}{16}$ in). Europe, the temperate belt in Asia.
3. *Lagria hirta:* 7—10 mm ($\frac{9}{32}$—$\frac{13}{32}$ in). Europe, the temperate belt in Asia.

1 *Cteniopus sulphureus* L. Alleculidae
2 *Rhinosimus ruficollis* L. Salpingidae
3 *Pytho depressus* L. Pythidae

Cteniopus sulphureus was formerly termed *C. luteus* or *C. flavus,* but the users of all three names were referring to the same feature – the beetle's yellow colouring. This species produces several colour forms, in which some parts of the body, including the pronotum and the elytra, turn darker at the expense of the yellow. The beetles fly well and they like flowers; they sit on umbelliferous plants, milfoil and scabious, eating pollen. From May to July they occur, primarily in lowlands, in sunny meadows, on grass verges, at the edges of woods and in clearings; in hilly country they live on sunny slopes. The larvae live in the topsoil, mainly on sandy and gravelly terrain, where they eat the remains of plants. They overwinter in the ground.

Among the many other beetles which live in rotting wood in deciduous trees, *Rhinosimus ruficollis* is conspicuous for its strikingly wide head and long rostrum. The imagos appear in April and May, sometimes on sap escaping from damaged trees.

Pytho depressus is a very distinctive forest beetle. It occurs chiefly in pine woods and sometimes in woods, but seldom in deciduous woods. It is rare in both lowlands and mountains, although it can be found at altitudes of over 2,000 m (6,560 ft). In the spring the female lays her eggs in batches by thrusting her ovipositor underneath the bark of dead trees. The larvae are well adapted for life under these conditions. They have a flat body and explore the passages made by various other insects, such as longhorns and bark beetles. As they go, they eat rotten bark, debris, the excrement of other insects and micro-organisms. They grow slowly. Eventually they fashion a chamber for themselves below the bark and pupate in it. The imago, which emerges in the autumn, hibernates in the chamber.

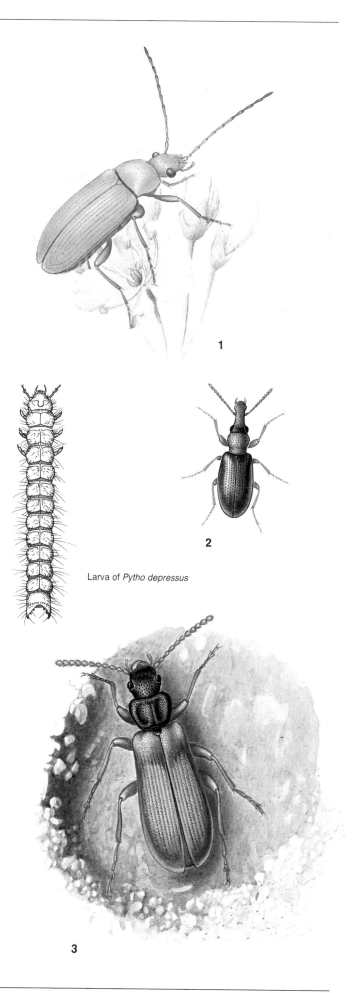

Larva of *Pytho depressus*

1. *Cteniopus sulphureus:* 7—9 mm ($\frac{9}{32}$—$\frac{3}{8}$ in). Europe, the temperate belt in Asia.
2. *Rhinosimus ruficollis:* 3.3—4.5 mm ($\frac{5}{32}$—$\frac{7}{32}$ in). Europe (far to the north).
3. *Pytho depressus:* 7—16 mm ($\frac{9}{32}$—$\frac{5}{8}$ in). Central and northern Europe, the Caucasus, Siberia.

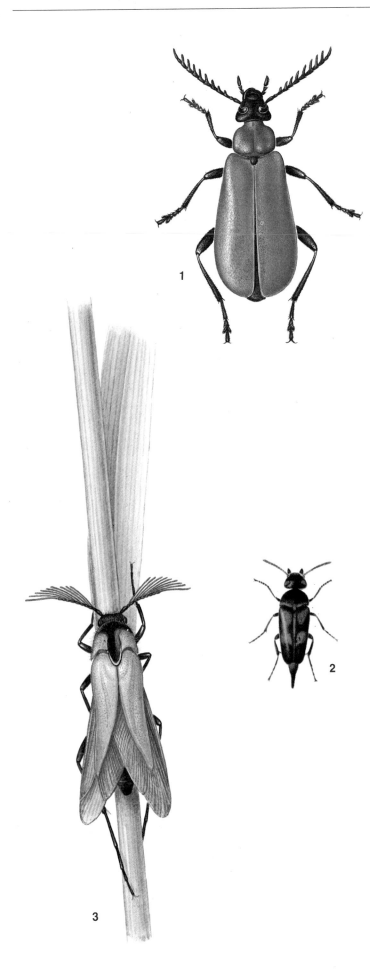

1 *Pyrochroa coccinea* L.   Pyrochroidae
Cardinal Beetle

2 *Variimorda fasciata* F.   Mordellidae

3 *Metoecus paradoxus* L.   Rhipiphoridae

The Cardinal Beetle (*Pyrochroa coccinea*), the largest member of the family in Europe, inhabits deciduous woods from lowlands to the subalpine zone in mountains. The beetles fly over clearings and at the margins of woods on sunny days in May and June. Having a liking for sweet juices, they visit flowering bushes (e.g. hawthorn) or herbaceous plants (they are very common on Umbelliferae), settle on leaves with sticky aphid honeydew on them and often gather together on fresh birch stumps with sap oozing from them. The long, flat-bodied larva lives below the bark of dry deciduous trees or stumps and in stacks of timber; it is mostly to be found in oak or beech. It crawls along the passages of insects living under bark, but also tunnels a passage of its own. It catches various insects, *inter alia* the larvae of bark beetles, and if nothing else is available it will eat the larvae of its own species. The fully grown larva nibbles a 'cradle' between the bark and the wood and pupates in it.

The members of the family Mordellidae have a ventrally convex abdomen tapering to a sharp point at the tip. Other characteristics are their small size and the wriggling movements they perform when disturbed. They live on flowers and are generally difficult to identify. *Variimorda fasciata* can be distinguished fairly easily, however, by its silvery or golden tomentum. In some places it is particularly common in June and July on the flowers of Umbelliferae.

The larva of *Metoecus paradoxus* can develop only in the specific microclimate of a wasp's nest (usually the nest of *Vespula vulgaris*). The newly hatched larva, which is minute in size, waits on rotting wood for a wasp to come along and carry it back to its nest. The larva develops in the nest as a parasite and pupates inside it. When the beetle emerges it leaves the nest, but lives only a few days.

1. *Pyrochroa coccinea:* 14—18 mm ($\frac{9}{16}$—$\frac{3}{4}$ in). A large part of Europe.
2. *Variimorda fasciata:* 5.5—8 mm ($\frac{1}{4}$—$\frac{5}{16}$ in). Europe, the Caucasus, Asia Minor, the Near East.
3. *Metoecus paradoxus:* 8—12 mm ($\frac{5}{16}$—$\frac{1}{2}$ in). Europe, the Caucasus; carried to North America.

1 *Meloe violaceus* Marsh.
Meloidae

2 *Calopus serraticornis* L.
Oedemeridae

3 *Oedemera virescens* L.

Beetles with a complicated metamorphosis have to lay a large number of eggs, since many of the young larvae die before they can reach an environment where their development can continue. This applies to oil beetles (Meloidae), whose numbers are steadily decreasing. *Meloe violaceus,* once a common species, is now rare. It is a springtime beetle. It is phytophagous and lives in little cultivated meadows. The young larvae, known as triungulins, crawl onto various kinds of flowers (e.g. anemones and dandelions) and wait for solitary bees to visit them. The bee gives the larva a free ride back to its nest and there the larva completes its development by hypermetamorphosis.

The strikingly large, long-bodied *Calopus serraticornis* is highly reminiscent of a longhorn beetle. It is a forest species and occurs at submontane and montane altitudes, where it ascends to the limit of the forest belt. It is active at night and spends the daytime hidden under bark, in old wood or under felled trunks. The larvae develop in rotting wood in conifers and deciduous trees, but chiefly spruce and pine. Their development takes several years. The young beetles hibernate.

In the species *Oedemera virescens,* the males have thickened femurs. The beetles like direct sunshine. They live in dry meadows, in clearings, on grass verges, along footpaths in fields and on the outskirts of woods. They are known in lowlands, in foothills and on mountains up to 2,000 m (6,560 ft). They occur from April to July, when they settle on dandelions and the flowers of other herbaceous plants, sucking nectar and nibbling pollen. The larvae develop in the lower part of the stems of different plants, such as monkshood, ragwort and lupins.

1

2

1. *Meloe violaceus:* 10—32 mm ($\frac{3}{8}$—$1\frac{1}{4}$ in). Europe (far to the north), Siberia.
2. *Calopus serraticornis:* 18—20 mm ($\frac{3}{4}$—$\frac{13}{16}$ in). Europe, Siberia.
3. *Oedemera virescens:* 8—11 mm ($\frac{5}{16}$—$\frac{7}{16}$ in). Europe (to the northern limit of the continent), Siberia.

3

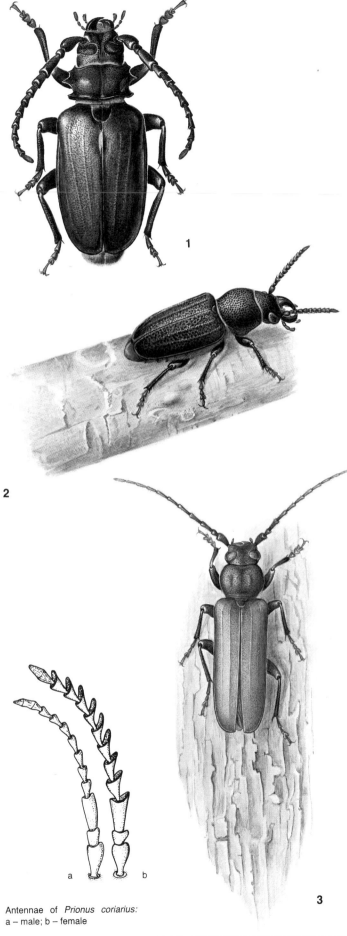

1 *Prionus coriarius* L.

2 *Spondylis buprestoides* L.

3 *Arhopalus rusticus* L.

Cerambycidae

The differences between male and female longhorn beetles are manifested mainly in the length and form of the antennae and sometimes in the number of antennal segments. This is the case with *Prionus coriarius,* which lives in old deciduous and mixed woods in lowlands and on the lower slopes of mountains. The imagos crawl on the ground and sit on tree stumps and logs. They fly during the night, but often fall prey to predacious nocturnal birds. The beetle stridulates audibly by rubbing the inner surface of its hind femora against the edge of its elytra. The imagos occur mainly in July and August, though they sometimes survive until September. The female has a protrusile ovipositor which is extended full length when she lays her eggs. At first, the larvae live under the bark on old stumps, but then descend to the roots and travel underground to find other roots. They generally pupate in the soil in a large cocoon; their development takes at least three years.

With its cylindrical body and short antennae, *Spondylis buprestoides* does not look very much like a longhorn. It lives in clearings in pine woods and is active in the afternoon and evening; otherwise it hides under the bark of tree stumps and under felled trunks. The imago lives for about three weeks, but its development takes two to three years. The female lays her eggs on the roots of stumps (pines and other conifers). As it develops, the larva moves up the stump from the roots. This species is considered to be a preglacial relic.

Arhopalus rusticus is another longhorn inhabitant of conifer forests. During the daytime it hides under bark on the trunks and is active in the evening and at night. It occurs from June to September and lives for six to seven weeks. The female lays her eggs in spruce, pine and larch stumps and dry trunks. The larvae pupate in the wood or in thick bark. The beetles sometimes emerge in timber yards.

Antennae of *Prionus coriarius:*
a – male; b – female

1. *Prionus coriarius:* 18—45 mm ($\frac{3}{4}$—1$\frac{3}{4}$ in). Europe (except the north), the Caucasus, Asia Minor, the Near East, Siberia, northern Africa; carried to North America.
2. *Spondylis buprestoides:* 12—24 mm ($\frac{1}{2}$—$\frac{15}{16}$ in). Europe (without Great Britain), the temperate belt in Asia.
3. *Arhopalus rusticus:* 10—30 mm ($\frac{3}{8}$—1$\frac{3}{16}$ in). The Palaearctic region, in the north beyond the Arctic Circle.

1 *Tetropium castaneum* L.
Cerambycidae
2 *Rhagium bifasciatum* F.
3 *Rhagium inquisitor* L.

Tetropium castaneum is a variably coloured longhorn beetle with brown or black elytra and a marked likeness to a few related species. It is particularly widely distributed in spruce woods at low and high altitudes, but is also known in forests with silver fir, pine or larch growths. The beetles are most abundant from April to September; they do not visit flowers. The larvae develop in the lower part of trees attacked by bark beetles or fungi, or in trunks damaged by the wind. They first of all tunnel under the bark and then penetrate into the wood. At a depth of about 2–4 cm ($\frac{13}{16} - 1\frac{9}{16}$ in) they gnaw a chamber for themselves in the wood and pupate in it; the head of the pupa faces in the direction of the exit hole. This species produces one generation a year.

The members of the genus *Rhagium* all have a similarly shaped body and short antennae, but can easily be distinguished by their colouring. *Rhagium bifasciatum* occurs mainly in hills and mountains and mostly inhabits conifer forests. Beetles which hibernate reappear sometimes at the end of April and then disappear in July. They settle on felled trees, on stacked timber and sometimes on flowers. The polyphagous larva develops mainly in old spruce and pine stumps and rotting trunks, but has also been found in beech, oak and alder.

Rhagium inquisitor is another hibernator which reappears in the spring. It sits on stumps, felled trees and stacked timber and occurs from lowlands up to the limit of the forest zone. The female lays approximately 150 eggs in stumps of spruce and pine trunks and occasionally silver fir, larch or oak trunks. The larva pupates between the bark and the wood, where it fashions an oval 'cradle' for itself out of splinters. The imago, which emerges in the autumn, may either hibernate in the cradle, or fly about for a short time and then seek refuge from the cold in rotting wood. The development of this species takes two to three years.

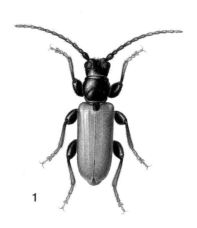

1

2

3

Rhagium inquisitor pupa under bark

1. *Tetropium castaneum:* 9—19 mm ($\frac{3}{8}$—$\frac{3}{4}$ in). The Palaearctic region.
2. *Rhagium bifasciatum:* 12—22 mm ($\frac{1}{2}$—$\frac{7}{8}$ in). Europe, the Caucasus, Transcaucasia, Asia Minor.
3. *Rhagium inquisitor:* 10—21 mm ($\frac{3}{8}$—$\frac{13}{16}$ in). Europe, the temperate zone in Asia (in Europe far to the north).

1 *Toxotus cursor* L.　　　Cerambycidae

2 *Gaurotes virginea* L.

3 *Leptura rubra* L.

Toxotus cursor mostly inhabits spruce forests at both low and high altitudes. The imagos, which appear from May to August, sit on felled timber, on old stumps and on flowers. The larvae develop in old trunks, branches and roots rotting on the ground and in rotting spruce stumps (less often in pine or silver fir stumps or the stumps of deciduous trees).

Gaurotes virginea, a small longhorn, usually has a black pronotum and metallic-blue or -green elytra. The elytra may sometimes be violet and in exceptional cases black, while the pronotum may be marked with red spots of different sizes or be completely red. This species abounds in forest meadows and on the outskirts of woods. It visits flowers and has a head well shaped for this purpose. From May to July the beetles frequent white-flowering umbelliferous plants and growths of hawkweed, thistles and masterwort.

Leptura rubra is undoubtedly one of the most common longhorns. It occurs from low to high altitudes – sometimes appearing as high as the forest limit. It is most abundant in July and August. The beetle is characterised by marked diurnal activity. The males are to be found in large to very large numbers on flowers, such as white-flowering Umbelliferae, hemp agrimony, thistles and flowering shrubs (e.g. elder). The females also visit flowers, but much less than the males; they prefer to sit on felled and stacked timber or crawl under bark. They lay eggs in old spruce or pine stumps and in logs; the larvae live in rotten wood. The imagos stridulate audibly.

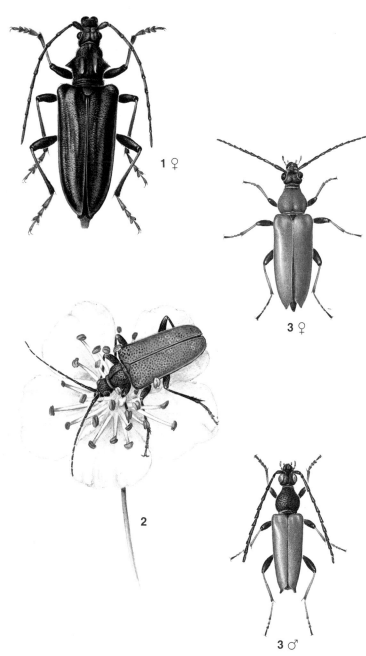

1. *Toxotus cursor:* 16—32 mm ($\frac{5}{8}$—$1\frac{1}{4}$ in). A large part of Europe (right to the north of the continent), western Siberia.
2. *Gaurotes virginea:* 9—12.5 mm ($\frac{3}{8}$—$\frac{15}{32}$ in). The northern part of the Palaearctic region.
3. *Leptura rubra:* 10—19 mm ($\frac{13}{32}$—$\frac{3}{4}$ in). Large territories in the Palaearctic region; imported into North America.

1 *Judolia cerambyciformis* Schr. Cerambycidae
2 *Strangalia maculata* Poda
3 *Strangalia melanura* L.

Beetles with spotted elytra have very variable colouring. *Judolia cerambyciformis* is known in a number of colour forms with light to predominantly dark elytra. This beetle inhabits hills and the lower slopes of mountains, where it flies from June to August. It visits the flowers of many kinds of shrubs and herbaceous plants and is frequently seen on the flowers of Umbelliferae, ragwort, ox-eye daisies and spiraea. The larvae develop in the thinner roots of various deciduous trees and conifers, in which they gnaw narrow passages about 30 cm (12 in) long; sometimes they cross over from one root to another via the soil. The fully grown larva pupates in the ground.

Strangalia maculata is also known for the marked colour variability of its elytra. It likes sunshine and flies in meadows and clearings, on the outskirts of woods and along forest footpaths from lowlands to mountains. From June to August the beetles settle on the flowers of shrubs and herbaceous plants. They are common on elder, milfoil, brambles, scabious and many other plants. The polyphagous larva develops in damp, rotting wood in the branches, thin trunks and roots of different deciduous trees, but seldom in conifers.

Strangalia melanura is a small longhorn occurring in lowlands and in mountains up to the forest boundary. It inhabits forest meadows, clearings and footpaths and may stray into gardens. The imagos abound from May to September on various kinds of flowers, from which they gather pollen, but which they also help to pollinate. They settle on milfoil, ox-eye daisies, hawkweed, brambles and chives. The female lays her eggs, and the larvae develop, in thin oak, maple, spruce and pine twigs rotting on the ground. The larvae grow to a length of up to 15 mm ($\frac{5}{8}$ in).

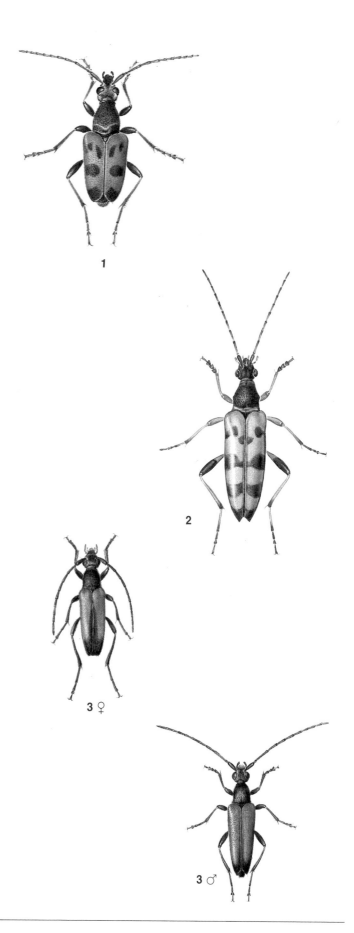

1. *Judolia cerambyciformis:* 6.5—11.5 mm ($\frac{9}{32}$ — $\frac{13}{32}$ in). Chiefly central and south-eastern Europe, the Caucasus, Transcaucasia, Asia Minor.
2. *Strangalia maculata:* 14—20 mm ($\frac{9}{16}$ — $\frac{13}{16}$ in). Mainly central and southern Europe, the Caucasus, Transcaucasia, Asia Minor, the Near East.
3. *Strangalia melanura:* 6—9.5 mm ($\frac{1}{4}$ — $\frac{3}{8}$ in). The Palaearctic region.

167

1 *Cerambyx cerdo* L.   Cerambycidae

2 *Molorchus minor* L.

Cerambyx cerdo, one of the biggest longhorns in Europe, inhabits old oakwoods, but also settles in solitary oaks, in which one generation follows the other in unbroken succession. The imagos live from May to August, but are most numerous in June and July. They sit on felled timber, stumps and living trees. They are not interested in nectar, but fly to injured trees to lick the sap. The beetle's development takes a long time – at least three years, but usually more (up to five). The larva's chief host tree is the oak, but it also develops in beech, hornbeam, elm and false acacia. The female lays a total of about a hundred eggs, in groups of one to three, in cracks in the bark. The young larva bites its way through the thick bark and overwinters under it; the following year it penetrates into the phloem and sapwood and a year after that into the heartwood. There it finally excavates a hook-shaped chamber and pupates inside it. The beetle emerges the same autumn, but remains in the chamber for the winter and does not come out until late in the spring. A decrease in its natural habitats has caused this handsome beetle to disappear from many of its original haunts; both deserve more effective protection.

A few longhorn beetles have such short elytra that the membraneous hindwings protrude beyond them. *Molorchus minor,* which is to be found at both low and high altitudes, is one of the most common of these species. The imagos can be encountered from the early spring – in some places in April, but mostly from May to July. They visit flowering umbelliferous plants, trees and shrubs (rowan, hawthorn, and spiraea). The larva develops in dead spruce and less often in silver fir, pine and larch. It lives in thin trunks and branches, gnaws winding passages under the bark and finally penetrates into the wood, where it pupates in a hook-shaped chamber.

1. *Cerambyx cerdo:* 24—53 mm ($\frac{15}{16}$—$2\frac{3}{32}$ in). Central and southern Europe, the Caucasus, Asia Minor, northern Africa.
2. *Molorchus minor:* 6—16 mm ($\frac{1}{4}$—$\frac{5}{8}$ in). Europe, the temperate belt in Asia.

1 *Aromia moschata* L.
Musk Beetle

Cerambycidae

2 *Rosalia alpina* L.

The pungent musky smell and metallic-green or coppery colouring of the Musk Beetle (*Aromia moschata*) are so distinctive that this species could never be mistaken for any other. It lives at low to medium altitudes and the beetles occur from June to August. They fly slowly and often settle on willow leaves, trunks, sun-warmed stones and flowering herbaceous plants and shrubs (Umbelliferae, spiraea, and yarrow); they also relish the sap oozing from injured willows, maples and birches. The larvae develop in old willows growing near rivers and streams and occasionally in poplars or alders. Their development takes several years; affected trees are riddled with their passages and with the exit holes of the beetles. The larva is often described as a pest of willows. Today this pretty longhorn is disappearing owing to river regulation schemes and the felling of its host tree, the willow.

In many countries *Rosalia alpina* is a protected species. Indeed, if this pretty longhorn and its habitats are not strictly protected, it will soon disappear altogether. The beetle is very variably coloured and the shape and number of the spots on its elytra and pronotum likewise vary, with the result that many different colour forms have been described and named. *Rosalia alpina* occurs on hills and mountains up to about 1,500 m (4,920 ft) and inhabits old beech woods. The imagos fly actively in the midday sunshine from June to August. They settle on felled and stacked timber, on stumps and on sun-warmed stones and sometimes visit flowers (such as elder). The female lays her eggs in dying standing beeches or in tall beech stumps and, in southern Europe, in hornbeam, ash or walnut. The larva gnaws passages between the sapwood and the heartwood and pupates in a hook-shaped chamber; its development takes several years.

1

2

1. *Aromia moschata:* 13—34 mm ($\frac{9}{16}$—1$\frac{3}{8}$ in). Europe, the temperate belt in Asia.
2. *Rosalia alpina:* 15—38 mm ($\frac{5}{8}$—1$\frac{1}{2}$ in). Central and southern Europe, the Caucasus, Transcaucasia, the Near East.

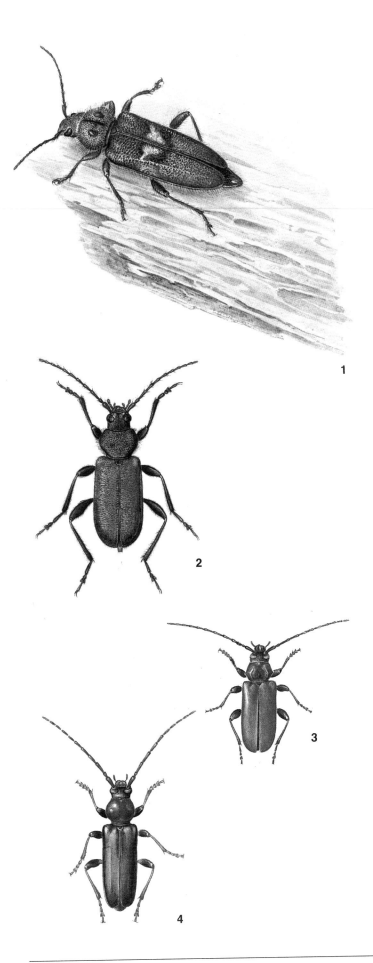

1 *Hylotrupes bajulus* L. — Cerambycidae
House Longhorn

2 *Callidium violaceum* L.

3 *Pyrrhidium sanguineum* L.

4 Phymatodes testaceus L.

Some longhorn beetles live in close proximity to people. The House Longhorn (*Hylotrupes bajulus*) could be said to be almost synanthropic, although on rare occasions it is also to be found in the open. The imagos live from June to August and sometimes longer. For its development the larva requires dry conifer wood (mainly spruce) which has already been made into beams, rafters, staircases, furniture and telegraph poles. Sometimes the beetle appears in timber yards. The larva devours the wood, mainly just below the surface, but sometimes deeper. The beetle leaves the wood through an oval opening.

Callidium violaceum is sometimes to be found in the lofts of new houses, where successive generations develop in rafters pre-infested with larvae and pupae. Otherwise, this is a beetle of conifer forests, where the imagos occur in the greatest numbers from May to July on stacked and felled timber; they do not visit flowers. The larvae develop in the outer wood of dead spruces, pines, silver firs and larches, but penetrate further inwards before pupating. Their development takes two years.

The body of *Pyrrhidium sanguineum* is covered with a very fine red tomentum. The beetle inhabits deciduous woods (especially oak woods), where it lives from April to July. It settles on felled and stacked timber, but not on flowers. The larva develops in oak and other hardwoods.

Phymatodes testaceus also inhabits deciduous woods. The very variably coloured beetle remains in hiding during the daytime and comes out at night. The larvae develop in dead oak, beech, hornbeam and fruit tree branches and trunks.

1. *Hylotrupes bajulus:* 7—21 mm ($\frac{9}{32}$—$\frac{13}{16}$ in). Over the entire globe.
2. *Callidium violaceum:* 8—16 mm ($\frac{5}{16}$—$\frac{5}{8}$ in). The Palaearctic region (far to the north), the Nearctic region.
3. *Pyrrhidium sanguineum:* 8—12 mm ($\frac{5}{16}$—$\frac{1}{2}$ in). Central and southern Europe, the Caucasus, Asia Minor, the Near East, northern Africa.
4. *Phymatodes testaceus:* 6—17 mm ($\frac{1}{4}$—$\frac{11}{16}$ in). Central and southern Europe, the southern part of northern Europe, the Caucasus, Transcaucasia, Asia Minor, the Near East, northern Africa; carried to North America.

1 *Plagionotus arcuatus* L.
Cerambycidae
2 *Plagionotus detritus* L.
3 *Anaglyptus mysticus* L.

Plagionotus arcuatus and *P. detritus* are both camouflaged to look like wasps, the purpose of this colouring being to scare away would-be enemies. *P. arcuatus* is abundant in oak woods. It likes sunshine and warmth and on fine days, from May to July, it runs about on felled oak trunks, settles on stumps and flies from one tree to another; it tends to avoid flowers, but has been seen on them. The larva develops chiefly in oak trunks felled before the advent of winter. The female lays her eggs in cracks in the bark. The larvae live under the bark and gnaw wide, winding passages which they choke up with the resultant debris. At the end of their development they penetrate about 5 cm (2 in) deep into the wood, where they pupate in a 'cradle'. Their development takes two years. *Plagionotus detritus* is likewise a beetle of oak woods, where it flies from May to July. It lives and develops similarly to the preceding species. The larva has also been found in birch and sweet chestnut, but the oak remains its main host plant.

Anaglyptus mysticus is a persistent visitor on the flowers of various kinds of herbaceous and woody plants. In May and June (at higher altitudes up to August) it can be encountered along forest paths, on the outskirts of woods and on grass verges, where it settles on flowering umbelliferous plants, hawthorn, dogwood and elder. The beetles' tricoloured elytra are very variable, with either red or black being predominant. The larva develops in dead branches and stumps of various deciduous trees and bushes, the chief types being oak, beech, maple, lime and false acacia, in different kinds of fruit trees and in hazel, hawthorn and spindle-trees. The beetles overwinter in rotting trunks or under bark.

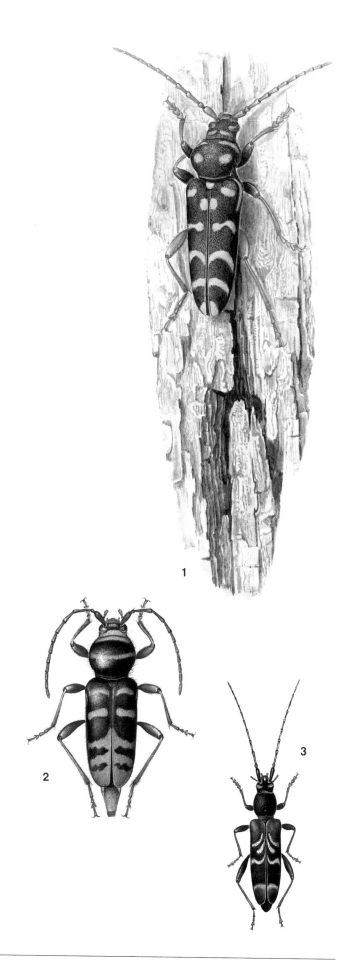

1. *Plagionotus arcuatus:* 6—20 mm ($\frac{1}{4}$—$\frac{13}{16}$ in). The western part of the Palaearctic region.
2. *Plagionotus detritus:* 10—19 mm ($\frac{3}{8}$—$\frac{3}{4}$ in). Central and southern Europe, the southern part of northern Europe, the Caucasus, Asia Minor, northern Africa.
3. *Anaglyptus mysticus:* 6—13 mm ($\frac{1}{4}$—$\frac{9}{16}$ in). Central and southern Europe, Transcaucasia, northern Africa.

1 *Monochamus sutor* L.   Cerambycidae
2 *Leiopus nebulosus* L.

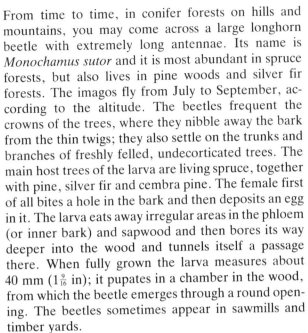

From time to time, in conifer forests on hills and mountains, you may come across a large longhorn beetle with extremely long antennae. Its name is *Monochamus sutor* and it is most abundant in spruce forests, but also lives in pine woods and silver fir forests. The imagos fly from July to September, according to the altitude. The beetles frequent the crowns of the trees, where they nibble away the bark from the thin twigs; they also settle on the trunks and branches of freshly felled, undecorticated trees. The main host trees of the larva are living spruce, together with pine, silver fir and cembra pine. The female first of all bites a hole in the bark and then deposits an egg in it. The larva eats away irregular areas in the phloem (or inner bark) and sapwood and then bores its way deeper into the wood and tunnels itself a passage there. When fully grown the larva measures about 40 mm ($1\frac{9}{16}$ in); it pupates in a chamber in the wood, from which the beetle emerges through a round opening. The beetles sometimes appear in sawmills and timber yards.

Leiopus nebulosus is a small, but common and widespread longhorn inhabiting growths of deciduous trees from low to high altitudes. The imagos can be seen from the end of April to July. The beetles fly short distances and alight on piles of dry twigs or undecorticated wood; they do not settle on flowers. The polyphagous larvae live on dead and often rotting undecorticated branches or on weak trunks that are still standing. Their chief host plants are oak, hornbeam and beech, but they often also appear on fruit trees, maples, hazels, willows, sweet chestnuts, poplars and walnuts. Under the bark, the larva eats away a passage for itself and then blocks it up with the debris. It pupates in the wood, sometimes in the autumn, in which case the imago overwinters. Hibernating pupae, from which the imago emerged at the beginning of the spring, have also been found.

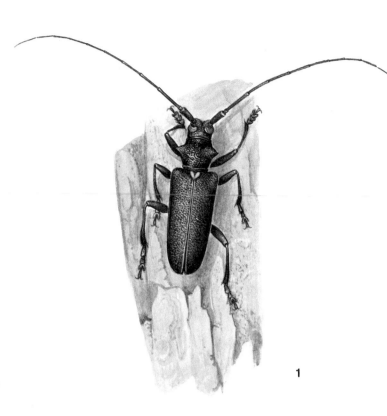

1

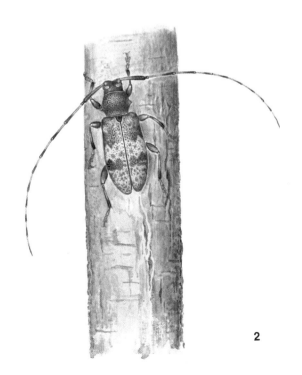

2

1. *Monochamus sutor:* 15—24 mm ($\frac{5}{8}$—$\frac{15}{16}$ in). The northern part of the Palaearctic region.
2. *Leiopus nebulosus:* 6—10 mm ($\frac{1}{4}$—$\frac{3}{8}$ in). Central Europe, the northern part of southern Europe.

1 *Acanthocinus aedilis* L.   Cerambycidae
Timberman Beetle

The Timberman Beetle (*Acanthocinus aedilis*) is surely the prototype of all longhorns. The male's antennae are about five times longer than his body and are thus relatively longer than those of any other beetle; the female's antennae are only double the length of her body. The development of the ovipositor is unusual for a beetle; the female can extend it, but cannot retract it into her body. Three other similar species still live in central Europe, but they are much rarer – although today we can no longer claim that even the Timberman Beetle is common. This species inhabits conifer forests (mainly pine woods) from lowlands to mountains. It appears very early in the spring – often in March on sunny days. These are beetles which emerged during the previous year and spent the winter below the bark of felled trees. They settle on undecorticated trunks and on stumps. The male beetle stalking along a pine log with its antennae pointing stiffly forwards is an imposing sight. When the beetle rests, pressed against the bark of a trunk, its grey colouring blends perfectly with its background and only a practised eye, looking specifically for the beetle, can detect it. These beetles do not settle on flowers and for food they are content to gnaw bark with their mandibles. The main host plants of the larvae are different kinds of pines, but the larvae can also develop in spruce, silver fir or larch. The female lays a total of 30–50 eggs in stumps with tightly fitting bark, in the bark of felled dead trees or in the trunks of trees which have just died. She first bites a hole in the bark, makes it deeper with her ovipositor and then deposits an egg in it. The larva lives and tunnels in the bark. When fully grown, with a length of about 35 mm ($1\frac{3}{8}$ in), it pupates in the bark or the wood. From the length of the antennal sheaths on the pupa it is easy to tell whether the beetle will be a male or a female. The imago emerges in the autumn. It usually remains underneath the bark for the winter, but in a warm season it may leave its shelter and not actually hibernate until later.

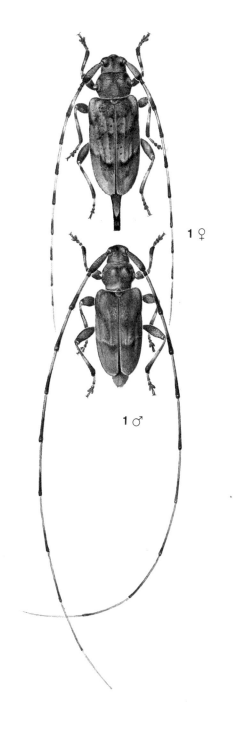

1 ♀

1 ♂

1. *Acanthocinus aedilis:* 12—20 mm ($\frac{1}{2}$—$\frac{13}{16}$ in). The western part of the Palaearctic region.

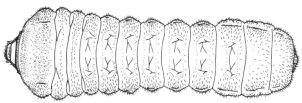

Larva of the Timberman Beetle (*Acanthocinus aedilis*)

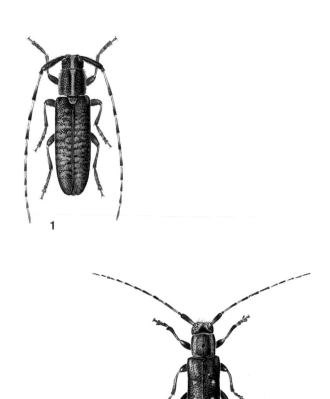

1

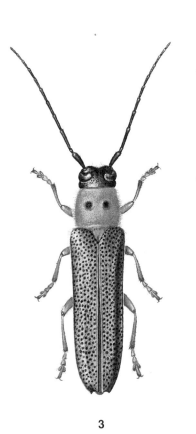

3

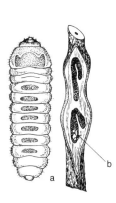

Larva (a) and pupa (b) of
Saperda populnea

1 *Agapanthia villosoviridescens* Deg.

2 *Saperda populnea* L.

3 *Oberea oculata* L.

For *Agapanthia villosoviridescens* and related species, life without herbaceous plants would be impossible, since they are essential for the development of the larvae. The forest-dwelling imagos live along paths and in clearings and from May to July they settle on various plants (but not on flowers) with their antennae pointing forwards and the tips curving downwards. They are mostly to be found on thistles, ragwort, hemp agrimony and stinging nettles. The imagos gnaw the tissues of the flower stalks. The female lays the eggs in the stem of the plant; the larva lives in the pith and travels down the stem to the base of the plant, sometimes as far as the root. It spends the winter in the hollow stem, just above the ground, and pupates there in the spring. One plant may contain several pupae.

Saperda populnea is characterised by the careful provision it makes for its brood. The female gnaws a few transverse grooves in living bark on an aspen or a poplar and round them she forms a horseshoe with a hole reaching at its apex to the sapwood. In the hole she deposits a single egg. Irritated by the gnawing and the presence of the egg, the tissues begin to proliferate and form a ridge of cells which provide the larva with its first food. The larva then penetrates between the bark and the sapwood, excavates a circular passage and invades the sapwood. The presence of the larva is betrayed externally by the formation on the branch of a bulging gall in which the larva eventually pupates. Since the female makes several such horseshoes, the number of galls on the host plant can be quite large. The beetle's development takes two years.

Oberea oculata also cares for its offspring. The female, which lays her eggs in living willow branches, likewise makes gashes and a hole in the bark. The imagos occur at low and subalpine altitudes and live on willow (mostly sallow) leaves. They do not visit flowers.

1. *Agapanthia villosoviridescens:* 10—22 mm ($\frac{13}{32}$—$\frac{7}{8}$ in). Central and southern Europe, the Caucasus, Siberia.
2. *Saperda populnea:* 9—15 mm ($\frac{3}{8}$—$\frac{5}{8}$ in). The Palaearctic region.
3. *Oberea oculata:* 15—21 mm ($\frac{5}{8}$—$\frac{13}{16}$ in). The Palaearctic region (in the north to the Arctic Circle).

1 *Bruchus pisorum* L.   Bruchidae
Pea Beetle

2 *Orsodacne cerasi* L.   Chrysomelidae

3 *Donacia aquatica* L.

The larva of the Pea Beetle (*Bruchus pisorum*) is an unpleasant pest whose eating activities and excrement make green peas unfit as seed as well as for consumption. The egg is stuck to the outer surface of a young pod. The larva bores its way inside and gnaws a passage in the pod; it then settles in one of the peas and devours it steadily from within. One pea may be invaded by several larvae, but there is only room for one of them to complete its development. The young and the fully grown larvae are very different from each other. The newly hatched larva is pink and has legs, while the mature larva is whitish and legless (in any case legs would not be of any use to it inside the pea). The larva finally pupates in the pea, which can be recognised by the thinly disguised hole in its surface. The imago emerges in the autumn; sometimes it overwinters in the pea, but if the autumn is fine it leaves the pea in September and flies into woods sometimes as much as 5 km (3 mi) away. There it hides under bark, in lichen growing on trees or in moss. In the spring the beetles fly back to the pea-fields, where they eat the young leaves and pollen; the pollen is particularly important for the female, since it stimulates maturation of her ovaries before egg-laying starts.

The leaf beetle *Orsodacne cerasi* frequents flowering umbelliferous plants and shrubs from April into the summer. It is very variably coloured, some beetles being yellow to reddish-brown and others black-spotted to black.

On plants growing beside water you can sometimes see above the surface (or even below it) metallic-coloured leaf beetles resembling small longhorns. *Donacia aquatica,* a very beautifully coloured beetle, lives on bur-reed, great spearwort and sedge. It is not a common species.

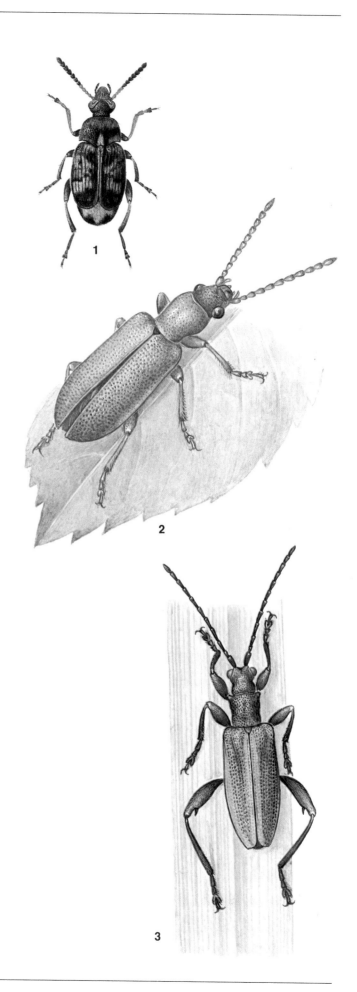

1. *Bruchus pisorum:* 4—4.5 mm ($\frac{5}{32}$ — $\frac{7}{32}$ in). Over most of the globe.
2. *Orsodacne cerasi:* 4.5—8 mm ($\frac{7}{32}$ — $\frac{5}{16}$ in). A large part of Europe.
3. *Donacia aquatica:* 6—10 mm ($\frac{1}{4}$ — $\frac{3}{8}$ in). Europe (far to the north).

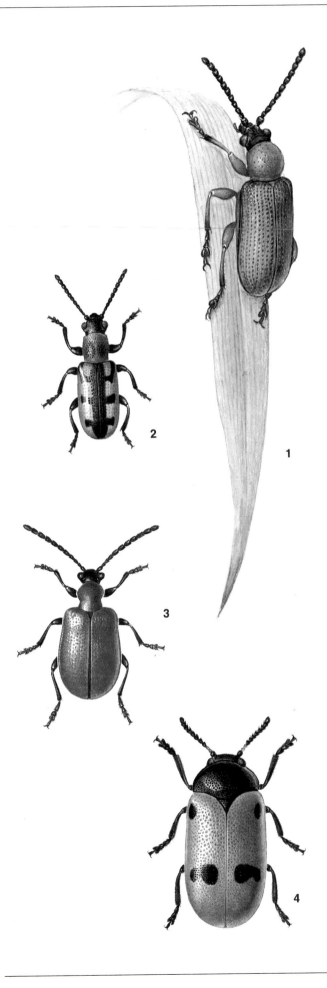

1 *Oulema melanopus* L. Chrysomelidae
2 *Crioceris asparagi* L.
3 *Lilioceris lilii* Scop.
4 *Clytra quadripunctata* L.

The imagos and larvae of *Oulema melanopus* spend the whole of their lives on wild grasses and cereals. Hibernating beetles reappear when the temperature rises to about 17 °C (60 °F). They settle on grasses and bite strips about 1 mm ($\frac{1}{32}$ in) wide out of them. The larvae also eat leaves, but in a different manner. They nibble the cuticle on one side only, leaving a transparent patch in the leaf.

The beautifully marked, but variably coloured *Crioceris asparagi* lives on cultivated and wild types of asparagus. The beetles overwinter under old leaves, stones or bark, or in old asparagus stalks; they appear in the spring and nibble the young shoots. The female lays her eggs perpendicularly to the stem of the host plant. The larvae develop very fast, so that the young beetles appear in June. Another generation of imagos hatches in July and it is these beetles that hibernate.

Lilioceris lilii and the very similar *L. merdigera* are a striking shade of bright red. The former lives chiefly on madonna lilies in gardens and parks, but also on other lilies and on fritillaries. Imagos are to be found throughout practically the whole of the vegetation season, since this species produces up to three generations in a year. It is also able to emit sounds.

Clytra quadripunctata occurs from May to August on bushes and trees, where it eats the tissues. Its actual development takes place in the nests of large ants belonging to the genus *Formica*. The egg (which the ants carry to the nest themselves) is wrapped in secretion, and the larva is also encased, to protect it from the ants' jaws. The beetle, which leaves the anthill after hatching, is likewise clad in chitin armour.

1. *Oulema melanopus:* 4—4.5 mm ($\frac{5}{32}$—$\frac{7}{32}$ in). The Palaearctic region; carried to North America.
2. *Crioceris asparagi:* 5—6.5 mm ($\frac{3}{16}$—$\frac{9}{32}$ in). The western part of the Palaearctic region; carried to North America.
3. *Lilioceris lilii:* 6—8 mm ($\frac{1}{4}$—$\frac{5}{16}$ in). The Palaearctic region.
4. *Clytra quadripunctata:* 7—11 mm ($\frac{9}{32}$—$\frac{7}{16}$ in). A large part of Europe (in the north to the northern part of Finland and Scandinavia).

1 *Cryptocephalus sericeus* L. Chrysomelidae
2 *Cryptocephalus sexpunctatus* L.
3 *Adoxus obscurus* L.

The genus *Cryptocephalus* comprises several dozen species whose imagos have short, wide bodies and filiform antennae and keep their heads tucked under their bodies. Many of them have bright markings and others – such as *Cryptocephalus sericeus,* one of the best known species – have metallic colouring. This species lives in meadows, on warm, grassy hillsides, on the grass beside field footpaths, at the edges of woods and on sunny railway embankments. It can be seen from May to July, sitting on flowering hawkweed and dandelions, its body frequently powdered with yellow pollen grains.

A characteristic specimen of the leaf beetle *Cryptocephalus sexpunctatus* should have a total of six black spots on its elytra (from the Latin *sex* = six and *punctum* = spot). Some individuals have only two black spots, however, while in others the spots unite across the body or down it, with the result that, in some cases, black predominates. This beetle occurs from May to August on different kinds of bushes and trees, such as hazel, hawthorn, oak, birch and willow.

The tubby-bodied *Adoxus obscurus* appears on the ground in the spring. The imago appears in May and will then be found up to late autumn. It lives on grapevines, where it has a special form, and on other plants. The imagos often occur on rosebay willowherb and hawkweed and on the leaves and inflorescences of grasses, but if you touch the plant they drop to the ground. The beetles bite thin strips, up to 15 mm ($\frac{5}{8}$ in) long, out of the plant tissues. The specimens one comes across are females; this species reproduces in a manner unusual in beetles, i.e. parthenogenetically. The larvae live in the soil.

1

2

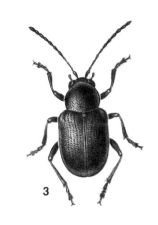

3

1. *Cryptocephalus sericeus:* 6.5—8 mm ($\frac{9}{32}$—$\frac{5}{16}$ in). A large part of Europe.
2. *Cryptocephalus sexpunctatus:* 4.5—6.5 mm ($\frac{7}{32}$—$\frac{9}{32}$ in). Europe, the temperate belt in Asia.
3. *Adoxus obscurus:* 5—6 mm ($\frac{3}{16}$—$\frac{1}{4}$ in). Europe (except the extreme north), northern Africa, North America, Mexico.

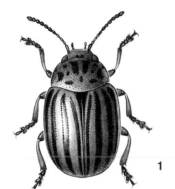

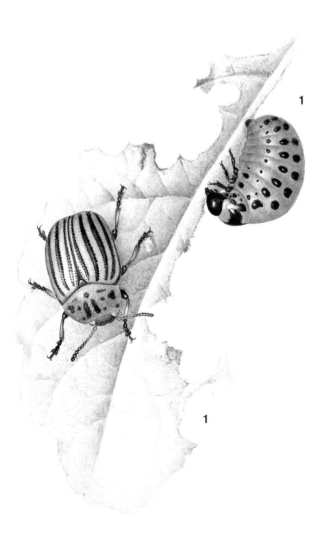

1 *Leptinotarsa decemlineata* Say
Chrysomelidae
Colorado Beetle

The scientific name of the Colorado Beetle *(Leptinotarsa decemlineata)* tells us that it has ten stripes on its body (Latin *decem* = ten and *lineatus* = striped), but its vernacular name tells us where it originally came from.

The Colorado Beetle was first described in 1824 on *Solanum rostratum,* a wild plant of the nightshade group growing in the state of Colorado in North America. As more and more potatoes were cultivated, the beetle changed over to this new host plant, which must have seemed to have been put there for its direct convenience. After spreading throughout America, it began to travel round the world settling in potato fields. Its spread was partly aided by people, but the beetle also migrated and spread of its own accord. In Europe it was soon assimilated into the native fauna.

The Colorado Beetle produces one or two generations per year, according to local conditions. The beetles hibernate in the ground and make their appearance in the spring. The female lays her eggs in large groups, usually on the underside of potato leaves. One female lays several hundred. At first white, the eggs soon turn yellow. The bright red, black-spotted young larva is very conspicuous; the full-grown larva is orange, measures about 15 mm ($\frac{5}{8}$ in) and crawls underground to pupate. After emerging, the beetle remains a few days in the soil and does not come out until its body tegument has hardened sufficiently. Both the beetles and the larvae live on the plant tissues above the ground and do not attack the potato tubers. They thus strip the host plant of its green tissues and if there are too many of them and tissue losses are too great, the results for the growth of the plants and for the potato harvest are disastrous. The big ground beetles *Carabus auratus, C. cancellatus* and *C. granulatus* are of great significance in combating the Colorado Beetle, since they devour the beetles and the larvae in potato fields.

1. *Leptinotarsa decemlineata:* 6—10 mm ($\frac{1}{4}$—$\frac{3}{8}$ in). Over practically the whole globe.

1 *Chrysomela caerulans* Scriba   Chrysomelidae
2 *Chrysolina staphylea* L.
3 *Chrysolina sanguinolenta* L.

Chrysomela caerulans glows with a metallic lustre, but is very variably coloured. Sometimes it is a metallic-blue, bluish-violet or bluish-green and sometimes bluish-black, coppery or copper with a greenish sheen. It likes a damp environment and we must therefore look for it in wet meadows, beside streams and on damp ground at the edges of forests, in hills and mountains rather than in lowlands; its host plant is water mint. The imagos live from May to August.

If you wish to identify the leaf beetle *Chrysolina staphylea* and differentiate it from other similar glossy-brown species, you must look for a somewhat unusual characteristic: *C. staphylea* has membraneous hindwings, which similar species lack. The imagos of this leaf beetle live from the spring to the autumn. They crawl over field footpaths and frequent waterside vegetation and damp meadows. They favour plants of the family Labiatae, in particular mint, sweet balm, basil and the like.

A few species of dark-coloured leaf beetles have a red border of varying widths round their pronotum and elytra. At first glance they all look alike, the difference lying in the characteristic of the stippling on their elytra and the marks on their pronotum. *Chrysolina sanguinolenta* seems to be the most common of these red-bordered leaf beetles. It occurs from early spring until late autumn. It inhabits sandy areas and can sometimes be seen in fields or footpaths, but it is not particularly abundant. The larva's host plant is toadflax.

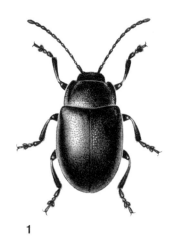

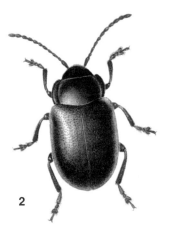

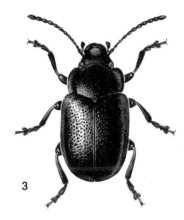

1. *Chrysomela caerulans:* 6.5—9 mm ($\frac{9}{32}$—$\frac{3}{8}$ in). Chiefly central and southern Europe, Asia Minor, central Asia.
2. *Chrysolina staphylea:* 6.5—9 mm ($\frac{9}{32}$—$\frac{3}{8}$ in). The Palaearctic region (in Europe far to the north), North America.
3. *Chrysolina sanguinolenta:* 6—9 mm ($\frac{1}{4}$—$\frac{3}{8}$ in). A large part of Europe, Siberia.

1 *Chrysolina fastuosa* Scop.   Chrysomelidae
2 *Chrysochloa cacaliae* Schrank
3 *Gastrophysa polygoni* L.
4 *Plagiodera versicolora* Laichart.

The tiny *Chrysolina fastuosa* attracts attention by the beauty of its variable metallic colouring, whose shades range from green and golden green to bluish-violet and coppery-red. This species is abundant from spring to autumn on hemp-nettles, deadnettles and stinging nettles almost everywhere, on grass verges and field and forest footpaths, beside roads and ditches and on rubble.

Chrysochloa cacaliae is a mountain beetle that is usually coloured green or blue. The beetles are common in the summer and autumn. Their host plants belong to the Asteraceae (Compositae) and the chief ones are ragwort and *Adenostylis*.

Gastrophysa polygoni is a strikingly coloured leaf beetle common on sorrel and knotgrass. It appears from the end of May to September at the edge of fields and on footpaths and grass verges. It is less abundant than the related, green-coloured *G. viridula,* which inhabits the same localities. Its larvae reduce the leaves to skeletons.

Plagiodera versicolora has widely oval contours and metallic colouring. The colouring is variable, so that some individuals are blue or bluish-green and others are green or copper-coloured. The imagos occur at both low and high altitudes; they are most often found on willows and poplars, where they live on the leaf tissues. The female lays her eggs on the undersides of leaves. The larvae remain on the leaves and eat them down to a skeleton. They also pupate on the leaves, hanging head downwards attached by the tips of their abdomens. The imago hibernates.

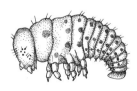

Larva of *Plagiodera versicolora*

1. *Chrysolina fastuosa:* 5—6 mm ($\frac{3}{16}$—$\frac{1}{4}$ in). Europe, the temperate belt in Asia.
2. *Chrysochloa cacaliae:* 7.5—10.5 mm ($\frac{5}{16}$—$\frac{7}{16}$ in). The massifs of central Europe.
3. *Gastrophysa polygoni:* 4—5 mm ($\frac{5}{32}$—$\frac{3}{16}$ in). A large part of Europe, North America.
4. *Plagiodera versicolora:* 2.5—4.5 mm ($\frac{3}{32}$—$\frac{7}{32}$ in). The Palaearctic region (in Europe right to the north of the continent), the Nearctic region, part of the Oriental region.

1 *Chrysomela aenea* L.

Chrysomelidae

2 *Chrysomela populi* L.
Red Poplar Leaf Beetle

3 *Phytodecta viminalis* L.

Chrysomela aenea is a common beetle on alders growing beside running and stagnant water, in marshy forest meadows and alongside forest paths from springtime onwards. It is generally metallic-green, greenish-gold or blue and less often reddish-gold. The beetles and the larvae live on the tissues of alder leaves and the larvae pupate on them. The imagos begin to emerge in August and overwinter in plant litter or old leaves.

The Red Poplar Leaf Beetle (*Chrysomela populi*), which is distributed from lowlands to mountains, finds food and shelter on different kinds of poplars. Since it can form two or three generations in one year, the first beetles appear in the spring and the last individuals vanish in October, to hibernate under bark, in moss or in fallen leaves. The female lays several hundred eggs on the undersides of leaves, in batches of 30–60 covered with a protective secretory substance. The voracious larvae sometimes eat the leaves down to the ribs. From their dorsal glands they can release drops of a fluid smelling strongly of carbolic acid. The larvae pupate on the leaves. Two more similar species differ from the Red Poplar Leaf Beetle in the absence of the dark spot at the tip of the elytra.

The pronotum and elytra of *Phytodecta viminalis* are very variably coloured. The large black spot at the base of the pronotum may disappear or break up into several separate spots. The spots on the elytra are likewise variable; sometimes they are missing and sometimes they unite and almost blot out the original red colour. The beetles occur from May to July on the leaves of different kinds of willows, but especially goat willows and other *Salix* species (*S. aurita*, *S. cinerea*). The larvae live on the same plants.

1

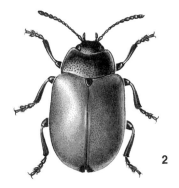

2

3

---

1. *Chrysomela aenea:* 6.5—8.5 mm ($\frac{9}{32}$—$\frac{11}{32}$ in). Europe (to beyond the Arctic Circle, but not in the Mediterranean region), the temperate belt in Asia.
2. *Chrysomela populi:* 10—12 mm ($\frac{3}{8}$—$\frac{1}{2}$ in). The Palaearctic region.
3. *Phytodecta viminalis:* 5.5—7 mm ($\frac{1}{4}$—$\frac{9}{32}$ in). The Palaearctic and Nearctic regions.

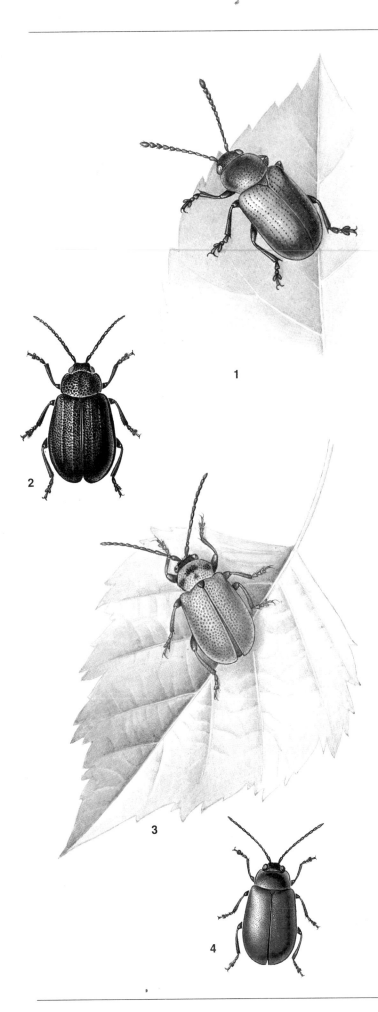

1 *Phyllodecta vitellinae* L. Chrysomelidae

2 *Galeruca tanaceti* L.

3 *Lochmaea caprea* L.

4 *Agelastica alni* L.
Alder Leaf Beetle

The tiny, variably coloured *Phyllodecta vitellinae* is sometimes dark green, dark blue or coppery, or occasionally black. The beetles and the larvae live on alder, willow and poplar leaves, which they reduce to a skeleton. The imagos abound from May to September. The full-grown larva drops to the ground and pupates in the topsoil.

From the summer onwards, we may see black, wide-bodied leaf beetles flying over field footpaths, pastures, dry hillsides and grass verges. Some of them have a large abdomen protruding from below their elytra. They are females of the species *Galeruca tanaceti*. The beetles occur until late in the autumn and are sometimes still to be encountered on fine days in November; they come out mainly on dull days and early in the evening. The female lays her eggs in the late autumn on the stems, leaves and dry flowers of various herbaceous plants. The eggs are wrapped in a protective secretory substance. The larvae are hatched in the spring; they measure about 12–14 mm ($\frac{1}{2}$ in) and pupate in the ground.

The rather inconspicuously coloured *Lochmaea caprea* is found on birches and poplars, but mainly on willows from spring to autumn. It lives on leaves, as do the larvae, which pupate in the ground.

Although the Alder Leaf Beetle (*Agelastica alni*) occasionally occurs on other deciduous trees, the alder is its main host plant. Beetles which have hibernated begin to eat the leaves in April. The female lays large batches of eggs on the undersides of leaves. The larvae all live together at first and then disperse among the leaves; they pupate in cells in the ground. The young beetles appear on the leaves at the end of July and retire for the winter in September.

1. *Phyllodecta vitellinae:* 4—5 mm ($\frac{5}{32}$—$\frac{3}{16}$ in). Europe (right to the north of the continent), the temperate belt in Asia.
2. *Galeruca tanaceti:* 6.5—11 mm ($\frac{9}{32}$—$\frac{7}{16}$ in). The western part of the Palaearctic region.
3. *Lochmaea caprea:* 4.5—6 mm ($\frac{7}{32}$—$\frac{1}{4}$ in). A large part of the Palaearctic region (in Europe right to the north of the continent).
4. *Agelastica alni:* 6—7 mm ($\frac{1}{4}$—$\frac{9}{32}$ in). The Palaearctic region; carried to the Nearctic region.

1 *Phyllotreta undulata* Kutsch.   Chrysomelidae

2 *Hispella atra* L.

3 *Cassida viridis* L.
Green Tortoise Beetle

4 *Platystomus albinus* L.   Anthribidae

1

Flea-beetles (*Phyllotreta*) are tiny jumping leaf beetles with thick femora. There are many species – light-coloured and black with yellow stripes on their elytra. *Phyllotreta undulata,* which often appears in masses in fields and gardens, is one of the last type. It attacks wild and cultivated Cruciferae. The beetles nibble the leaf tissues and do considerable damage in large numbers. The larvae live in the ground on the small roots.

Among the beetles of the temperate belt, *Hispella atra* is something of a curiosity. Its body is covered with spiny processes, so that it looks like a minute hedgehog. Movements of its head are accompanied by stridulation, as the anterior edge of the pronotum scrapes on ridges across the vertex. The larvae develop in the leaves of grasses (e.g. meadow-grass and couch-grass).

The bright green *Cassida viridis* is sometimes separated from the leaf beetles and placed in a family of its own (Cassididae). It lives on labiate plants, especially mint and betony. Against their background of leaves, the green beetles are invisible. The female makes doubly sure that the eggs are safe. She wraps each small batch in a layer of secretion and then covers the whole clutch up again. At the tip of its abdomen the larva has a forked appendage on which it carries its frass and exuviae as camouflage. The larva pupates on a leaf.

Platystomus albinus blends perfectly with its environment. It sits on mouldy stumps, on branches and on stacks of timber in deciduous woods. The larva lives in dead wood (oak, beech, birch, alder and willow), in which it gnaws a passage; it also pupates in the wood.

2

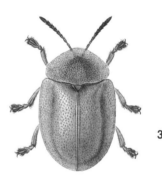

3

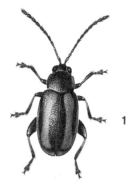

4

1. *Phyllotreta undulata:* 1.8—2.5 mm ($\frac{1}{16}$ — $\frac{3}{32}$ in). Europe, the temperate belt in Asia.
2. *Hispella atra:* 3—4 mm ($\frac{1}{8}$ — $\frac{5}{32}$ in). A large part of the Palaearctic region.
3. *Cassida viridis:* 7—10 mm ($\frac{9}{32}$ — $\frac{13}{32}$ in). The Palaearctic region.
4. *Platystomus albinus:* 6—12 mm ($\frac{1}{4}$ — $\frac{1}{2}$ in). Europe, Asia Minor, Siberia, the Near East.

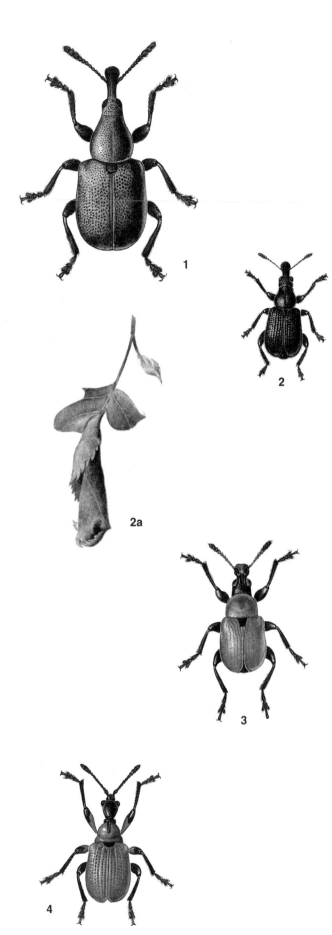

1 *Byctiscus betulae* L. — Attelabidae

2 *Deporaus betulae* L.
Birch Leaf Roller

3 *Attelabus nitens* Scop.
Oak Leaf Roller

4 *Apoderus coryli* L.

Leaf-rollers live on deciduous trees. The females have a very strong protective instinct and 'stitch' a capsule for their eggs from one or more leaves. This protects the egg and provides food for the larva. The capsule then falls from the tree and the larva leaves it and pupates in the ground. Different females make their capsules in different ways.

The female *Byctiscus betulae* makes the capsule from one or more leaves. By drilling the petiole and nibbling the blade in several places she causes the leaf to wilt and then rolls it into a tube containing one to six eggs.

The female Birch Leaf Roller (*Deporaus betulae*) has a different and more complicated technique. On one side of a birch leaf she begins to bite an 'S'-shaped curve which continues to the midrib. She then makes a cut in the midrib and proceeds to the opposite edge of the leaf, all the time damaging the blade with her claws to cause it to wither and make it easier to work with. She then twists the rest of the leaf into a kind of cornet and closes the lower end (2a). In the tissue of the cornet she bites special pockets, each to hold a single egg.

The female Oak Leaf Roller (*Attelabus nitens*) makes her capsules from oak leaves. She makes a cut from the edge to the midrib about one third of the way along the leaf, which she bites, but does not sever; she also chews the blade to make it wither. She then repeats the process on the other side of the leaf, brings the two halves of the leaf together with their upper surfaces facing and rolls the whole into a tube from tip to base. As a rule, the capsule contains only one egg.

Apoderus coryli makes tubular capsules from hazel (and, less often, from oak and birch) leaves and places one or two eggs in each.

1. *Byctiscus betulae:* 4.6—6 mm ($\frac{7}{32}$—$\frac{1}{4}$ in). Europe, Asia Minor, the Near and Middle East, Siberia, northern China.
2. *Deporaus betulae:* 2.5—4 mm ($\frac{3}{32}$—$\frac{5}{32}$ in). Europe, the temperate belt in Asia, northern Africa.
3. *Attelabus nitens:* 4—6 mm ($\frac{5}{32}$—$\frac{1}{4}$ in). Europe, the Caucasus, Asia Minor, the Near and Middle East, Siberia.
4. *Apoderus coryli:* 6—8 mm ($\frac{1}{4}$—$\frac{5}{16}$ in). Europe, the temperate belt in Asia.

1 *Apion apricans* Herbst   Apionidae
2 *Otiorhynchus fuscipes* Oliv.   Curculionidae
3 *Otiorhynchus ligustici* L.

Until quite recently, apionids, like leaf-rollers, were included in the weevil family (Curculionidae). These tiny beetles are very similar to one another in appearance. *Apion apricans* is a common and widespread species inhabiting clover fields from low to high altitudes. The beetles sit on the leaves and bite holes in them. The female lays eggs in clover inflorescences, at the base of the calyx of individual flowers; one inflorescence contains seven to ten eggs and one female, in the course of her lifetime, lays over 200. The larva nibbles the inside of the calyx and the axis of the flower and pupates in the inflorescence. This species forms two generations in southern and central Europe, but only one in northern Europe, where the beetles hibernate twice and sometimes three times.

The members of the weevil genus *Otiorhynchus* are slow walkers. They are also unable to fly and their elytra are joined together along the suture. *Otiorhynchus fuscipes* is a characteristic species of submontane and mountain forests and abounds on all kinds of plants. Neither the beetles nor the larvae are fussy in their choice of host plants.

Otiorhynchus ligustici is likewise polyphagous, but prefers plants belonging to the vetch family, in particular clover and lucerne. It is also to be found in sugar beet fields and on strawberry plants and grapevines. The male beetles are known, but they are very rare and reproduction takes place by parthenogenesis. The female lays 30–50 eggs in the topsoil. The larvae eat small roots. By the autumn they are usually fully grown; they then hibernate and pupate the following year. The beetle remains in the ground and does not appear until it also has hibernated. It occurs in fields, meadows and vineyards from lowlands to mountains.

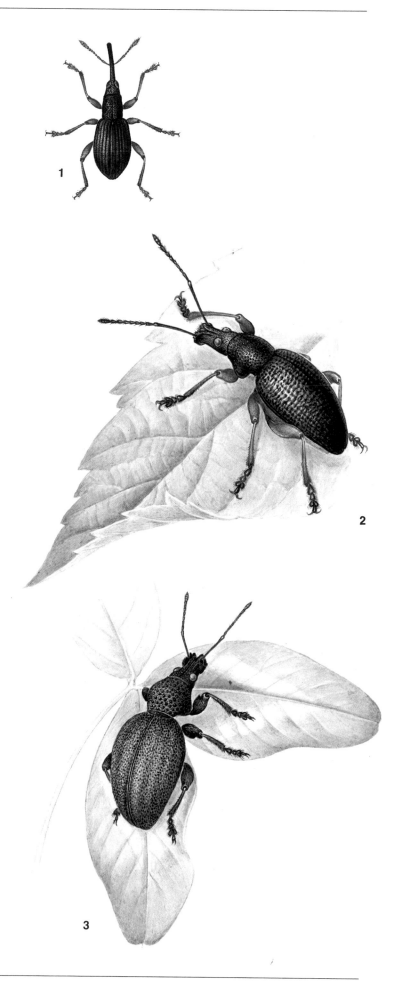

1. *Apion apricans:* 1.9—2.4 mm ($\frac{1}{16}$—$\frac{3}{32}$ in). The Palaearctic region (in Europe beyond the Arctic Circle), the Near and Middle East, northern Africa.
2. *Otiorhynchus fuscipes:* 9—12 mm ($\frac{3}{8}$—$\frac{1}{2}$ in). Central and western Europe.
3. *Otiorhynchus ligustici:* 8—12.5 mm ($\frac{5}{16}$—$\frac{15}{32}$ in). Central and southern Europe, the Caucasus, Transcaucasia, Asia Minor; carried to North America.

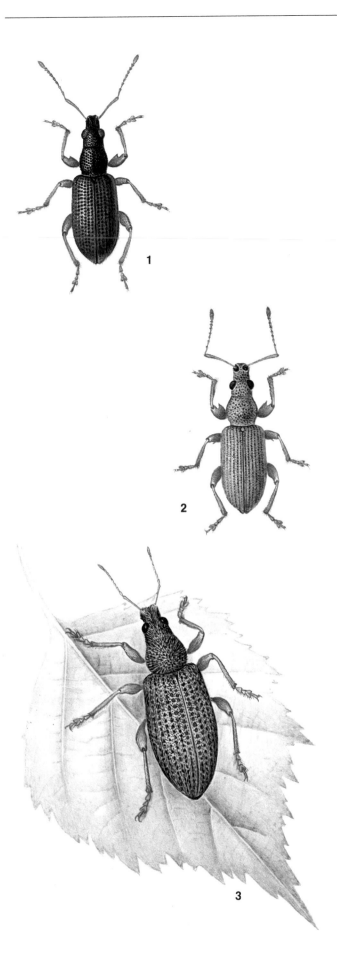

1 ***Phyllobius oblongus*** L. Curculionidae
2 ***Phyllobius argentatus*** L.
3 ***Polydrusus mollis*** Stroem

Phyllobius oblongus is a common beetle found in deciduous woods and gardens in May and June. The rows of long, light-coloured, slanting hairs on its elytra make it easily recognisable. It occurs on many deciduous trees and bushes, including oaks, beeches, maples, limes, bird-cherry, poplars and hawthorn, and in gardens on cherry, pear, apple and apricot trees. The beetles have a healthy appetite and nibble leaves, buds and petals. The female lays the eggs in the ground, several at a time. The larvae live on the roots of various plants (grasses, sorrel and deadnettles) and hibernate before pupating.

Many weevils, even when not related, are green. *Phyllobius argentatus* is one of the most common. It lives in the spring and summer and occurs at low to mountain altitudes. It frequents many ligneous plants, including fruit trees.

Polydrusus mollis is a gleaming, coppery, robust weevil which appears early in the spring as soon as the leaves on the trees begin to sprout. If you examine it with a magnifying glass, you can see the coppery or greenish-grey scales which cover the beetle's body. It inhabits woods, the outskirts of forests and gardens. Occasionally the beetles congregate on birches, hazels, oaks or fruit trees and eat the leaves. The beetles we encounter are mostly females; males are very rare and, like a number of other weevils, this species reproduces parthenogenetically. *Phyllobius pyri* is a similar species but has a tooth on its front femora.

1. *Phyllobius oblongus:* 3.8—5.5 mm ($\frac{5}{32}$—$\frac{1}{4}$ in). Europe, Siberia, northern Africa; carried to North America.
2. *Phyllobius argentatus:* 3.8—5.5 mm ($\frac{5}{32}$—$\frac{1}{4}$ in). Europe, the Caucasus, Siberia, Japan.
3. *Polydrusus mollis:* 6—8.5 mm ($\frac{1}{4}$—$\frac{11}{32}$ in). Europe, Siberia.

1 *Sitona lineatus* L.
Pea Weevil

2 *Hylobius abietis* L.
Large Pine Weevil

3 *Liparus germanus* L.

The Pea Weevil (*Sitona lineatus*) may have light bands down its elytra. It is a pest of pea plants, but it is not monophagous and lives also on vetches, beans and other leguminous plants, where the beetles can be found from May to July. They bite little semi-circles from the leaf edges, leaving them frilly-edged like postage stamps. The female lays her eggs at the base of the plant and on the leaves, either singly or in groups. She is extremely prolific and can lay over 1,000 eggs. The larva burrows in the ground; at first it lives in root nodules on the roots, later on fine rootlets and then, as it grows, on the inner tissues of thick roots, with possible fatal results for the host plant. The larva pupates in the ground in an earthen cell. The young beetles hibernate.

The Large Pine Weevil (*Hylobius abietis*) is common in conifer forests in general and in pinewoods in particular, in lowlands, hills and mountains. For an insect it is long-lived, since it has a life span of three years. The imagos appear in the second half of April and on warm days they fly mainly in the late afternoon and the evening. They eat the fresh inner bark of young shoots and stunt their growth. The female lays the eggs at the roots of fresh stumps, in a hollow she herself has made in the bark. The larva tunnels first in the inner bark and later in the sapwood; it hibernates and does not pupate in the stump until the following year. The beetles hibernate in litter or in moss.

The stout-bodied *Liparus germanus* occurs sporadically from May to July in subalpine and alpine regions. It favours damp localities and you are therefore most likely to find it beside mountain streams and ditches and at the margins of forests. It frequents the leaves of plants which like moisture, such as butterbur, hogweed and wild angelica. The larvae live on roots.

1

2

3

1. *Sitona lineatus:* 3.4—4.7 mm ($\frac{5}{32}$—$\frac{7}{32}$ in). The Palaearctic region; carried to North America.
2. *Hylobius abietis:* 7.3—13.5 mm ($\frac{9}{32}$—$\frac{9}{16}$ in). Europe, the temperate belt in Asia.
3. *Liparus germanus:* 12—15.5 mm ($\frac{1}{2}$—$\frac{5}{8}$ in). Central and western Europe.

1a

1

2

3

1 *Anthonomus pomorum* L.
Apple Blossom Weevil

2 *Furcipus rectirostris* L.

3 *Curculio nucum* L.
Nut Weevil

Clusters of apple blossom often include a few unopened buds with rusty-looking petals (1a). If you carefully remove the petals, you can see in the bud a legless larva about 5–6 mm ($\frac{1}{4}$ in) long, or, if you come a little later, a yellowish pupa. Both belong to the Apple Blossom Weevil (*Anthonomus pomorum*). With patience you might even be able to watch the beetle bite its way out through a hole in the side of the bud. The beetles live on the apple trees for about two to three weeks and then aestivate; in the autumn they retire below bark or into leaves or lichen and hibernate. The female lays her eggs in young flower buds in the spring.

Furcipus rectirostris, on the other hand, is found in wild and cultivated cherries, bird-cherry, blackthorn and other *Prunus* species. The imago leaves its winter quarters early in the spring and lives until June. It eats the leaf tissues and petals. The female lays her eggs in unripe fruit, while the larva penetrates into the stone and eats the kernel; it then pupates in the stone. The imago emerges in July or August, leaves the fruit and retires for the winter at the end of September or the beginning of October.

On the ground under a hazel tree you may occasionally find nuts with a round hole in them, showing that they have been attacked by the Nut Weevil (*Curculio nucum*). The beetles appear on the trees in May and June and bite small holes in the leaves and the young nuts. The eggs are laid in hazelnuts or acorns. The kernel grows normally but is then destroyed by the larva. The nut falls prematurely from the tree; the larva then leaves it, burrows in the ground, hibernates and pupates in the spring at a depth of about 25 cm (10 in). In places where hazels are cultivated, the Nut Weevil can be a serious nuisance.

1. *Anthonomus pomorum:* 3.4—4.3 mm ($\frac{5}{32}$—$\frac{7}{32}$ in). A large part of the Palaearctic region; carried to North America.
2. *Furcipus rectirostris:* 3.7—4.5 mm ($\frac{5}{32}$—$\frac{7}{32}$ in). Large territories in Eurasia as far as Japan.
3. *Curculio nucum:* 5.5—7 mm ($\frac{1}{4}$—$\frac{5}{16}$ in). A large part of the Palaearctic region.

1 *Pissodes castaneus* De Geer Curculionidae

2 *Sitophilus granarius* L.
Granary Weevil

3 *Ceutorhynchus assimilis* Payk.

4 *Cionus scrophulariae* L.

Pissodes castaneus is a weevil which develops and lives in pinewoods at lowish altitudes. It is mostly to be found on Scots pines, but develops equally well on other pine species. From the spring to the autumn the imagos nibble the buds and the young shoots. The female lays her eggs in young trees: she makes grooves in the bark at the base of the trunks and lays a few eggs in each. The larva gnaws a winding passage between the bark and the wood and pupates in a chamber at the end. The beetles have a life span of up to four years and overwinter in leaf litter.

Products which need to be stored have a great many pests. The Granary Weevil (*Sitophilus granarius*), one of the most common, abounds in grain stores and mills. The larva develops in the actual grain, devours its contents and then pupates in it. The number of generations depends mainly on the temperature; in central Europe there are two or three, but in the south there are more.

Ceutorhynchus assimilis is a very common pest of wild and cultivated cruciferous plants, including kohlrabi, oilseed rape, charlock, white mustard and radishes. The beetles eat small holes in the plant's organs. The larva lives in the fructifications, but pupates a little way down in the ground.

Cionus scrophulariae is to be found wherever figwort grows – in clearings, on hillsides and beside forest tracks. The slime-covered larvae bite holes in the leaves. The pupa, which is enclosed in a cocoon and is attached to a plant, resembles a figwort seed pod.

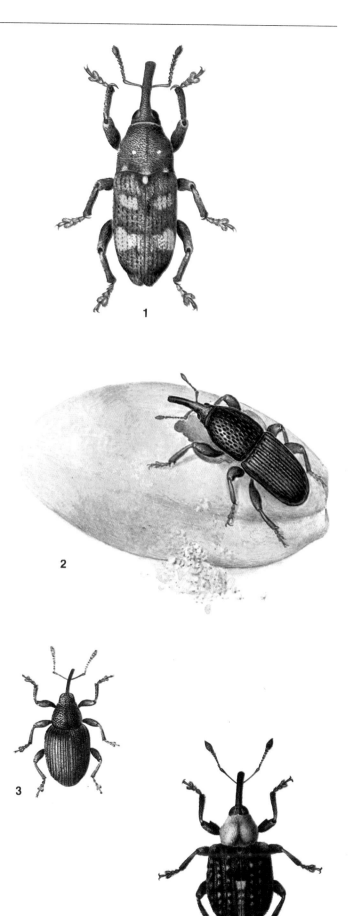

1. *Pissodes castaneus:* 4.5—7.2 mm ($\frac{7}{32}$—$\frac{9}{32}$ in). Europe (beyond the Arctic Circle), Siberia, northern Africa.
2. *Sitophilus granarius:* 3—4 mm ($\frac{1}{8}$—$\frac{3}{16}$ in). Over the whole globe.
3. *Ceutorhynchus assimilis:* 1.9—2.8 mm ($\frac{1}{16}$—$\frac{1}{8}$ in). Europe, the Caucasus, the Near East, northern Africa; carried to North America.
4. *Cionus scrophulariae:* 3.9—5 mm ($\frac{3}{16}$—$\frac{1}{4}$ in). Europe, the Caucasus, Asia Minor; carried to North America.

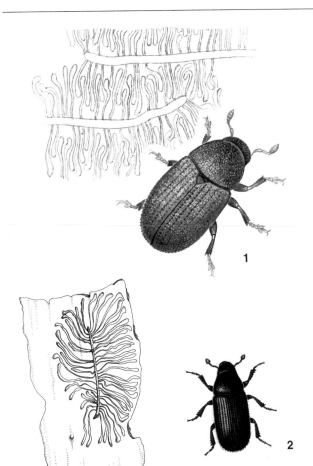

1 *Hylesinus fraxini* Panz.   Scolytidae

2 *Tomicus piniperda* L.
Large Pine Shoot Beetle

3 *Ips typographus* L.
Engraver Beetle, Spruce Bark Beetle

4 *Xenos vesparum* Rossi   Stylopidae

Female bark and ambrosia beetles construct passages for their offspring under bark or in wood. This system of maternal and larval tunnels or galleries is often so characteristic that it tells us which species made it.

Hylesinus fraxini lives on ash trees (*Fraxinus* is the generic name of the ash). It makes a light cross-gallery in freshly felled trees, fresh stumps and the branches of old trees, with densely arranged larval passages projecting from it on either side. The young beetles, which appear at the end of June and the beginning of July, excavate passages in the branches of young trees until they reach sexual maturity.

The galleries of the Large Pine Shoot Beetle (*Tomicus piniperda*) have a completely different appearance. This is a monogamous species, with one female to one male. It settles in felled pines, pine stumps and diseased standing trees. In the pre-maturity phase, the beetles fly to the crowns of the trees, where they eat passages a few centimetres long in young twigs.

The Engraver Beetle (*Ips typographus*) develops primarily in trees damaged by gales or weakened by some other pest. It attacks healthy trees only in times of a mass incidence. Its host plant is a spruce tree of at least 60–70 years old. The beetle is polygamous. The male excavates a nuptial chamber and is then joined by two or more females. The number of females determines the appearance of the maternal passage; if there are two, one passage leads upwards from the nuptial chamber and the other downwards. The larval galleries lead bilaterally from the maternal passage, at right angles to it. The young beetles develop in the phloem.

A small, scale-like structure can sometimes be seen protruding between the abdominal segments of wasps belonging to the genus *Polistes*. The 'scale' is a female beetle of the species *Xenos vesparum*, which has wingless females, but winged males.

Gallery of *Tomicus piniperda* larvae

Xenos vesparum (male)

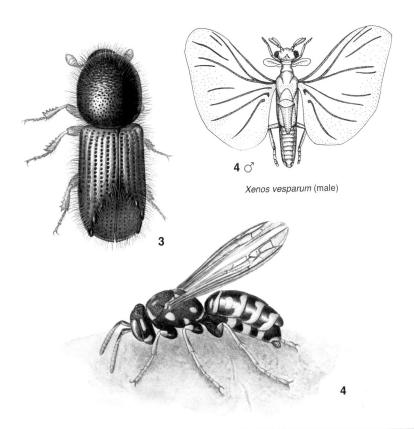

1. *Hylesinus fraxini:* 2.5—3.5 mm ($\frac{3}{32}$—$\frac{5}{32}$ in). A large part of Europe.
2. *Tomicus piniperda:* 3.5—5.8 mm ($\frac{5}{32}$—$\frac{1}{4}$ in). The Palaearctic region (in Europe right to the north and in the Mediterranean region).
3. *Ips typographus:* 4.2—5.5 mm ($\frac{3}{16}$—$\frac{1}{4}$ in). Europe, the temperate belt in Asia.
4. *Xenos vesparum:* ♂ 3 mm, ♀ 7—9 mm (♂ $\frac{1}{8}$ in, ♀ $\frac{9}{32}$—$\frac{3}{8}$ in). Europe (up to 50 ° latitude north).

1 *Acantholyda erythrocephala* L. Pamphiliidae
2 *Cephalcia abietis* L.
3 *Sirex juvencus* L. Siricidae

The two members of the family Pamphiliidae depicted here live in different types of woods. *Acantholyda erythrocephala* inhabits young pine woods, while *Cephalcia abietis* occurs in old spruce woods. There are colour differences between the sexes in both species, but they are more pronounced in *A. erythrocephala*, in which the females have a red head and the males a blue head.

A. erythrocephala imagos fly from the end of April to the beginning of May. The female lays her eggs in pine needles. The larvae all live together in a web nest, feeding on the pine needles, until they measure about 20 mm ($\frac{13}{16}$ in) long. Then they leave the nest, burrow in the ground and pupate there in a chamber. The development of this species takes one to three years.

Cephalcia abietis imagos may appear in the middle of June, depending on local conditions. The female, which is usually fertilised by several males, lays about a hundred eggs on spruce needles in the crown of the tree. The larvae live gregariously on a branch, in a web nest in which they deposit their exuviae and their faeces. When fully grown they burrow deep in the ground, where they live for one to two years in an earthen cell before pupating.

The life of large horntails is bound up with conifer forests. Some species, such as *Sirex juvencus*, favour pine woods, where the imagos can be seen in clearings on sunny days. The female, which is differently coloured from the male, lays her eggs in dry wood which has been damaged by some pest, weather or fire. At the same time as laying the eggs, she introduces fungal spores into the wood; as the larva tunnels, the spores germinate. The fungi break down the wood and the larvae can then digest it more easily. When fully grown, the larva returns towards the surface of the wood and pupates just below it. Its development takes two to three years.

1 ♀

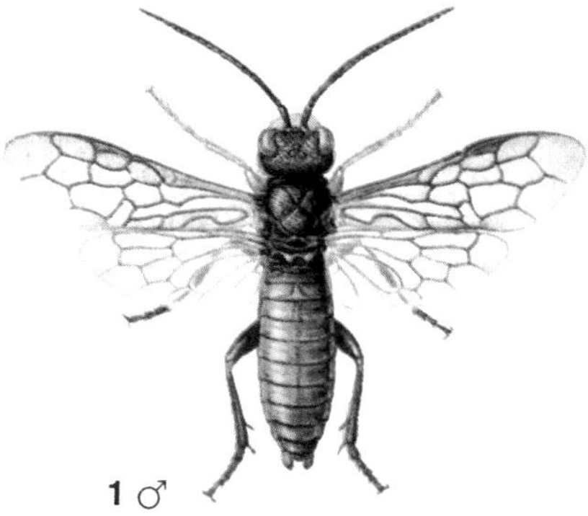

1 ♂

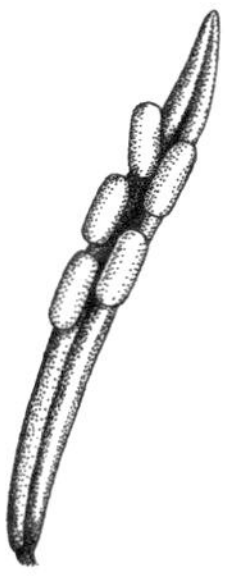

Eggs of *Cephalcia abietis* on a spruce needle

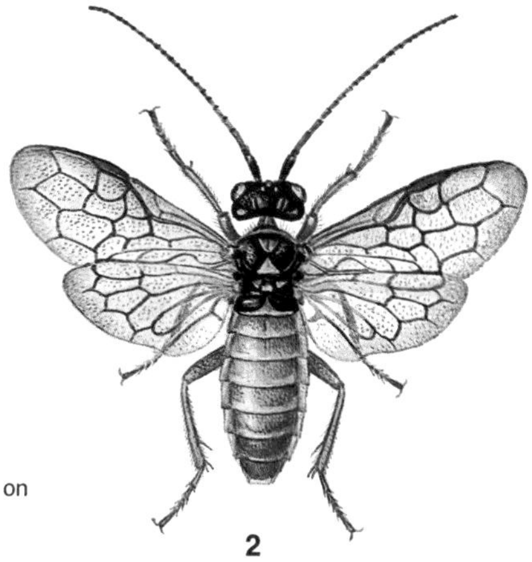

2

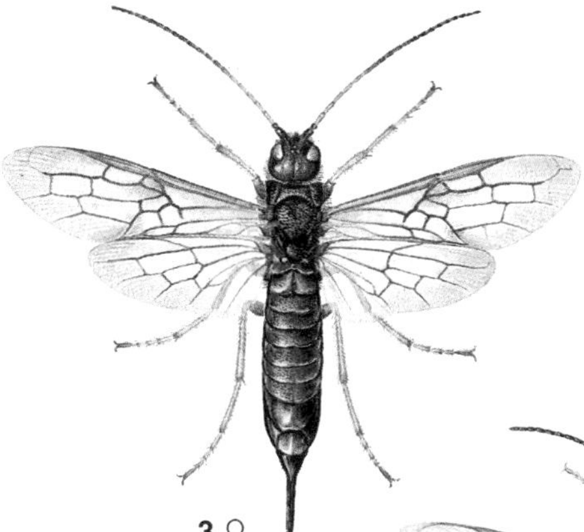

3 ♀

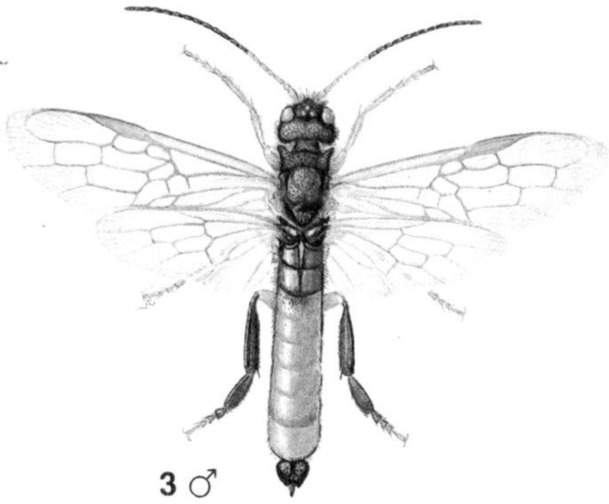

3 ♂

1. *Acantholyda erythrocephala:* 10—12 mm, wing span 20—26 mm ($\frac{3}{8}$—$\frac{1}{2}$ in, wing span $\frac{13}{16}$—$1\frac{1}{16}$ in). Europe; carried to North America.
2. *Cephalcia abietis:* ♂ 11 mm, ♀ 14 mm (♂ $\frac{7}{16}$ in, ♀ $\frac{9}{16}$ in). Central and northern Europe, Siberia, northern China.
3. *Sirex juvencus:* ♂ 12—28 mm, ♀ 15—30 mm (♂ $\frac{1}{2}$—$1\frac{1}{8}$ in, ♀ $\frac{5}{8}$—$1\frac{3}{16}$ in). A large part of Europe, the temperate belt in Asia, northern Africa; carried to Australia.

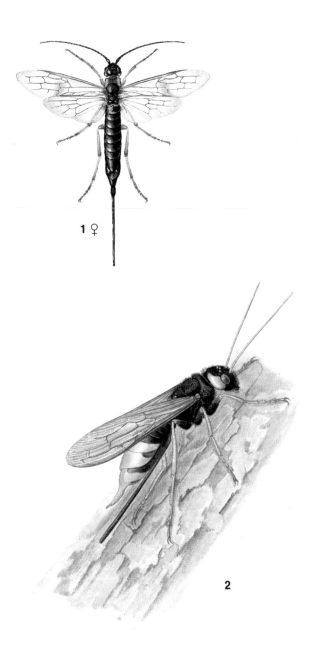

1 ♀

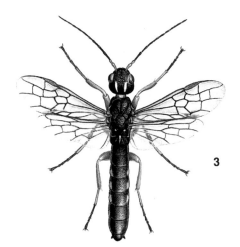

3

1 *Xeris spectrum* L.   Siricidae

2 *Urocerus gigas* L.
Giant Horntail

3 *Xiphydria camelus* L.   Xiphydriidae

In addition to the larvae of *Sirex juvencus,* conifer forests are also inhabited by the larvae of several other large wasps, the most common of which are *Xeris spectrum* and *Urocerus gigas.* The former lives mainly in pine woods. When laying eggs, the female makes use of cracks in the trunks. The larva, which tunnels in the wood, feeds on cellulose. It also over-winters in the wood. The total development of this species takes two to three years.

In size and colouring, the Giant Horntail (*Urocerus gigas*) resembles a hornet. It is one of the largest members of the family and one of the largest European hymenopterans in general. Its 'waspish' colouring is sometimes a disadvantage, since it is often persecuted and killed by ignorant human beings. It does not sting, however, and is only very distantly related to the Hor-net. This handsome forest species frequents light, sun-ny places where freshly felled, undecorticated coni-fers are to be found. In these, and in diseased standing trunks, the female progressively lays 50 –350 eggs at a depth of only 5–10 mm ($\frac{3}{16} - \frac{3}{8}$ in). As in the preced-ing species, the larva tunnels in the wood and lives on cellulose. When fully grown it returns towards the surface of the wood and pupates there. The imago leaves the trunk through a round opening. Horntails (or wood wasps) also appear quite frequently in timber yards or in stocks of firewood. The larvae of this (and other) horntails have a serious enemy in the parasitic larvae of the ichneumon fly *Rhyssa persuasoria.*

Xiphydria camelus is probably the best known species of the small Xiphydriidae family. It lives in growths of deciduous trees and the larvae develop in the wood of alders and birches.

1. *Xeris spectrum:* 30 mm (1$\frac{3}{16}$ in). A large part of Europe, Siberia, China, Japan.
2. *Urocerus gigas:* ♂12—32 mm, ♀ 24—44 mm (♂ $\frac{1}{2}$—1$\frac{1}{4}$ in, ♀ $\frac{15}{16}$—1$\frac{3}{4}$ in). A large part of Europe, the temperate belt in Asia, northern Africa.
3. *Xiphydria camelus:* 10—21 mm ($\frac{3}{8}$—$\frac{13}{16}$ in). Europe, the temperate belt in Asia.

1 *Arge ochropus* Gmelin
Argidae
2 *Cimbex luteus* L.
Cimbicidae
3 *Cimbex femoratus* L.
Birch Sawfly

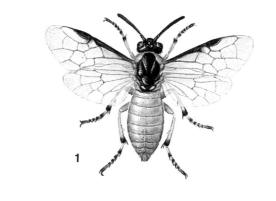

Arge ochropus is a frequent species among the many insects which visit flowering Umbelliferae. It is to be found here from the spring to the height of summer, since it produces two generations a year. The imagos of the first generation appear in May and those of the second generation in July and August. The larvae develop on roses. The female lays eggs in a row on a young shoot of a briar rose or cultivated rose bush, where they lie on the twig like a long chain. The larvae live on the leaves and when they measure about 20 mm ($\frac{13}{16}$ in) they retire underground and pupate.

Cimbicid sawflies (Cimbicidae) are a small, but very distinctive hymenopteran family whose members can be recognised by their club-tipped antennae and their general appearance. The two species depicted here – *Cimbex luteus* and *C. femoratus* – represent two colour extremes, the former being yellow and black and the latter black. Both species live in close association with deciduous trees and reproduce in a similar manner. The female lays her eggs in a leaf; with her ovipositor she makes a kind of pocket in the leaf, inside which the egg is protected from predators and bad weather. The larvae live on the leaves and eat their tissues; in the case of *C. luteus* they are willow and poplar leaves and in the case of *C. femoratus* birch leaves. The imagos feed on juices they obtain from the branches. The fully grown larva is plump and up to 40 mm ($1\frac{9}{16}$ in) long or more. It wraps itself in a large cocoon for the winter and does not pupate until the following spring. The pupal stage is very short and the imagos live only a few days.

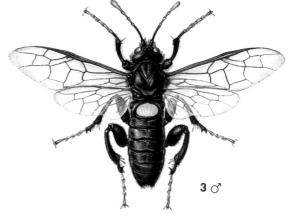

1. *Arge ochropus:* 7—10 mm ($\frac{9}{32}$—$\frac{13}{32}$ in). The whole of Europe, Siberia, Asia Minor.
2. *Cimbex luteus:* 16—25 mm ($\frac{5}{8}$—1 in). A large part of the Palaearctic region.
3. *Cimbex femoratus:* 16—25 mm ($\frac{5}{8}$—1 in). The whole of Europe, Siberia.

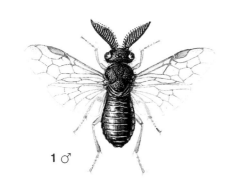

1 ♂

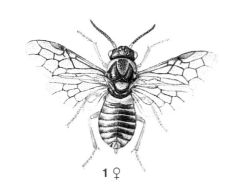

1 ♀

Eggs of the Pine Sawfly (*Diprion pini*) on a pine needle

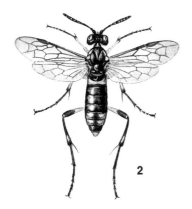

2

1 *Diprion pini* L.   Diprionidae
Pine Sawfly

2 *Macrophya montana* Scop.   Tenthredinidae

Not so very long ago the Pine Sawfly (*Diprion pini*) was still considered to be a pest of pine woods. Its incidence today is very sporadic, however, and in many localities it has disappeared altogether. The male and the female are differently coloured and have different antennae. This species occurs in young pine woods struggling for existence on a poor soil. It may form one or two generations in a year (June–July or April–May and July–August). Before laying the eggs, the female makes an incision in a pine needle with her ovipositor and deposits up to twenty eggs in it. The larvae live on the needles gregariously. They first of all nibble the sides of the needles, leaving the main rib intact; later they eat the whole of the needles and sometimes gnaw the bark of the young shoots. The larva is relatively large compared with the imago and when fully grown measures up to 26 mm ($1\frac{1}{16}$ in); it then wraps itself in a tubby brown cocoon and afterwards pupates inside it. The pupae of the first generation are usually to be found in cracks in the bark and those of the second generation in the ground at the foot of the tree.

The typical sawflies (Tenthredinidae) are a very large family comprising small and moderately large species, most of which have short antennae with only a small number of segments. The antennae are serrate (toothed), plumate (feathery) or clavate (club-tipped). In the spring and summer sawflies regularly visit the inflorescences of umbelliferous plants. Many species are harmless, but others are of some, but not serious, importance as pests. *Macrophya montana* is one of the indifferent species. The femora of its hindlegs are strikingly long and are the same length as the tibiae. Several dozen other related species live in Europe.

1. *Diprion pini:* ♂ 7—8 mm, ♀ 7.5—10 mm (♂ $\frac{9}{32}$ in, ♀ $\frac{5}{16}$—$\frac{3}{8}$ in). A large part of Europe, northern Africa.
2. *Macrophya montana:* 10—12 mm ($\frac{3}{8}$—$\frac{1}{2}$ in). The whole of Europe, Asia Minor, northern Africa.

1 *Tenthredo campestris* L.
2 *Tenthredo zonula* Klug.
3 *Tenthredo amoena* Grav.

Tenthredinidae

Tenthredo campestris (formerly often described under the name *T. flavicornis*) is one of the commonest, largest and most strikingly coloured sawflies. From May to August the imagos visit the flowers of all kinds of herbaceous plants and shrubs in meadows and gardens and sit on the leaves. An excessive spread of goutweed (*Aegopodium podagraria*), the host plant of the larvae, leads to a high incidence of this sawfly. The full-grown larvae, which are about 20 mm ($\frac{13}{16}$ in) long, retire underground, make a cocoon for themselves and pupate in it.

In many hymenopteran families, but also in other insect orders, such as beetles and two-winged flies, there are quite a few species whose combined dark and yellow colouring is reminiscent of wasps. Among sawflies there are also a number of species which no doubt benefit from this 'waspish' colouring. Animals, especially insectivorous birds, which have had unpleasant experiences with true wasps will give any creature with these striking markings a wide berth. *Tenthredo zonula* is one of these wasp-like species. The male and female differ as regards the proportion of yellow on their abdomen (the female has more yellow segments than the male). The imagos are common everywhere on grass verges and in meadows and they regularly visit the inflorescences of umbelliferous plants. The larvae live on St John's Wort. The black and yellow colouring of *Tenthredo amoena*, another typical sawfly, is even more vivid. This species occurs during the summer in quite large numbers in similar localities to the preceding species and the two are often found together.

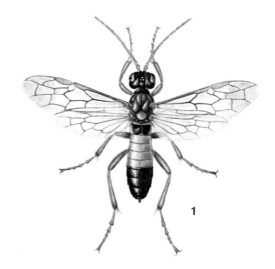

1

2

3

1. *Tenthredo campestris:* 13—14 mm ($\frac{9}{16}$ in). Practically the whole of Europe.
2. *Tenthredo zonula:* 9—10 mm ($\frac{3}{8}$ in). Europe, Asia Minor, northern Africa.
3. *Tenthredo amoena:* 10—12 mm ($\frac{3}{8}$—$\frac{1}{2}$ in). Central, southern and western Europe.

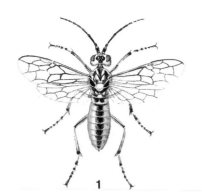

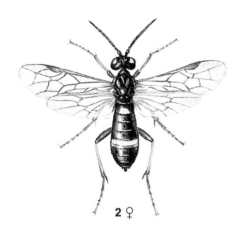

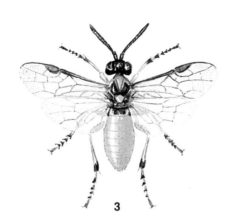

1 *Rhogogaster viridis* L. Tenthredinidae

2 *Allantus cinctus* L.

3 *Athalia rosae* L.
Turnip Sawfly

In Europe several species are coloured similarly to *Rhogogaster viridis*. The imagos of this species fly over meadows and grass verges and settle on shrubs and herbaceous plants; they prey on various other insects. The larvae are phytophagous and live on the leaf tissues of trees and herbaceous plants.

The imagos of *Allantus cinctus* sit on or near rose bushes. The females lay their eggs on rose leaves (but sometimes on strawberry leaves) and the larvae develop on them and eat them. When at rest, the larvae lie coiled up on the leaves, but if they are disturbed they drop to the ground. When fully grown, they do not retire underground as most other sawflies do, but penetrate a twig and bite out a short passage inside it. The larvae sometimes leave the host plant and pupate in cracks in walls and fences. This species produces two generations in a year.

The Turnip Sawfly (*Athalia rosae*) is a regular member of the fauna of flowering Umbelliferae, Cruciferae and Compositae. The imagos are often to be seen from the spring until late in the autumn, according to how many generations there are. There are usually two generations, but sometimes there may be three or even four. The imagos gather pollen and nectar, but are not very active. The female lays about 300 eggs on wild and cultivated Cruciferae. With her ovipositor she separates the upper and lower surface of a leaf at its edge and lays a single egg in the resultant cavity. At first the larvae live in a passage inside the leaf and then on the underside of the blade, which they perforate in different places. Lastly, they are to be seen at the edge of the leaves and on their upper surfaces. They pupate in the ground in a silk-lined earthen cocoon.

1. *Rhogogaster viridis:* 10—13 mm ($\frac{3}{8}$—$\frac{9}{16}$ in). A large part of the Palaearctic region.
2. *Allantus cinctus:* 7—10 mm ($\frac{9}{32}$—$\frac{3}{8}$ in). Europe, Siberia; carried to North America.
3. *Athalia rosae:* 6—8 mm ($\frac{1}{4}$—$\frac{5}{16}$ in). Eurasia, northern and southern Africa, South America.

196

1 *Phymatocera aterrima* Klug   Tenthredinidae
Solomon's Seal Sawfly

2 *Blennocampa pusilla* Klug

3 *Caliroa cerasi* L.

The slow-flying Solomon's Seal Sawfly (*Phymatocera aterrima*), which closely resembles a true fly, appears early in the spring on and near wild and cultivated Solomon's seal and lily-of-the-valley. The imagos soon disappear, but not long afterwards the greyish-blue, long-bodied larvae appear on the leaves, in which they bite holes and sever the ribs. The holes grow larger and larger, until all that is left of the leaf are the main veins. The full-grown larva pupates in the ground.

Blennocampa pusilla is another sawfly which frequents roses. It is inconspicuous, dark and very small. In May and June, if you fail to find the imagos, twisted rose leaves – the work of the larvae – are a sure sign of its presence. The young larvae roll the leaf up from the edge towards the main rib, forming a tube housing one or two larvae. The larvae eat the leaf tissue and when they are fully grown they leave the plant and retire underground. Here they form a cocoon in which, after hibernating, they pupate. This is a common species, and it is very unpopular with gardeners because of the way it spoils the appearance of rose bushes.

Like the preceding species, *Caliroa cerasi* can be traced more easily by its larvae, which live on the leaves of cherry, apple, rowan and other deciduous trees. The young larva looks like a slug and is covered with a slimy substance smelling strongly of ink. The last larval instar, however, does not secrete any slime; it leaves the host plant and, a little way down in the soil, spins a cocoon for itself and pupates in it. The larvae also make themselves conspicuous by reducing the upper surface of the leaves to a skeleton. *C. cerasi* produces two generations in a year and can be a pest, according to the circumstances.

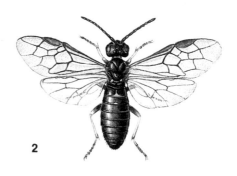

1 ♀

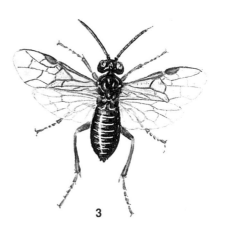

2

3

---

1. *Phymatocera aterrima:* 8—9 mm ($\frac{5}{16}$—$\frac{3}{8}$ in). Chiefly central and southern Europe.
2. *Blennocampa pusilla:* 4 mm ($\frac{5}{32}$ in). A large part of the Palaearctic region.
3. *Caliroa cerasi:* 5 mm ($\frac{3}{16}$ in). Over practically the whole globe.

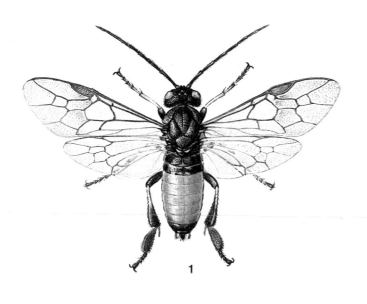

1

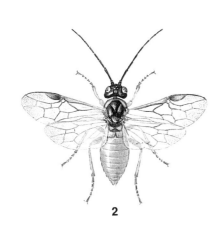

2

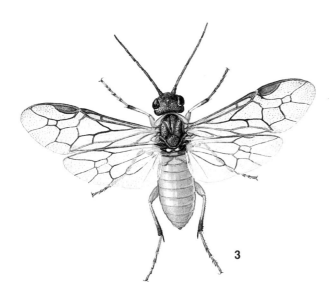

3

1 *Croesus septentrionalis* L.   Tenthredinidae
2 *Trichiocampus viminalis* Fall.
3 *Nematus ribesii* Scop.

The larvae of *Croesus septentrionalis* are far more conspicuous than the imagos. They are brightly coloured and live mostly (though not solely) on birch and alder leaves, the edges of which they nibble. If disturbed, they are instantly on the alert, holding their bodies stiffly erect like question marks. If that is not sufficient warning, they all begin to sway. The imagos fly during May. The larvae pupate in the soil.

In May, *Trichiocampus viminalis* can often be encountered in poplar avenues. The female lays her eggs in the petioles and the malodorous larvae live on the leaves. The larvae have a collective instinct which causes them to live gregariously. Sometimes they appear on the leaves in such numbers that the tree is stripped bare. When they have attained a length of about 20 mm ($\frac{13}{16}$ in), they creep into cracks in the bark, wrap themselves in cocoons and pupate.

One might say that every deciduous tree or shrub has its typical sawfly. *Nematus ribesii* is common on red currants and gooseberries, for example. Since it produces several generations in a year, you will come across it from the spring to the autumn. The imagos of the first generation emerge in the spring and fly about in gardens during April. The female lays her eggs in the veins on the undersides of leaves. After slitting the tissue with her ovipositor, she lays a few eggs in it in a row, leaving them partly protruding; in all she lays about 50 eggs. The larvae consume large amounts of leaf tissue and are so voracious that the bushes are sometimes stripped. When fully grown they disappear underground, wrap themselves in a blackish-brown cocoon and then pupate in it.

1. *Croesus septentrionalis:* 7—10 mm ($\frac{9}{32}$—$\frac{13}{32}$ in). The whole of Europe.
2. *Trichiocampus viminalis:* 9 mm ($\frac{3}{8}$ in). Central and northern Europe.
3. *Nematus ribesii:* 14—16 mm ($\frac{9}{16}$—$\frac{5}{8}$ in). Central and northern Europe; carried to North America.

1 *Rhyssa persuasoria* L. Ichneumonidae
Giant Ichneumon Fly, Persuasive Burglar

2 *Megarhyssa superba* Schr.

The Giant Ichneumon Fly (*Rhyssa persuasoria*) is one of the biggest ichneumon flies in Europe. Like several others of its kind it inhabits spruce woods. The imagos fly at the edges of the woods and in clearings with felled timber on the ground. The female can be distinguished from the male by her long, thin ovipositor. Her senses are remarkable. She runs over a trunk, stops from time to time, feeling it with her antennae, and then, at a given spot, makes a longer pause. That is because she has detected a large horntail or wood wasp larva in the wood, which she needs as food for her future brood. Without wasting time, she thrusts her thin, flexible, but strong ovipositor into the wood, aiming it slowly, but surely, at the body of the larva, which as yet has no idea of the fate awaiting it. Oviposition takes about half an hour. This is a critical time for the female ichneumon fly, because in the event of danger she would be unable to withdraw the ovipositor quickly and fly away. An egg is deposited on the sawfly larva and when the ichneumon fly larva is hatched it slowly consumes the body of its still living host until practically nothing is left. The ichneumon fly larva overwinters in the wood and pupates in the spring. There is only one generation in a year. In the spring, when the imagos emerge, the males appear a few days sooner and wait for the females.

Unlike the Giant Ichneumon Fly, *Megarhyssa superba* inhabits deciduous woods. The female of this species looks for horntail and sawfly larvae of the families Siricidae and Xiphydriidae (usually the species *Xiphydria camelus* and *Tremex fuscicornis*) as food for its brood. The larvae of *M. superba* are also ectoparasites, i.e. they live on the surface of their host's body and slowly work their way inwards. The present decrease in the number of large wood wasps and sawflies means that the number of these handsome ichneumon flies is also diminishing.

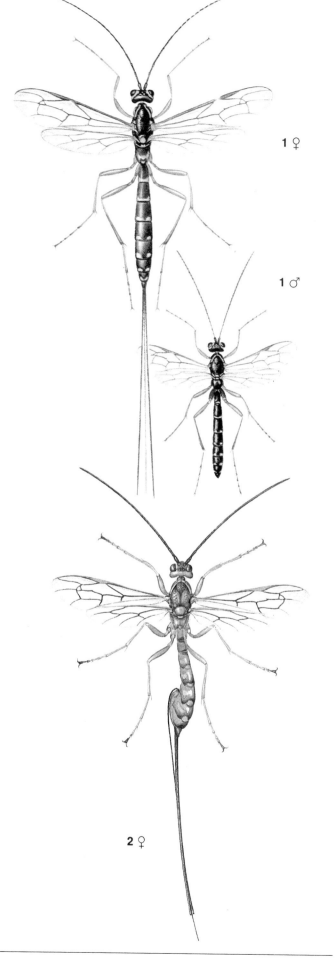

1 ♀

1 ♂

2 ♀

1. *Rhyssa persuasoria:* 18—40 mm, ♀ plus ovipositor up to 80 mm ($\frac{3}{4}$—1$\frac{9}{16}$ in, ♀ plus ovipositor up to 3$\frac{1}{3}$ in). The Palaearctic and Nearctic regions.
2. *Megarhyssa superba:* 19—34 mm, ♀ plus ovipositor up to 90 mm ($\frac{3}{4}$—1$\frac{3}{8}$ in, ♀ plus ovipositor up to 3$\frac{9}{16}$ in). Europe, the temperate belt in Asia.

1 *Pimpla instigator* F.   Ichneumonidae

2 *Enicospilus ramidulus* L.

3 *Amblyteles armatorius* Först.

Marked individual differences in body length among insects are determined by the nutritional value of the food consumed by the larva during growth. In some groups of insects these differences are negligible, but in ichneumon flies they are considerable. In the species *Pimpla instigator,* the smallest specimens measure only 10 mm ($\frac{3}{8}$ in), but the largest can be 25 mm (1 in). This black ichneumon fly lives in forests and, like other species, smells of asphalt. The imagos live on flowers, but are also tempted by living insects. The female in particular has no difficulty in sucking haemolymph from pupae stabbed by her ovipositor. Lepidopteran pupae are also of prime importance for the nutrition of her offspring, since they are the food of the larvae. The female is not particular as regards the species of the pupa, but she must be sure that it is sufficiently nutritious and that it will last the larva for the whole of its development. She therefore usually lays her eggs in pupae of species such as the Lackey Moth (*Malacosoma neustria*) and the Gypsy Moth (*Lymantria dispar*), and sometimes in the pupae of cimbicid sawflies (Cimbicidae). For oviposition she needs a temperature of over 20 °C (70 °F). The imagos overwinter, often together, under the bark of trees and logs.

A great many ichneumon flies are rusty-brown and have flat-sided bodies, so that at first glance they all look the same and are difficult to identify. *Enicospilus ramidulus* has two rust-coloured spots on its first pair of wings. Its larvae live on the caterpillars of the Pine Beauty (*Panolis flammea*).

The male and female of many ichneumon flies are often different in colour. In the species *Amblyteles armatorius* this is the case with the abdomen and limbs. In the summer the imagos occur on flowers. The larvae live on the caterpillars of various owlet moths (Noctuidae). The female hibernates.

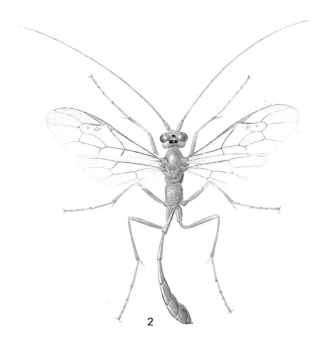

1 ♀

2

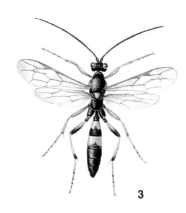

3

1. *Pimpla instigator:* 10—25 mm ($\frac{3}{8}$—1 in). The Palaearctic region.
2. *Enicospilus ramidulus:* 18—20 mm ($\frac{3}{4}$—$\frac{13}{16}$ in). The central and southern part of the Palaearctic region.
3. *Amblyteles armatorius:* 12—16 mm ($\frac{1}{2}$—$\frac{5}{8}$ in). A large part of the Palaearctic region.

1 *Spathius exarator* L. Braconidae
2 *Apanteles glomeratus* L.
3 *Biorhiza pallida* Ol. Cynipidae

Spathius exarator is to be found from spring to autumn in dwellings with old, worm-eaten floorboards, old doorposts and furniture; if there is central heating it will be found there the whole year round. It flies and settles on furniture, walls and window-panes. The larvae can develop only in wood attacked by woodworm (in particular the larvae of *Anobium punctatum*). The few eggs are minute in size, but compared with the size of the female they are huge; the female deposits them beside a woodworm larva, which she stuns with her ovipositor. The braconid larva lives on the body of the woodworm and consumes almost all of it; it then pupates in the wood in a cocoon.

In years with an abundance of Cabbage White butterflies (*Pieris brassicae*), groups of yellow silky cocoons appear in the vicinity of its motionless caterpillars. They belong to *Apanteles glomeratus*, whose female lays 15–50 eggs in a living caterpillar. The larvae begin to eat the contents of the caterpillar's body while it is still alive. As a rule, however, the caterpillar eventually leaves its host plant, comes to rest on a fence or a wall and stops moving. The fully grown larvae crawl out through small holes in its body, wrap themselves in a cocoon and hibernate. This braconid is a good regulator of the Cabbage White population – unless, of course, it is destroyed by insecticides.

Biorhiza pallida is not one of the best known gallwasps, but its galls attract attention. During its complex development it forms two generations, each of which has a different gall. The one shown here grows on oak branches. It is called an oak apple. This type gives rise in the summer to males and females. The fertilised females burrow in the ground and lay their eggs on oak roots, where the other type of gall is formed. These galls give rise in the following winter to agamous (parthenogenetic) females, which produce the first type of gall on the branches, thereby completing the cycle.

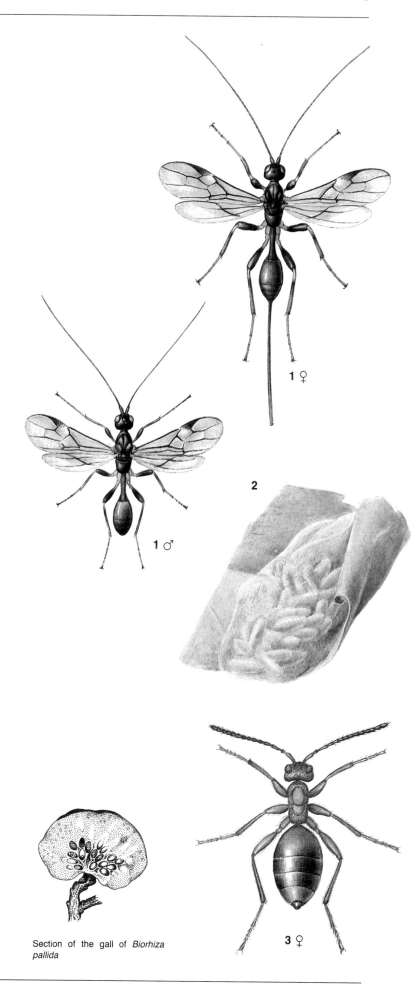

1 ♀

1 ♂

2

Section of the gall of *Biorhiza pallida*

3 ♀

1. *Spathius exarator:* 5—9 mm ($\frac{3}{16}$—$\frac{3}{8}$ in). A large part of Europe.
2. *Apanteles glomeratus:* 3—4 mm ($\frac{1}{8}$—$\frac{5}{32}$ in). Europe; introduced into North America.
3. *Biorhiza pallida:* branch gall: 20—40 mm, root gall about 5 mm; the agamous ♀ 3.5—6 mm, in the summer generation ♂ 1.9—2.3 mm, ♀ 1.7—2.8 mm (branch gall $\frac{13}{16}$—$1\frac{9}{16}$ in, root gall about $\frac{3}{16}$ in; the agamous ♀ $\frac{5}{32}$—$\frac{1}{4}$ in, in the summer generation ♂ $\frac{1}{16}$ in, ♀ $\frac{1}{16}$—$\frac{3}{32}$ in). A large part of Europe, Asia Minor, northern Africa.

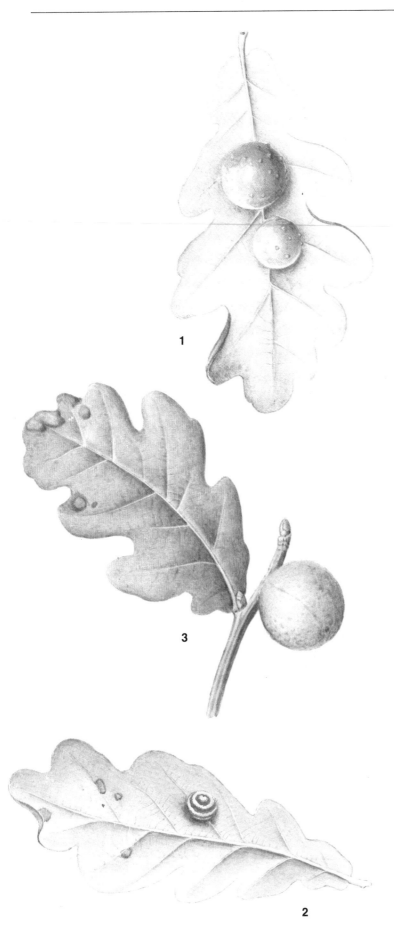

1 *Cynips quercusfolii* L.   Cynipidae
2 *Cynips longiventris* Hart.
3 *Andricus kollari* Hart.

From the height of summer to autumn the spherical galls of *Cynips quercusfolii* can be seen on the undersides of oak leaves, where they are joined to the veins by a short stalk. They are often called cherry galls. Initially green, they later turn yellow or reddish. Each gall contains a chamber with a single gall-wasp developing in it. The larva lives on the tissues of the gall; the gall-wasp (always a female) emerges in the winter. Without being fertilised, these females lay eggs in dormant buds on oak branches and trunks and the small velvety galls which develop at the places where they have laid them give rise in May and June to males and females. The fertilised females lay eggs on the undersides of oak leaves, where the spherical galls are formed again. Both generations develop in the same year.

Cynips longiventris develops similarly to the previous species but its galls are quite differently coloured, although they likewise grow on oak leaves.

Andricus kollari also forms two types of galls and two generations, but it is also known to change its host plant. Its striking spherical galls, which are hard when they mature, grow on oak twigs. They are called marble galls. A single female develops in the gall and leaves it at the end of the summer through a round hole; this female, which is agamous and unfertilised, lays eggs on Turkey oak, where another type of gall – a tiny bud gall – is formed. In April and May, imagos of both sexes emerge from these galls. These females, which are fertilised, lay eggs in common oak buds and thereby initiate formation of the first type of gall.

---

1. *Cynips quercusfolii:* $\varnothing$ of leaf gall 10—20 mm, length of bud gall about 3 mm; the agamous $\female$ 3.4—4 mm, in the sexual generation $\male$ 2—2.5 mm, $\female$ 2.3—2.7 mm ($\varnothing$ of leaf gall $\frac{3}{8}$—$\frac{13}{16}$ in, of bud gall about $\frac{1}{8}$ in; the agamous $\female$ $\frac{5}{32}$—$\frac{3}{16}$ in, in the sexual generation $\male$ $\frac{1}{16}$—$\frac{3}{32}$ in, $\female$ $\frac{1}{16}$ in). Europe, Asia Minor.
2. *Cynips longiventris:* $\varnothing$ of leaf gall 8—10 mm, length of bud gall 2 mm; the agamous $\female$ 2.9—3.6 mm, in the sexual generation $\male$ 2—2.5 mm, $\female$ 2.3—2.7 mm ($\varnothing$ of leaf gall $\frac{5}{16}$—$\frac{3}{8}$ in, of bud gall $\frac{1}{16}$ in; the agamous $\female$ $\frac{1}{8}$—$\frac{5}{32}$ in, in the sexual generation $\male$ $\frac{1}{16}$—$\frac{3}{32}$ in, $\female$ $\frac{1}{16}$—$\frac{1}{8}$ in). Central, western and south-western Europe, the southern regions of the USSR, the Near East.
3. *Andricus kollari:* $\varnothing$ of spherical gall 10—25 mm, of bud gall 2—3 mm; the agamous $\female$ 4.8—6 mm, in the sexual generation $\male$ and $\female$ 2 mm long ($\varnothing$ of spherical gall $\frac{7}{32}$—$\frac{1}{4}$ in, of bud gall $\frac{1}{16}$—$\frac{3}{32}$ in; the agamous $\female$ $\frac{3}{16}$—$\frac{1}{4}$ in, in the sexual generation $\male$ and $\female$ $\frac{1}{16}$ in long). Central, southern and western Europe, Asia Minor, northern Africa.

1 *Andricus quercuscalicis* Burgsd.   Cynipidae

2 *Neuroterus quercusbaccarum* L.
Spangle Gall

3 *Diplolepis rosae* L.
Robin's Pin-cushion Wasp, Bedeguar Gall-wasp

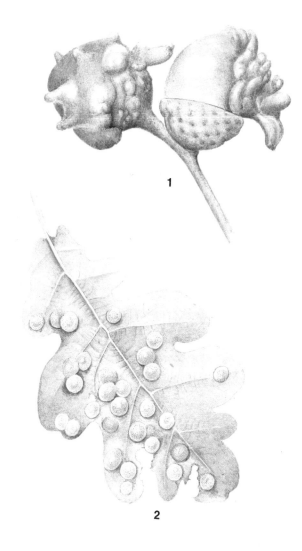

1

Some ripening acorns may be seen to be misshapen and covered with a green, extremely sticky substance, which eventually turns brown, hardens, adheres to the acorn and drops with it to the ground. This is the gall of the gall-wasp *Andricus quercuscalicis* and it is irregularly shaped and of variable size. Inside the gall there is a cavity, with an agamous female developing in an inner gall seated on its floor. This unfertilised female founds a new generation whose galls are attached to the male catkins of Turkey oaks and give rise to males and females; these females again initiate the formation of acorn galls, which are also called knopper galls.

The development of *Neuroterus quercusbaccarum* is similarly complex, with alternation of two generations and two types of galls. The lenticulate leaf galls ('spangles') are usually attached in large numbers to the undersides of oak leaves and fall together with them. The larva living in the gall pupates inside it in the spring and an agamous female emerges during March. The galls of the new generation, which are attached to oak leaves and male catkins, are spherical and fairly conspicuous. They are commonly called currant galls. They give rise to gall-wasps of both sexes, whose fertilised females lay the eggs on the undersides of oak leaves, where the spangle galls are then formed again.

Bedeguar galls, also known as Robin's pin-cushions, are very common on roses. They can be green, yellow or red and be situated on leaves, petioles and young shoots. The bedeguar is produced by the gall-wasp *Diplolepis rosae* and contains a large number of chambers in each of which a single gall-wasp develops. During the vegetation season it is fresh, but in the autumn it turns darker and dries and hardens. The pupae overwinter in the chambers and the imagos emerge in the spring. They do not change their host plant and form only one type of gall. The imagos are mostly females; males are very rare.

2

3

1. *Andricus quercuscalicis:* the acorn gall 15—20 mm high, 18—25 mm wide; $\varnothing$ of the catkin gall 1—2 mm; the agamous $\female$ up to 5 mm, in the sexual generation $\male$ and $\female$ 1.3—1.5 mm (the acorn gall $\frac{5}{8}$—$\frac{3}{16}$ in high, $\frac{3}{4}$—1 in wide, $\varnothing$ of the catkin gall $\frac{1}{16}$ in; the agamous $\female$ up to $\frac{3}{16}$ in, in the sexual generation $\male$ and $\female$ $\frac{1}{16}$ in). Southern, western and central Europe, Asia Minor.
2. *Neuroterus quercusbaccarum:* $\varnothing$ of lenticulate gall 5—6 mm, of spheric gall 5—8 mm; the agamous $\female$ 2.5—2.8 mm, in the sexual generation $\male$ 2.7—2.9 mm, $\female$ 2.5—2.8 mm ($\varnothing$ of lenticulate gall $\frac{3}{16}$—$\frac{1}{4}$ in, of spheric gall $\frac{3}{16}$ — $\frac{5}{16}$ in; the agamous $\female$ $\frac{3}{32}$ in, in the sexual generation $\male$ $\frac{3}{32}$—$\frac{1}{8}$ in, $\female$ $\frac{3}{32}$ in). A large part of Europe, Asia Minor, northern Africa.
3. *Diplolepis rosae:* 3.7—4.3 mm ($\frac{5}{32}$—$\frac{7}{32}$ in). Practically the whole of Europe.

1 ♀

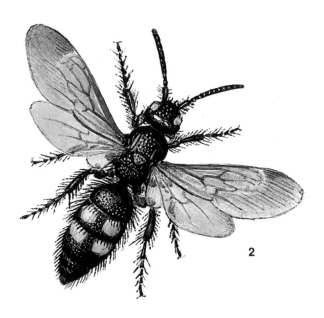

2

1 *Scolia maculata* Dr.   Scoliidae
2 *Scolia quadripunctata* F.

Scolia maculata is one of the longest and largest hymenopterans in Europe. As in many other species of this order, the male and the female have a different number of antennal segments (the female twelve and the male thirteen). The female also has a sting, the male has not. This species likes plenty of warmth. The imagos fly from June to the beginning of August, but only on sunny days. They suck the nectar of various flowers. For its development, this beetle-wasp needs the larvae of the Rhinoceros Beetle (*Oryctes nasicornis*). When the female has located a larva, she burrows until she has reached it and then paralyses it with her sting, but does not kill it. This process is common among many hymenopterans. The beetle-wasp then cleans the larva and attaches an egg to the underside of its body, so that when its own larva is hatched it has sufficient nutritious food close at hand; all it has to do is to bite a hole in the beetle larva's cuticle and suck its juices. The beetle-wasp larva has to develop quickly before its food supply begins to decompose; it moults three times and finally wraps itself in silken threads which eventually form a cocoon. It hibernates before pupating. This is another species which is becoming steadily rarer.

Scolia quadripunctata looks like a miniature replica of *S. maculata* and it also likes warmth. It inhabits steppe and wooded steppe country, where the imagos live on flowers and suck nectar. They settle on thyme, wood angelica and mountain clover. They fly only at temperatures of over 20 °C (70 °F); at night, or if the temperature falls below this level, they retire underground. The females make provision for their brood by seeking out the larvae of lamellicorn beetles, including small species (of the genera *Anomala, Anoxia, Epicometis, Oxythyrea* and others) and large rose chafers (*Cetonia, Liocola*).

1. *Scolia maculata:* ♂ 26—32 mm, ♀ 32—40 mm (♂ $1\frac{1}{16}$— $1\frac{1}{4}$ in, ♀ $1\frac{1}{4}$—$1\frac{9}{16}$ in). Europe except the north, the Caucasus, central Asia, northern Africa.
2. *Scolia quadripunctata:* ♂ 9—14 mm, ♀ 10—15 mm (♂ $\frac{3}{8}$—$\frac{9}{16}$ in, ♀ $\frac{13}{32}$—$\frac{5}{8}$ in). A large part of Europe (except the north), central Asia, northern Africa.

1 *Chrysis ignita* L.
Rubytail, Firetail

Chrysididae

2 *Hedychrum nobile* Scop.

3 *Mutilla europaea* L.
Velvet Ant

Mutillidae

4 *Smicromyrme rufipes* F.

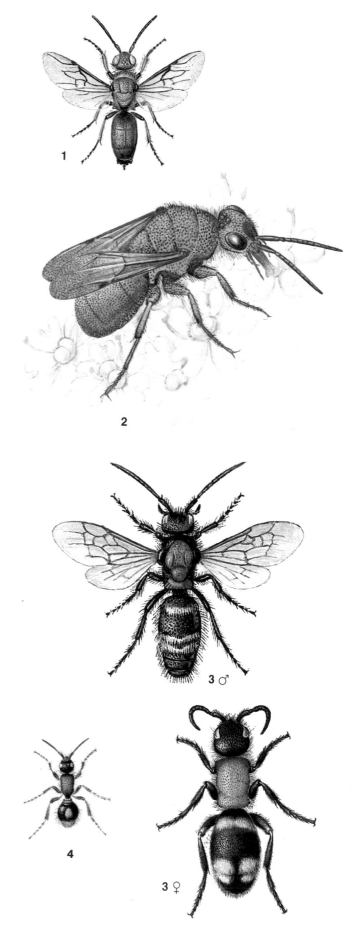

Among the hymenopterans, the distinctive feature of cuckoo wasps is the range of their dazzling metallic colours, although their habits are also interesting. From spring to autumn, Rubytails (*Chrysis ignita*) settle on flowering Umbelliferae, the sun-warmed walls of wooden country buildings and wooden fences, etc. The imagos suck nectar, but their development takes place in the larvae of various solitary wasps (Eumenidae) and ′solitary bees (Colletidae, Megachilidae, Anthophoridae). The cuckoo wasp forces its way into the host's nest, deposits an egg and leaves in a hurry. In time, the cuckoo wasp larva devours the larva of its host and any food supplies prepared for its use.

The cuckoo wasp *Hedychrum nobile* is abundant in sandy localities. The imagos are common on umbelliferous plants and on milfoil. They develop in the larvae of a great many other hymenopterans, including solitary wasps (*Cerceris, Odynerus*) and solitary bees (*Halictus*).

Mutillids (Mutillidae) also develop parasitically, such as the common Velvet Ant (*Mutilla europaea*). Inter-sex differences in this species are made clear by the illustrations, although it should be pointed out that the female has a sting which she uses without hesitation if picked up. The males sit on flowers; the females run about on the ground and even stray onto asphalt roads in towns. The larvae develop in the nests of various bumblebees and live on bumblebee larvae. The imagos leaves the bumblebee's nest as soon as they are hatched.

Smicromyrme rufipes is a smaller mutillid inhabiting sandy localities. It develops in the nests of other hymenopterans belonging to the families Sphecidae and Pompilidae.

1. *Chrysis ignita:* 4—13 mm ($\frac{3}{16}$—$\frac{9}{16}$ in). The whole of Europe (including Scandinavia), the temperate belt in Asia, northern Africa.
2. *Hedychrum nobile:* 6—10 mm ($\frac{1}{4}$—$\frac{3}{8}$ in). The Palaearctic region.
3. *Mutilla europaea:* ♂ 11—17 mm, ♀ 10—16 mm (♂ $\frac{7}{16}$—$\frac{11}{16}$ in, ♀ $\frac{3}{8}$—$\frac{5}{8}$ in). The Palaearctic region.
4. *Smicromyrme rufipes:* 4—6 mm ($\frac{3}{16}$—$\frac{1}{4}$ in). The Palaearctic region.

1 ♀

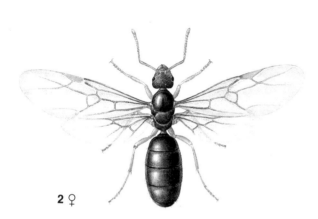

2 ♀

2 ♀

1 *Lasius fuliginosus* Latr.   Formicidae
2 *Lasius flavus* F.
Yellow Meadow Ant

Ants, together with bees, are undoubtedly the best known hymenopterans. They live in different environments and have their own specific customs, but they all have one thing in common – they form a state. The state is headed by one or more queens and is inhabited by workers whose number varies with the species; at certain times males are also present. Ants can be black, yellow or reddish-brown, but their colour is not, as a rule, an adequate criterion for their exact identification.

The nest of *Lasius fuliginosus* is constructed differently from the nests of other European ants. It may be hung in a hollow tree or hidden in a stump, under the roots of trees or occasionally under a stone. It is often to be found in old walls. It is made of wood debris and soil particles stuck together by the workers and looks like a grubby bath sponge. Well-kept tracks lead from the nest to the surrounding parts. Quite often we find several nests in close proximity to one another, new nests being formed as offshoots of the maternal nest. The colony is monogynous or oligogynous (i.e. it has one or just a few queens). The ants search eagerly for aphids and lick the sweet honeydew they excrete. Together with insects, honeydew forms a substantial part of their diet.

Mounds of earth, of varying heights, in meadows, on grass verges and in gardens, usually belong to *Lasius flavus*. The anthills are shut off from the outside world and their most important part is the subterranean nest stretching a long way underground. Life in the dark has weakened the vision of these ants, which are guided chiefly by their sense of smell when looking for food. They live mainly on honeydew and actually breed the aphids on the roots of grasses growing into the nest. They swarm on summer afternoons. Small holes appear in the previously closed anthill and males and females come streaming out on their nuptial flight. There is usually only one queen in the nest of this ant.

1. *Lasius fuliginosus:* ♀ 4—6 mm, ♀ 5—6.8 mm, ♂ 3.8—5.2 mm (♀ $\frac{5}{32}$ — $\frac{1}{4}$ in, ♀ $\frac{3}{16}$ — $\frac{5}{16}$ in, ♂ $\frac{5}{32}$ — $\frac{3}{16}$ in). Europe, the Caucasus, Siberia, China, Japan, western India.
2. *Lasius flavus:* ♀ 1.7—4 mm, ♀ 7—9 mm, ♂ 3—4 mm (♀ $\frac{1}{16}$ — $\frac{3}{16}$ in, ♀ $\frac{5}{16}$ — $\frac{3}{8}$ in, ♂ $\frac{1}{8}$ — $\frac{5}{32}$ in). Europe, the temperate belt in Asia, northern Africa, the eastern part of North America.

1 *Lasius niger* L.
Black Ant, Garden Ant
2 *Lasius emarginatus* Oliv.

The Black Ant (*Lasius niger*) is one of the most common European ants. Its environmental requirements are modest and it can thus be found in both dry and damp localities. Its nests are built in meadows, on grass verges, on the outskirts of woods, in gardens and in the walls of country cottages. Most often they lie under a stone, in an old stump or below bark on a tree trunk. In the absence of sufficient stones the Black Ant nests in the ground. The underground nest communicates with the outer world via little holes ringed round by small ridges which can often be observed on well-trodden earthen tracks; as a rule, it is surmounted by an earthen mound reinforced with blades of grass. Otherwise the workers keep the mound more or less free of grasses. The underground nest and its earthen superstructure are riddled by a maze of passages and chambers in which the life of the colony takes place. The ants swarm in the summer, when males and females leave the nest en masse and set out on the nuptial flight. The fertilised female then sheds her wings and secludes herself in a chamber, where she lays the first eggs and rears the first workers, the foundations of a new colony with a single queen at its head. The Black Ant lives on insects and aphid and coccid honeydew. It breeds the aphids itself and builds shelters round their colonies for their protection. In the country it invades dwellings in search of sweet foodstuffs.

Lasius emarginatus is a strikingly bicoloured ant which likes a dry environment. It mainly frequents cracks in rocks and since it finds similar places in the walls of houses, it is very common in the vicinity of people; it also lives in dry spots under the bark of stumps and in dead wood. It swarms from June to August, during the night. It hunts caterpillars and other insects, but it also likes aphid honeydew and by gathering seeds with oily outgrowths on them (e.g. sweet violet seeds), it helps to spread the plants to new localities.

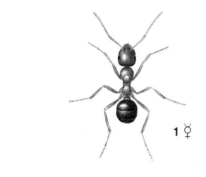

1 ⚲

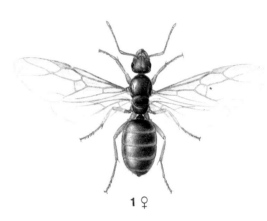

1 ♀

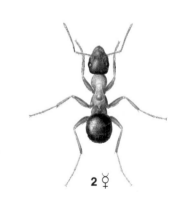

2 ⚲

1. *Lasius niger:* ⚲ 2—5 mm, ♀ 6.6—10 mm, ♂ 3.5—4.7 mm (⚲ $\frac{1}{16}$—$\frac{3}{16}$ in, ♀ $\frac{9}{32}$—$\frac{13}{32}$ in, ♂ $\frac{5}{32}$—$\frac{7}{32}$ in). Eurasia, northern Africa, North America; carried to southern Africa.
2. *Lasius emarginatus:* ⚲ 3—4 mm, ♀ 7—9 mm, ♂ 3.2—4.2 mm (⚲ $\frac{1}{8}$—$\frac{5}{32}$ in, ♀ $\frac{9}{32}$—$\frac{3}{8}$ in, ♂ $\frac{1}{8}$—$\frac{5}{32}$ in). Central and southern Europe, south-western Asia.

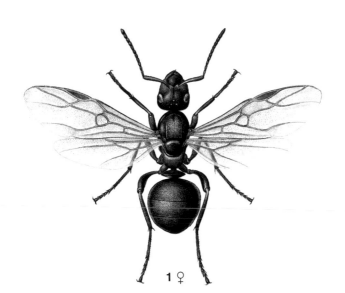

1 ♀

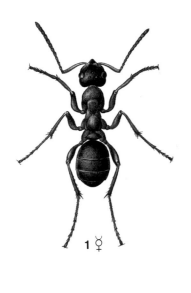

1 ☿

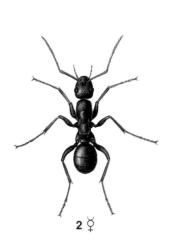

2 ☿

2 ♀

1 *Formica polyctena* Först.

2 *Formica fusca* L.

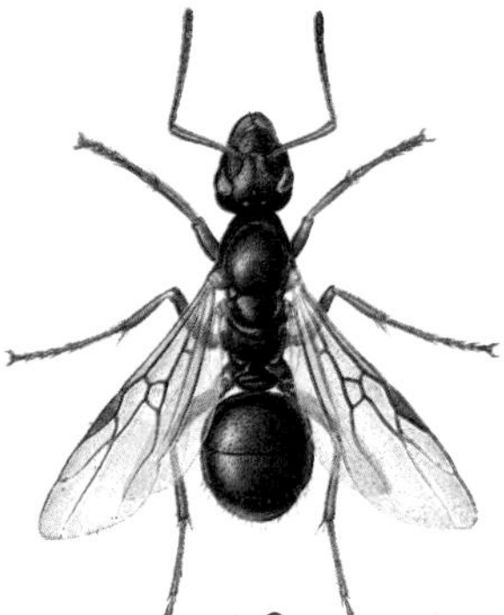

Formicidae

Among the large forest ants which build extensive, tall nests, the most common today in Europe is *Formica polyctena*. It is not so long ago that large forest anthills were normally ascribed to the Red Wood Ant (*Formica rufa*), but detailed studies showed that this species is not very common. *F. polyctena* chiefly inhabits spruce woods, but also occurs in deciduous woods. The nest is built round the foot of a tree or a stump, but its foundations lie underground. It is a polygynous nest (i.e. ruled by many queens). The ants appear outside on the anthill on the first warm days in March and swarm early in the spring. After the nuptial flight the female sheds her wings and sets about forming a new colony. This is often an offshoot of the old colony, with the result that several anthills may be found over a relatively small area. *F. polyctena* is an aggressive and predacious species which hunts insect imagos and larvae in its immediate vicinity, but also likes sweet juices. *F. polyctena* is established artificially in forests, under the supervision of experts, to combat insect pests.

Formica fusca builds its nest in shady localities. The nest is in the ground, often in an old stump, behind bark or under a stone. If there are not sufficient stones available, the ants build a mound. Swarming takes place from June to August. The female hibernates before laying the eggs and rearing the workers. One nest may contain several queens living together in harmony. This is a predacious species which hunts various kinds of insects, including smaller ants, together with their larvae and pupae; in addition, it likes aphid honeydew. The nest is often raided by ants of the species *Formica sanguinea* and *Polyergus rufescens*.

1. *Formica polyctena:* ☿ 4—8 mm, ♀ and ♂ 8—10 mm (☿ $\frac{5}{32}$—$\frac{5}{16}$ in, ♀ and ♂ $\frac{5}{16}$—$\frac{13}{32}$ in). Central Europe, the temperate belt in Asia.
2. *Formica fusca:* ☿ 4.4—7.5 mm, ♀ 7—10 mm, ♂ 7—11 mm (☿ $\frac{7}{32}$—$\frac{9}{32}$ in, ♀ $\frac{9}{32}$—$\frac{13}{32}$ in, ♂ $\frac{9}{32}$—$\frac{7}{16}$ in). Europe, the temperate belt in Asia, North America.

1 *Camponotus ligniperda* Latr.   Formicidae
2 *Myrmica rubra* L.   Myrmicidae
3 *Monomorium pharaonis* L.
Pharaoh Ant

The genus *Camponotus* has only a few species, all resembling one another, but comprises some of the biggest ants. *Camponotus ligniperda* is to be seen in dry clearings at low altitudes. The workers build a nest in a dead spruce, silver fir or pine trunk or an old stump (seldom in living wood). The nest is a system of chambers and passages bitten away by the workers in the annual rings in the centre of the trunk. This species also nests in the ground under stones. Apart from workers of average size, the nest further contains large workers with large heads, which are sometimes incorrectly described as 'soldiers'. Swarming takes place in the afternoon at the beginning of June. These ants live on juices, in particular aphid honeydew and the juices of young shoots of deciduous trees.

The ants of the Myrmicidae family have a sting, the stab of which is more painful than the bite of other ants. *Myrmica rubra*, a rusty-brown ant, is one of the commoner members of the family. It lives in woods, fields, meadows and gardens and its nests are very varied in appearance. Each nest usually contains several queens – sometimes hundreds. They may lie in the ground under a stone, in a tussock of moss, a clump of grass or an old stump, or below bark; sometimes they are surmounted by a mound. The ants suck nectar, lick honeydew and forage for seeds; occasionally they catch insects. They swarm during the summer.

The Pharaoh Ant (*Monomorium pharaonis*) is familiar to many people who live in modern blocks of flats or work in bakeries, restaurants, hothouses and hospitals, in all of which it finds sufficient warmth and nourishment. Its primitive nest is hidden under flooring, in cracks in the walls or in other convenient shelters. Since the Pharaoh Ant forms a large number of secondary nests, it often seems to be ubiquitous in many places. The ant is omnivorous and is guided to food by its excellent sense of smell. This ant came originally from Africa and is unable to survive out of doors in the British climate.

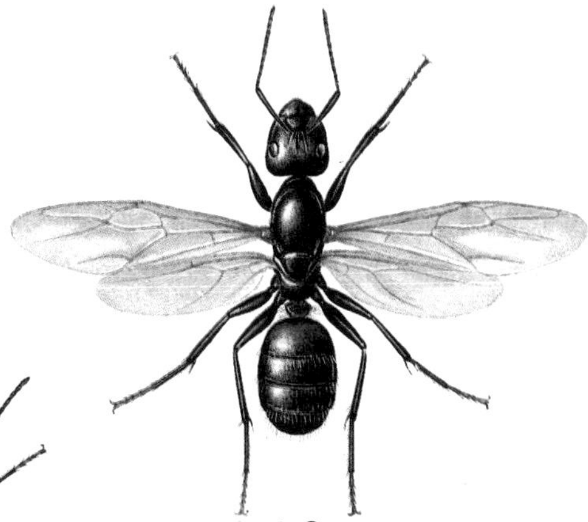

1 ♀

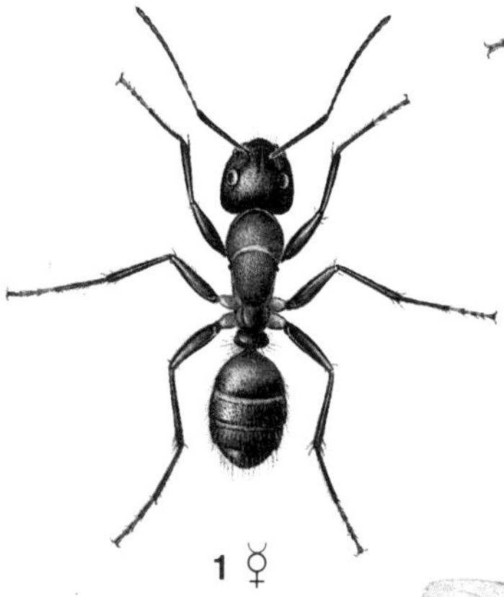

1 ☿

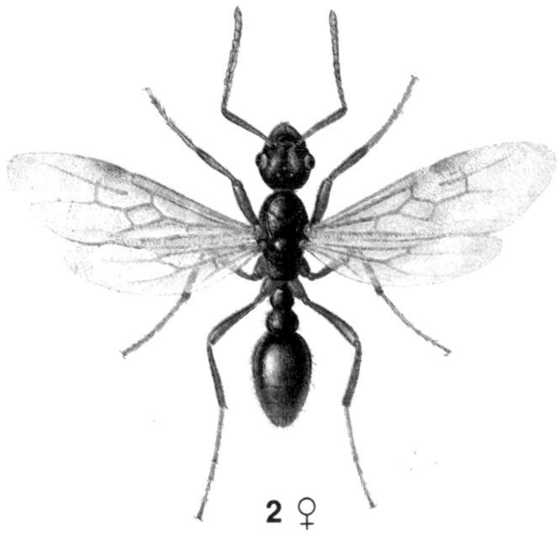

2 ♀

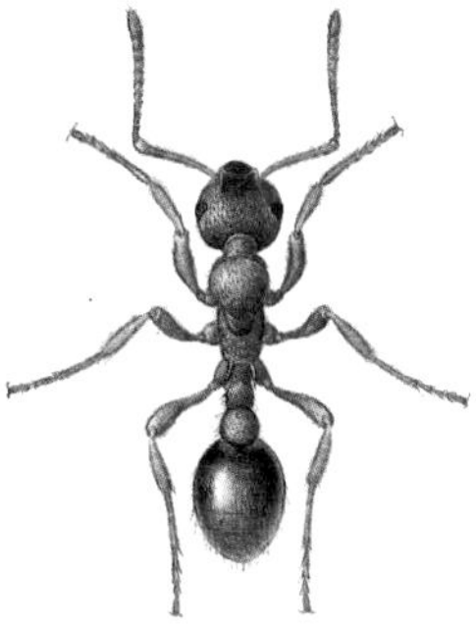

2 ☿

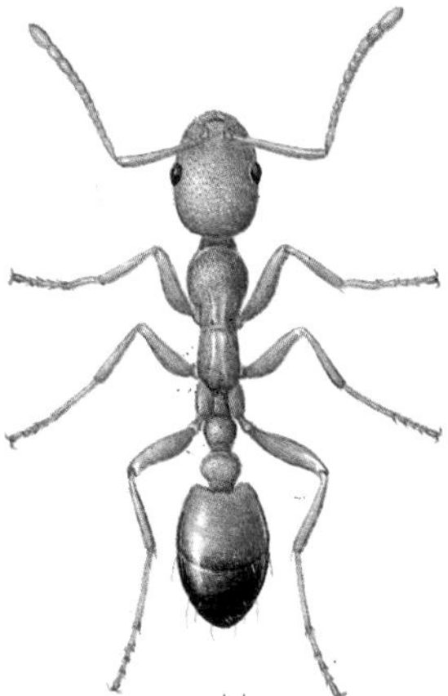

3 ☿

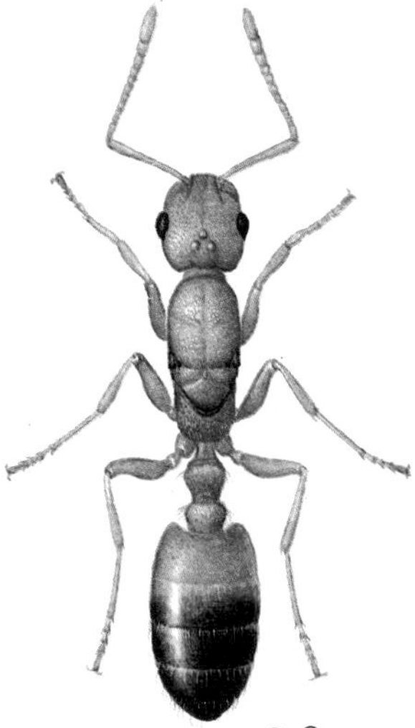

3 ♀

1. *Camponotus ligniperda:* ☿ 7—14 mm, ♀ up to 18 mm, ♂ 9—12 mm (☿ $\frac{9}{32}$ — $\frac{9}{16}$ in, ♀ up to $\frac{3}{4}$ in, ♂ $\frac{3}{8}$ — $\frac{1}{2}$ in). Central and southern Europe, Asia, North America.
2. *Myrmica rubra:* ☿ 4—5.3 mm, ♀ 4.5—6 mm, ♂ 4.5—5 mm (☿ $\frac{5}{32}$ — $\frac{7}{32}$ in, ♀ $\frac{7}{32}$ — $\frac{1}{2}$ in, ♂ $\frac{7}{32}$ — $\frac{3}{16}$ in). Almost the whole of Europe (in the south mainly in mountains), the temperate belt in Asia, Japan.
3. *Monomorium pharaonis:* ☿ 2—2.5 mm, ♀ 3.5—5 mm, ♂ 2.8—3 mm (☿ $\frac{1}{16}$ — $\frac{3}{32}$ in, ♀ $\frac{5}{32}$ — $\frac{3}{16}$ in, ♂ $\frac{1}{8}$ in). Over most of the globe.

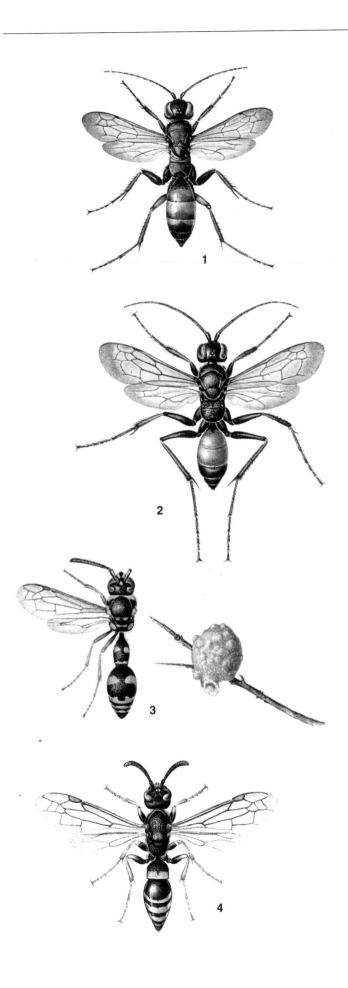

1 *Anoplius fuscus* L. Pompilidae

2 *Cryptocheilus notatus* Rossius

3 *Eumenes pomiformis* F. Eumenidae

4 *Symmorphus murarius* L.

Care of the offspring, which attains different levels in many hymenopterans, is very pronounced in spider wasps (Pompilidae). *Anoplius fuscus* and *Cryptocheilus notatus,* depicted here, both like warmth, frequent flowering Umbelliferae, and care for their brood in the same way. They run about on the ground, fly short distances and search for wolf spiders (Lycosidae). Having caught one, they stun it with their sting, dig an underground chamber, drag the prey into it and deposit an egg on it. The spider wasp larva lives on the spider's body and finally pupates in the chamber.

Potter and mason wasps (Eumenidae), which are related to the social wasps (Vespidae), have a very distinctive way of caring for their brood and their mode of life is also remarkable. *Eumenes pomiformis* is one of the most common potter wasps. The imagos fly from spring to autumn in lowlands and hills. For the development of the larvae the female makes neat, fat-bellied earthen cells with a narrow neck and sticks them to the undersides of stones, in various crevices and to the stems of plants. Each cell contains a single egg suspended on a filament and is stocked with a few small caterpillars paralysed by the female to prevent them from escaping; lastly, the potter wasp seals the entrance to the cell.

Symmorphus murarius is a mason wasp. Its females hunt leaf beetles, paralyse them and place them in nest cells, which are usually hidden in cracks in walls. Like other potter and mason wasps, this one is parasitised by cuckoo wasps, which like to lay their eggs in its nests.

1. *Anoplius fuscus:* 7—20 mm ($\frac{9}{32}$—$\frac{13}{16}$ in). The Palaearctic region.
2. *Cryptocheilus notatus:* 9—15 mm ($\frac{3}{8}$—$\frac{5}{8}$ in). Europe, Asia Minor, central Asia, Transcaucasia.
3. *Eumenes pomiformis:* ♂ 10—11 mm, ♀ 11—16 mm (♂ $\frac{7}{16}$ in, ♀ $\frac{7}{16}$—$\frac{5}{8}$ in). A large part of Europe (except the north), northern Africa.
4. *Symmorphus murarius:* ♂ 9—11 mm, ♀ 11—17 mm (♂ $\frac{3}{8}$—$\frac{7}{16}$ in, ♀ $\frac{7}{16}$—$\frac{11}{16}$ in). Central, western and southern Europe, Asia Minor.

1 *Vespa crabro* L.
Hornet

Vespidae

People are afraid of the Hornet because of its size, but it will not attack unless it is provoked. It lives in a communal nest (1a), which is usually built in a hollow deciduous tree in a wood. The number of such trees is diminishing, however, and the Hornet is beginning to settle with increasing frequency in the vicinity of humans. It now also nests in dark attics, in wooden partition walls in country cottages, in nesting-boxes and in old trees in gardens. Like all wasps, it forms one-year colonies. The workers, the old queen and the males die in the autumn and only the fertilised young females survive the winter in various refuges – although many of them are killed by frosts. In the spring, the female begins to build a nest, but the bulk of the work is done later by the workers.

The female makes a papery substance out of old, rotting wood mixed with saliva, forms a stalk, part of the first comb with a few cells, and part of the outer envelope, and then sticks an egg in each cell. She feeds the larvae herself, but as soon as the first workers appear in the nest she is relieved of her building and feeding duties. The workers complete the first comb and then build further tiers, with bars between them for reinforcement, and cover the whole nest with a very decorative outer envelope. The nest has about five combs, each roughly 20 cm (8 inches) in diameter, while the total number of cells is in the region of 1,500. The cells open downwards, but the larvae do not fall out, at first because they are stuck to the cell and later because they are so plump that they are completely wedged in; eventually they also pupate in it. The Hornet preys on various insects, but particularly on flies, which form about 90 per cent of its diet; on rare occasions it attacks larger insects, such as dragonflies. It also sucks nectar and the juices of injured trees, etc. The workers carry the food they gather in a kind of crop; when they return to the nest they feed the larvae and the young Hornets, which then pass on some of the food to others. The Hornet is a very useful insect and deserves to be strictly protected.

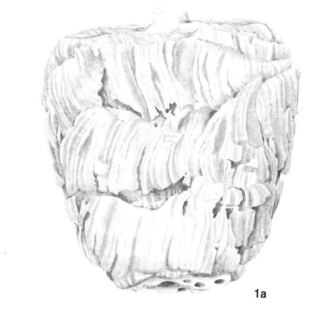

1a

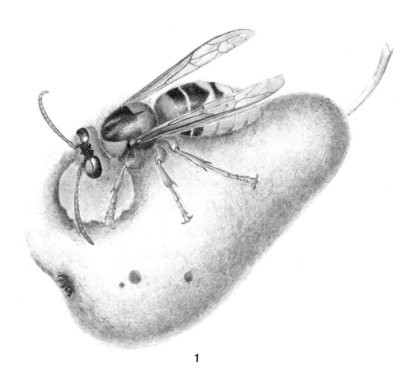

1

1. *Vespa crabro:* ♀ 18—25 mm, ♀ 23—35 mm, ♂ 21—28 mm (♀ $\frac{3}{4}$—1 in, ♀ $\frac{15}{16}$—1$\frac{3}{8}$ in, ♂ $\frac{13}{16}$—1$\frac{1}{8}$ in). A large part of Eurasia, North America.

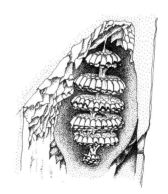

Scheme of Hornets' (*Vespa crabro*) nest

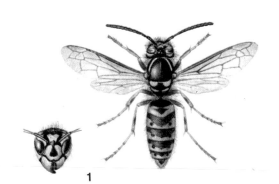

1

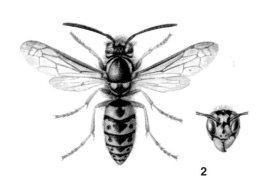

2

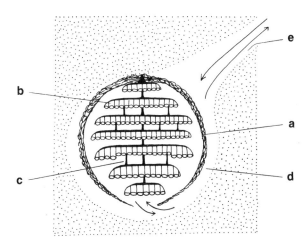

Diagram of underground wasps' nest: (arrows indicate wasps flying in and out) a – covering, b – comb, c – strengthening bars, d – air space, e – entrance tunnel

1 *Vespula vulgaris* L.
Common Wasp

Vespidae

2 *Vespula germanica* L.
German Wasp

The Common Wasp (*Vespula vulgaris*) and the German Wasp (*Vespula germanica*) are the best known and most common European wasps. They are very much alike and both nest in the dark – most often in a hole in the ground. The differences between them are clearly discernible, however, irrespective of colour variability. On their clypeus, the female and the worker of the Common Wasp have a black mark shaped roughly like an anchor, while the German Wasp has three dark spots. The nest of *V. vulgaris* is light ochre while that of *V. germanica* is grey in colour. Both belong to 'long-lived' species, since their nesting season lasts from spring until late in the autumn. In the spring, after hibernating, the queen looks for a place for the nest. As soon as she has found a convenient hole she begins to build the foundations, but as the workers hatch they take over the building of the nest, keep it clean, regulate the temperature and humidity and feed the queen and the larvae. The completed nest is suspended from a stalk, the combs are interconnected by bars and the whole is covered with a multi-layer paper envelope. The cells in the uppermost combs (where the workers develop) are small, while in the lower (i.e. later) combs they are large and contain developing queens and males. The number of cells in the nests of both wasps is large and in each case several thousand individuals are hatched during one season.

We often hear about the damage done by wasps, but what do they actually eat? While they are feeding the larvae – and that is most of the time while they inhabit the nest – they catch various insects, such as flies, mosquitoes and different kinds of caterpillars. Wasps lie in wait for their prey, pounce on it, bite off its legs, wings and head and then parcel up the rest and fly back with it to the nest. During the feeding season they destroy large quantities of insects and in this respect are unquestionably useful. In the autumn, however, they settle on over-ripe fruit. Although this has generally fallen to the ground, wasps are still therefore regarded as partial pests. The males mainly frequent flowers and belong to the regular fauna of flowering Umbelliferae.

1. *Vespula vulgaris*: ♀ 11—14 mm, ♀ 16—19 mm, ♂ 13—17 mm (♀ $\frac{7}{16}$ — $\frac{9}{16}$ in, ♀ $\frac{5}{8}$ — $\frac{3}{4}$ in, ♂ $\frac{9}{16}$ — $\frac{11}{16}$ in). A large part of the globe.
2. *Vespula germanica*: ♀ 12—16 mm, ♀ 17—20 mm, ♂ 13—17 mm (♀ $\frac{1}{2}$ — $\frac{5}{8}$ in, ♀ $\frac{11}{16}$ — $\frac{13}{16}$ in, ♂ $\frac{9}{16}$ — $\frac{11}{16}$ in). All the continents; in Europe missing only in the north of Finland and Scandinavia.

1 *Vespula rufa* L.
Red Wasp

Vespidae

2 *Dolichovespula saxonica* F.

The Red Wasp (*Vespula rufa*) shows a preference for open, hilly country. It nests in woods, but is also to be found in gardens. The nest is built in a small, dark space in the ground. The queen lays the foundations in the spring, in a cavity under grass roots, in an old stump or a hollow log, under the roots of trees or in a garden bed. The nest is grey because the workers use old, but sound wood from telegraph poles, fence posts and dry spruce trunks, etc., for its construction; it is reached by a short passage and is relatively small. The three to four combs contain just a few hundred cells, the first of which are small, while the later ones, in which males and females develop, are larger.

The Red Wasp's life is of only short duration and between the end of August and the middle of September it dies. Like other wasps, the Red Wasp is useful, although it is less abundant than the Common Wasp and the German Wasp. The imagos visit flowers; they are common on snowberry and raspberry and on various herbaceous Umbelliferae, etc. They do not enter dwellings.

Of all the wasps found in the vicinity of man, *Dolichovespula saxonica* is probably the most frequent. It likes to nest in attics, chalets, church towers and nesting-boxes. It also nests, though less often, in the open, e.g. in feeding troughs for game, forest shelters, clumps of grass or moss. The nest is grey and is partly or completely visible. Its size varies, large nests being the size of a human head. Quite often you will find tiny nests with only a few cells; these are incomplete nests whose queen came to a premature end. The protective envelope of the mature nest covers about five combs with 1,300 cells. The colony is of short duration and exists only from May to August. This is an unaggressive and very useful wasp and ought to be given every protection.

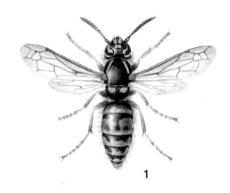

1

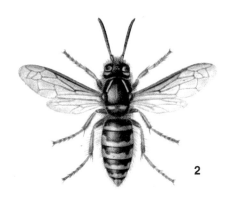

2

 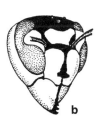

a   b

Head of *Dolichovespula saxonica*
(a) and *Vespula vulgaris* (b)

1. *Vespula rufa:* ♀ 10—14 mm, ♀ 16—20 mm, ♂ 13—16 mm (♀ $\frac{3}{8}$—$\frac{9}{16}$ in, ♀ $\frac{5}{8}$—$\frac{13}{16}$ in, ♂ $\frac{9}{16}$—$\frac{5}{8}$ in). The whole of Europe (far to the north in Finland and Scandinavia, in mountains in the south, common in the British Isles).
2. *Dolichovespula saxonica:* ♀ 11—14 mm, ♀ 15—18 mm, ♂ 13—15 mm (♀ $\frac{7}{16}$—$\frac{9}{16}$ in, ♀ $\frac{5}{8}$—$\frac{3}{4}$ in, ♂ $\frac{9}{16}$—$\frac{5}{8}$ in). A large part of Europe (except the north and the British Isles).

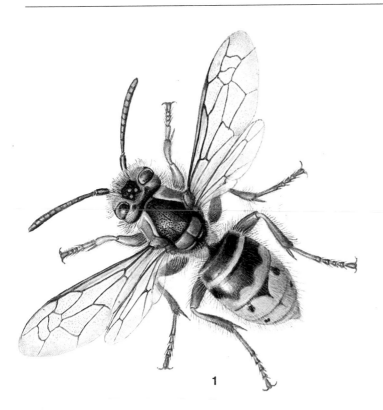

1 *Dolichovespula media* Retz.   Vespidae

2 *Dolichovespula sylvestris* Scop.
Tree Wasp

In *Dolichovespula media*, the typical black and yellow wasp colouring is supplemented by red. In size and colouring, this wasp resembles a Hornet. Being fond of light, it does not nest in an enclosed space, but chooses a garden hedge, shrubs, rocks or the crown of a tree. The workers like to scrape building material from living poplars. The nest is shaped like a lemon and has a tubular extension, especially in the early phase of its construction; it is covered with a pale grey to whitish envelope resembling parchment paper. The imagos fly from the end of May to about the middle of October. *D. media* is a great predator; it catches insects and is not particular in its choice of prey. Sometimes it visits snowberry flowers or flowering Umbelliferae and sucks the nectar.

The Tree Wasp (*Dolichovespula sylvestris*), which likes warmth, inhabits wooded hilly country. It prefers a damp environment for its nest, but otherwise has no special requirements as regards light or sunshine. Its nests are situated to catch at least a little light; they are mostly suspended on trees, in nesting-boxes, in deserted beehives, on wooden rafters in attics or on dormer windows. The workers obtain the nest material from fence posts or decorticated poplar trunks. The nest itself is greyish-yellow. The combs contain several hundred cells. The colony is short-lived; the queen founds it during May, but by the end of August it is already moribund. *Dolichovespula sylvestris* is predacious, like other species, but it also likes to visit flowers where it encounters other hymenopterans. It keeps out of the way of human beings, does not attack them and does not fly into dwellings.

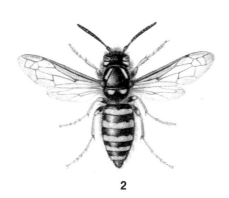

Dolichovespula media – variability of the abdominal marking

1. *Dolichovespula media:* ♀ 15—19 mm, ♀ 18—22 mm, ♂ 15—19 mm (♀ $\frac{5}{8}$—$\frac{3}{4}$ in, ♀ $\frac{3}{4}$—$\frac{7}{8}$ in, ♂ $\frac{5}{8}$—$\frac{3}{4}$ in). A large part of Europe (to the Arctic Circle in the north, in mountains in the south).
2. *Dolichovespula sylvestris:* ♀ 13—15 mm, ♀ 15—19 mm, ♂ 14—16 mm (♀ $\frac{9}{16}$—$\frac{5}{8}$ in, ♀ $\frac{5}{8}$—$\frac{3}{4}$ in, ♂ $\frac{9}{16}$—$\frac{5}{8}$ in). Europe (to 64° latitude north), northern Africa.

1 *Polistes nimpha* Christ.
2 *Polistes gallicus* L.

Vespidae

Polistes wasps are a separate subfamily of Vespidae. Their abdomen is differently shaped from that of typical wasps and narrows to a point both in front and behind. At the base of the hindwings there is a small lobe, which is absent in typical wasps. The nest is also different, since it consists of a single comb without a protective envelope. The sting of these wasps is much less painful than the sting of typical wasps.

The workers of *Polistes nimpha* and *Polistes gallicus* can be differentiated quite easily by the colour of the antennal flagellum and the ventral surface of the last abdominal segment. In *P. nimpha* the antennal flagellum and the underside of the last abdominal segment have a smoky tinge, while in *P. gallicus* the flagellum is orange and the last abdominal segment is yellow. After hibernating, the queen founds a new nest in the spring. She lays a few eggs and rears a few workers, which then continue to build the nest, keep it clean and feed the larvae. As a rule, *Polistes nimpha* builds its light grey, fragile nests close to the ground, where it is damper. The nest is attached to a stone, a piece of wood, the stem of a plant or the outer wall of a house. Further south in Europe this wasp builds its nests in sheltered spaces, where they are protected from the sun; it also impregnates them with a secretion from its salivary glands to protect and strengthen them.

In central Europe, *Polistes gallicus* nests in enclosed spaces, such as attics, where, as a rule, several nests can be found close together.

Polistes wasps are predacious like typical wasps; they also catch various kinds of insects as food for their larvae and they often sit on flowers drinking nectar. In the autumn they find plenty of sweet juice in fallen over-ripe fruit.

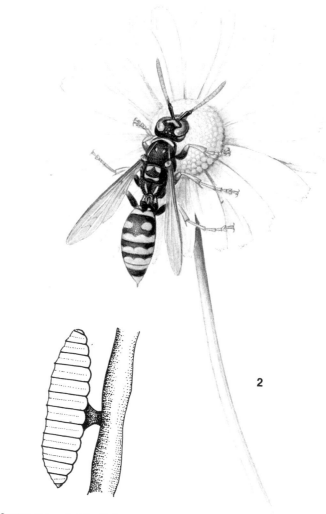

2

Section of a nest of the *Polistes* wasp

1

1. *Polistes nimpha:* ♀ 14 mm, ♀ 16 mm, ♂ 12—15 mm (♀ $\frac{9}{16}$ in, ♀ $\frac{5}{8}$ in, ♂ $\frac{1}{2}$—$\frac{5}{8}$ in). Central and southern Europe and the southern part of northern Europe. Absent from Great Britain, Denmark and the north of Finland and Scandinavia.
2. *Polistes gallicus:* ♀ 15 mm, ♀ 18 mm, ♂ 14—16 mm (♀ $\frac{5}{8}$ in, ♀ $\frac{3}{4}$ in, ♂ $\frac{9}{16}$—$\frac{5}{8}$ in). Europe (except the north), Asia (as far as Japan).

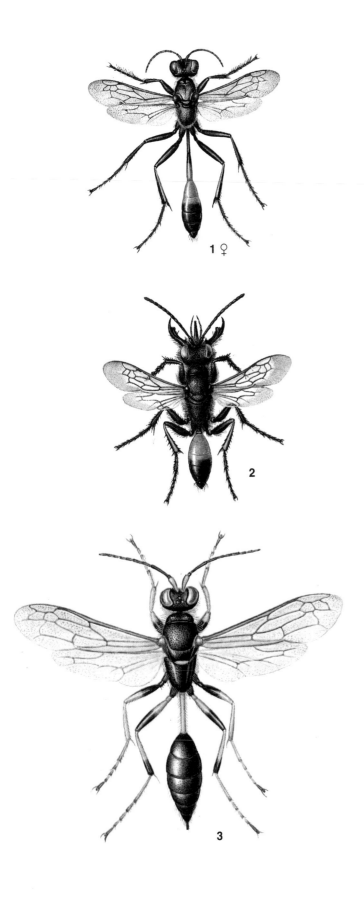

1 ♀

2

3

1 *Ammophila sabulosa* L.   Sphecidae
Red-bearded Sand Wasp

2 *Podalonia hirsuta* Scop.

3 *Sceliphron destillatorium* L.

Digger wasps are very shapely insects which develop in an extremely interesting manner and make very careful provision for their brood. *Ammophila sabulosa*, the most common large species, inhabits sandy banks, hillsides and clearings. The imagos can be seen during the summer and autumn, sitting on thyme, willowherb, scabious, melilot and many other plants, sucking nectar. The female runs about on the ground, flying short distances from time to time, searching for caterpillars, which she needs as food for the larvae. Before laying her eggs she digs an underground nest and then goes hunting. When she has found a caterpillar, she stings it to immobilise it, carries it back to the nest, drags it inside and deposits an egg on it. She then seals the nest, carefully masking the entrance to make it invisible, and leaves the rest to the larva. The larva, which is hatched soon afterwards, devours the caterpillar and pupates in the ground; when the digger wasp later emerges it has to force its way out.

The very similar, but more robust *Podalonia hirsuta* also lives in warm localities and cares for its offspring in a similar manner. This wasp catches its prey before it digs a nest for the egg. It feeds its larvae mainly on the caterpillars of owlet moths.

The large, handsome *Sceliphron destillatorium* is no ordinary species. It occurs in explicitly warm localities during the summer and makes an earthen nest for its brood. It provides the larvae with food like other species, but the food itself is different. The female catches spiders, paralyses them, carries them back to the nest and places a single egg on each.

1. *Ammophila sabulosa:* ♂ 16—23 mm, ♀ 20—28 mm (♂ $\frac{5}{8}$—$\frac{15}{16}$ in, ♀ $\frac{13}{16}$—$1\frac{1}{8}$ in). The entire Palaearctic region.
2. *Podalonia hirsuta:* ♂ 14—19 mm, ♀ 16—23 mm (♂ $\frac{9}{16}$—$\frac{3}{4}$ in, ♀ $\frac{5}{8}$—$\frac{15}{16}$ in). A large part of the Palaearctic region.
3. *Sceliphron destillatorium:* ♂ ♀ 17—30 mm (♂ ♀ $\frac{11}{16}$—$1\frac{3}{16}$ in). Eurasia (in Europe no further north than Austria and the south of Czechoslovakia).

1 *Philanthus triangulum* F.
2 *Cerceris arenaria* L.
3 *Gorytes laevis* Latr.

Sphecidae

1

Many of the digger wasps look very much like typical social wasps. At rest, however, they hold their wings flat rather than folded longitudinally. One digger wasp, *Philanthus triangulum,* lives from June to September in warm, sandy localities, where it settles on flowers. The female hunts Honeybees, which are useful to her in two ways. Firstly, she licks the sweet juices released from the mouthparts of the paralysed bee and secondly, she utilises the bee as food for her offspring. In sandy ground she excavates a main burrow with several side passages (1a), each of which terminates in a chamber. There are five to seven such chambers in the nest and in each of them the digger wasp places two or three bees and one egg. The larvae, which hatch in only three days, live on the bees and then overwinter in the chamber in a flask-like cocoon, but do not pupate until the following spring. The imago emerges at the beginning of June. Once described as a pest of bees, this is now a rare species in many areas.

The digger wasps of the genus *Cerceris,* which are characterised by laterally constricted abdominal segments, likewise frequent sandy localities. *Cerceris arenaria* is one of the most common. It visits melilot, black medick, willowherb and thistles. The female makes a nest in sand and catches weevils as food for the larvae; sometimes she tries to take possession of the nest of another digger wasp.

Gorytes laevis, another species liking warm, sandy localities, cares for its brood in a similar manner. The female excavates a nest in the sand and stocks it with froghoppers and leafhoppers.

1a

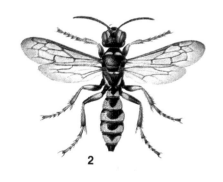

2

3

1. *Philanthus triangulum:* ♂ 8—10 mm, ♀ 13—17 mm (♂ $\frac{5}{16}$—$\frac{3}{8}$ in, ♀ $\frac{9}{16}$—$\frac{11}{16}$ in). The Palaearctic region.
2. *Cerceris arenaria:* ♂ 8—12 mm, ♀ 11—15 mm (♂ $\frac{5}{16}$—$\frac{1}{2}$ in, ♀ $\frac{7}{16}$—$\frac{5}{8}$ in). Central and southern Europe, eastwards beyond the Caspian Sea, northern Africa.
3. *Gorytes laevis:* 7—9.5 mm ($\frac{5}{16}$—$\frac{3}{8}$ in). Eurasia (from the British Isles to Turkestan).

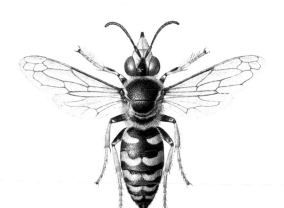

1

1 *Bembix rostrata* L.   Sphecidae
2 *Mellinus arvensis* L.
3 *Trypoxylon figulus* L.

Bembix rostrata carries the care of its offspring further than most other digger wasps, since it keeps the larvae constantly supplied with fresh food (large hover-flies, horse-flies and others). The nest lies in sand, but at no great depth. One female manages to feed about six larvae. The imagos appear in July and August. Like many other digger wasps, this one is becoming steadily rarer, owing to increasing destruction of its natural habitats.

Mellinus arvensis, one of the most common European digger wasps, also feeds its brood on various dipterans. In a single day it digs a nest in sandy soil at a depth of about 75 cm (29 in). The larvae are fully grown in nine to eleven days and then wrap themselves in cocoons and pupate.

The imagos of the species *Trypoxylon figulus* are to be seen from April to August. The larvae develop in passages bitten by the female in a stem of a bramble, or in tunnels left by insects living in wood, etc. The female partitions off the nest into separate cells containing spiders paralysed by her sting; the number of spiders varies according to their size and as many as 40 have been found in one cell. The larva hatches soon afterwards, lives on the spiders while it is developing and then pupates in the cell.

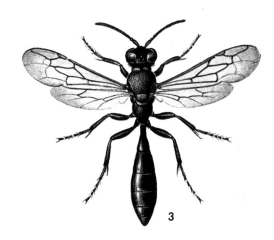

2

3

1. *Bembix rostrata:* 15—22 mm, wing span 32 mm ($\frac{5}{8}$—$\frac{7}{8}$ in, wing span $1\frac{1}{4}$ in). A large part of the Palaearctic region.
2. *Mellinus arvensis:* ♂ 7—11 mm, ♀ 11—14 mm (♂ $\frac{5}{16}$— $\frac{7}{16}$ in, ♀ $\frac{7}{16}$—$\frac{9}{16}$ in). A large part of Europe.
3. *Trypoxylon figulus:* ♂ 5—10 mm, ♀ 6—12 mm (♂ $\frac{3}{16}$— $\frac{3}{8}$ in, ♀ $\frac{1}{4}$—$\frac{1}{2}$ in). Practically the whole Palaearctic region.

1 *Colletes daviesanus* Sm. Colletidae
2 *Andrena flavipes* Panz. Andrenidae
3 *Andrena fulva* Müller
4 *Panurgus calcaratus* Scop.

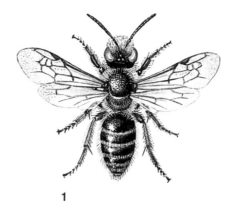

1

Many hundreds of species of different solitary bees, apart from the Honeybee, play an important role in nature as pollinators. Most of them look very much alike and are not easy to identify. *Colletes daviesanus* is often to be found during the summer on flowering yarrow or tansy. It nests gregariously in earth banks. The female supplies the larvae with pollen and the larvae overwinter.

Andrena flavipes, which flies at the end of March, is one of the first pollinators of spring flowers. In July and August it is followed by the bees of the second generation, which visit umbelliferous plants. They nest in sand and earth banks and the size of their colonies varies.

Andrena fulva is another solitary springtime bee, which flies only from the middle of April to the middle of May. It is to be found in urban parks and gardens, where it pollinates fruit trees (chiefly cherry and apple), various herbaceous plants such as hellebore and cinquefoil, and trees such as maple. It is often to be seen around gooseberry and currant bushes. The entrances to its underground nest, guarded by little cones of soil, can sometimes be seen on well-trodden footpaths.

In the summer, on hawkweed and dandelion flowers, you will often see small bees crawling on their sides between the individual florets, their dark bodies smothered in pollen. They belong to the species *Panurgus calcaratus,* which nests, often gregariously, on field paths.

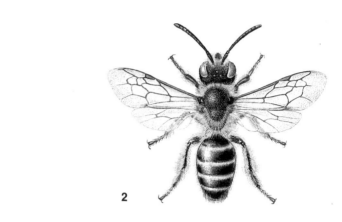

2

3

4

1. *Colletes daviesanus:* 8—11 mm ($\frac{5}{16}$—$\frac{7}{16}$ in). Europe, Siberia.
2. *Andrena flavipes:* 11—13 mm ($\frac{7}{16}$—$\frac{9}{16}$ in). Most of Europe, Asia Minor, central Asia, northern Africa.
3. *Andrena fulva:* 12 mm ($\frac{1}{2}$ in). Central and north-western Europe, the Balkans.
4. *Panurgus calcaratus:* 8—9 mm ($\frac{5}{16}$—$\frac{3}{8}$ in). The whole of Europe.

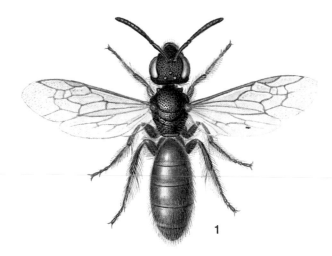

1 *Lasioglossum malachurum* K.   Halictidae

2 *Lasioglossum albipes* F.

3 *Sphecodes gibbus* L.

On sandy slopes, during the whole of the spring and summer season, you will often come across small holes with inconspicuous little bees coming out of them from time to time. The holes lead to the nests of *Lasioglossum malachurum* or some other related species, since many species often nest in close proximity. *L. malachurum* forms numerically large colonies comprising up to 250 individuals. The foundations of the nest are laid by a fertilised female who spent the winter hibernating. The entrance hole, which is also the exit hole, opens into a narrow passage about 70 cm (28 in) long; this leads to a chamber containing the cells of the nest, which open in the direction of the passage. The female fills the cells with pollen and lays her eggs. In central and western Europe this species produces three generations in a single season. The nest cells of the first generation are only a few centimetres underground. The workers which are hatched from them build more cells for further offspring, but deeper down, to protect the future generation from the rising temperature and ensure greater humidity. The last generation consists of young females and males. The females are fertilised, overwinter in the maternal nest and then, in the spring, disperse to found their own nests.

Lasioglossum albipes occurs from spring to autumn on flowers growing in meadows and gardens. It is common on flowering dandelions.

Being unable to build a nest of their own, the members of the genus *Sphecodes* are dependent on the nests of other solitary bees for the development of their larvae. The imagos of the species *Sphecodes gibbus* fly in the autumn. The males die before the onset of winter; the fertilised females hibernate and reappear in spring on flowering dandelions and willow catkins. The eggs are laid in the nests of *Halictus* species, e.g. *Halictus maculatus* and *H. quadricinctus*, etc.

1. *Lasioglossum malachurum:* ♂ 7.5—9 mm, ♀ 8—8.5 mm ($\circlearrowleft \frac{9}{32}$—$\frac{3}{8}$ in, ♀ $\frac{5}{16}$—$\frac{11}{32}$ in). Europe, the Caucasus.
2. *Lasioglossum albipes:* ♂ 7—8.5 mm, ♀ 8.5—9 mm ($\circlearrowleft \frac{9}{32}$—$\frac{11}{32}$ in, ♀ $\frac{11}{32}$—$\frac{3}{8}$ in). A large part of the Palaearctic region.
3. *Sphecodes gibbus:* 7—13 mm ($\frac{9}{32}$—$\frac{9}{16}$ in). Europe.

1 *Melitta leporina* Panz.

Melittidae

2 *Dasypoda altercator* Harris
Hairy-legged Mining Bee

When springtime solitary bees have disappeared from the scene, their place is taken by explicitly summer pollinators. Like most bees, the two species depicted here have a hairy 'brush' on their hindlegs for collecting pollen. *Melitta leporina* often flies over fields of flowering lucerne, but also visits other flowers. Its underground nest is a vertical shaft with nest cells along the sides. The female places a supply of pollen in each cell, with an egg on top of it, and then closes the cell with an earthen lid. This bee produces one generation a year.

Some solitary bees have a very strikingly developed collecting apparatus; they include the Hairy-legged Mining Bee (*Dasypoda altercator*) and related species, whose hind tibiae and first tarsal joint are thickly overgrown with long hairs. In addition to collecting pollen, the hairs are used in the building of the nest, which is situated in a sandy bank. The bee burrows to a depth of about 60 cm (24 in) and removes surplus sand by crawling out backwards, throwing the sand behind her out of the entry hole. Her hindlegs act as brooms, which sweep away the sand to right and left. This leaves a kind of path, with banked-up sand on each side, leading from the entry hole, which is also the exit hole. Several side passages, each terminating in a nest cell, lead from the main shaft. In each of the cells the female places a supply of pollen, kneaded into a ball supported by 'legs' of sand to keep it off the ground and prevent it from becoming mouldy. After placing an egg on top of each of the pollen balls, the female seals off the nest with sand and leaves it to its fate. The larvae live on the pollen, overwinter in the cells and pupate the following spring. This bee also forms only one generation a year. It visits flowering hawkweed, chicory and other herbaceous plants and lives primarily in sandy localities.

1

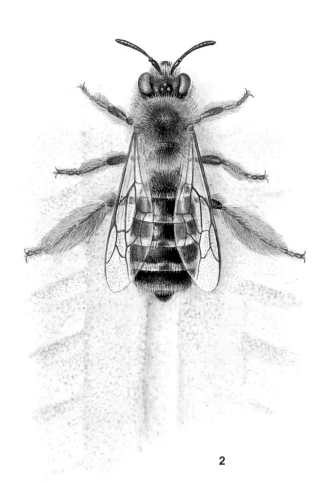

2

1. *Melitta leporina:* 11—13 mm ($\frac{7}{16}$—$\frac{9}{16}$ in). A large part of Europe.
2. *Dasypoda altercator:* 12—15 mm ($\frac{1}{2}$—$\frac{5}{8}$ in). A large part of the Palaearctic region.

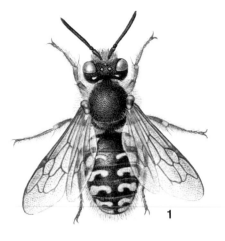

1

1 *Anthidium manicatum* L.   Megachilidae
2 *Hoplitis adunca* Panz.
3 *Osmia rufa* L.
Mason Bee
4 *Megachile maritima* Kirby

On the underside of their bodies, the moderately large to large bees of the family Megachilidae have brushes, formed of hairs of different lengths, for sweeping pollen from flowers. *Anthidium manicatum* is a summer bee with striking yellow markings. It frequents certain labiate plants, such as woundwort, sage and trefoil. It nests in the ground and also in chinks in walls or wooden beams. The cells are made of pieces of plant fluff stuck together.

Hoplitis adunca is a common visitor in Europe on flowering viper's bugloss. It nests in cracks in walls and old beams and carries viper's bugloss pollen to the nest, where it kneads it into hemispherical piles, on each of which it places an egg.

In the early spring, the Mason Bee (*Osmia rufa*) settles on flowering lungwort, violets, willow and poplar catkins and, in gardens, on crocuses or hyacinths. It nests in holes in wood, in cracks in walls and in the deserted nests of other solitary bees. The female partitions off the nest into chambers, in each of which she places a pile of kneaded pollen.

In the summer, flowering thistles and cornflowers attract a striking bee with large mandibles. *Megachile maritima* is one of a series of related and similar species called leaf-cutter bees. The nest is built under stones and the cells are lined with fragments of leaves, which the bee cuts off most efficiently with its jaws. The presence of such 'trimmed' leaves is a sure sign that the bees are not very far away.

2

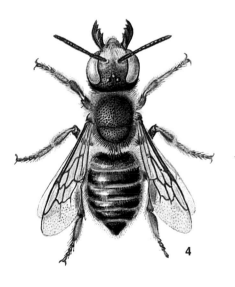

3

1. *Anthidium manicatum:* ♂ 14—17 mm, ♀ 11—13 mm (♂ $\frac{9}{16}$—$\frac{11}{16}$ in, ♀ $\frac{7}{16}$—$\frac{9}{16}$ in). The western part of the Palaearctic region.
2. *Hoplitis adunca:* 9—13 mm ($\frac{3}{8}$—$\frac{9}{16}$ in). The western part of the Palaearctic region.
3. *Osmia rufa:* 8—13 mm ($\frac{5}{16}$—$\frac{9}{16}$ in). Central and southern Europe, Transcaucasia.
4. *Megachile maritima:* 14—17 mm ($\frac{9}{16}$—$\frac{11}{16}$ in). Central and northern Europe.

1 *Nomada fulvicornis* F. Anthophoridae

2 *Epeolus cruciger* Panz.

3 *Eucera longicornis* L.

Hymenopteran markings consisting of yellow spots on a dark ground are often very variable, as in typical wasps (Vespidae), digger wasps (Sphecidae) and bees. *Nomada fulvicornis*, illustrated here, is another example; it is one of many species of the same genus which are not easy to tell apart. These bees do not build a nest of their own and their offspring are reared by various solitary bees belonging to different genera. *Nomada fulvicornis* forms two generations a year; the bees of the spring generation appear in April and May and are usually to be found on sallows and currant bushes, while the summer generation flies in August and visits ragwort, goldenrod and clover. The off-spring of this species are reared in the nests of solitary bees of the genus *Andrena* (e.g. *A. tibialis, A. bimaculata* and others).

The beautiful and strikingly coloured *Epeolus cruciger* is another parasite and its offspring are reared by primitive solitary bees of the genus *Colletes*.

The males of *Eucera longicornis* and related species are characterised by extremely long antennae. The imagos fly in May and are still to be found in suitable grassy localities, despite the gradual disappearance of this bee, owing to the decrease in the number of such habitats. The males appear much sooner than the fe-males. The imagos visit flowering vetches and alka-net. They nest in the ground. The female excavates a burrow, with nest cells round the sides, so that the whole can be compared to the shape of a bunch of grapes. Each cell contains pollen and an egg. *Eucera longicornis* is a host of the parasitic bee *Nomada sex-fasciata* and rears its offspring.

1. *Nomada fulvicornis:* 10—14 mm ($\frac{3}{8}$—$\frac{9}{16}$ in). The western part of the Palaearctic region.
2. *Epeolus cruciger:* 5—8 mm ($\frac{3}{16}$—$\frac{5}{16}$ in). Europe.
3. *Eucera longicornis:* 12—15 mm ($\frac{1}{2}$—$\frac{5}{8}$ in). Practically the whole of Europe.

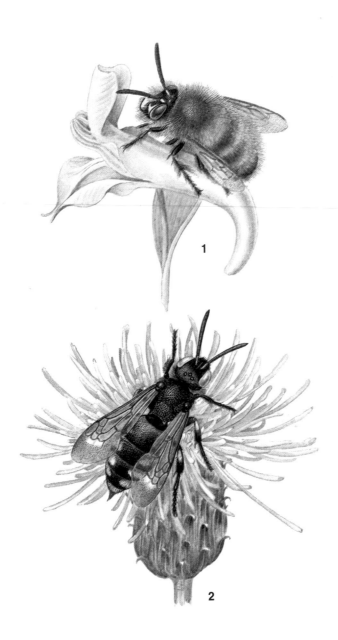

1 *Anthophora acervorum* Pallas <small>Anthophoridae</small>

2 *Thyreus orbatus* Lep.

3 *Xylocopa violacea* L.
   Blue Carpenter Bee

The first warm days of spring also tempt solitary bees out of hiding, among them the strikingly stout-bodied, hirsute *Anthophora acervorum,* which is covered with black or greyish-brown hairs and pollinates lungwort, corydalis, primroses, willow and poplar catkins, and later deadnettles, at the end of March and in April. It flies quite fast and close to the ground; if it feels itself to be in danger, it flies away, but later returns to its territory. The female builds a nest in clay walls, often close to country dwellings, e.g. in barns and cowsheds.

The family Anthophoridae contains quite a few bees which do not rear their broods themselves, but lay eggs in the nests of other bees and let the next generation develop there. The offspring of *Thyreus orbatus,* whose imagos visit summer flowers, develop in the nests of the species *Anthophora pubescens* and *A. quadrimaculata.*

The Blue Carpenter Bee (*Xylocopa violacea*) and *Xylocopa valga,* which are very similar in both colour and appearance, are two of the largest solitary bees. *X. violacea* imagos (males and females) overwinter and make their appearance in May. They like considerable warmth and inhabit steppe-type localities and gardens. They visit the flowers of thistles, viper's bugloss, sallows, sicklewort and other plants. They are very fast fliers. Bees are known for their highly developed care of their offspring and in this species it is very pronounced. The female builds a nest in an old hollow tree. Basically it is a shaft 15–30 cm (6–12 in) long, divided by partitions into ten to fifteen chambers, each containing a supply of pollen and one egg. The imagos, often in single file, fly out through a hole bitten in the wood by the first bee. Carpenter bees frequently nest in the same place where they were born.

Scheme of the nest of the Blue Carpenter Bee (*Xylocopa violacea*)

1. *Anthophora acervorum:* 14—16 mm ($\frac{9}{16}$—$\frac{5}{8}$ in). The western part of the Palaearctic region.
2. *Thyreus orbatus:* 8.5—11 mm ($\frac{11}{32}$—$\frac{7}{16}$ in). A large part of Europe.
3. *Xylocopa violacea:* 20—23 mm ($\frac{13}{16}$—$\frac{15}{16}$ in). Southern and central Europe.

1 *Apis mellifera* L.

Honeybee, Hive Bee

Apidae

The nest of the Honeybee (*Apis mellifera*) has the reputation of being the most perfectly organised state known among insects. It is ruled by a single queen, the mother of all the occupants of the hive, which can number up to 80,000 and which all have strictly defined functions. The queen lays the eggs. The workers, which live only a short time, perform different tasks. In the first phase of their life they keep the nest clean and, while their pharyngeal glands function, they feed the young grubs. During the next ten days they are kept busy building the regular hexagonal cells of the comb from wax produced by their wax glands; they also concentrate nectar and fill the cells with pollen. At the end of this period they act for a short time as guards. In the last phase of their life they collect pollen and nectar; the pollen is carried back to the hive in 'pollen baskets' on the tibiae of their hindlegs. The hive contains males only in the spring and at the beginning of the summer; their sole function is to fertilise the new queen.

In the hive, the bees develop from eggs laid singly by the queen in the cells of the comb. Workers develop in small cells, males (drones) in large cells. Future queens develop in special cells shaped like a bunch of grapes. When the new queens are ready to emerge, the old queen either dies of old age or leaves the hive with about half of the workers (a swarm) to allow the new queen to take her place. The bee-keeper usually finds this swarm hanging from a branch and can then transfer it to a new hive. In the old hive, the first queen to emerge stings the other queens, still in their cells, to death and thus becomes the undisputed ruler of the hive. From a human point of view, Honeybees are crueller than wasps and bumblebees, which let the young queens remain in the nest. From the point of view of bees, however, there is no other alternative, since the presence of several queens would, in time, lead to destruction of the community owing to the presence of too many individuals in the nest.

Bees have excellent orientation skills and can communicate by means of specific 'dances', which inform other workers of the quality and amount of food in the neighbourhood. They can also distinguish colours and, lastly, they are among the most important pollinators.

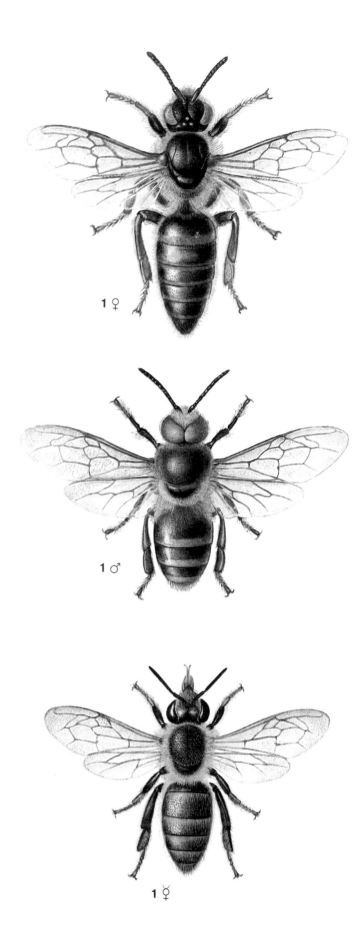

1 ♀

1 ♂

1 ☿

1. *Apis mellifera:* ☿ 12—15 mm, ♀ 16—20 mm, ♂ 14—18 mm (☿ $\frac{1}{2}$—$\frac{5}{8}$ in, ♀ $\frac{5}{8}$—$\frac{13}{16}$ in, ♂ $\frac{9}{16}$—$\frac{3}{4}$ in). The entire globe.

1

2

3

1 *Bombus pascuorum* Scop.

2 *Bombus pomorum* Panzer

3 *Bombus subterraneus* L.

Apidae

After Honeybees, bumblebees are the second most important pollinators. They are irreplaceable for the pollination of trumpet-shaped flowers, for which Honeybees have too short a proboscis. *Bombus pascuorum* is one of the most common species which fly from the spring to the autumn; it is often to be seen on vetches, clover, various Compositae and fruit trees. Like all bumblebees, it lives in one-year colonies. In the spring, the queen founds the nest in moss, grass, deserted birds' and mammals' nests or old straw, in a wood, field, garden or even close to people, e.g. in a barn, wood-shed or cow-shed. In the nest, the female first kneads pollen into a lump, usually lays eight eggs on it, coats the whole with a layer of wax and then makes a wax receptacle for the nectar. The eggs and larvae are kept warm by the heat of her body. The larvae grow quickly and pupate in a cocoon shaped like a hazelnut. These pupae give rise to the first workers, which are very small because they have had only just enough food for their development. In the summer, young queens and males appear in the nest, which contains a total of about 100–200 individuals. In the summer the colony dies out and only the young naked queens survive the winter.

In some places in Europe, *Bombus pomorum* is a fairly common species in fields, meadows, gardens and woods. It is rather variably coloured. It nests in the ground (frequently in voles' nests), and is mostly to be found on labiate and composite plants. It is important as a pollinator of clover.

Bombus subterraneus nests in the ground. The females do not leave their winter quarters until May, which is relatively late. This bumblebee has a very long proboscis. It likes clover and deadnettles and is common on thistles.

1. *Bombus pascuorum:* ♀ 14—16 mm, ♀ 18—22 mm, ♂ 13—18 mm (♀ $\frac{9}{16}$—$\frac{5}{8}$ in, ♀ $\frac{3}{4}$—$\frac{7}{8}$ in, ♂ $\frac{9}{16}$—$\frac{3}{4}$ in). The whole of Europe (right to the north), Siberia, the Caucasus, central Asia.
2. *Bombus pomorum:* ♀ 16—18 mm, ♀ 20—24 mm, ♂ 18—20 mm (♀ $\frac{5}{8}$—$\frac{3}{4}$ in, ♀ $\frac{13}{16}$—$\frac{15}{16}$ in, ♂ $\frac{3}{4}$—$\frac{13}{16}$ in). The temperate parts of Eurasia (not present in northern and southern Europe).
3. *Bombus subterraneus:* ♀ 14—16 mm, ♀ 17—30 mm, ♂ 15—20 mm (♀ $\frac{9}{16}$—$\frac{5}{8}$ in, ♀ $\frac{11}{16}$—1$\frac{3}{16}$ in, ♂ $\frac{5}{8}$—$\frac{13}{16}$ in). Europe, the temperate belt in Asia.

1 ***Bombus hortorum*** L.

Apidae

2 ***Bombus lapidarius*** L.

Large Red-tailed Bumblebee

3 ***Bombus muscorum*** F.

There are several bumblebees whose bodies are covered with alternating bands of black, yellow and white hairs. *Bombus hortorum* is one of these. The queen begins to look for a place for the nest about halfway through April. It may be above or under the ground, in a deserted mouse's nest, in a nesting-box, in a pile of old rags or under floorboards, etc. This bumblebee is to be encountered in meadows, gardens, parks and thickets, on grass verges and beside footpaths. The nest is occupied by a few dozen to a few hundred individuals. *B. hortorum* is a well-known pollinator of fruit-trees, but it also visits foxgloves, corydalis, lungwort, thistles and many other herbaceous plants, trees and bushes.

The queens and workers of the Large Red-tailed Bumblebee (*Bombus lapidarius*) can be identified from their velvety black, hairy bodies and red-tipped abdomens. The females (future queens) appear early in the spring and look for somewhere to nest. They nest in holes (abandoned mammals' nests), nesting-boxes and crevices in rocks and houses and their nest comprises 100–300 inhabitants. The bumblebees fly in open country, in meadows and pastures, on the outskirts of woods, in gardens and in parks. The young queens and the males fly up to the end of October. The Large Red-tailed Bumblebee is an important pollinator of 250 known types of host plants; in particular, it is an important pollinator of clover.

Bombus muscorum is one of the most handsome bumblebees, but is now rare. After hibernating, the queen appears in the middle of May. This species likes damp surroundings and occurs in damp meadows, fens, moorland and coastal areas. It nests outside, in a clump of grass or moss, but also under cover, in a nesting-box or a deserted bird's nest. Its own nest is small and contains only a few dozen individuals. These bumblebees visit deadnettles, woundwort, thistles and many other plants. The colouring of this species does not vary.

1

2

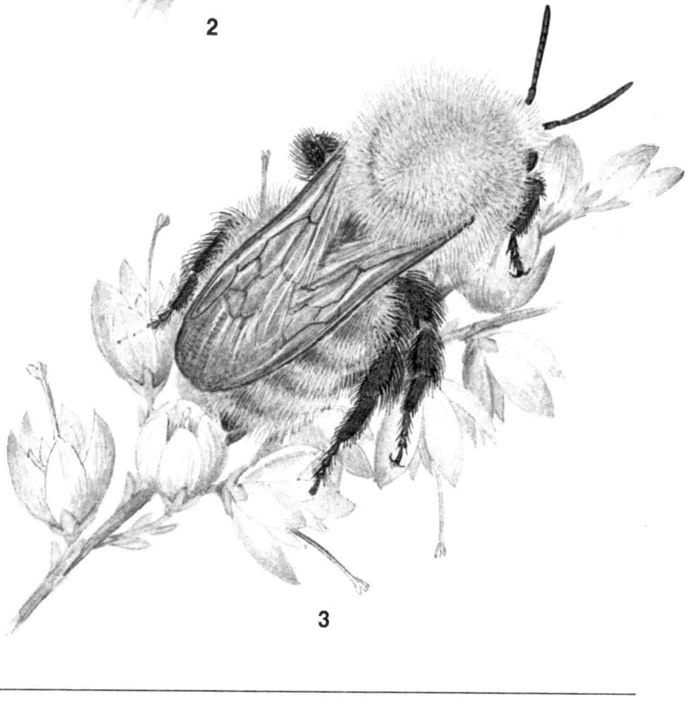

3

1. *Bombus hortorum:* ☿ 12—20 mm, ♀ 17—24 mm, ♂ 15—20 mm (☿ $\frac{1}{2}$—$\frac{13}{16}$ in, ♀ $\frac{11}{16}$—$\frac{15}{16}$ in, ♂ $\frac{5}{8}$—$\frac{13}{16}$ in). The temperate belt in Eurasia.
2. *Bombus lapidarius:* ☿ 15—20 mm, ♀ 20—27 mm, ♂ 14—18 mm (☿ $\frac{5}{8}$—$\frac{13}{16}$ in, ♀ $\frac{13}{16}$—$1\frac{1}{16}$ in, ♂ $\frac{9}{16}$—$\frac{3}{4}$ in). A large part of Europe (in the north to Lapland, in the Alps to about 2,000 m (6,561 ft).
3. *Bombus muscorum:* ☿ 12—18 mm, ♀ 17—22 mm, ♂ 13—16 mm (☿ $\frac{1}{2}$—$\frac{3}{4}$ in, ♀ $\frac{11}{16}$—$\frac{7}{8}$ in, ♂ $\frac{9}{16}$—$\frac{5}{8}$ in). A large part of Europe (except the north and south), northern Asia.

1 ***Bombus terrestris*** L.   Apidae
Buff-tailed Bumblebee

2 ***Psithyrus rupestris*** F.

3 ***Psithyrus campestris*** Panz.

The Buff-tailed Bumblebee (*Bombus terrestris*) and *Bombus lucorum* are very similarly coloured and are often confused. The yellow hairs on *B. terrestris* are more a yellowish-brown shade, however, while on *B. lucorum* they are lemon-yellow. Weather permitting, the first female Buff-tailed Bumblebees appear in the middle of March and look for a suitable site for a nest; their search is accompanied by a deep buzzing. This species lives mostly in holes, in deserted mammals' nests, often as much as 1 m (3 ft) deep in the ground. Its nest is numerically one of the largest, with several hundred inhabitants (in the south up to one thousand). The bumblebees fly over meadows, pastures, fields and gardens and on the outskirts of woods and are common in town parks. They pollinate a great many plants, in particular bilberries, cranberries, raspberries, deadnettles, sage, thistles and fruit trees.

In size and colouring, cuckoo bees (genus *Psithyrus*) resemble bumblebees so closely that a layman is generally unable to tell the difference. They do not nest in colonies and do not build a nest, but let their offspring be reared by bumblebees. *Psithyrus rupestris* closely resembles the Large Red-tailed Bumblebee, in whose nest it lays its eggs. In May and June the imagos fly about, looking for the nests of their hosts. The second generation of cuckoo bees appears at the end of the summer, when the males occur in abundance on thistles. The young females hibernate. There are no workers.

Psithyrus campestris lays its eggs in the nests of *Bombus pascuorum,* *B. pomorum* and other bumblebees. Females which have hibernated search for nests in May and June. The new generation is hatched at the height of summer; in September the males appear in large numbers on thistles.

1. *Bombus terrestris:* ♀ 15—19 mm, ♀ 20—23 mm, ♂ 14—22 mm (♀ $\frac{5}{8}$—$\frac{3}{4}$ in, ♀ $\frac{13}{16}$—$\frac{15}{16}$ in, ♂ $\frac{9}{16}$—$\frac{7}{8}$ in). The whole of Europe, Asia Minor, northern Africa.
2. *Psithyrus rupestris:* ♂ 10—18 mm, ♀ 18—25 mm (♂ $\frac{3}{8}$—$\frac{3}{4}$ in, ♀ $\frac{3}{4}$—1 in). Central and northern Europe.
3. *Psithyrus campestris:* ♂ 11—16 mm, ♀ 15—17 mm (♂ $\frac{7}{16}$—$\frac{5}{8}$ in, ♀ $\frac{5}{8}$—$\frac{11}{16}$ in). A large part of Europe.

1 *Philopotamus variegatus* Scop.   Philopotamidae

2 *Phryganea grandis* L.   Phryganeidae

3 *Limnephilus griseus* L.   Limnephilidae

Caddis-flies are known to us primarily through their larvae, most of which spend the whole of their development in a self-made individual case. The larvae of *Philopotamus variegatus* and related species, however, make a common tubular nest over 50 mm (2 in) long, out of secretory filaments. The imagos, which fly from June to August, live mainly in montane and submontane regions.

Phryganea grandis, which is one of the largest caddis-flies, is to be found from lowland to alpine altitudes. During the daytime the imagos sit on stones and wood, etc., with their wings folded roof-wise over their bodies; at night they are attracted by sources of artificial light and often settle near them, e.g. on illuminated cottage walls. This is still a common species. The larvae make themselves a case out of plant fragments whose length is many times greater than their width and which are arranged in a gradual spiral. The case is open at both ends. Older larvae live among plants, where they lie in wait for prey; they are highly rapacious and catch any aquatic insect larvae which venture near them. They overwinter and, after making a few constructional modifications, pupate in their cases the following spring. The pupal stage is brief; in the final phase the pupa rises to the surface and the imago emerges shortly afterwards.

Many caddis-flies are still to be seen in the autumn. *Limnephilus griseus* still occurs in November – and in favourable years until December. The first imagos appear in May. This caddis-fly is to be found chiefly round the ponds and pools in which its larvae develop. The larva makes a case of diverse plant fragments all stuck together. Europe is inhabited by many related and similar species.

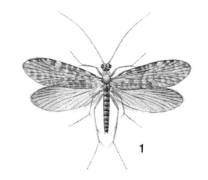

1

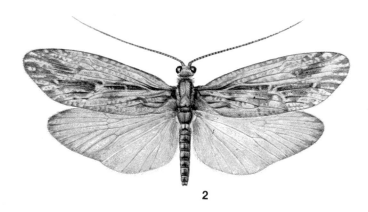

2

Case of the caddis-fly larva of the genus *Phryganea*

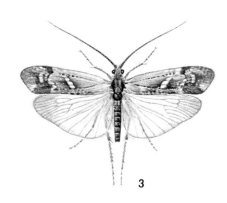

3

1. *Philopotamus variegatus:* 7—9 mm, forewing span 21—29 mm ($\frac{9}{32}$—$\frac{3}{8}$ in, forewing span $\frac{13}{16}$—1$\frac{1}{8}$ in). Europe.
2. *Phryganea grandis:* 15—21 mm, forewing span 40—60 mm ($\frac{5}{8}$—$\frac{13}{16}$ in, forewing span 1$\frac{9}{16}$—2$\frac{3}{8}$ in). Palaearctic region.
3. *Limnephilus griseus:* 6.5—12 mm, forewing span 19—30 mm ($\frac{9}{32}$—$\frac{1}{2}$ in, forewing span $\frac{3}{4}$—1$\frac{3}{16}$ in). Eurasia.

1 *Hepialus humuli* L. Hepialidae
Ghost Moth

2 *Nemophora degeerella* L. Incurvariidae

At the beginning of the lepidopteran system, alongside families of tiny moths, is the family Hepialidae, which belongs to the numerically small suborder Jugatae. In the moths of this suborder, the two pairs of wings are joined together by a lobe on the forewings, as in the Ghost Moth (*Hepialus humuli*), their best known representative. The males and females of this species are very differently coloured. The imagos fly over mountain and submontane meadows and frequently appear in gardens; during the daytime they rest. The males are more active than the females; they fly in the evening, showing themselves to females, which mostly sit on the vegetation, but will then rise up to meet the males. At egg-laying time, however, the females are more active; they fly about the countryside and successively release eggs – several hundred in all. The caterpillars burrow in the ground, where they live on the roots of various kinds of plants, such as sorrel, stinging nettles and wild and cultivated hops. The caterpillar hibernates twice and pupates in a loose cocoon in the ground in the spring. The single generation of moths flies from May to August.

The second lepidopteran suborder, Heteroneura (formerly Frenatae), comprises the vast majority of species. Distinct from the preceding suborder, the wings of these lepidopterans are joined together by a special organ known as a frenulum. The Incurvariidae are one of the more primitive families of this suborder. *Nemophora degeerella* is a very common species. It is relatively small, but has very long antennae, which, in the male, are up to five times the length of his wing. The imagos fly in May and June over damp clearings, along forest paths and at the margins of deciduous and mixed woods; they often settle on the vegetation. The caterpillar lives on anemones; it first of all mines passages in a leaf and later spins a long, bag-like cocoon round itself, in which to spend the winter.

1. *Hepialus humuli:* forewing span 40—70 mm ($1\frac{9}{16}$—$2\frac{3}{4}$ in). Eurasia (the temperate belt).
2. *Nemophora degeerella:* forewing span 16—21 mm ($\frac{5}{8}$—$\frac{13}{16}$ in). Europe (in the east to the Caucasus).

1 *Tineola bisselliella* Hum.   Tineidae
Common Clothes Moth

2 *Psyche casta* Pall.   Psychidae

3 *Lepidopsyche unicolor* Hfn.

4 *Phyllonorycter blancardella* F.   Gracillariidae

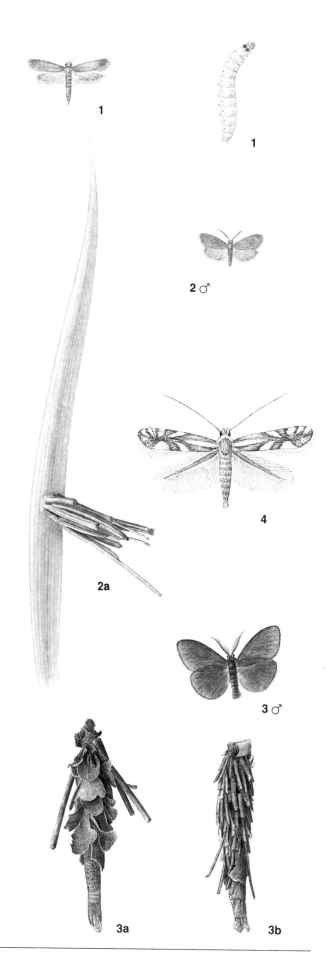

Tineola bisselliella, the familiar, widespread and dreaded Common Clothes Moth, flies from May to September in the open, but appears in households the whole year round. Outdoors the caterpillars eat various remains in birds' and mammals' nests, but indoors they wreak havoc in woollen fabrics, clothes and furs, spoiling or completely destroying them. Today there are sufficient chemical preparations available for combating them, but regular examination and airing of cupboards and wardrobes are equally important.

In the imago stage, bagworm moths (Psychidae) are generally inconspicuous. The males can fly, but the females are wingless. These moths are much better known from the cases which the caterpillars ('bagworms') stick together around themselves and which identify the species to which they belong. *Psyche casta* caterpillars make a small case and stick it to all sorts of plants (2a). *Lepidopsyche unicolor*, on the other hand, makes large bags, with differences between the bags of future males (3a) and females (3b). The caterpillars hibernate; the moths emerge the following year and appear from June to August.

The tiny moths of the family Gracillariidae are characterised by unusually narrow hindwings with long, fine fringes all the way round them. The forewings are very prettily patterned, but it needs a strong magnifying glass to see all the delicate details. The caterpillars of these moths are leaf miners and live in the leaf tissues. The species *Phyllonorycter blancardella* mines on the undersides of apple leaves. The caterpillars of the last generation overwinter in the leaves and pupate in the spring.

---

1. *Tineola bisselliella:* forewing span 10—16 mm ($\frac{3}{8}$—$\frac{5}{8}$ in). Over practically the whole globe.
2. *Psyche casta:* forewing span of ♂ 12—15 mm ($\frac{1}{2}$—$\frac{5}{8}$ in). Europe (in the east to the Caucasus).
3. *Lepidopsyche unicolor:* forewing span 25—30 mm (1—$1\frac{3}{16}$ in). The temperate part of Europe.
4. *Phyllonorycter blancardella:* forewing span 6—8 mm ($\frac{1}{4}$—$\frac{5}{16}$ in). The Palaearctic region.

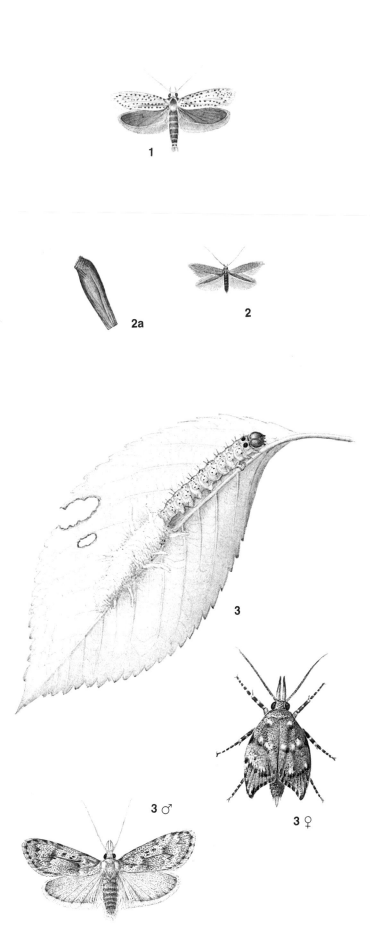

1 *Yponomeuta evonymella* L.   Yponomeutidae
Bird-cherry Ermine

2 *Coleophora laricella* Hb.   Coleophoridae
Larch Case Bearer

3 *Diurnea fagella* Schiff.   Oecophoridae

Several species of small moths have white forewings marked with dark spots. The distinctive feature of the Bird-cherry Ermine Moth (*Yponomeuta evonymella*) is that the spots are arranged in five rows. The moth forms a single generation which flies in July and August from lowlands to mountains, where it reaches the upper deciduous forest limit. The caterpillars live on rowan, birch-cherry or buckthorn, on which they weave large nests made of white filaments, where they all live together. They move rapidly, but they do not abandon the nest and eventually they pupate in it. In large numbers they can strip the tree bare.

The Larch Case Bearer (*Coleophora laricella*) is a tiny, inconspicuous moth whose single generation flies in June and July. It inhabits larch woods, mainly in hilly country. The moth easily escapes notice, but the caterpillar rather attracts it. It lives in a longish case (2a) and mines larch needles in the autumn and spring; when it has finished eating, the needles are white and hollow and soon dry up. If there are too many caterpillars, the tree is stripped bare.

The members of the family Oecophoridae are all small, but often very brightly coloured moths. Although not one of the most conspicuous, *Diurnea fagella* is one of the best known species. The males have normally developed wings; the females have stunted wings. The moths appear very early in the spring (during March) and are still to be seen in May. They inhabit forests from low to high altitudes, where they ascend to the upper deciduous forest limit. The caterpillars live on the leaves of various deciduous trees and shrubs, on which they spin a protective case for themselves. This species produces one generation a year.

1. *Yponomeuta evonymella:* forewing span 22—24 mm ($\frac{7}{8}$—$\frac{15}{16}$ in). The Palaearctic region.
2. *Coleophora laricella:* forewing span 8—10 mm ($\frac{5}{16}$—$\frac{3}{8}$ in). Eurasia.
3. *Diurnea fagella:* forewing span 19—20 mm ($\frac{3}{4}$—$1\frac{1}{8}$ in). Europe (in the east into central Asia.)

1 *Sesia apiformis* Cl.
Hornet Moth

Sesiidae

2 *Tortrix viridana* L.
Green Oak Tortrix

Tortricidae

3 *Cydia pomonella* L.
Codlin Moth

With its protective 'waspish' colouring, striped body and transparent membraneous wings, the Hornet Moth (*Sesia apiformis*) does, indeed, look remarkably like a wasp. It likes damp and warm localities with growths of poplars and therefore occurs primarily in lowlands, although it is also known in mountains. Its single generation flies from May to June (sometimes until August). As distinct from most lepidopterans, the caterpillars do not live on leaves, but inside the roots and the lower parts of the trunks of different kinds of poplars or sallows. They usually hibernate twice.

In some summers, Green Oak Tortrix (*Tortrix viridana*) caterpillars appear on young oak leaves in such quantities that the blades soon disappear and in a short time the tree is left bare. Such invasions occur chiefly in places where the woods have been treated with chemicals and the natural enemies of the caterpillars have been destroyed. This is a good example of how dangerous it can be for people to interfere with the natural balance of nature. After completing their development, the *Tortrix* caterpillars pupate in rolled-up leaves and the moths emerge during June and July. The female lays eggs in pairs on oak twigs, where they remain during the winter.

If you cut open an apple, you might find inside it the caterpillar of a Codlin Moth (*Cydia pomonella*), sure proof that the apple has not been treated with chemicals. The caterpillar tunnels through the apple, but does not complete its development inside it. In the autumn it crawls out, spends the winter under bark or in a crack in a trunk and pupates in the spring. The moths fly from the end of May; sometimes there are two generations. The female usually lays the eggs singly on young apples and the caterpillar bores its way inside.

1. *Sesia apiformis:* forewing span 30—40 mm ($1\frac{3}{16}$—$1\frac{9}{16}$ in). The warmer part of Eurasia, North America.
2. *Tortrix viridana:* forewing span 18—23 mm ($\frac{3}{4}$—$\frac{15}{16}$ in). Europe, the Caucasus, Asia Minor, northern Africa.
3. *Cydia pomonella:* forewing span 14—18 mm ($\frac{9}{16}$—$\frac{3}{4}$ in). Over the entire globe.

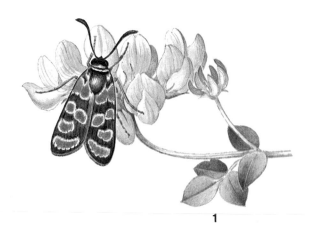

1

1 *Zygaena carniolica* Scop.   Zygaenidae
2 *Zygaena filipendulae* L.
Six-spot Burnet

3 *Zygaena ephialtes* L.

It is not difficult to distinguish burnet moths from other lepidopterans, but sometimes it is difficult to tell which species they belong to, as many of them are very variably coloured. *Zygaena carniolica* has red, white-bordered spots on its forewings. It flies from June to August in warm, sunny lowland localities on a limestone base. The caterpillars live on leguminous plants, in particular sainfoin, overwinter in a cocoon and pupate late in the spring of the following year.

The Six-spot Burnet (*Zygaena filipendulae*) is the most common member of the genus. From June to August it flies over meadows, forest clearings, grass borders in fields and meadows and sunny slopes from lowlands to altitudes of about 2,000 m (6,560 ft). The female lays yellowish eggs in clusters. The caterpillars live on leguminous plants (chiefly trefoil and sainfoin). After hibernating, they pupate in the spring in a cocoon attached to a plant; sometimes they hibernate twice.

Zygaena ephialtes is exceptionally variably coloured. The typical form has white spots and a few red or orange spots on its wings. In some forms, however, the spots are all on the forewings and the hindwings are red or orange. The band across the abdomen is the same colour as the spots. This burnet moth flies from June to August in places where it is warm – sunny hillsides, the outskirts of woods, clearings and steppes, etc. The caterpillars live mainly on leguminous plants. They hibernate (sometimes twice) and pupate in the spring in a light yellow cocoon.

2

3

3

3

3

1. *Zygaena carniolica:* forewing span 25—32 mm (1—$1\frac{1}{4}$ in). Central and southern Europe, Asia as far as the Altai Mts.
2. *Zygaena filipendulae:* forewing span 30—38 mm ($1\frac{3}{16}$—$1\frac{1}{2}$ in). Europe, extending into central Asia.
3. *Zygaena ephialtes:* forewing span 30—40 mm ($1\frac{3}{16}$—$1\frac{9}{16}$ in). The temperate part of Eurasia.

1 *Cnaemidophorus rhododactyla* Den. et Schiff.

Pterophoridae

2 *Cossus cossus* L.
Goat Moth

Cossidae

3 *Zeuzera pyrina* L.
Leopard Moth

Plume moths (Pterophoridae) immediately attract attention because of their split fore- and hindwings. *Cnaemidophorus rhododactyla* flies from May to August at the margins of forests and over meadows and bushy hillsides. The caterpillar lives in the flowers of wild and cultivated roses; it hibernates and pupates in May among the leaves of the host plant. This moth is now rare in many places.

The caterpillars of most lepidopterans live on the leaves of their host plants. The caterpillars of the Goat Moth (*Cossus cossus*) and the Leopard Moth (*Zeuzera pyrina*) are something of an exception, however, since they burrow in wood. The nocturnal Goat Moth is most abundant in June and July (sometimes a little sooner or later). It chiefly inhabits deciduous woods, riparian copses and gardens. At first, the caterpillars live gregariously on a branch or trunk; later they invade the wood, where each excavates its own passage. They generally infest willows and poplars, but have also been found in oaks and fruit trees. The caterpillar usually hibernates twice, but sometimes three or four times; its presence can be detected by the strong goat-like smell emanating from the wood. It mostly pupates in the wood in a cocoon.

The Leopard Moth (*Zeuzera pyrina*) has very variable markings on its wings; its size is also variable and depends on the amount and quality of the food eaten by the caterpillar. The moths are active at night; they fly from June to August in gardens, parks, woods and fruit-tree nurseries. The caterpillars live in wood, but, unlike the preceding species, they favour thin trunks and branches. Apples and pears stand at the head of their long list of host plants. The caterpillar hibernates twice and then pupates in a cocoon, usually in a passage in the wood.

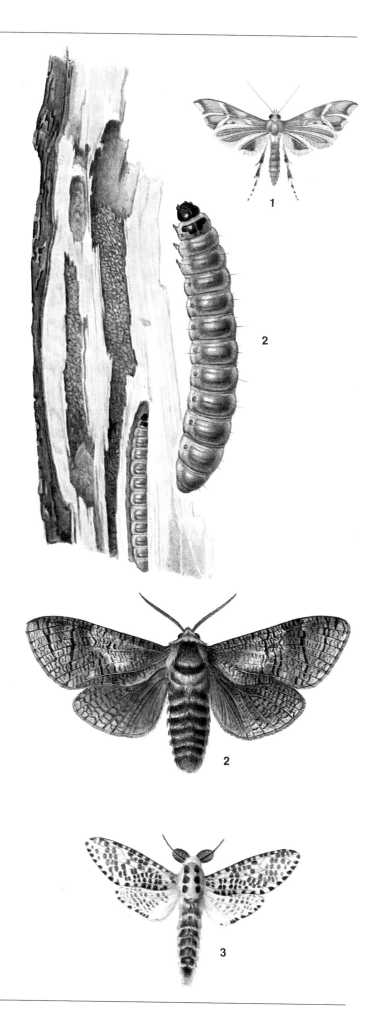

1. *Cnaemidophorus rhodadactyla:* forewing span 18—25 mm ($\frac{3}{4}$—1 in). The Palaearctic and Nearctic regions.
2. *Cossus cossus:* forewing span 65—80 mm ($2\frac{9}{16}$—$3\frac{1}{8}$ in). The Palaearctic region.
3. *Zeuzera pyrina:* forewing span 35—60 mm ($1\frac{3}{8}$—$2\frac{3}{8}$ in). Europe, the temperate belt in Asia; carried to North America.

1 *Malacosoma neustria* L.
Lackey Moth

2 *Poecilocampa populi* L.
December Moth

3 *Lasiocampa quercus* L.
Oak Eggar

Lasiocampidae

From time to time, in certain places, the Lackey Moth (*Malacosoma neustria*) appears in large numbers. It is equally at home in orchards, tree-lined avenues and woods. The imagos fly from June to September. The female lays her eggs in characteristic rings round thin twigs. The rings are of varying widths and may contain several hundred eggs. The eggs overwinter. The caterpillars, which are hatched in the spring, at first live gregariously in silken nests; later they disperse all over the tree. They eat the leaves of various trees, but have a special predilection for fruit trees. They pupate among the leaves in a yellowish cocoon.

As the winter approaches, the number of lepidopterans to be seen in the open rapidly decreases, but there are some which explicitly like the chill of autumn. The December Moth *Poecilocampa populi*, which flies from October to the end of the year, actually tolerates slight frosts. It lives in gardens and woods and often flies towards the light of lamps. Eggs are laid during the flight stage. The caterpillars, which begin to hatch in March or April, are at their most numerous from May to July. They devour the leaves of different deciduous trees, such as ash and various types of alders, poplars, willows, elms, limes and fruit trees.

The male and female Oak Eggar (*Lasiocampa quercus*) differ markedly from each other as regards size and colouring. This species is a relatively rare inhabitant of oak woods, mixed woods, heaths and grassy places, but its numbers tend to be greater at higher altitudes. The male flies during the daytime, the female in the evening. The imagos live from June to August. The female lays her eggs at the end of the summer. The caterpillars, which hatch the same year, live on oak, willow, birch, blackthorn, bilberry, bramble, raspberry and heather leaves and, after hibernating, continue feeding during the following year; they pupate at the end of May. At high altitudes the caterpillars hibernate twice.

---

1. *Malacosoma neustria:* forewing span 25—35 mm (1—1$\frac{3}{8}$ in). The Palaearctic region.
2. *Poecilocampa populi:* forewing span 30—36 mm (1$\frac{3}{16}$—1$\frac{7}{16}$ in). The temperate part of Eurasia (not present in the most southerly part of Europe).
3. *Lasiocampa quercus:* forewing span ♂ 55—65 mm, ♀ 70—85 mm (forewing span: ♂ 2$\frac{3}{16}$—2$\frac{9}{16}$ in, ♀ 2$\frac{3}{4}$—3$\frac{3}{8}$ in). Europe, Asia Minor, Siberia.

1 *Macrothylacia rubi* L.
Fox Moth

Lasiocampidae

2 *Gastropacha quercifolia* L.
Lappet

3 *Dendrolimus pini* L.
Pine-tree Lappet

The males of the Fox Moth (*Macrothylacia rubi*) fly from the early evening until nightfall; the somewhat larger females sit on vegetation during the daytime and fly during the night, when they are attracted by lamplight. The moths frequent woodland clearings, the margins of woods and meadows, where they live from May to July, although they are not normally seen. You are much more likely to come across the caterpillar, which is large, plump and covered with brown hairs; it occurs in grass and often wanders along field paths or grass borders in search of food. It eats bramble, dogrose, strawberry, clover and heather leaves. After hibernating, followed by a short spring feed, it pupates in a greyish-white cocoon.

The Lappet (*Gastropacha quercifolia*) is most often found on a woodland floor among the debris, but may also spend some time on a branch or a wall, posed to look like a dry leaf. In southern Europe it forms two generations, but elsewhere only one, whose imagos live from June to August. Northern European moths are generally darker than southern specimens. This species inhabits open woods, orchards, avenues and parks, but is rapidly becoming rare, chiefly because it is sensitive to various chemicals used by fruit-growers. The eggs are laid singly or in small groups. The caterpillars appear from August on oaks, hawthorn, plum, morello cherry, apple and pear trees, willows and hazels. They hibernate and pupate in the summer of the following year on a branch, in a loose grey cocoon.

The Pine-tree Lappet (*Dendrolimus pini*) is known for its highly variable colouring. There are size and colour differences between the male and female. It inhabits conifer (chiefly pine) forests from lowlands to altitudes of about 1,500 m [4,920 ft]). The imagos fly in July and August. The female lays her eggs in large groups. The caterpillars live on conifer needles taken from the trees. They appear in August and then hibernate. They pupate in June of the following year in a strong yellowish cocoon.

1. *Macrothylacia rubi*: forewing span ♂ 45—50 mm, ♀ 55—70 mm (♂ $1\frac{3}{4}$—2 in, ♀ $2\frac{3}{16}$—$2\frac{3}{4}$ in). A large part of temperate Eurasia.
2. *Gastropacha quercifolia*: forewing span 56—90 mm ($2\frac{7}{32}$—$3\frac{9}{16}$ in). The temperate part of Eurasia.
3. *Dendrolimus pini*: forewing span 50—75 mm (2—3 in). Europe (minus the British Isles), western Asia, northern Africa.

1 *Smerinthus ocellatus* L.
Eyed Hawkmoth

2 *Sphinx ligustri* L.
Privet Hawkmoth

In Europe there are only about twenty species of hawkmoths, all of them noted for their elegant form, beautiful markings and outstanding skill as fliers. The caterpillars are also striking; many of them have an outgrowth projecting from the ends of their bodies and many of them are brightly coloured.

During the daytime, the Eyed Hawkmoth (*Smerinthus ocellatus*) can be found sitting motionless on a tree trunk or a fence post, close to the ground, with its wings spread and the forewings largely overlapping the hindwings. If in danger, the moth shifts its forewings forwards to show the large coloured eyespots on its hindwings and starts to jerk in a menacing manner. When the danger has gone, it resumes its resting position again. The imagos, which emerge early on spring mornings, live only a few days. As a rule there is one generation, which appears from April to June, but sometimes a partial second generation is formed from July to October. The imagos sometimes stray into gardens. The main host plants of the caterpillars are different types of willows, together with fruit trees, blackthorn and poplars. The pupa overwinters.

The Privet Hawkmoth (*Sphinx ligustri*) rests on bark with its wings folded roof-wise over its back, i.e. quite differently from the Eyed Hawkmoth. It inhabits bushy country, parks and gardens and occasionally appears in cities. It becomes active when it is almost dark and visits flowers to suck their nectar. In central Europe it forms only one generation, which flies from May to July, but in the south it produces a second generation. The female lays her eggs singly on the undersides of leaves of the host plant. The caterpillar is not choosy and devours snowberry, lilac, guelder-rose, ash, rowan, elder, privet and many other leaves with equal impartiality. When resting it adopts a sphinx-like position. After four to six weeks it buries itself deep in the ground, pupates and spends the winter in this state. The moths generally emerge during the daytime.

1. *Smerinthus ocellatus:* forewing span 90—120 mm ($3\frac{9}{16}$—$4\frac{3}{4}$ in). The Palaearctic region.
2. *Sphinx ligustri:* forewing span 90—120 mm ($3\frac{9}{16}$—$4\frac{3}{4}$ in). The Palaearctic region.

1 *Acherontia atropos* L.
Death's-head Hawkmoth

Sphingidae

2 *Hyloicus pinastri* L.
Pine Hawkmoth

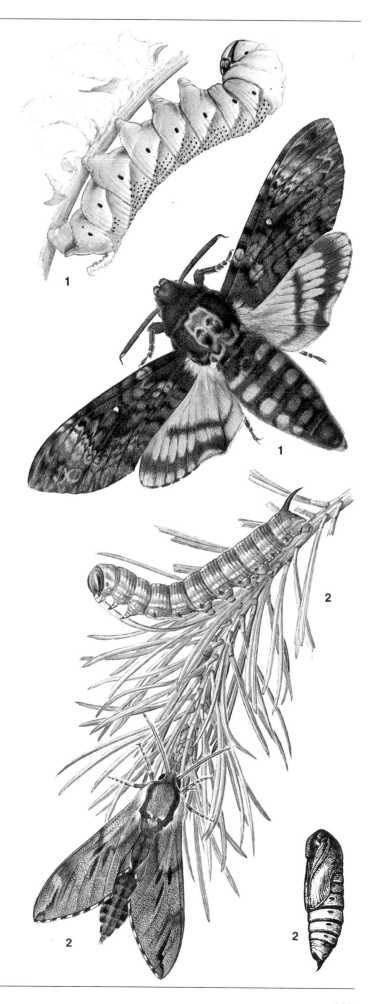

The Death's-head Hawkmoth (*Acherontia atropos*) attracts attention because of the strange markings on its thorax, where the scales form a pattern like a skull. Although a native of tropical Africa and south-west Asia, this outstanding flier regularly migrates to Europe and often to Britain. It produces two to three generations in the south of Europe, but only one or two further north, according to local conditions. The imago flies long into the night and is sometimes attracted by artificial lights. It sucks the nectar of certain flowers and is known to be tempted by the smell of honey; a raid on a bee hive usually proves fatal, however. The caterpillar is polyphagous; it lives chiefly on potatoes and other solanaceous plants, but on many other plants as well. If irritated, it whistles and its head darts from side to side. It pupates in the ground in a large earthen case. The moth sometimes emerges before the onset of winter, but in that case does not survive it. In central Europe most of the pupae die during the winter, even in the ground, as they are killed by frosts.

When resting on the bark of a coniferous tree, the Pine Hawkmoth (*Hyloicus pinastri*) matches its background perfectly. It inhabits dry conifer forests, but being an excellent flier it also appears far from them. It flies in the evening and at night and sucks nectar from flowers on the wing; it is particularly fond of evening primrose and viper's bugloss. As a rule, it produces only one generation whose imagos fly from May to July, but sometimes a partial second generation is formed in August. The female attaches her eggs to conifer needles. The caterpillar usually lives on pine needles, but does not ignore the needles of other conifers. The young caterpillars bite off the tips, but the older caterpillars eat the whole needles. When fully grown, the caterpillar descends from the tree and pupates in needles or moss at its foot. The pupa hibernates, sometimes twice. The imago emerges in the spring or summer during the daytime.

1. *Acherontia atropos:* forewing span 80—120 mm ($3\frac{1}{8}$—$4\frac{3}{4}$ in). Tropical Asia and Africa, southern Europe.
2. *Hyloicus pinastri:* forewing span 65—80 mm ($2\frac{9}{16}$—$3\frac{1}{8}$ in). The Palaearctic region; carried to North America.

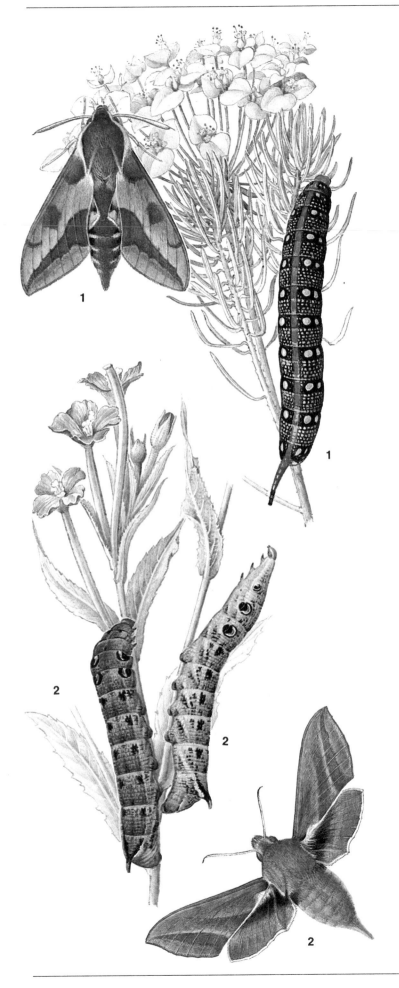

1 *Hyles euphorbiae* L. Sphingidae
Spurge Hawkmoth

2 *Deilephila elpenor* L.
Elephant Hawkmoth

The Spurge Hawkmoth (*Hyles euphorbiae*) visits flowering viper's bugloss, sage and campion and, in gardens, flowering phlox. Predominantly pink individuals are termed *Hyles euphorbiae* f. *rubescens*. The imagos fly from May to July, but in some years, especially in southern Europe, a second, partial generation appears from August to October. This species inhabits dry localities such as the edges of fields, sandbreaks, grassy hillsides and meadows, etc. The female lays about 200 minute, light green eggs from which the caterpillars hatch about a week later. This is one of the most brightly coloured and beautiful hawkmoths. Its most frequent host plant is cypress spurge, together with other types of spurge, dog's mercury, plantain and knotgrass, etc. The full-grown caterpillar retires into moss, leaves or the topsoil, where it pupates in a cocoon. As a rule the pupal stage hibernates, but in a few cases the moths emerge in the autumn (the second generation); the pupa may also remain dormant for two to five years before the imago emerges. Not so very long ago this hawkmoth was still relatively common, but now it is rare and in some places it has disappeared altogether. The caterpillars are evidently sensitive to chemical treatment of their habitats.

In the evening, flowering phlox entices the Elephant Hawkmoth (*Deilephila elpenor*) into gardens. However, it also sucks nectar from many other flowers, such as viper's bugloss, common soapwort, honeysuckle and willowherb. The moths fly mainly from May to July, but a second generation sometimes appears in August and September. They are mostly to be found in meadows, on wooded hillsides, near streams and in gardens. The female lays about a hundred eggs on the undersides of the leaves of host plants – most frequently different kinds of willowherb, bedstraw and balsam, but also honeysuckle and loosestrife. The caterpillar, which has distinctive markings on the front of its body, occurs in a grey and a green form.

1. *Hyles euphorbiae*: forewing span 55—75 mm (2$\frac{3}{16}$—3 in). Europe (except the north), western Asia, northern India, northern Africa, North America.
2. *Deilephila elpenor*: forewing span 45—60 mm (1$\frac{3}{4}$—2$\frac{3}{8}$ in). The Palaearctic region.

1 *Hippotion celerio* L.
Silver-striped Hawkmoth

Sphingidae

2 *Macroglossum stellatarum* L.
Hummingbird Hawkmoth

3 *Hemaris fuciformis* L.
Broad-bordered Bee Hawkmoth

In the tropical belt, the Silver-striped Hawkmoth (*Hippotion celerio*) forms one generation after another and is one of the commonest hawkmoths. In Europe, it inhabits the Mediterranean region and forms two generations. On rare occasions it strays into central Europe and Britain, where a careful record is kept of its appearances. After nightfall it sucks nectar from various flowers, especially petunias and common soapwort. The caterpillar is polyphagous and feeds on grapevine, bedstraw, sorrel and willowherb, etc. It pupates in or on the soil, but in central Europe it does not survive the winter frosts.

As distinct from the large nocturnal hawkmoths, the Hummingbird Hawkmoth (*Macroglossum stellatarum*) and Broad-bordered Bee Hawkmoth (*Hemaris fuciformis*) fly during the daytime. The Hummingbird Hawkmoth is a migrant; it not only flies far to the north, but also high up in mountains, to the upper vegetation limit. It chiefly inhabits meadows, grass verges and gardens with sufficient flowers to provide it with nectar, which it sucks while hovering. It visits central Europe in June, where its offspring appear in July. Its larval food plant is usually bedstraw. The caterpillars pupate in a loose cocoon in the ground, but in central Europe they seldom survive the hard winters.

The Broad-bordered Bee Hawkmoth (*Hemaris fuciformis*) is notable for its transparent, dark-bordered wings. It flies from May to July and a partial second generation appears in August. The female lays about a hundred eggs. The caterpillars live chiefly on various kinds of bedstraw, honeysuckle and snowberry; the pupae overwinter once or twice.

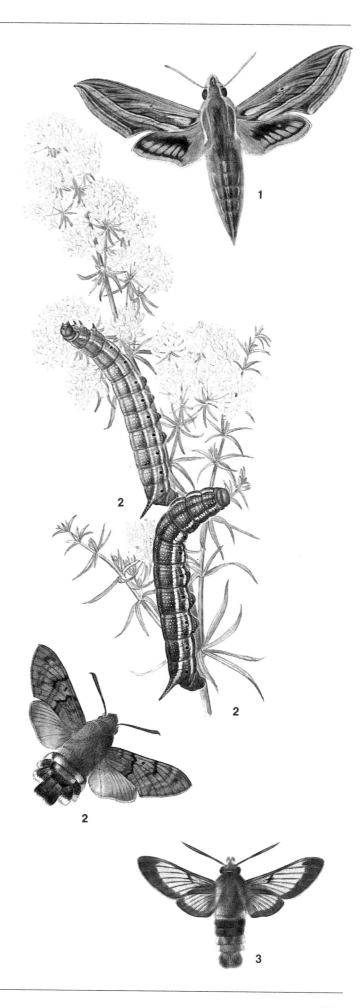

1. *Hippotion celerio:* forewing span 70—80 mm ($2\frac{3}{4}$—$3\frac{1}{8}$ in). Tropical Africa, Asia, Australia, the Mediterranean region.
2. *Macroglossum stellatarum:* forewing span 40—50 mm ($1\frac{9}{16}$—2 in). Warm parts of the Palaearctic region, North America.
3. *Hemaris fuciformis:* forewing span 40—47 mm ($1\frac{9}{16}$—$1\frac{7}{8}$ in). The temperate part of Europe and Asia as far as the Altai Mts.

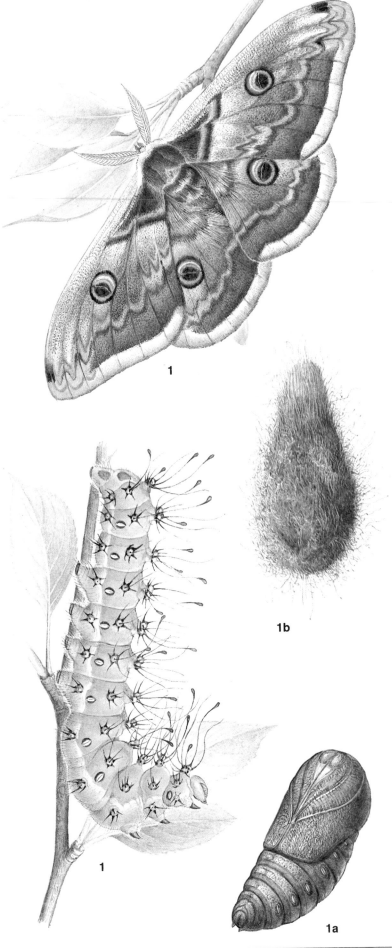

1 *Saturnia pyri* Den. et Schiff.   Saturniidae
Giant Peacock Moth

The Giant Peacock (*Saturnia pyri*) is the biggest European moth. Its single generation appears from the end of April or the beginning of May to the beginning of June. It is active at night and by day sits on a trunk or a wall, often close to a street-lamp, having been attracted by the light. It rests with its wings half open, showing the large coloured eye-marks. The sexes can be differentiated by their antennae, which are pectinate in the male and bristle-like in the female. The moths do not suck nectar; in fact, they take no food at all and derive nutrition from the fat in their own stout bodies, which was accumulated during the caterpillar stage.

Originally an inhabitant of forest-grassland regions, the Giant Peacock is to be seen with increasing frequency in orchards. The female lays large, oval eggs, measuring about 3 mm ($\frac{1}{8}$ in) in groups. The young caterpillars are brownish-black, with reddish tubercles; later they are greenish-yellow and have rows of tubercles with long, club-tipped spines growing from them. The caterpillars are voracious and because of their size their food consumption is considerable. If they live in orchards or gardens they mainly eat pear, cherry and almond tree leaves and, in warmer regions, the leaves of the trees of citrus fruits. Elsewhere they eat ash, willow and poplar leaves. The caterpillar is to be found on its host plants from June to August; when fully grown it is thick-bodied and about 100–120 mm ($3\frac{15}{16}$–$4\frac{3}{4}$ in) in length. At the beginning of August it stops feeding and looks for a suitable place in which to pupate, usually on a forked branch or near the foot of a tree. It then spins brown or greyish-white silken threads round itself and pupates in the resultant cocoon (1b). The cocoon is elongate and pear-shaped; the pupa (1a) is brown, with dark wing sheaths. The pupa overwinters, but it is not uncommon for two or even more years to elapse before the moth emerges in the spring.

1b

1a

1. *Saturnia pyri*: forewing span 100—130 mm ($3\frac{15}{16}$—$5\frac{1}{8}$ in). The Mediterranean region (extending into central Europe in the north), the Caucasus, Transcaucasia, the Near East.

1 *Saturnia pavonia* L.
Emperor

Saturniidae

2 *Aglia tau* L.
Tau Emperor

The male Emperor (*Saturnia pavonia*) can likewise be distinguished from the female by his pectinate antennae, but equally by his differently coloured wings. In addition there are differences between the habits of the sexes, since the male flies in the afternoon and the female at night. The moths appear early in the spring (in March or April, according to local climatic conditions) and remain until June. They frequent warm, sunny, steppe-like slopes, heathland or the outskirts of woods, commonly visit gardens and occur at both low and high altitudes. The eggs are greyish to olive-green. The newly hatched caterpillars are black, but later they acquire orange tubercles and finally they are predominantly green, with black spots. They live from May to August, chiefly on brambles, raspberries, roses, bilberries, blackthorn, heather, birches and willows. The full-grown caterpillar wraps itself in a brown pear-shaped cocoon, where it is transformed to a violet-brown pupa. The moth emerges in spring, but before that the pupa may remain dormant for two or more winters.

As distinct from the female, the male Tau Emperor (*Aglia tau*) has pectinate antennae; it is also differently coloured. The female is a little larger than the male and is less active, although at night she may fly to lights. This species inhabits deciduous woods (mostly beech) from lowlands to altitudes of about 1,600 m (5,250 ft). Its single generation flies from the early spring and in mountains it is still to be seen in July. Young and older caterpillars are differently coloured; they live from May to August on the leaves of beech, hornbeam, oak and other deciduous trees. When fully grown, the caterpillar hides in old leaves on the ground and pupates in a thinly spun cocoon. The dull, blackish-brown pupa spends the winter in the cocoon on the ground.

1 ♂

1 ♀

1

1

1. *Saturnia pavonia:* forewing span 40—60 mm ($1\frac{9}{16}$—$2\frac{3}{8}$ in). A large part of Eurasia.
2. *Aglia tau:* forewing span 50—65 mm (2—$2\frac{9}{16}$ in). The Palaearctic region.

2

1 *Pyrgus malvae* L. Hesperiidae
Grizzled Skipper

2 *Erynnis tages* L.
Dingy Skipper

3 *Ochlodes venata* Brem. et Grey
Large Skipper

4 *Hesperia comma* L.
Silver-spotted Skipper

The members of the family Hesperiidae (skippers) are traditionally ranked among the butterflies because they fly during the daytime, although they are not closely related to the other families regarded as typical butterflies. They are not very vividly coloured and their wings are often marked with light spots, as in the Grizzled Skipper (*Pyrgus malvae*). In flight skippers are very quick and difficult to follow with the eye. The butterflies fly over meadows and pastures at low to mountain altitudes and, from April to August, form two generations. The caterpillar lives on cinquefoil, strawberry plants, brambles and mallows. The pupa overwinters. The Dingy Skipper (*Erynnis tages*), which inhabits grassland, likewise produces two generations; its caterpillars live chiefly on leguminous plants and also on field eryngo.

A few skippers are a rusty-orange colour with light spots on their wings. They include the Large Skipper (*Ochlodes venata*) and the Silver-spotted Skipper (*Hesperia comma*), which resemble each other. The males of both species, but not the females, have a strip of dark, scented scales on the upper surfaces of their forewings. The imagos of *Ochlodes venata* fly over meadows, pastures, the margins of woods, forest paths and grass verges, visiting flowers. The number of generations varies with the climate, from one in the north to three in southern Europe. This species ascends to altitudes of about 2,000 m (6,560 ft). *Hesperia comma* forms only one generation, whose imagos fly in July and August and ascend to still higher altitudes than the preceding species. They inhabit open woods, meadows and grassy slopes, often on a limestone base. The caterpillars of these two skippers live mainly on grasses.

1. *Pyrgus malvae:* forewing span 18—22 mm ($\frac{3}{4}$—$\frac{7}{8}$ in). Europe, the temperate belt in Asia.
2. *Erynnis tages:* forewing span 23—26 mm ($\frac{15}{16}$—$1\frac{1}{16}$ in). A large part of Eurasia.
3. *Ochlodes venata:* forewing span 25—32 mm (1—$1\frac{1}{4}$ in). The temperate part of Eurasia.
4. *Hesperia comma:* forewing span 25—30 mm (1—$1\frac{3}{16}$ in). Europe, the temperate belt in Asia, northern Africa, North America.

244

1 *Papilio machaon* L.
Swallowtail

Papilionidae

2 *Iphiclides podalirius* L.
Scarce Swallowtail

The Swallowtail (*Papilio machaon*) and the very similar Scarce Swallowtail (*Iphiclides podalirius*) have a great deal in common. Their colours are the same and in both species the hindwings are produced to a prominent 'tail'. In Europe they are both threatened with extinction in several places and are therefore protected by law in various countries. That sounds very nice, but has very little meaning if the places where the butterflies live and develop are not protected. In Britain the Swallowtail is found only in marshy areas such as the Norfolk Broads. Both butterflies like to fly to the highest points of the landscape, but whereas the Swallowtail likes grassy localities, the Scarce Swallowtail prefers dry hillsides and wooded steppes with plenty of thornbushes. As a rule, both species produce two generations in a year, but sometimes, especially in the south, there may be a third generation. Both the caterpillars are very brightly coloured and if they feel themselves to be in danger they protrude from the front of their bodies a forked process known as an osmeterium, which is connected to a scent gland and has a repellent function. The caterpillars' diets are not the same, however. Swallowtail caterpillars feed on umbelliferous plants (chiefly fennel, dill, carrots and caraway), while those of the Scarce Swallowtail live on blackthorn, cherry, bird-cherry, pear and plum leaves. Interestingly, the pupae of the two species are again similarly coloured, the pupae of the summer generation being green and those of the second generation (which overwinters) brown.

European swallowtails form only a fraction of the members of the family as a whole, which is represented on a worldwide scale by about 700 species, often very large and fantastically coloured, and which include the biggest butterflies in existence.

1. *Papilio machaon:* forewing span 50—75 mm (2—3 in). A large portion of the Palaearctic region (in Europe right to the north of the continent).
2. *Iphiclides podalirius:* forewing span 50—70 mm (2—2¾ in). The Palaearctic region (to 54 ° latitude north).

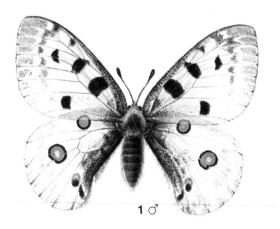

1 ♂

1 ♀

1 *Parnassius apollo* L. Papilionidae
Apollo

2 *Parnassius mnemosyne* L.
Clouded Apollo

Not so long ago, the Apollo (*Parnassius apollo*), one of the most beautiful butterflies, used to be caught as a souvenir of an outing in mountains, or as something that could be sold at a profit. Catching it does not present any problems, since its flight is slow and fluttering and it settles on flowers. Its beauty, combined with a certain blundering awkwardness, has in many places proved its undoing and has led to its actual or imminent disappearance. It is now so rare that its name has been entered in the World Red Book of endangered species. It inhabits flowering meadows at low mountain altitudes, mainly on limestone. It is to be seen mostly in July and August. The female lays her eggs singly on succulent plants (stonecrop, house-leek) and on saxifrage, where they overwinter. The strikingly coloured caterpillars are to be found most frequently on white stonecrop. They like sunshine and on cloudy days go into hiding. If irritated they protrude their osmeterium in the same way as swallowtails. They pupate on the ground between stones. This species occurs in over 200 colour forms and geographical races over its large distribution area.

Unlike other apollos, the Clouded Apollo (*Parnassius mnemosyne*) has no red spots on its hindwings. It lives mainly in lowlands in the north of its range, but does not avoid mountainous country and ascends to altitudes of about 1,500 m (4,920 ft) elsewhere. It flies clumsily, like the Apollo. The butterflies are most abundant from May to July, although in favourable localities they may appear as early as April. The eggs overwinter and the caterpillars hatch early in the spring; they live on *Corydalis* species. Like other apollos, the Clouded Apollo is protected by law in many countries.

2 ♂

1

1. *Parnassius apollo:* forewing span 65—75 mm (2$\frac{9}{16}$—3 in). From western Europe to Lake Baikal in the east.
2. *Parnassius mnemosyne:* forewing span 45—60 mm (1$\frac{3}{4}$—2$\frac{3}{8}$ in). A large part of Europe, the Caucasus, central Asia, Iran.

1 *Aporia crataegi* L.
Black-veined White

2 *Pieris brassicae* L.
Large (Cabbage) White

Until quite recently, the Black-veined White (*Aporia crataegi*) was classified as a serious fruit-tree pest. In some places its caterpillars still devastate orchards, but in central Europe it is, in the main, a rare species, which has now completely disappeared from the fruit-growing regions where it was once common. It is extinct in Britain, but often occurs in large numbers in southern Europe. The imagos fly in open country from May to July. This is a migratory species whose imagos appear suddenly in the most unexpected places. The caterpillars live on blackthorn, spiraea, hawthorn and fruit-tree leaves. They hibernate in collective nests and complete their development in the spring. This butterfly forms only one generation a year.

Unlike the vanishing Black-veined White, the Large White (*Pieris brassicae*) is a common and widespread species. The female (but not the male) has two black spots on her forewings. The incidence of this white coincides with regions where vegetables are grown. The caterpillars live mainly on Cruciferae, including kohlrabi, cabbages, cauliflowers and radishes, etc. The female deposits her 200–300 eggs in largish groups on the undersides of leaves of the host plant, where the young caterpillars live gregariously, grow quickly and consume vast amounts of leaf tissue, sometimes leaving nothing but the thick veins. In three to four weeks they are fully grown, leave the host plant and pupate on a fence, on the wall of a wood-shed or under a windowsill etc. In central Europe, in the course of the year, there are usually two generations, whose imagos fly from April to August. The pupae (chrysalises) hibernate. In favourable years there may be a partial third generation and in the south the number of generations is even greater. A high incidence of these butterflies is usually attended by the appearance of their braconid parasite, *Apanteles glomeratus*, whose larvae develop in the caterpillars (see p. 201).

1. *Aporia crataegi:* forewing span 50—65 mm (2—2$\frac{9}{16}$ in). Central and southern Europe (to 62 ° latitude in the north), northern Africa. Now extinct in Great Britain.
2. *Pieris brassicae:* forewing span 50—65 mm (2—2$\frac{9}{16}$ in). Europe, Asia as far as the Himalayas, northern Africa.

247

1 ♂

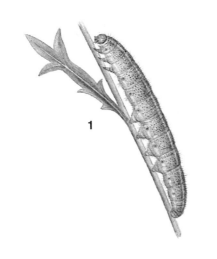

1

1 *Pieris rapae* L.
Small White

Pieridae

2 *Pieris napi* L.
Green-veined White

The Small White (*Pieris rapae*), one of the most common butterflies, flies from March to October. The female – like the female of the Large White, Green-veined White and other pierids – has more black spots on her wings than the male. The Small White inhabits gardens, fields, meadows and the outskirts of woods at low and high altitudes. The butterflies often gather round drying puddles in fields and on footpaths. The caterpillars are to be found mostly on cruciferous plants, but also on mignonette and other plants. Most often they attack *Brassica* species, on which they have been carried all over the world. They have become acclimatised to conditions wherever these vegetables are cultivated. The 150 eggs are laid, one or two at a time, on the leaves of the host plants, so that the caterpillars also occur singly. In central Europe this species generally forms two generations in a year, but at high altitudes only one. Summer butterflies are larger than spring individuals. The pupae hibernate.

The Green-veined White (*Pieris napi*) is another common member of the genus. Although not strikingly marked, it has produced a number of colour forms and geographical races. It flies in open country, in open deciduous woods and on their outskirts, in clearings, near streams and in meadows, fields and gardens, from lowlands to mountains. During the year, according to the altitude, it forms one to three generations whose imagos fly from early in the spring until late in the autumn. The female lays the greenish eggs singly on the leaves of the host plants (mostly wild Cruciferae). The caterpillars are fully grown in two to three weeks and pupate on the plant head upwards. The pupae of the first generation are yellowish-green with black spots, while those of the autumn generation (which hibernate) have no spots.

2 ♂

2 ♀

1. *Pieris rapae:* forewing span 40—50 mm ($1\frac{9}{16}$—2 in). Over practically the whole globe.
2. *Pieris napi:* forewing span 35—45 mm ($1\frac{3}{8}$—$1\frac{3}{4}$ in). The Palaearctic region, North America.

1 *Anthocharis cardamines* L.
Orange-tip

Pieridae

2 *Colias hyale* L.
Pale Clouded Yellow

The males and females of some lepidopterans are very much alike, but in other species there are marked inter-sex differences in size and/or colouring. In the case of the Orange-tip (*Anthocharis cardamines*), the colour differences are considerable. The imagos fly from April to June over meadows and fields, along woodland paths, at the margins of woods and in gardens. It is most common in lowlands, but is also known to occur in mountain valleys at altitudes of about 2,000 m (6,560 ft). The eggs are skittle-shaped and are almost always laid on flowers or flower buds (usually lady's smock, river, winter and rock cress, or shepherd's purse, etc.). The caterpillar, which hatches in a few days, is fully grown at about five weeks and pupates on the plant. The boat-shaped pupa, which has tapering ends and is positioned right way up, is green to begin with, but then turns brown. This species produces one generation in a year and hibernates in the pupal stage.

The Pale Clouded Yellow (*Colias hyale*) is far less familiar than the Brimstone (*Gonepteryx rhamni*), although it is quite common and is relatively easily distinguishable from similar species. The female is paler than the male. This species inhabits grassland and wooded steppes, fallow ground and flowering meadows and regularly visits clover fields. It generally produces two generations in close succession; the first flies from April to June and the second from July to September. Sometimes there is a third generation, whose imagos fly until November. The female lays the skittle-shaped eggs singly on various leguminous plants. The caterpillars' commonest host plants are vetches, trefoil and clover. The caterpillars hibernate when only half-grown and pupate on the plant the following spring. The pupae are girdled and in an upright position.

1♂

1♀

2

2

2

1. *Anthocharis cardamines:* forewing span 35—45 mm ($1\frac{3}{8}$—$1\frac{3}{4}$ in). A large part of Eurasia, northern Africa.
2. *Colias hyale:* forewing span 40—45 mm ($1\frac{9}{16}$—$1\frac{3}{4}$ in). From central Europe to the Altai Mountains in the east.

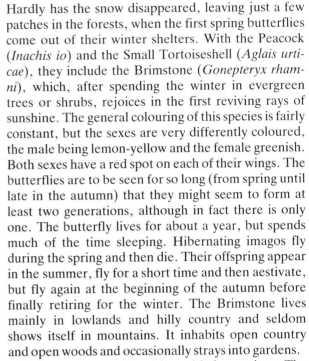

1 *Gonepteryx rhamni* L.
Pieridae
Brimstone

Hardly has the snow disappeared, leaving just a few patches in the forests, when the first spring butterflies come out of their winter shelters. With the Peacock (*Inachis io*) and the Small Tortoiseshell (*Aglais urticae*), they include the Brimstone (*Gonepteryx rhamni*), which, after spending the winter in evergreen trees or shrubs, rejoices in the first reviving rays of sunshine. The general colouring of this species is fairly constant, but the sexes are very differently coloured, the male being lemon-yellow and the female greenish. Both sexes have a red spot on each of their wings. The butterflies are to be seen for so long (from spring until late in the autumn) that they might seem to form at least two generations, although in fact there is only one. The butterfly lives for about a year, but spends much of the time sleeping. Hibernating imagos fly during the spring and then die. Their offspring appear in the summer, fly for a short time and then aestivate, but fly again at the beginning of the autumn before finally retiring for the winter. The Brimstone lives mainly in lowlands and hilly country and seldom shows itself in mountains. It inhabits open country and open woods and occasionally strays into gardens.

The eggs are greyish-white, with four stripes. The female deposits them singly on the host plant, so that the caterpillars also occur singly; they can be encountered from April to July. When newly hatched the caterpillars are greenish; later they are bluish-green, with a dense and finely granular cuticle. Their diet is limited to the leaves of common and alder buckthorn. As a rule, the caterpillar sits on the midrib of the leaf, where it spins a kind of cushion for itself. When young, it bites holes in the leaf, but later eats it from the edges. In only three to five weeks it is fully grown and pupates on a twig or a leaf. The green pupa blends perfectly with its surroundings; it is girdled and the head is directed upwards. The pupal stage lasts two to three weeks.

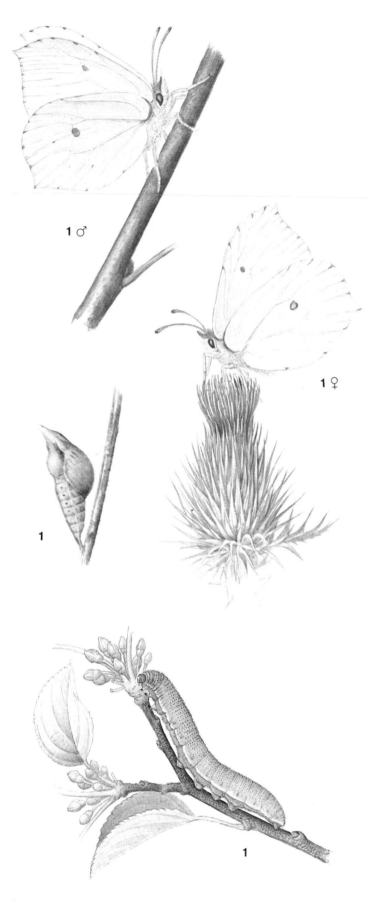

1♂

1♀

1

1

1

1. *Gonepteryx rhamni*: forewing span 50—55 mm (2—2$\frac{3}{16}$ in). Eurasia, northern and western Africa.

1 *Quercusia quercus* L.
Purple Hairstreak

2 *Callophrys rubi* L.
Green Hairstreak

3 *Lycaena phlaeas* L.
Small Copper

The family Lycaenidae mainly comprises predominantly blue-coloured species, but some species are orange or dark and many have spots and lines on their wings, so that collectively they are known as blues, coppers and hairstreaks. The sexes are sometimes differently coloured. The male Purple Hairstreak (*Quercusia quercus*) has a purple sheen all over its wings, the female has only a small patch of purple on her forewings. Distinctive for this species is the underside of the wings. The imago flies in oak woods from July to August, but is seldom to be seen, as it spends most of its time in the crowns of the trees. The eggs overwinter. The caterpillars, which are hatched in the spring, live on oak leaves and pupate on the ground under old leaves.

From above, the Green Hairstreak (*Callophrys rubi*) is a very plain butterfly, but when it folds its wings their bright green underside distinguishes it from all other species (except Chapman's Green Hairstreak from southern Europe). It flies from April onwards, in different localities – on hillsides covered with thornbushes, over heaths and moorland, and sometimes high up in mountains. It forms one or two generations in a year, depending on local climatic conditions. The dark green caterpillar is polyphagous and is common on gorse, rockrose, bilberry, bird's-foot trefoil and the flowers of dogwood. When fully grown, it crawls under old leaves or moss, but hibernates before pupating.

The Small Copper (*Lycaena phlaeas*) is one of the most common lepidopterans. It inhabits dry localities with sufficient flowers (but not woods) and even ascends to alpine altitudes. It appears in March and, depending on whether it forms two or three generations, it can still be seen late in the autumn, sitting on dry, sun-warmed footpaths in fields. The caterpillars live on a frugal diet of sorrel leaves and hibernate before pupating.

1. *Quercusia quercus:* forewing span 28—33 mm ($1\frac{1}{8}$—$1\frac{5}{16}$ in). Europe, Transcaucasia, the Near East, northern Africa.
2. *Callophrys rubi:* forewing span 24—28 mm ($\frac{15}{16}$—$1\frac{1}{8}$ in). The Palaearctic region.
3. *Lycaena phlaeas:* forewing span 22—27 mm ($\frac{7}{8}$—$1\frac{1}{16}$ in). The Palaearctic region, North America.

1 *Heodes virgaureae* L.
Scarce Copper

Lycaenidae

2 *Plebejus argus* L.
Silver-studded Blue

3 *Polyommatus icarus* Rott.
Common Blue

The Scarce Copper (*Heodes virgaureae*) is one of the reddish-orange lycaenids. It likes meadows full of flowers and if it finds sufficient flowering plants on the banks of streams, it can be encountered there too; it also occurs at the edges of woods. The male is very different from the female; the sun emphasises the fiery glow of his wings, but she has black-spotted wings and sometimes occurs in a dark (melanistic) form. The imagos of the single generation fly from June to August and live at various altitudes. The caterpillars' food plant is sorrel.

The Silver-studded Blue (*Plebejus argus*) is characterised by marked sexual dichroism and the brown female is totally unlike the blue-coloured male. The butterflies like open country; from June to August they fly over damp and dry meadows, heathland, at the margins of woods or in clearings, and congregate round drying puddles. The female lays the white eggs singly. The caterpillar lives on clover, milk-vetch, gorse or heaths. It secretes a substance relished by ants of the genera *Lasius* and *Formica* and is therefore often surrounded by them. It pupates in the ground, under a stone or even in an anthill.

The Common Blue (*Polyommatus icarus*) is characterised by similar sexual dichroism. A common and abundant species, it flies over meadows, on the outskirts of woods and over fields and flowery hillsides. It forms one to three generations, according to local climatic conditions; the caterpillars of the last generation hibernate. If there are three generations, the imagos can be seen from April to October. The caterpillars live on various leguminous plants, in particular bird's-foot trefoil, spiny restharrow, lucerne, greenweed, broom and clover. Like those of the preceding species, they are surrounded by ants which lap up the caterpillars' sugary secretions.

---

1. *Heodes virgaureae:* forewing span 27—32 mm ($1\frac{1}{16}$—$1\frac{1}{4}$ in). A large part of the Palaearctic region (excluding Great Britain).
2. *Plebejus argus:* forewing span 20—23 mm ($\frac{13}{16}$—$\frac{15}{16}$ in). Europe, the temperate belt in Asia.
2. *Polyommatus icarus:* forewing span 25—30 mm (1—$1\frac{3}{16}$ in). The Palaearctic region.

1 *Charaxes jasius* L.　　　　　Nymphalidae

2 *Apatura iris* L.
　Purple Emperor

3 *Limenitis populi* L.
　Poplar Admiral

The Nymphalidae butterflies include some of the best known and most popular species. Some have exceedingly beautifully coloured wings and many are still common, despite the decline of their natural environment. The sharp spurs on its hindwings give *Charaxes jasius* something of the appearance of a swallowtail. The butterfly, which likes warmth, flies in two distinctly separate generations (May–June and August–September). The caterpillars live on arbutus (strawberry-trees).

The male Purple Emperor (*Apatura iris*) is conspicuous for the bluish-violet lustre formed by the diffraction of light rays on the scales on his wings. This very handsome and lively butterfly produces a single generation which flies in July and August. It likes the damp atmosphere of deciduous woods, the banks of streams and damp woodland footpaths, where several butterflies often gather together; it is also attracted by fresh horse or cow dung on forest paths. It is most abundant in lowlands, but occurs in mountains at low altitudes. The eggs are laid singly. The caterpillar has two bluish horns on its head. It lives on various kinds of willows and hibernates and completes its development in the spring. It pupates upside down under leaves.

The Poplar Admiral (*Limenitis populi*) is a distinctive species of open woods with streams and rivers running through them; it also flies at the margins of forests. On sunny mornings and also before thunderstorms in the afternoon, the imagos settle on damp paths. Otherwise they mostly remain in the crowns of the trees, although they are attracted by decaying dead organisms and by excrement. The greenish eggs are laid singly. The bizarre-looking caterpillar lives mainly on aspen leaves, hibernates when it is half-grown and pupates on a twig or a leaf; the brownish-orange pupa is marked with dark spots.

1. *Charaxes jasius:* forewing span 75—85 mm (3—3$\frac{3}{8}$ in). Mediterranean region, tropical and northern Africa.
2. *Apatura iris:* forewing span 55—65 mm (2$\frac{3}{16}$—2$\frac{9}{16}$ in). Europe, the temperate belt in Asia.
3. *Limenitis populi:* forewing span 65—80 mm (2$\frac{9}{16}$—3$\frac{1}{8}$ in). From central Europe, across central Asia, to Japan.

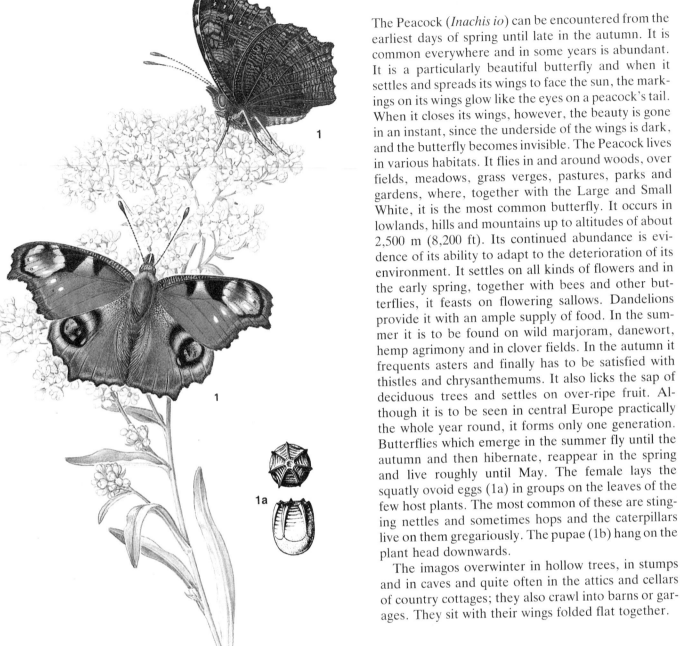

1 *Inachis io* L.

Nymphalidae

Peacock

The Peacock (*Inachis io*) can be encountered from the earliest days of spring until late in the autumn. It is common everywhere and in some years is abundant. It is a particularly beautiful butterfly and when it settles and spreads its wings to face the sun, the markings on its wings glow like the eyes on a peacock's tail. When it closes its wings, however, the beauty is gone in an instant, since the underside of the wings is dark, and the butterfly becomes invisible. The Peacock lives in various habitats. It flies in and around woods, over fields, meadows, grass verges, pastures, parks and gardens, where, together with the Large and Small White, it is the most common butterfly. It occurs in lowlands, hills and mountains up to altitudes of about 2,500 m (8,200 ft). Its continued abundance is evidence of its ability to adapt to the deterioration of its environment. It settles on all kinds of flowers and in the early spring, together with bees and other butterflies, it feasts on flowering sallows. Dandelions provide it with an ample supply of food. In the summer it is to be found on wild marjoram, danewort, hemp agrimony and in clover fields. In the autumn it frequents asters and finally has to be satisfied with thistles and chrysanthemums. It also licks the sap of deciduous trees and settles on over-ripe fruit. Although it is to be seen in central Europe practically the whole year round, it forms only one generation. Butterflies which emerge in the summer fly until the autumn and then hibernate, reappear in the spring and live roughly until May. The female lays the squatly ovoid eggs (1a) in groups on the leaves of the few host plants. The most common of these are stinging nettles and sometimes hops and the caterpillars live on them gregariously. The pupae (1b) hang on the plant head downwards.

The imagos overwinter in hollow trees, in stumps and in caves and quite often in the attics and cellars of country cottages; they also crawl into barns or garages. They sit with their wings folded flat together.

1. *Inachis io:* forewing span 50—60 mm (2—2$\frac{3}{8}$ in). The temperate part of Eurasia.

1 *Nymphalis antiopa* L.
Camberwell Beauty

Nymphalidae

2 *Vanessa atalanta* L.
Red Admiral

The light-coloured border of both pairs of wings clearly differentiates the Camberwell Beauty (*Nymphalis antiopa*) from all other nymphalids. At first the border is yellow; in older butterflies it fades to whitish and some of the scales are rubbed off. The Camberwell Beauty is one of the largest European butterflies. It lives mostly in woods, in lowlands and in mountains, and prefers a damp environment with stagnant or flowing water, where it flies from early in the spring. These are butterflies which spent the winter in various shelters, such as attics in cottages, hollow trees and caves. They die at the end of May and the new generation, which appears at the end of July, hibernates over the following winter. The butterfly is thus to be seen almost the whole year round. The elongate eggs, which have seven ridges on them, are laid in groups. The caterpillar is similar to the caterpillars of other nymphalids, but has conspicuous red spots along its back. The caterpillars live gregariously on willows, birches, aspens and various kinds of poplars; the pupa is suspended from a plant.

Stinging nettles are an important host plant of the caterpillar of several nymphalids, including the Peacock (*Inachis io*), the Small Tortoiseshell (*Aglais urticae*), the Painted Lady (*Vanessa cardui*), the Comma (*Polygonia c-album*), the Map (*Araschnia levana*) and the Red Admiral (*Vanessa atalanta*). The last of these species flies over flowering meadows from the spring to the autumn and regularly visits gardens. It is a migrant and a superb flier, which seldom overwinters north of the Alps, but regularly flies there; it inhabits both lowlands and mountains. It likes to sit on felled timber and on the ground. It licks the sap of deciduous trees and in the autumn it settles on over-ripe fruit (mainly pears and plums) in gardens, where it meets other lepidopterans, together with wasps and other insects. The caterpillar lives alone on the host plant, wrapped in a twisted leaf.

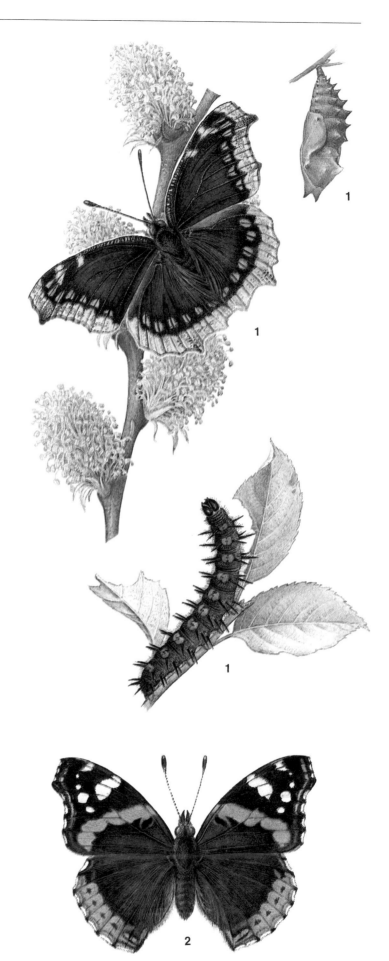

1. *Nymphalis antiopa:* forewing span 55—75 mm ($2\frac{3}{16}$—3 in). Europe, the temperate belt in Asia, North America.
2. *Vanessa atalanta:* forewing span 50—60 mm (2—$2\frac{3}{8}$ in). A large part of Europe, Asia Minor, Iran, northern Africa. Central America, Haiti, New Zealand.

1 *Vanessa cardui* L.
Painted Lady

2 *Aglais urticae* L.
Small Tortoiseshell

3 *Polygonia c-album* L.
Comma

The Painted Lady (*Vanessa cardui*) is a prominent migratory species. It is an outstanding flier, is at home in the tropics and subtropics and usually arrives in central and northern Europe from southern Europe and northern Africa in May. It likes open country – fields, steppes and the outskirts of woods. It produces two or three generations in a year. The eggs are dark green, the caterpillars eat stinging nettles and different kinds of thistles and the pupa hangs from a leaf of the host plant. In the autumn, the newly emerged butterflies migrate southwards; they do not overwinter in central Europe.

The Small Tortoiseshell (*Aglais urticae*), the most common nymphalid, is also one of the first species to appear in the spring. It occurs at all altitudes and in the Alps is still to be found at about 3,000 m (9,840 ft). It flits from flower to flower and in the spring it regularly visits flowering sallows; it is common in gardens and parks and even appears in the streets of towns. It forms two to three generations during the year. The female lays the eggs in groups, so that the caterpillars live gregariously. They are to be found on stinging nettle leaves, which they sometimes nibble away completely. The butterflies hibernate in hollow trees and stumps, in cellars and in attics. Like the Peacock, the Small Tortoiseshell can withstand environmental changes, which do not reduce its numbers.

The Comma (*Polygonia c-album*) takes both its scientific and its vernacular name from the white mark like a letter C, or a comma, on the underside of the hindwings. The Comma develops differently from other nymphalids. The eggs laid in the spring give rise to some imagos which eventually hibernate and to others which produce a further generation during the summer. The two groups differ in colour. What happens is that the overwintered butterflies lay eggs which can follow one of two patterns. Slow developers mature in late summer and hibernate. Fast-breeders produce pale adults in early to mid summer and then new adults produce a second generation in early autumn, which then hibernates together with the slow developers. The caterpillars live on stinging nettles, hops and brambles.

---

1. *Vanessa cardui:* forewing span 45—60 mm ($1\frac{3}{4}$—$2\frac{3}{8}$ in). Over most of the globe.
2. *Aglais urticae:* forewing span 40—50 mm ($1\frac{9}{16}$—2 in). The temperate part of Eurasia.
3. *Polygonia c-album:* forewing span 42—50 mm ($1\frac{11}{16}$—2 in). The Palaearctic region, except the extreme north.

1 *Araschnia levana* L.

Map

Nymphalidae

The vernacular name of the Map (*Araschnia levana*) is meant to express the intricacy of its markings. This is further emphasised by the occurrence of two generations so differently coloured that each was originally thought to be a separate species (sometimes an extra [intermediary] generation is formed). The development of a given type of generation depends on the length of the day (i.e. on the season) during the caterpillar stage and can be influenced artificially. The spring generation, whose imagos have brown, black-spotted wings, flies from April to July; this is the *levana* form. The imagos of the *prorsa* form (the summer generation) appear in July and August and have black wings very variably marked with red and white spots. The intermediary generation is termed f. *porima;* it appears in September and October, but only in climatically favourable years.

The butterflies fly in and around open woods, on flowering hillsides, over damp meadows and near water, etc. They are common and abundant and, unlike many other species whose numbers are rapidly decreasing, their populations seem to be increasing. Nowadays they even appear in places where they were formerly never observed. This is a primarily lowland species and the maximum altitude of its incidence is about 1,000 m (3,280 ft). The eggs are spherical, green and grooved and are laid in chains. The caterpillars at first live gregariously on stinging nettles (their food plant), but towards the end of their development they disperse over the plant and live on the undersides of the leaves. They crawl slowly and if disturbed will drop to the ground. They are black, are covered with forked spines and might easily be mistaken for Peacock caterpillars, which are likewise black and live on stinging nettle leaves. Caterpillars of both generations are to be found on the plants from the spring to the beginning of the autumn. They moult four times. As in other nymphalid species, the pupa is attached to the plant and hangs head downwards. It remains in this state during the winter and the *levana* form emerges the following spring.

1. *Araschnia levana:* forewing span 28—40 mm ($1\frac{1}{8}$—$1\frac{9}{16}$ in). Europe, the temperate belt in Asia.

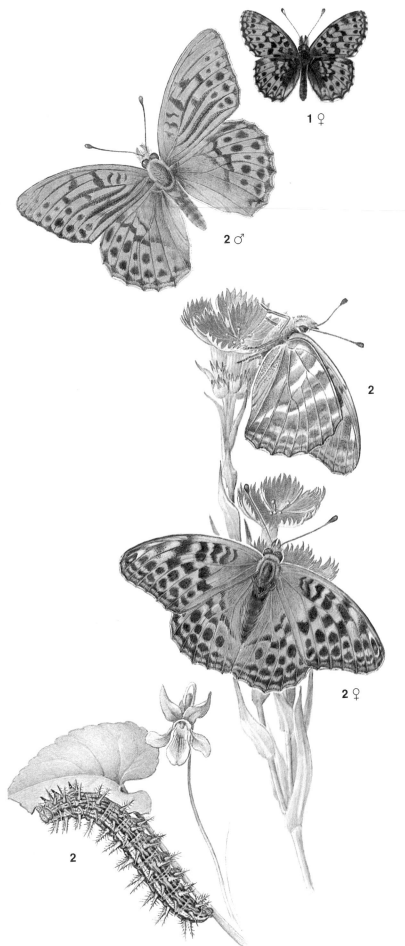

1 *Clossiana dia* L.
Weaver's or Violet Fritillary

Nymphalidae

2 *Argynnis paphia* L.
Silver-washed Fritillary

1 ♀

2 ♂

2

2 ♀

2

According to the scientific nomenclature, fritillaries belong to different genera, but they are all very similarly coloured, with brownish-orange wings marked with black spots and stripes. Many species have distinctive pearly spots on the undersides of their wings. The Weaver's or Violet Fritillary (*Clossiana dia*) is one of the smallest. From above it closely resembles other small species, but its hindwings are violet-brown on the underside. It flies over woodland meadows, clearings and heaths from lowlands up to altitudes of about 1,200 m (3,930 ft). It settles on various flowers and likes thyme, brambles and scabious. Since it forms two to three generations in the course of the year, the butterflies are to be seen throughout practically the whole vegetation season, from April to October. The caterpillars live on violets (mainly sweet violets), raspberries and brambles. They hibernate and pupate in the spring.

The Silver-washed Fritillary (*Argynnis paphia*) is one of the most beautiful and best known fritillary species. Its wings are usually brownish or russet; the female's are darker than the male's. The male can be identified relatively easily from the dark rows of scented scales along the veins on the upper surface of its forewings. Females in which dark colours preponderate are known as the *valesina* form. The imagos fly from June to September in forest clearings, over wet meadows, beside streams, over woodland footpaths and at the margins of woods; they occur in lowlands and at low mountain altitudes up to about 1,200 m (3,930 ft) or possibly higher. They settle on flowers, with their wings outspread, and can be observed at close quarters; if disturbed, they immediately fly away. They are very common on hemp agrimony, danewort and thistles. The surface of the eggs, which are laid singly, is richly sculptured with longitudinal and transverse ribs. The caterpillars live on different kinds of violets (mainly dog violets), wild raspberries and other *Rubus* species. Young caterpillars hibernate and then continue developing until May.

1. *Clossiana dia:* forewing span 27—35 mm ($1\frac{1}{16}$—$1\frac{3}{8}$ in). The temperate part of Eurasia.
2. *Argynnis paphia:* forewing span 55—65 mm ($2\frac{3}{16}$—$2\frac{9}{16}$ in). A large part of the Palaearctic region.

1 *Fabriciana adippe* Schiff.   Nymphalidae
High Brown Fritillary

2 *Issoria lathonia* L.
Queen of Spain Fritillary

3 *Brenthis ino* Rott.
Lesser Marbled Fritillary

The High Brown Fritillary (*Fabriciana adippe*) has many colour forms and geographical races; sometimes it even lacks the typical pearly spots, in which case it is described as the *cleodoxa* form. It flies during the summer at the edges of woods, along woodland footpaths and over clearings. It occurs mainly in hilly country, but in mountains it ascends to the limit of the forest. It is attracted by flowering thistles and sucks nectar from their flowers. The caterpillars live on different kinds of violets.

Among the fritillaries, the Queen of Spain Fritillary (*Issoria lathonia*) has the most striking and most brightly gleaming pearly spots. Although the underside of its wings is like that of many other species, the pearly patches are nevertheless quite distinctive. It is also the only migratory fritillary and in Europe it flies far to the north. From north to south the number of its generations increases from one to three; the individual generations overlap one another. This species likes dry and preferably sandy localities. It flies over fields and steppes and on the outskirts of woods and settles on the ground or on thistle, scabious, clover and other flowers. It occurs at low and high altitudes. The eggs are light grey; the caterpillars, which are hatched in June, live mainly on violets. This species seldom overwinters in central Europe.

The smaller Lesser Marbled Fritillary (*Brenthis ino*) inhabits damp, cool meadows and marshes from lowland to mountain altitudes and flies from June to August. It flies slowly and settles on different kinds of flowers. The long, yellow, longitudinally grooved eggs are laid singly. The caterpillars live on various plants which like damp surroundings, such as meadowsweet, burnet, goatsbeard and brambles. They hibernate and complete their development in the spring. This species produces one generation in a year.

1. *Fabriciana adippe:* forewing span 42—55 mm ($1\frac{11}{16}$—$2\frac{3}{16}$ in). A large part of the Palaearctic region.
2. *Issoria lathonia:* forewing span 35—45 mm ($1\frac{3}{8}$—$1\frac{3}{4}$ in). The Palaearctic region.
3. *Brenthis ino:* forewing span 32—40 mm ($1\frac{1}{4}$—$1\frac{9}{16}$ in). The temperate part of Eurasia.

1 *Mellicta athalia* Rott.   Nymphalidae
Heath Fritillary

2 *Melanargia galathaea* L.   Satyridae
Marbled White

3 *Maniola jurtina* L.
Meadow Brown

Like many other nymphalids, the imagos of the Heath Fritillary (*Mellicta athalia*) like to gather round puddles on footpaths in fields. This species prefers damp localities and inhabits open woods and meadows. It flies from May to September in one or two generations which follow each other in close succession. Its wings are rather variably marked, making its differentiation from related species somewhat difficult. The eggs are laid in clusters. The caterpillars live mainly on plantain, but sometimes on cow-wheat. They hibernate and pupate in the spring.

Although five more similar species live in Europe, the Marbled White (*Melanargia galathaea*) occurs further north than the others, as far as the Baltic. The dark markings on its wings are variable and even the ground colour is not constant, being sometimes white and sometimes yellow. The butterflies appear from June to August over clearings, dry hillsides, steppes, meadows, woodland paths and uncultivated ground. They settle on scabious, wild marjoram and many other herbaceous plants. While in flight the female drops the eggs singly onto the ground. The caterpillars live on various grasses, including timothy grass, couch-grass, meadow-grass, Yorkshire fog and wheat. They hibernate and complete their development in the spring.

The Meadow Brown (*Maniola jurtina*) is characterised by interesting sexual dichroism. The dark eyespot on the male's forewings has an orange border, while in the female it lies in a wide orange-coloured area. The female is also generally more brightly coloured than the male. This species used to be more abundant than it is today, but it is still common in meadows, pastures and open woods. It flies from June to October and visits flowering plants such as scabious, brambles and wild marjoram, etc. The caterpillars develop on grasses, their chief food plant being meadow-grass.

1. *Mellicta athalia:* forewing span 25—38 mm (1—$1\frac{1}{2}$ in). The temperate part of Eurasia.
2. *Melanargia galathaea:* forewing span 37—52 mm ($1\frac{7}{16}$—$2\frac{1}{16}$ in). Europe, the Caucasus, the Near East, Iran, northern Africa.
3. *Maniola jurtina:* forewing span 40—48 mm ($1\frac{9}{16}$—$1\frac{7}{8}$ in). Europe, eastwards to the Urals, the Near East, Iran.

1 *Aphantopus hyperantus* L.
Ringlet

Satyridae

2 *Coenonympha pamphilus* L.
Small Heath

The wings of the male and female Ringlet (*Aphantopus hyperantus*) are not very different in colour, but the species *per se* can be distinguished from other browns by its typical markings – black eye-spots (ocelli) with a white centre and yellow border – on the undersides of both pairs of wings. When the butterfly sits on a flower, the wings are folded so that the upper surfaces meet, leaving the markings on the underside clearly visible. This species frequents the margins of forests, forest paths and tracks, damp meadows and clearings and is still common. It mainly inhabits lowlands and hills but also ascends mountains up to altitudes of about 1,500 m (4,920 ft). The imagos occur from June to August and sometimes later. They sit on the flowers of various forest plants, such as flowering brambles and wild raspberries. The eggs are dropped singly by the female while in flight. The caterpillars live on grasses (chiefly meadow-grass and millet grass); they hibernate before they are fully developed and pupate the following year.

The Small Heath (*Coenonympha pamphilus*), the best known of the thirteen *Coenonympha* species in Europe, is common from the spring to the autumn, since it is resistant to environmental changes which have taken a heavy toll of many other species. It forms two to three generations, according to local climatic conditions, but in mountains only one. The various generations overlap. The Small Heath inhabits heathland, meadows and grassland of all kinds and is often to be seen there in large numbers. The eggs have fine longitudinal grooves and cross-ridges. The caterpillars occur throughout the whole of the summer and autumn (they belong to different generations). As with other browns, the food plants of the Small Heath are grasses, in particular meadow-grass, mat-grass and dog's tail, etc. The caterpillars of the last generation hibernate and complete their development and pupate in the spring.

1 ♀

1 ♂

1

2

2

2

1. *Aphantopus hyperantus:* forewing span 35—42 mm (1$\frac{3}{8}$—1$\frac{11}{16}$ in). The temperate part of Eurasia.
2. *Coenonympha pamphilus:* forewing span 23—33 mm ($\frac{15}{16}$—1$\frac{5}{16}$ in). The western part of the Palaearctic region.

1 *Pararge aegeria* L. Satyridae
Speckled Wood

2 *Lasiommata maera* L.
Large Wall Brown

3 *Lasiommata megera* L.
Wall Brown

Speckled Wood (*Pararge aegeria*) imagos appear early in the spring before the oak and beech woods have donned their leaves. These are butterflies belonging to the first generation, whose offspring fly from July to September. The Speckled Wood occurs at low altitudes and ascends mountains no higher than the deciduous wood limit. It forms differently coloured geographical races. South European butterflies have orange spots on their wings; in central and northern Europe the spots are creamy-white. The caterpillars develop on meadow-grass, wheat, couch-grass and other grasses.

The Large Wall Brown (*Lasiommata maera*) is to be found in lowlands and up to altitudes of about 2,000 m (6,560 ft). It flies in and around open woods and over woodland paths and meadows. It settles on felled trees and sunlit patches on the ground, warming itself with outspread wings. The imagos fly from May to September in two consecutive generations. The caterpillars occur from June to August and again from September; these last caterpillars hibernate. Their food plants are various grasses, but particularly meadow-grass, barley-grass, fescue and rye-grass.

The Wall Brown (*Lasiommata megera*) inhabits open country with warm, dry, stony places, where the butterflies appear early in the spring. As a rule there are two generations, but where the climate is favourable there may be three, so that the imagos can be seen until late in the autumn. The imagos like to sit on sun-warmed rocks and warm walls. The caterpillars occur from June to September; those of the last generation overwinter and complete their development the following spring. They likewise live on grasses, in particular meadow-grass, fescue, cock's-foot and rye-grass.

1. *Pararge aegeria:* forewing span 32—42 mm ($1\frac{1}{4}$—$1\frac{11}{16}$ in). From western Europe into central Asia, northern Africa.
2. *Lasiommata maera:* forewing span 37—50 mm ($1\frac{7}{16}$—2 in). Europe, the Near East, central Asia, Iran, northern Africa.
3. *Lasiommata megera:* forewing span 35—45 mm ($1\frac{3}{8}$—$1\frac{3}{4}$ in). A large part of the Palaearctic region.

1 *Anagasta kuehniella* Zell. Pyralidae
Mediterranean Flour Moth

2 *Plodia interpunctella* Hb.
Indian Meal Moth

3 *Pyralis farinalis* L.
Meal Moth

4 *Crambus lathoniellus* Zincken. Crambidae

2   **1**

Stores of agricultural products and larders in dwellings have provided many insects with a very advantageous habitat. They offer sufficient food, a favourable temperature and the right humidity, so that the generations can follow one another in unbroken succession. The chief insects here are small beetles and moths. The beetles tend to remain hidden, but the moths often draw attention to themselves by settling on walls, fluttering round lights or investigating receptacles with liquid contents. The Mediterranean Flour Moth (*Anagasta kuehniella*), one of the least welcome of these guests, forms up to five generations under good conditions. Except for the winter months, the moths are abundant, especially from May to August. The caterpillars live in flour.

The Indian Meal Moth (*Plodia interpunctella*), a member of the same family, is generally thought to be a clothes moth, probably because of its size and its presence in dwellings. It is a very persistent pest. It appears in stores and households from June to September. The moth is harmless, but the voracious caterpillars devour anything from fruit to cooking ingredients and chocolate.

The Meal Moth (*Pyralis farinalis*) is another well-known pest of mills, foodstores with flour products and households, but it also occurs in the open. The caterpillars live and hibernate in tubular silken capsules.

Crambus lathoniellus is one of many small moths called grass moths, living in meadows. It occurs in both lowlands and mountains and the caterpillars live on various grasses; after hibernating, they pupate in the spring.

3

4 ♂

4 ♀

1. *Anagasta kuehniella:* forewing span 20—25 mm ($\frac{13}{16}$—1 in). The entire globe.
2. *Plodia interpunctella:* forewing span 15—20 mm ($\frac{5}{8}$—$\frac{13}{16}$ in). The entire globe.
3. *Pyralis farinalis:* forewing span 18—30 mm ($\frac{23}{32}$—1$\frac{3}{16}$ in). The entire globe.
4. *Crambus lathoniellus:* forewing span 19—22 mm ($\frac{3}{4}$—$\frac{7}{8}$ in). The Palaearctic region.

1 *Drepana falcataria* L.　　　Drepanidae
Pebble Hook-tip

2 *Habrosyne pyritoides* Hufn.　　Thytiridae
Buff Arches

3 *Thyatira batis* L.
Peach Blossom

4 *Polyploca flavicornis* L.
Yellow Horned

The scientific name of the Pebble Hook-tip (*Drepana falcataria*) is taken from the Latin word *'falx'*, meaning sickle. And indeed, the moth's forewings are curved like sickles. This characteristic also occurs in related species, however. The Pebble Hook-tip lives at both low and high altitudes. It forms two generations. The moths of the spring generation fly from April to June and those of the summer generation from July to August. They are to be found in clearings and deciduous woods, beside streams, on heaths and in urban parks. The caterpillars likewise appear at different times – in June and from August to October. They devour the leaves of young birches, alders and poplars. This species spends the winter in the pupal stage.

The Buff Arches (*Habrosyne pyritoides*) has very delicately marked forewings whose pattern resembles agate. The imagos, in a single generation, fly from June to August on the outskirts of woods, over sunny bushy slopes and in parks and gardens. The caterpillars live on wild raspberry and bramble leaves; the pupae overwinter.

The markings of the Peach Blossom (*Thyatira batis*) are unique. The imagos, in one or two generations, are active in the evening, when they fly at the margins of forests and on hillsides overgrown with brambles and raspberry bushes, the food plants of the caterpillars. This species also overwinters in the pupal stage.

Early in the spring, when the sallows are in flower, the Yellow Horned (*Polyploca flavicornis*) appears in birchwoods, mixed woods and parks. The caterpillars live on birches and pupate before hibernating.

1. *Drepana falcataria:* forewing span 27—35 mm ($1\frac{1}{16}$—$1\frac{3}{8}$ in). Central and northern Europe.
2. *Habrosyne pyritoides:* forewing span 35—40 mm ($1\frac{3}{8}$—$1\frac{9}{16}$ in). The temperate part of Eurasia.
3. *Thyatira batis:* forewing span 32—38 mm ($1\frac{1}{4}$—$1\frac{1}{2}$ in). The temperate part of Eurasia.
4. *Polyploca flavicornis:* forewing span 35—40 mm ($1\frac{3}{8}$—$1\frac{9}{16}$ in). The temperate part of Eurasia.

1 *Archiearis parthenias* L.   Geometridae
Orange Underwing

2 *Alsophila aescularia* Schiff.
March Moth

3 *Spargania luctuata* Schiff.
White-banded Carpet

Geometers (Geometridae) are thin-bodied moths whose relatively large wings are very often marked with incredibly fine and intricate patterns, so that they are comparatively easy to identify. The caterpillars (inchworms or loopers), which often resemble dry twigs, 'inch' their way along. They have fewer legs than most other caterpillars.

The Orange Underwing (*Archiearis parthenias*) appears in open birchwoods at the end of February and remains until May, when it is followed on the trees by the caterpillars. The caterpillars complete their development during the summer and then spin themselves a cocoon, in which they pupate. The pupae remain in the cocoons during the winter.

The March Moth (*Alsophila aescularia*) is another very early geometer. The males can be seen flying in February; the females are wingless and bear no resemblance to a moth. This geometer inhabits deciduous and mixed woods and is quite common in gardens. The polyphagous caterpillars live on the leaves of various deciduous trees. They pupate during the summer and the pupae overwinter.

Its striking appearance and the markings on its wings make the White-banded Carpet (*Spargania luctuata*) fairly easy to identify. The markings are very intricate, especially on the forewings, so that, understandably, the course of the lines and bands is relatively very variable. This geometer appears much later than the other two species. The first moths fly in June, while the last can still be encountered in August. This species forms one or two generations, according to the type of country and the climate. It prefers a cool environment and in the south is to be found at higher altitudes. The caterpillars live during the summer and early autumn on different kinds of willowherb and on bilberry plants. The winter is spent in the pupal stage.

1

2 ♂

2 ♀

3

1. *Archiearis parthenias:* forewing span 30—40 mm (1$\frac{3}{16}$— 1$\frac{9}{16}$ in). The cold and temperate parts of Eurasia.
2. *Alsophila aescularia:* forewing span of ♂ 25—35 mm 1—1$\frac{3}{8}$ in). The temperate part of Eurasia.
3. *Spargania luctuata:* forewing span 22—28 mm ($\frac{7}{8}$—1$\frac{1}{8}$ in). Central and northern Europe.

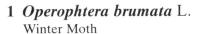

1 *Operophtera brumata* L.   Geometridae
Winter Moth

2 *Entephria caesiata* Schiff.
Grey Mountain Carpet

3 *Colostygia pectinataria* Kn.
Green Carpet

1

1♂

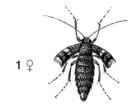

1♀

2

3

The male Winter Moth (*Operophtera brumata*) has normally developed wings, but the female has only wing stumps less than half the length of her body. This moth flies late in the autumn. The imagos appear in October and November and are often still to be seen in January. The males fly, but the females can only crawl about on the trees, where, in cracks in the bark and round the buds, they lay several hundred to a few thousand eggs. The caterpillars hatch in the spring. The young caterpillars force their way into the buds and chew them, while the older ones nibble the fruit, e.g. cherries. Large caterpillars bite holes in the leaves and in prolific years can strip the trees bare. They pupate in a cocoon in the topsoil or in grass. Only one generation is formed in a year.

Mountain geometers are represented by the Grey Mountain Carpet (*Entephria caesiata*), a beautiful and relatively large moth with very intricate markings, especially on its forewings (dark, or melanistic, specimens are also known). The single generation of moths appears from June to August, but is most abundant in June and July. The caterpillars live on heather, bilberry and cranberry plants. They hibernate and pupate among the leaves of their host plant in the spring.

The Green Carpet (*Colostygia pectinataria*) is a regular inhabitant of deciduous and mixed woods. It is a widespread species, but towards the south it occurs mainly in mountains. It produces only one generation in a year. The imagos fly from May to July. After they have flown for only a short time, the green tinge on their forewings disappears. The caterpillars have a relatively limited diet, since they live on various kinds of bedstraw and deadnettles. They appear in the autumn, but do not pupate until the spring; the imagos emerge in May.

1. *Operophtera brumata:* forewing span of ♂ 22—28 mm, length of ♀ 8—10 mm (forewing span of ♂ $\frac{7}{8}$—1$\frac{1}{8}$ in, length of ♀ $\frac{5}{16}$—$\frac{3}{8}$ in). Central Europe, eastern Siberia.
2. *Entephria caesiata:* forewing span 30—35 mm (1$\frac{3}{16}$—1$\frac{3}{8}$ in). Central and northern Europe, northern Asia.
3. *Colostygia pectinataria:* forewing span 22—27 mm ($\frac{7}{8}$—1$\frac{1}{16}$ in). Central and northern Europe; eastwards to the Altai Mts.

1 *Cosmorhoe ocellata* L.
Purple Bar

Geometridae

2 *Eulithis prunata* L.
Phoenix

3 *Cidaria fulvata* Forst.
Barred Yellow

4 *Rheumaptera subhastata* Nick.

5 *Rheumaptera undulata* L.
Scallop Shell

The Purple Bar (*Cosmorhoe ocellata*) is fairly common from May to September. The moths appear in two consecutive and overlapping generations. The caterpillars live from June up to the autumn on various kinds of bedstraw; those of the second generation complete their development in the same autumn, overwinter in a loosely spun cocoon and pupate the following spring.

The Phoenix (*Eulithis prunata*) inhabits the margins of deciduous woods, hillsides with plenty of shrubs and gardens. Although there is only one generation, the moths fly from June to September. The eggs overwinter and the caterpillars, which are hatched in the spring, eat the leaves of blackthorn, hawthorn and currant-bushes.

The food plants of the Barred Yellow (*Cidaria fulvata*) are roses, both wild and cultivated, so that this geometer is also to be found in gardens and parks. It is a lowland species and the imagos of the single generation fly from June to August. The eggs overwinter.

The pronounced intricacy of the markings on its wings predestines the geometer *Rheumaptera subhastata* to considerable variability. This species likes high altitudes and a rather cold environment. The imagos of the single generation fly from May to July. The caterpillars live on bilberry leaves, complete their development in the autumn and then pupate; the pupa hibernates.

The scientific name of the Scallop Shell (*Rheumaptera undulata*) describes the markings on the moth's wings (*undulata* = wavy). This species inhabits open woods and their outskirts, wooded valleys and gardens. The imagos fly mainly in June and July. The caterpillars live on sallow, aspen, alder and bilberry leaves. The pupal stage overwinters.

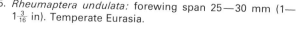

1. *Cosmorhoe ocellata:* forewing span 20—25 mm ($\frac{13}{16}$—1 in). The temperate part of Eurasia.
2. *Eulithis prunata:* forewing span 30—35 mm ($1\frac{3}{16}$—$1\frac{3}{8}$ in). The temperate part of Eurasia, North America.
3. *Cidaria fulvata:* forewing span 20—25 mm ($\frac{5}{16}$—1 in). The temperate part of Eurasia (as far as the Altai Mts).
4. *Rheumaptera subhastata:* forewing span 23—28 mm ($\frac{15}{16}$—$1\frac{1}{8}$ in). The northern part of the Palaearctic region, North America.
5. *Rheumaptera undulata:* forewing span 25—30 mm (1—$1\frac{3}{16}$ in). Temperate Eurasia.

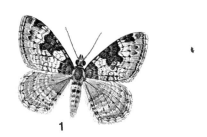

1

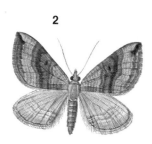

2

3

1 *Xanthorhoe fluctuata* L.   Geometridae
Garden Carpet

2 *Scotopteryx chenopodiata* L.
Shaded Broad-bar

3 *Epirrhoe alternata* Müll.
Common Carpet

The Garden Carpet (*Xanthorhoe fluctuata*), one of the most abundant geometers, inhabits fallow land, gardens and parks and frequents the outskirts of woods. The moths like to sit on tree trunks. There are two generations. The imagos of the first generation fly in the largest numbers in May and June (and sometimes sooner), while those of the second generation live from July to September. The Garden Carpet occurs in lowlands and foothills and in mountains is still to be encountered at altitudes of about 2,400 m (7,870 ft). The eggs are pale yellow, while the caterpillars are sometimes brown or reddish-brown and sometimes grey or greenish. The first generation of caterpillars lives in June and the second generation from August to October. Their food plants are various Cruciferae. They pupate in a fine cocoon. The second generation spends the winter in the pupal stage.

The Shaded Broad-bar (*Scotopteryx chenopodiata*) is one of the abundant geometer species. It mainly inhabits meadows, heaths, the margins of forests and gardens from lowlands up to the alpine zone. The imagos of the single generation fly mostly in July and August, but sometimes until September. The caterpillars have a large menu, but show a preference for leguminous plants. They abound on tufted vetch, meadow pea and dyer's greenweed and are commonly to be found on grasses. They appear from August onwards, hibernate, complete their development the following year and pupate in June.

A list of the common geometers would not be complete without the Common Carpet (*Epirrhoe alternata*), whose wing markings are characterised by pronounced variability. It normally inhabits deciduous woods, but has learnt to settle in cultivated areas; being adaptable, it thus has a better chance of survival than other species. At high altitudes it is scarcer. Since there are one or two generations, the imagos can be seen from April to September. The caterpillars, which occur from the summer to the autumn, live on various kinds of bedstraw.

1. *Xanthorhoe fluctuata:* forewing span 18—25 mm ($\frac{3}{4}$—1 in). The temperate part of Eurasia, North America.
2. *Scotopteryx chenopodiata:* forewing span 25—30 mm (1—1$\frac{3}{16}$ in). Europe, the temperate belt in Asia.
3. *Epirrhoe alternata:* forewing span 20—25 mm ($\frac{13}{16}$—1 in). Europe, the temperate belt in Asia.

1 *Camptogramma bilineata* L. Geometridae
Yellow Shell

2 *Aplocera plagiata* L.
Treble-bar

3 *Cyclophora punctaria* L.
Maiden's Blush

4 *Timandra griseata* Petersen
Blood-vein

The strikingly coloured Yellow Shell (*Camptogramma bilineata*) is very common in most localities, especially near streams. The moths fly from May to August in either one or two generations. The polyphagous caterpillars live on dock, chickweed and deadnettles; they hibernate and pupate in the spring.

The caterpillars of the Treble-bar (*Aplocera plagiata*) live on St John's wort as their food plant. The warmth-loving imagos have somewhat variable markings on their wings, so that, as in related species, several forms have been described. The moths can be seen from May to October and during this time form two generations. The caterpillars of the second generation hibernate.

The Maiden's Blush (*Cyclophora punctaria*) was no doubt given its scientific name because of the tiny spots on its wings (in Latin, *punctum* = spot). The markings of this common species are very variable. It inhabits deciduous woods, where the moths occur from April to August in two consecutive generations. The caterpillars live mostly on oak leaves, but occasionally eat birch leaves.

The Blood-vein (*Timandra griseata*) is notable for the shape of its wings and for their markings. The oblique dark stripe on the forewings continues without a break onto the hindwings. The moths fly over meadows and untilled land and often appear in gardens. Since there are two overlapping generations, they can be seen from May to October. The caterpillars have a fairly specialised diet and live chiefly on dock, sorrel and knotgrass; the second caterpillar generation hibernates.

1. *Camptogramma bilineata:* forewing span 20—25 mm ($\frac{13}{16}$—1 in). The Palaearctic region.
2. *Aplocera plagiata:* forewing span 27—40 mm ($1\frac{1}{16}$—$1\frac{9}{16}$ in). The Palaearctic region.
3. *Cyclophora punctaria:* forewing span 18—25 mm ($\frac{3}{4}$—1 in). Europe, Asia Minor, Iran.
4. *Timandra griseata:* forewing span 23—28 mm ($\frac{15}{16}$—$1\frac{1}{8}$ in). Eurasia.

1 *Abraxas grossulariata* L. Geometridae
Magpie Moth

2 *Scopula ornata* Scop.
Lace Border

3 *Lomaspilis marginata* L.
Clouded Border

The Magpie Moth (*Abraxas grossulariata*) can be glimpsed, here and there, in gardens, in parks and sometimes in meadows. The markings on its wings are rather variable and a number of colour forms have been described. The imagos of the single generation fly from June to August. The polyphagous caterpillars live on currant and gooseberry bushes, blackthorn, bird-cherry, sallows, hazels and other deciduous trees. The caterpillars hibernate, continue their development the following spring and then pupate.

The formerly common Lace Border (*Scopula ornata*) has now become much rarer. It inhabits warm lowland slopes, steppe-type localities and the margins of woods. The imagos, which form two or three generations, fly from May to September. The caterpillars live on aromatic plants, such as wild marjoram and thyme, together with dandelions, sorrel, speedwell and others. They hibernate and pupate the following spring.

Deciduous woods provide satisfactory living conditions for many geometer species, including the Clouded Border (*Lomaspilis marginata*). This species also appears in gardens, parks and meadows, however, and is still common everywhere; it also occurs in several colour forms. The imagos fly for a long time, during which one or sometimes two generations appear. The imagos of the first generation appear from April to June and those of the second (if any) in July and August. The caterpillars are polyphagous, but confine their feeding to various deciduous trees and shrubs (chiefly poplars, birches, hazels, willows and the like). They pupate in the autumn and the pupae overwinter.

1. *Abraxas grossulariata:* forewing span 35—40 mm (1$\frac{3}{8}$—1$\frac{9}{16}$ in). The Palaearctic region.
2. *Scopula ornata:* forewing span 18—25 mm ($\frac{3}{4}$—1 in). Eurasia (the temperate belt as far as the Amur).
3. *Lomaspilis marginata:* forewing span 20—25 mm ($\frac{13}{16}$—1 in). The Palaearctic region.

1 *Opisthograptis luteolata* L.   Geometridae
Brimstone Moth

2 *Ennomos autumnaria* Wernb.
Large Thorn

3 *Ourapteryx sambucaria* L.
Swallow-tailed Moth

The bright yellow of the Brimstone Moth (*Opisthograptis luteolata*) distinguishes this species from all other geometers. It inhabits shrub-covered hillsides, heaths, woods, parks and gardens and occurs in one or in two generations. Sometimes it appears in April, but more usually in May and, if a second generation is formed, it is still to be seen in September. The green, yellow-banded caterpillars have a wide range of food plants, of which blackthorn, hawthorn, honeysuckle, willows, hazels and bilberry plants are the most common. It is generally the pupae that hibernate, but sometimes the caterpillars of the second generation overwinter.

As indicated by its scientific name, the Large Thorn (*Ennomos autumnaria*) is an autumn species, whose single generation flies from August to October in and around deciduous woods and in parks and gardens. The male is smaller and darker than the female and has pectinate antennae. The dark brown *schultzi* form has a violet sheen on its wings. The moths live mainly in lowlands. Owing to the late appearance of the imagos, the eggs overwinter. The caterpillars, which develop in the spring, live on the leaves of various deciduous trees (chiefly birch, lime, alder, maple, oak, willow and plum). They pupate in the summer among the leaves, in a fine cocoon.

The Swallow-tailed Moth (*Ourapteryx sambucaria*) is another large geometer. It inhabits the warm margins of woods, meadows, the areas round streams and gardens and parks. It flies mainly from June to August, but if, as sometimes happens, it forms a second generation, these imagos fly from September to October. The caterpillars are polyphagous, but display a preference for common elder, lilac, blackthorn, aspen, clematis and ivy. They hatch in August, overwinter and continue their development in the spring; they pupate in June on the branches, in loosely spun cocoons. The slender pupa is fawn-coloured.

1. *Opisthograptis luteolata:* forewing span 32—37 mm ($1\frac{1}{4}$—$1\frac{7}{16}$ in). A large part of the Palaearctic region.
2. *Ennomos autumnaria:* forewing span 40—50 mm ($1\frac{9}{16}$—2 in). The Palaearctic region.
3. *Ourapteryx sambucaria:* forewing span 40—50 mm ($1\frac{9}{16}$—2 in). The western part of the Palaearctic region.

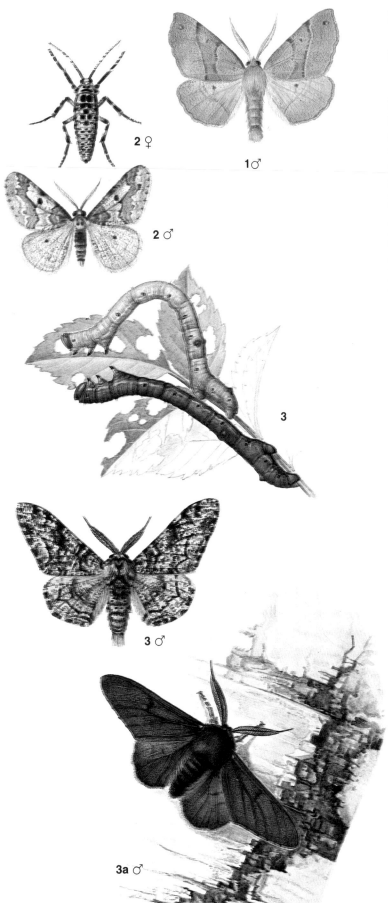

1 *Colotois pennaria* L. Geometridae
Feathered Thorn

2 *Erannis defoliaria* Clerck
Mottled Umber

3 *Biston betularia* L.
Peppered Moth

Many geometers find the late autumn the best time to live in. The Feathered Thorn (*Colotois pennaria*) is common in deciduous woods from September to November. The eggs, which are laid in the autumn, overwinter and the caterpillars are hatched the following spring; they live on the leaves of various woody plants.

The Mottled Umber (*Erannis defoliaria*) is another late autumn species; it appears in October and November and not infrequently is still to be seen in December. Sexual dimorphism is pronounced. The male has all the characters of a moth, but the female is wingless and can only crawl about on the trees. This geometer inhabits deciduous and mixed forests and sometimes visits gardens. The eggs hatch in the spring and the caterpillars live on the leaves of various trees, including beech, hornbeam, oak, elm, birch, lime and fruit trees. If there are too many of them, the trees may be completely defoliated.

In contrast to the two preceding species, which fly very late in the autumn, the Peppered Moth (*Biston betularia*) occurs from May to July. As distinct from the female, which has filiform antennae, the male has pectinate antennae. The Peppered Moth is an example of how industrial pollution can influence coloration. In the last century, black individuals, which produced black offspring, were found in industrial centres in the British Isles. This melanic form, which was named *carbonaria* (3a), was later discovered in industrial regions in other countries also; it was found to be more resistant to fumes and to have a better chance of survival owing to its protective colouring. The caterpillars, which eat the leaves of various deciduous trees, pupate in the autumn; the pupae hibernate.

1. *Colotois pennaria:* forewing span 35—45 mm ($1\frac{3}{8}$—$1\frac{3}{4}$ in). Europe and eastwards into central Asia.
2. *Erannis defoliaria:* forewing span 30—40 mm ($1\frac{3}{16}$—$1\frac{9}{16}$ in). Europe, the Caucasus.
3. *Biston betularia:* forewing span 35—60 mm ($1\frac{3}{8}$—$2\frac{3}{8}$ in). Europe, the temperate belt in Asia.

1 *Bupalus piniarius* L.
Bordered White or Pine Looper

Geometridae

2 *Psodos quadrifaria* Sulz.

3 *Geometra papilionaria* L.
Large Emerald

The Bordered White or Pine Looper (*Bupalus piniarius*) is a species in which the sexes are very differently coloured. Furthermore, the colouring of each sex is very variable, so that many different colour forms have been described. The Bordered White inhabits pine woods with an age of 25–70 years. The moths fly from May (sometimes from April) until July and there is only one generation. The female lays her eggs on the pine needles and the caterpillars hatch in about three weeks; they live on needles for about four months and pupate in the autumn. The pupae spend the winter in the ground, so that many of them fall prey to hungry animals. In prolific years, with too many caterpillars, this species can do considerable damage.

Many geometers fly from lowland up to mountain altitudes, but some are strictly specialised for life in the mountains. *Psodos quadrifaria* lives in the stunted pine and alpine meadow zone, where it flies from June to August. The caterpillars nibble many kinds of plants and then hibernate. Since the distribution of this geometer is not continuous, several geographical races can be distinguished.

Among lepidopterans, green wings are something of an exception, but among geometrids there are several green species. The largest of these, the Large Emerald (*Geometra papilionaria*), is most common in birch woods from lowlands to mountains, but also occurs on heaths and even in gardens. The imagos fly from June to August. The light-coloured markings on their wings are variable. As distinct from the female, the male has pectinate antennae. The green caterpillars live chiefly on birches, but also devour alder, hazel and other leaves. They appear in August, hibernate, complete their development in the spring and pupate in a thinly spun cocoon.

1 ♂

1 ♀

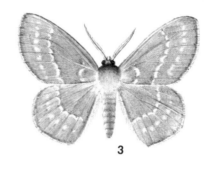

2

3

3

1. *Bupalus piniarius:* forewing span 28—35 mm (1$\frac{1}{8}$—1$\frac{3}{8}$ in). Europe, the temperate belt in Asia.
2. *Psodos quadrifaria:* forewing span 18—23 mm ($\frac{3}{4}$—$\frac{15}{16}$ in). The mountain massifs of Europe and the temperate part of Asia.
3. *Geometra papilionaria:* forewing span 40—50 mm (1$\frac{9}{16}$—2 in). Europe, the temperate belt in Asia.

273

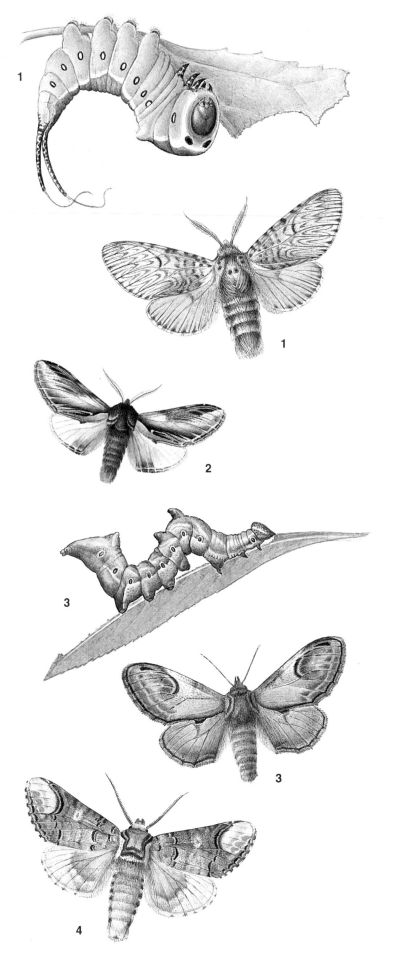

1 *Cerura vinula* L.   Notodontidae
Puss Moth

2 *Pheosia tremulae* Clerck
Swallow Prominent

3 *Eligmodonta ziczac* L.
Pebble Prominent

4 *Phalera bucephala* L.
Buff-tip

Some moths have very unusual and remarkable caterpillars. One of the most interesting is undoubtedly the caterpillar of the Puss Moth (*Cerura vinula*), which, if disturbed, adopts a menacing pose, withdraws its head into its prothorax and shoots out two whip-like, flesh-coloured processes from the tip of its abdomen. The moths fly from April to August in deciduous woods, where the female lays small groups of eggs on the leaves of willows or poplars. The caterpillars pupate in the autumn in a strong cocoon on a trunk or a branch.

The caterpillars of the Swallow Prominent (*Pheosia tremula*) also live on willows, poplars and birches. The moths fly in deciduous woods round streams and rivers, where they form one or two generations (only one in the north of its range). The Pebble Prominent (*Eligmodonta ziczac*) also produces one or two generations in a year – one from April to June and the other (if any) from July to September. The caterpillars, which occur from June to September, live on the leaves of poplars, willows and many other deciduous trees. Their form is striking in itself, but when resting they try to imitate a dry leaf or a gall. The differences in their colouring – grey, brownish, greenish, bluish and violet – are also interesting.

The Buff-tip (*Phalera bucephala*) inhabits deciduous woods and is also to be found in parks and avenues. The moths fly from May to August and if the climatic conditions are favourable they form a second generation in southern Europe. The caterpillars live in July and August; unlike those of the other species mentioned above, they are hairy. At first they all live together, but later disperse over the host plant. They eat the leaves of limes, elms, hazels, poplars, oaks and other deciduous trees. The pupal stage hibernates.

1. *Cerura vinula:* forewing span 45—70 mm ($1\frac{3}{4}$—$2\frac{3}{4}$ in). Most of the Palaearctic region.
2. *Pheosia tremulae:* forewing span 45—55 mm ($1\frac{3}{4}$—$2\frac{3}{16}$ in). Europe, southern Siberia.
3. *Eligmodonta ziczac:* forewing span 40—45 mm ($1\frac{9}{16}$—$1\frac{3}{4}$ in). Europe, the temperate belt in Asia.
4. *Phalera bucephala:* forewing span 45—55 mm ($1\frac{3}{4}$—$2\frac{3}{16}$ in). Europe, eastern Asia.

1 *Calliteara pudibunda* L.
Pale Tussock

Lymantriidae

2 *Orgyia antiqua* L.
Vapourer

1 ♂

1

2

2 ♀

2 ♂

The Pale Tussock (*Calliteara pudibunda*) flies in deciduous woods (especially beech woods), gardens and parks from April to June. Sometimes it forms a second generation in the autumn. The imagos are variably coloured and the markings on the wings are sometimes blurred, so that the moth seems to be almost the same colour; such individuals are named f. *concolor*. While the moth is inconspicuous, the same cannot be said about the caterpillar, which is also variably coloured, but can be unequivocally identified from the tufts of yellow hairs on its body and the bundle of recurved pink hairs at the end of its abdomen. The caterpillar is polyphagous and eats the leaves of various deciduous trees (e.g. beech, oak, birch and fruit trees). It lives from July to October and then pupates. The dark-coloured pupa is covered with yellow hairs and is wrapped in a yellowish-brown cocoon; it is this stage that hibernates.

In some tussock moths (Lymantriidae), inter-sex differences are manifested mainly in the shape of the antennae, in size and generally in colouring also. In the Vapourer (*Orgyia antiqua*) the differences go much further. The male has all the characteristics of a moth and is able to fly, while the tubby female has only wing stumps. The moths occur in lowlands, hills and mountains, where they ascend beyond the limit of the forest. They are not uncommon in towns. They live from May to the end of October, in one, two or three generations. After emergence, the female remains on her pupal cocoon and deposits all her eggs on it; the eggs of the last generation overwinter. The caterpillar is very striking in appearance, with tufts of yellow hairs all over its body, two bundles of long hairs behind its head and one at the end of its abdomen. Its food requirements are modest; it eats the leaves of various deciduous trees and shrubs, such as beech, oak, willow, blackthorn and bilberry, and also appears on spruces and herbaceous plants. Caterpillars of the different generations can be seen from April to September; when fully grown they pupate in a cocoon.

1. *Calliteara pudibunda:* forewing span 40—45 mm ($1\frac{9}{16}$—$1\frac{3}{4}$ in). Europe, the temperate belt in Asia.
2. *Orgyia antiqua:* forewing span of ♂ 25—30 mm (1—$1\frac{3}{16}$ in). Temperate Eurasia.

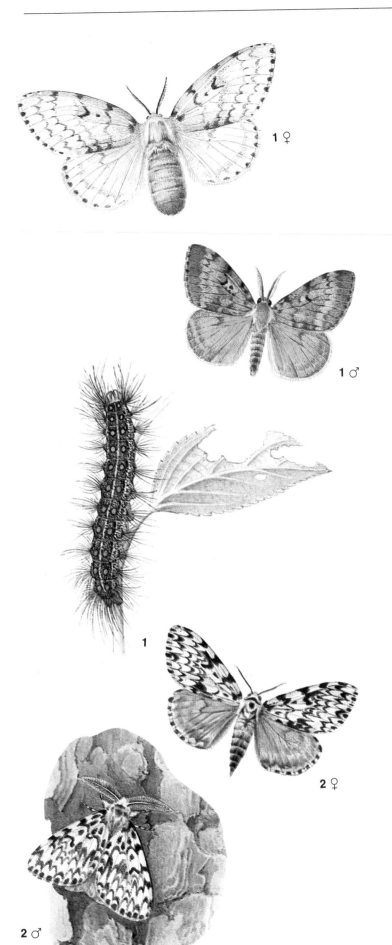

1 ♀

1 ♂

1

2 ♀

2 ♂

1 *Lymantria dispar* L.
Gypsy Moth

Lymantriidae

2 *Lymantria monacha* L.
Black Arches

The Gypsy Moth (*Lymantria dispar*) is one of the tussock moths whose male and female differ as regards their colour and size and the shape of their antennae. It is a typical inhabitant of deciduous woods, gardens and parks. (It is extinct in Britain.) The male flies in July and August and sometimes until September and is generally common (in some years abundant). The female cannot fly. She lays the eggs in a heap on the bark of the trunk or a branch of a deciduous tree and covers them with hairs. The resultant patch, which looks rather like a flat fungus, varies in size from as little as 7 sq cm (1 sq in) to as much as 100 sq cm (15 sq in). The eggs overwinter. The caterpillars, which live from April to June, are polyphagous; they mostly feed on oaks, but are also common on beeches and many other deciduous trees (in gardens on plum, apricot and nut trees). In prolific years they can do untold damage. They pupate in a loosely spun cocoon in a crack in the bark or a forked branch. The pupal stage is short and the moths emerge in ten to fourteen days.

It is not so long ago that the Black Arches (*Lymantria monacha*) still devastated spruce monocultures. The caterpillars live primarily on spruces, but sometimes on pines, and they are also known on oaks. In the history of forestry, the extent of the damage they have done in European spruce forests is incalculable. The eggs overwinter and the caterpillars, which hatch in the spring, are at their most voracious in May and June. They pupate in a loose cocoon in a crack in the bark or in litter. The moths emerge in July and fly until September. The caterpillars have natural enemies, however, such as searcher beetles (genus *Calosoma*), also known as caterpillar hunters, large ground beetles (genus *Carabus*) and the Four-spot Carrion Beetle (*Xylodrepa quadripunctata*), not to mention birds (particularly cuckoos). In prolific years they are also attacked by polyhedral disease, whose viruses transform the caterpillars' tissues to a brownish liquid.

1. *Lymantria dispar:* forewing span of ♂ 40—50 mm, of ♀ 60—90 mm (forewing span of ♂ $1\frac{9}{16}$—2 in, of ♀ $2\frac{3}{8}$—$3\frac{9}{16}$ in). The Palaearctic region; carried to North America.
2. *Lymantria monacha:* forewing span of ♂ 40—45 mm, of ♀ 50—55 m (forewing span of ♂ $1\frac{9}{16}$—$1\frac{3}{4}$ in, of ♀ 2—$2\frac{3}{16}$ in). The temperate part of the Palaearctic region.

1 *Syntomis phegea* L. Ctenuchidae
Nine-spotted

2 *Arctia caja* L. Arctiidae
Garden Tiger

3 *Panaxia dominula* L.
Scarlet Tiger

In the warmer parts of Europe, the Nine-spotted (*Syntomis phegea*), which is highly reminiscent of a burnet, can be seen in June and July on sunny slopes, in clearings and at the margins of woods. The moths sometimes appear *en masse* and settle on the flowers of various summer plants. The eggs are yellow. The caterpillars live on dandelions, deadnettles, plantain and other herbaceous plants, where they eat the leaves. After hibernating, they feed for a short time in the spring and then pupate.

Most tiger moths are characterised by vivid colouring. The resting Garden Tiger (*Arctia caja*) is almost invisible among the vegetation, but if disturbed it spreads its forewings, revealing the red, dark-spotted hindwings, whose colours are meant to deter enemies. This species is found more or less everywhere in both cultivated and rough areas. The moths fly during the night from June to August. Their mouthparts are vestigial, so that they are unable to take any food. The highly distinctive caterpillar is polyphagous. After hibernating, it resumes its feeding and then pupates on the ground in a cocoon.

The Scarlet Tiger (*Panaxia dominula*) appears sporadically in damp meadows, wooded valleys and the vicinity of streams. It flies during the daytime and the night from May to July or August. Unlike the Garden Tiger, it has well-developed mouthparts and is therefore able to drink nectar from flowers; it also settles on damp woodland paths and sucks water. The markings on its wings are very variable and in some individuals the hindwings are not red, but yellow, with dark spots. The caterpillars have a wide range of food plants and eat deadnettle, stinging nettle, forget-me-not, honeysuckle, raspberry and willow leaves. They hibernate and pupate in the spring in a fine, whitish cocoon.

1. *Syntomis phegea:* forewing span 35—40 mm ($1\frac{3}{8}$—$1\frac{9}{16}$ in). Europe, Asia Minor, Transcaucasia.
2. *Arctia caja:* forewing span 45—65 mm ($1\frac{3}{4}$—$2\frac{9}{16}$ in). The temperate part of Eurasia, North America.
3. *Panaxia dominula:* forewing span 45—55 mm ($1\frac{3}{4}$—$2\frac{3}{16}$ in). The temperate part of Europe and eastwards to the Caucasus.

1 *Parasemia plantaginis* L.　　Arctiidae
Wood Tiger

2 *Spilosoma lubricipeda* L.
White Ermine

Moths with spotted wings always display some degree of colour variability. The Wood Tiger (*Parasemia plantaginis*) shows exceptional variability. The hindwings of typical male specimens are yellowish, with dark spots, but in individuals living in mountains they are white with dark spots. The hindwings of typical females are red, with black spots, but in colour variants they are often predominantly dark, with only narrow strips of colour. Conversely, the black may almost disappear, leaving only tiny spots. Like other tiger moths, the male Wood Tiger has pectinate antennae. The moths fly from May to July or August, mainly in damp localities and in open country. They are more numerous at higher altitudes and in mountains ascend to 3,000 m (9,840 ft). The greenish eggs have crisscross sculpturing on their surface. The caterpillars are polyphagous, but prefer plantain as their host plant. With a break for hibernation, they live from August to May, when they pupate in a greyish-brown cocoon in various kinds of shelters, such as a crack in the bark of a tree, close to the ground, or under a stone, etc.

The White Ermine (*Spilosoma lubricipeda*), is one of the most common of the few white tiger moths (ermines). Its wings are sprinkled more or less thickly with dark spots, which sometimes disappear, however, giving rise to the *paucipuncta* form. From May to July, this ermine frequents the outskirts of forests, bushy hillsides and gardens and ascends mountains to altitudes of about 1,600 m (5,248 ft). As a rule it forms only one generation, but sometimes there is a second generation whose moths live from July to October. The female lays her eggs in small groups. The caterpillars, which are polyphagous, pupate the same year in a grey cocoon, so that the pupal stage hibernates.

1. *Parasemia plantaginis:* forewing span 32—38 mm ($1\frac{1}{4}$—$1\frac{1}{2}$ in). Europe, the temperate belt in Asia.
2. *Spilosoma lubricipeda:* forewing span 30—42 mm ($1\frac{3}{16}$—$1\frac{11}{16}$ in). Europe, the temperate part of Asia.

1 *Agrotis segetum* Schiff.
Turnip Moth

2 *Agrotis exclamationis* L.
Heart and Dart

3 *Noctua pronuba* L.
Large Yellow Underwing

Owlet moths (Noctuidae) are the largest lepidopteran family, with over 1,100 known species in Europe alone and over 20,000 in the world at large. Since they are considered to be the most advanced lepidopteran group, they stand, in the natural system, at the head of this order. On their forewings, many species have intricate and very fine markings which are a guide to their identification. They also include destructive species, among which the Turnip Moth (*Agrotis segetum*) is usually regarded as the chief pest. Its caterpillars devour the leaves and roots of various plants. Although this was originally a steppe species, it is now to be found mainly in fields. The moths appear in two generations; the full-grown caterpillars hibernate.

The Heart and Dart (*Agrotis exclamationis*) takes its name – scientific and vernacular – from the markings on its forewings, which look either like an exclamation mark or a heart and a dash, depending on whether you view it vertically or horizontally. From May to August the moths fly over meadows and pastures, as a rule in a single generation. The caterpillars are polyphagous; they eat the roots of various wild plants, in particular grasses. They overwinter in the soil and pupate in the spring.

Many owlet moths have grey or brown hindwings, but in some species the hindwings are yellow, red or blue, usually with dark markings. For instance, the Large Yellow Underwing (*Noctua pronuba*) has yellow hindwings. This large and beautiful moth lives in various types of localities and is still to be found at altitudes of about 3,000 m (9,842 ft). It occurs from the spring until late in the autumn. The females lay their eggs at the end of the summer on the leaves and stems of different plants. The polyphagous caterpillars eat various herbaceous plants, including vegetables. They hibernate and pupate in April. The yellowish-brown pupa has two spines at the end of the body.

1. *Agrotis segetum:* forewing span 27—40 mm ($1\frac{1}{16}$—$1\frac{9}{16}$ in). Europe, the temperate part of Asia, South Africa.
2. *Agrotis exclamationis:* forewing span 30—40 mm ($1\frac{3}{16}$—$1\frac{9}{16}$ in). Europe, the temperate belt in Asia.
3. *Noctua pronuba:* forewing span 45—55 mm ($1\frac{3}{4}$—$2\frac{3}{16}$ in). Europe, the temperate belt in Asia.

1 *Xestia c-nigrum* L.   Noctuidae
  Setaceous Hebrew Character

2 *Melanchra persicariae* L.
  Dot

3 *Mythimna pallens* L.
  Common Wainscot

4 *Cucullia artemisiae* Hbn.
  Scarce Wormwood

The Setaceous Hebrew Character (*Xestia c-nigrum*) is one of the commonest noctuids. As a rule, it flies in two consecutive generations, so that the moths are to be found from May until late in October. They are abundant in fields and gardens and at night they swirl round street lamps and settle on the walls of houses. The polyphagous caterpillars nibble the leaves of small herbaceous plants; those of the second generation hibernate.

The Dot (*Melanchra persicariae*) inhabits open country in lowlands and mountains up to about 1,000 m (3,280 ft). Its most distinctive feature is the white reniform spot on its dark forewings. There is only one generation, but the moths fly from the spring to the autumn and the polyphagous caterpillars appear from July to October. Some of the caterpillars hibernate, but the main hibernating stage is the pupa, which overwinters in a chamber in the ground. The egg is shown in illustration 2a.

The Common Wainscot (*Mythimna pallens*) spends its life in dry or damp grassy localities, where its two generations fly from May to October. The polyphagous caterpillars live on grasses and other herbaceous plants. They spend the day curled up under the leaves of their host plant. Those of the second generation hibernate.

The moths of the genus *Cucullia* all look very much alike and are hard to tell apart. The caterpillars, on the other hand, are endowed with protective colouring which makes them invisible against their normal background. The weird caterpillars of the Scarce Wormwood (*Cucullia artemisiae*), which live on mugwort (a kind of wormwood), are a fine example. Their backs are surmounted by protuberances which resemble the flowers of the host plant. The moth, which lives in dry localities, flies in June and July; the pupae hibernate.

1. *Xestia c-nigrum:* forewing span 38—42 mm ($1\frac{1}{2}$—$1\frac{11}{16}$ in). Europe, the temperate belt in Asia.
2. *Melanchra persicariae:* forewing span 37—40 mm ($1\frac{7}{16}$—$1\frac{9}{16}$ in). The temperate part of the Palaearctic region.
3. *Mythimna pallens:* forewing span 30—35 mm ($1\frac{3}{16}$—$1\frac{3}{8}$ in). Europe, the temperate belt in Asia, North America.
4. *Cucullia artemisiae:* forewing span 37—42 mm ($1\frac{7}{16}$—$1\frac{11}{16}$ in). Central and southern Europe.

1 *Xanthia togata* Esp.
Pink-barred Sallow

Noctuidae

2 *Acronicta aceris* L.
Sycamore

3 *Acronicta psi* L.
Grey Dagger

1

The autumn, as well as the spring and summer, has its characteristic lepidopterans, which are not to be encountered at any other time. The Pink-barred Sallow (*Xanthia togata*) is one of them. Its single generation flies from August to October in lowlands and mountains, as far as the deciduous forest limit. The eggs overwinter and the caterpillars, which hatch in the spring, live first of all on sallow flowers and later on the ground vegetation.

Many plainly coloured noctuids have brightly coloured and often very striking caterpillars. This is the case with the members of the genus *Acronicta*. The Sycamore (*Acronicta aceris*) flies from May to August and sometimes forms a second generation. It lives in deciduous woods in warm localities, in horse chestnut avenues and in urban parks. The long-haired caterpillars develop from July to September on various deciduous trees, but mostly on sycamores, horse chestnuts, oaks, beeches, different kinds of poplars, hazels and birches. In prolific years the trees may be defoliated. The pupae hibernate.

The Grey Dagger (*Acronicta psi*) was given its scientific name in the eighteenth century by the Swedish naturalist Linnaeus, with reference to the mark on its forewings which resembles the Greek letter *psi*. It likes dry habitats, where it occurs in one or two generations. The hairy and very brightly coloured caterpillar lives on various deciduous trees or bushes, including, for instance, pear trees, hawthorn, blackthorn, hazels, poplars, willows, limes and elms. Before the advent of winter it pupates in a grey cocoon, so that the pupal stage hibernates.

2

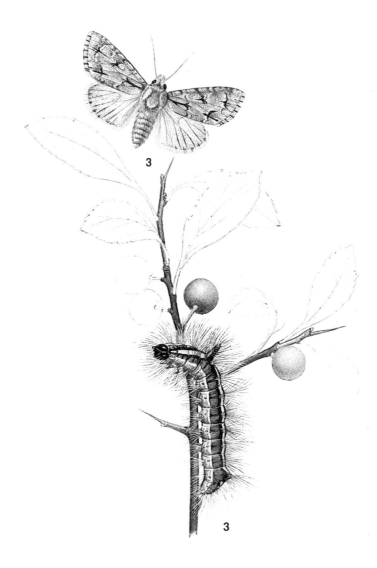

3

3

1. *Xanthia togata:* forewing span 27—30 mm ($1\frac{1}{16}$—$1\frac{3}{16}$ in). The temperate and northern part of the Palaearctic region, North America.
2. *Acronicta aceris:* forewing span 35—45 mm ($1\frac{3}{8}$—$1\frac{3}{4}$ in). The temperate part of Europe and eastwards into central Asia.
3. *Acronicta psi:* forewing span 33—38 mm ($1\frac{5}{16}$—$1\frac{1}{2}$ in). Central and southern Europe, temperate Asia.

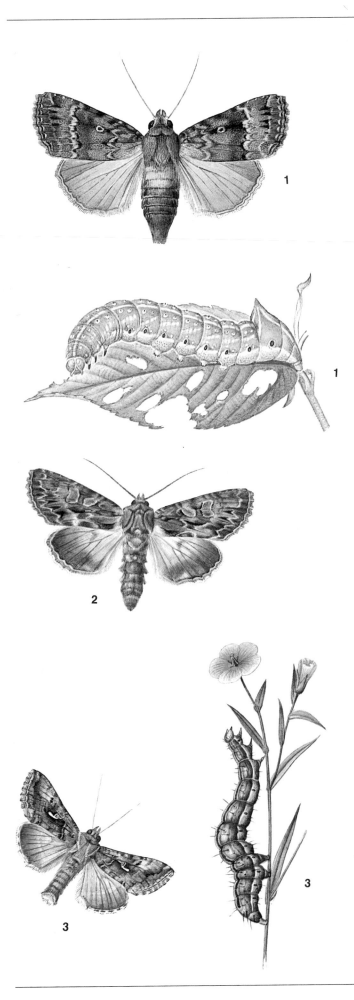

1 *Amphipyra pyramidea* L. Noctuidae
Copper Underwing

2 *Apamea monoglypha* Hufn.
Dark Arches

3 *Autographa gamma* L.
Silver Y

Deciduous woods are the habitat of many lepidopterans, whose caterpillars find sufficient suitable food and shelter in them. The Copper Underwing (*Amphipyra pyramidea*) is one of these species. Its single generation flies from July to the beginning of October and it also appears in gardens and parks. At first violet, the eggs gradually turn orange during the winter; the caterpillars are hatched in the spring. They live from May to June on different kinds of deciduous trees, including fruit trees.

The Dark Arches (*Apamea monoglypha*) is very common from June to September, mainly in grassy localities. It is also abundant in fields and is known to visit gardens. The moths are variably coloured, some being predominantly light-coloured and others mainly dark; the markings on the wings may also fade. In general, the males are darker than the females. The caterpillars hatch in the autumn. They live on the basal parts of different grasses, hibernate in a clump of grass or a clod of earth and by May, when they pupate, measure about 60 mm ($2\frac{3}{8}$ in). The pupa is chestnut-brown.

The Silver Y (*Autographa gamma*), one of the commonest noctuids, was given both its names because of the light-coloured spot on its forewings (the small Greek *gamma* is much the same shape as the letter Y). The moth has no special environmental requirements; it occurs almost everywhere, even high up in mountains. It also flies during the daytime, but appears in the greatest numbers after dusk. The Silver Y is a migratory species. Many individuals from subtropical regions have already reached central Europe in April. They reinforce and mix with the local population. One or two generations are formed. The imagos of the second generation fly south again.

---

1. *Amphipyra pyramidea:* forewing span 40—52 mm ($1\frac{9}{16}$—$2\frac{1}{16}$ in). Europe, the temperate belt in Asia.
2. *Apamea monoglypha:* forewing span 45—55 mm ($1\frac{3}{4}$—$2\frac{3}{16}$ in). Europe, the temperate belt in Asia.
3. *Autographa gamma:* forewing span 35—40 mm ($1\frac{3}{8}$—$1\frac{9}{16}$ in). Eurasia.

1 *Catocala fraxini* L.
Clifden Nonpareil

Noctuidae

2 *Catocala nupta* L.
Red Underwing

In the eighteenth century, when the Swedish naturalist Linnaeus gave the Clifden Nonpareil (*Catocala fraxini*) its scientific name, he named it after the ash tree (in Latin *fraxinus*), one of the food plants of the caterpillar. The caterpillar does live on ash trees, but favours poplars more; it is rarely to be found on other deciduous trees, such as birches and oaks. The moths fly from July to October, mainly in riparian woods, but also in mountains up to the deciduous wood limit. The coloration of their forewings is very variable; moths which live in the north are in general darker than those in the south. The dark-coloured, grooved eggs (1a) overwinter and the caterpillars are hatched in May. By July they are full-grown, measure 80–90 mm ($3\frac{1}{8}-3\frac{9}{16}$ in) and pupate on a leaf (1b). The blue-dusted pupa is wrapped in a flimsy cocoon. The Clifden Nonpareil is a disappearing species.

Many underwings have red hindwings with a wide dark border and a dark zigzag stripe of varying widths. One of them is the Red Underwing (*Catocala nupta*), whose hindwings may be yellow instead of red (the *flava* form). When resting, the Red Underwing is practically invisible, but if it feels itself to be in danger it spreads its forewings and startles the enemy by exposing its red hindwings. Before the attacker has recovered from this surprise, the moth has zigzagged away. It inhabits deciduous woods near rivers and streams, but also occurs in parks and avenues and visits gardens. It is to be found from July to October and ascends mountainsides to altitudes of about 1,000 m (3,280 ft). The eggs are laid in groups or singly in cracks in willows and poplars (the caterpillars' food plants). The eggs overwinter and the caterpillars pupate in June; the pupa is wrapped in silk-bound leaves.

1. *Catocala fraxini:* forewing span 75—95 mm ($3-3\frac{3}{4}$ in). The temperate part of Eurasia, North America.
2. *Catocala nupta:* forewing span 66—75 mm ($2\frac{9}{16}-3$ in). The temperate part of Eurasia.

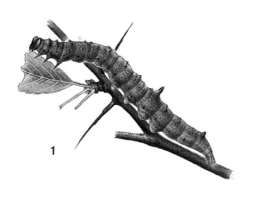

1 *Ephesia fulminea* Scop.

Noctuidae

2 *Scoliopteryx libatrix* L.
Herald

3 *Hypena proboscidalis* L.
Snout

Today, *Ephesia fulminea* is a severely endangered lepidopteran species, since it does not tolerate the violent inroads made by people in nature; in some places it has completely disappeared. It flies from May to August. In warm localities, including steppe formations, orchards, gardens and the outskirts of woods, it will fly even longer. The caterpillars, which hatch in the spring, have a characteristic outgrowth on their eighth segment. They live mostly on blackthorn and plum trees and occasionally on hawthorn, various kinds of fruit trees and oaks; they pupate in June.

Caves and cellars provide a whole series of animals with shelter for the winter. The Herald (*Scoliopteryx libatrix*) often spends the winter in such places in great numbers. In the spring the moths fly out and found a new generation. As a rule, there is a further, later generation and it is this one that hibernates. This species prefers damp woods and other localities near water and ascends mountains to about 2,000 m (6,560 ft). It also visits gardens. The caterpillars live on various kinds of willows and poplars.

The extremely long palps of the Snout (*Hypena proboscidalis*) are directed straight forwards and give the moth the appearance of having a long nose. It is a common species in lowland, hill and mountain forests. It also seems to be very adaptable, since it is still common everywhere. It usually produces two generations. The moths of the first generation fly in May and June and those of the second generation in August and September. The abundance of this noctuid is evidently also positively influenced by the abundance of stinging nettles, which are the chief food plant of the caterpillar. The caterpillars of the second generation hibernate and then pupate in April or May. The imagos emerge in the spring.

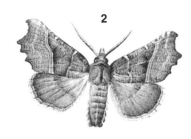

1. *Ephesia fulminea:* forewing span 45—52 mm (1¾—2 1/16 in). The warmer parts of Eurasia.
2. *Scoliopteryx libatrix:* forewing span 40—45 mm (1 9/16—1¾ in). The Palaearctic region, North America.
3. *Hypena proboscidalis:* forewing span 25—38 mm (1—1½ in). The Palaearctic region.

1 *Panorpa communis* L. Panorpidae
Scorpion-fly

2 *Panorpa alpina* Ramb.

3 *Boreus hiemalis* L. Boreidae
Snow-flea

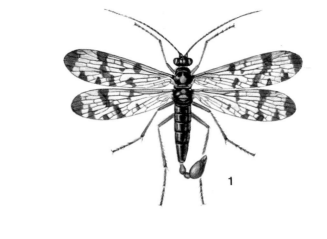

Forest undergrowth, the vegetation beside forest streams, damp meadows and sometimes gardens and parks form the habitat of the Scorpion-fly (*Panorpa communis*), which appears from May to September. It flies for only short distances and soon settles on a plant. The male entices the female with a kind of dance and a gift in the form of a solidified drop of a liquid released from its mouth; further gifts are presented during copulation. The female lays 25–75 eggs in a depression in the ground. The larvae at first live all together, but subsequently disperse. They live in leaf litter in a tunnel in which they can move both forwards and backwards. They feed on decaying animal organisms and plants and pupate in a chamber in the ground. Shortly before the imago emerges, the pupa breaks open the cover of the pupal chamber and actively forces its way towards the surface.

Panorpa alpina is commoner at higher altitudes. It is to be found near water from June to August.

The number of real winter insects is very small. Some merely prolong their appearance from autumn into December, but the Snow-flea (*Boreus hiemalis*) lives from October to April. It is most commonly to be seen on snow, on which it can jump short distances. It does not like heat and temperatures of over 20 °C (70 °F) are fatal for it. It occurs mainly in places where there is moss, whose juices are its chief food, although it also sucks dead insects dry. The female lays her eggs in moss. The development of the larvae takes two years. They live first of all on the fine moss rootlets and then on the leaves and finally they pupate in a cell in the ground. Towards the end of its development the pupa leaves the cell and crawls up to the surface.

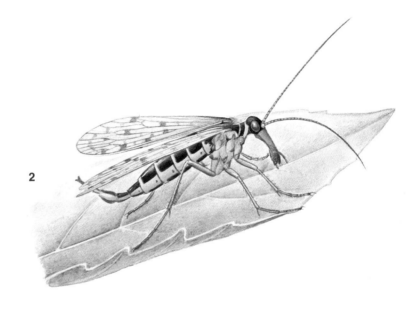

1

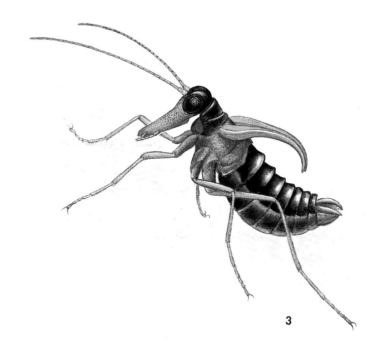

2

1. *Panorpa communis:* wing span 25—30 mm (1—1$\frac{3}{16}$ in). Europe, the temperate belt in Asia.
2. *Panorpa alpina:* wing span 25—30 mm (1—1$\frac{3}{16}$ in). Europe.
3. *Boreus hiemalis:* ♂ 2.5—3.5 mm, ♀ 4—5 mm (♂ $\frac{3}{32}$—$\frac{5}{32}$ in, ♀ $\frac{5}{32}$—$\frac{3}{16}$ in). Central and northern Europe.

3

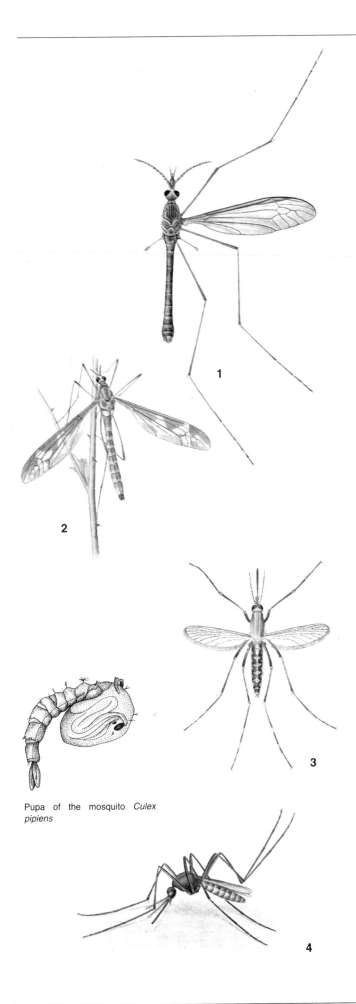

Pupa of the mosquito *Culex pipiens*

1 *Tipula oleracea* L.   Tipulidae
Daddy-long-legs

2 *Tipula maxima* Poda

3 *Aëdes caspius* Pallas   Culicidae

4 *Culex pipiens* L.

Crane-flies (Tipulidae) fly in the spring and summer in meadows, fields, gardens and woods. They like to rest on vegetation and the walls of houses. One of the most common species is the Daddy-long-legs (*Tipula oleracea*), whose first generation appears in April and May and the second in August and September. It flies in the early morning and before sunset, but only in calm weather. The female usually lays her eggs in spots where leguminous plants grow. The larvae live on the roots and in some places can be a nuisance. They pupate in the soil; the larvae of the second generation hibernate.

Tipula maxima is the largest European crane-fly. It can be recognised not only by its size, but also by the markings on its wings. It occurs from May to July in damp localities, preferably near a stream. It is not common.

Female mosquitoes are well known for the way they can ruin picnics. They molest human beings, stab them and suck their blood, while the harmless males suck only sweet plant juices. *Aëdes caspius* is one of the most common species in Europe. It inhabits the flood areas of rivers, where it occurs in vast numbers. The larvae develop in pools.

Culex pipiens sucks only bird blood. It can be seen from the spring to the autumn, when the females retire into cellars to hibernate. The larvae develop mostly in the vicinity of people, e.g. in rain-butts in gardens. These mosquitoes often enter houses in the autumn and hibernate there.

---

1. *Tipula oleracea:* 15—23 mm ($\frac{5}{8}$—$\frac{15}{16}$ in). Europe, northern Africa.
2. *Tipula maxima:* 26—42 mm (1$\frac{1}{16}$—1$\frac{11}{16}$ in). Europe.
3. *Aëdes caspius:* 4 mm ($\frac{5}{32}$ in). Europe, temperate Asia, North Africa.
4. *Culex pipiens:* 3.5—5 mm ($\frac{5}{32}$—$\frac{3}{16}$ in). Practically the entire globe.

1 *Chironomus plumosus* L.   Chironomidae
2 *Mikiola fagi* Hart.   Cecidomyidae
Beech Gall-midge
3 *Bibio marci* L.   Bibionidae
St Mark's-fly

Chironomus plumosus is a mosquito-like midge, but it does not bite. Its vestigial mouthparts make food intake impossible and it is very short-lived. The males form large swarms. The larva is called a bloodworm. It lives in water, where it makes itself a case of detritus and sand, mixed with the secretion of its salivary glands, and quickly spins a funnel inside the mouth. The movements of its body produce a current in the water, bringing various small particles which are caught in the funnel; the larva eats them together with the funnel, which it then replaces.

On beech leaves you will often come across elongate, lemon-shaped structures, which are at first green and later turn yellow or red; there are usually several on one leaf. These are galls (2a) whose formation is induced by the female Beech Gall-midge (*Mikiola fagi*) and each contains a developing larva. The tiny imago flies very early in the spring; it is common, but easily goes unnoticed.

The dark, slim-bodied St Mark's-fly (*Bibio marci*) emerges from the pupa when the fruit trees are in full flower. The males are the first to appear and they wait for the females to emerge. The females are larger and have darker wings; in the males, only the anterior edge of the wings is dark. The St Mark's-fly lives at both low and quite high altitudes and inhabits orchards, gardens, the outskirts of woods and wooded steppes. In favourable years the imagos are abundant. Several dozen eggs are laid in the ground and the larvae live here. They hibernate in the topsoil and are therefore not infrequently washed out by spring floods caused by melting snow. Although the larvae may do some damage by gnawing small roots, their useful activity in the formation of humus must also be taken into account. The adults are good pollinators.

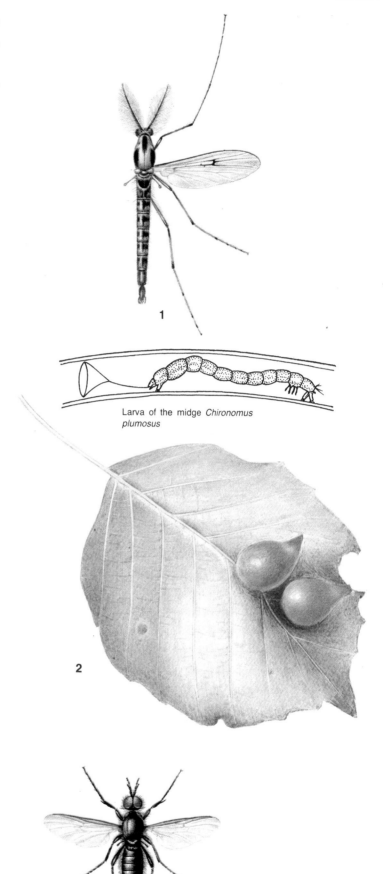

1

Larva of the midge *Chironomus plumosus*

2

3

1. *Chironomus plumosus:* 10—12 mm ($\frac{3}{8}$—$\frac{1}{2}$ in). The Palaearctic and Nearctic regions.
2. *Mikiola fagi:* imago 3.5—4 mm, gall 4—12 mm (imago $\frac{5}{32}$ in, gall $\frac{5}{32}$—$\frac{1}{2}$ in). Europe.
3. *Bibio marci:* 8—10 mm ($\frac{5}{16}$—$\frac{3}{8}$ in). Europe, extending eastwards into central Asia.

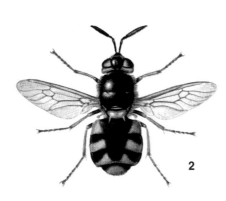

1 *Rhagio scolopacea* L. Rhagionidae

2 *Stratiomys chamaeleon* L. Stratiomyidae
Soldier-fly

3 *Chloromyia formosa* Scop.

The family Rhagionidae comprises a great many predacious species which sit head downwards on tree trunks and telegraph poles. *Rhagio scolopacea* flies from May to August at the margins of forests and in meadows and gardens. The larvae, which live in damp ground, are also predacious.

The very striking *Stratiomys chamaeleon* is one of a group of colourful flies called soldier-flies. They belong to the family Stratiomyidae. It is coloured somewhat like a hover-fly, but, unlike hover-flies, it has a flattened body and two teeth on its thorax. The imagos like damp localities and live from June to September. They sit on flowering plants, especially Umbelliferae. They occur in lowlands and foothills and in mountains they ascend to over 2,000 m (6,560 ft). The significance of a damp environment is that the female *S. chamaeleon* lays her eggs on the undersides of aquatic plants – mostly arrowhead, flowering rush, water plantain and the like. The larva lives in water, among the vegetation or in the mud. It has a very long abdomen with the spiracles at the tip; its development takes a long time. The pupa lies in the skin of the last larval instar (puparium) and floats on the water.

Chloromyia formosa is striking in its metallic colouring. The imagos fly in the spring and summer and sit on low vegetation and shrubs; they are common on flowering umbelliferous plants such as carrots, dill, chervil and fennel. They occur from lowlands to altitudes of over 2,000 m (6,560 ft). The light yellow larva grows to a length of up to 12 mm ($\frac{1}{2}$ in). It lives in soil, under stones and in garden compost and has often been found in cow dung. It hibernates before pupating.

1. *Rhagio scolopacea:* 13—18 mm ($\frac{9}{16}$—$\frac{3}{4}$ in). Central Europe.
2. *Stratiomys chamaeleon:* 12—16 mm ($\frac{1}{2}$—$\frac{5}{8}$ in). Europe except the north, the temperate belt in Asia.
3. *Chloromyia formosa:* 6.5—9 mm ($\frac{9}{32}$—$\frac{3}{8}$ in). The Palaearctic region.

1 *Chrysops caecutiens* L.   Tabanidae
Horse-fly

2 *Chrysops relictus* Meig.

3 *Haematopota pluvialis* L.
Cleg-fly

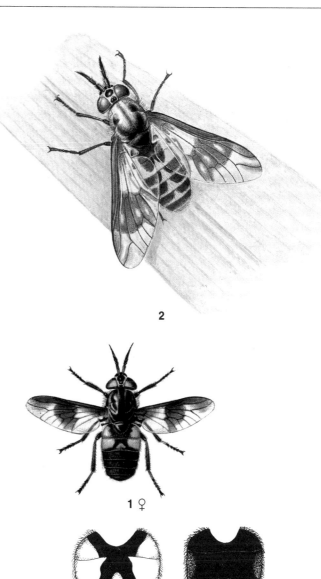

2

1 ♀

Abdomen of female (a) and male
(b) of *Chrysops caecutiens*

In addition to other characteristics, the horse-flies of the genus *Chrysops* can be identified by the distinctive dark markings on their abdomens, which are different in males and females. The female *Chrysops caecutiens* has characteristic markings on her abdomen. The first two abdominal segments are yellow and on the second there is a mark like an inverted capital V. The male, however, has a black abdomen. This common species flies in the summer in low-lying country near water. The females primarily attack people's heads, cattle and horses; they bite in the middle of the day and early evening. The males drink nectar from flowers and water from pools and puddles. The green-coloured larvae are predacious and live in water, mostly among vegetation.

In general appearance *Chrysops relictus* resembles the preceding species, but the markings on its abdomen are different at first glance. In the first place, the female's markings are similar to the male's. The imagos fly from June to August, usually close to water, but also in forests. The females suck the blood of human beings, horses, cattle, rodents and other animals.

The most common horse-fly to molest man is undoubtedly the Cleg-fly (*Haematopota pluvialis*), which appears from May onwards, but occurs in the greatest numbers in the summer. It flies in forests, meadows and gardens and attacks its victims – people and a whole series of animals – silently, punctures their skin with its proboscis and immediately starts sucking. Its bite is painful. It does not even mind rain. The larvae are to be found beside water and in other damp habitats. They are predacious and hunt various insects living in the ground. After hibernating, they pupate in the late spring or early summer of the following year.

1. *Chrysops caecutiens:* 7—10 mm ($\frac{5}{16}$—$\frac{3}{8}$ in). Europe, temperate Asia.
2. *Chrysops relictus:* 6—11 mm ($\frac{1}{4}$—$\frac{7}{16}$ in). Europe, temperate Asia.
3. *Haematopota pluvialis:* 8—12 mm ($\frac{5}{16}$—$\frac{1}{2}$ in). The Palaearctic region.

3

1

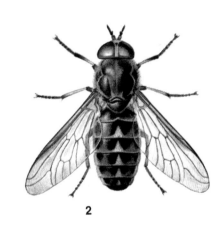

2

3

1 *Tabanus bromius* L. Tabanidae
2 *Tabanus bovinus* L.
3 *Hybomitra bimaculata* Macq.

Female horse-flies have a very bad name. They attack animals and human beings, suck their blood and make themselves a nuisance in general. The males sit on flowers and suck nectar. These flies have very striking eyes. In the live insect the eyes are marked with a rainbow pattern of coloured lines and spots, which disappear in dead and preserved specimens. *Tabanus bromius* is one of the most common *Tabanus* species. It flies from the end of May to the beginning of August, plagues people and domestic and wild animals and, via its bite, can transmit certain blood-borne diseases.

The female *Tabanus bovinus* specialises mainly in cattle and horses, which it attacks in pastures and meadows. It plagues them most in the middle of the day, sucks their blood and causes them to shy. The eggs are laid on vegetation on the banks of stagnant and flowing water, or are released directly onto the surface. The pale yellow, predacious larvae live in the mud on the bank. After hibernating, they pupate in the places where they developed. The imagos emerge in May and fly until August.

Hybomitra bimaculata flies in lowland fishpond regions. The females suck the blood of humans, cows and horses. The males appear very early in the morning, at sunrise, and wait for the females to emerge. After copulating, the female lays her black eggs, always in groups, on aquatic plants. The rust-brown larvae live in mud on the banks of fishponds, or among aquatic plants near the bank. The larvae hibernate, but have also been observed crawling about in the winter under the ice; they pupate on the bank early in the spring.

1. *Tabanus bromius:* 11—16 mm ($\frac{7}{16}$—$\frac{5}{8}$ in). Europe, temperate Asia, northern Africa.
2. *Tabanus bovinus:* 19—24 mm ($\frac{3}{4}$—$\frac{15}{16}$ in). Europe, the Caucasus, Transcaucasia, northern Africa.
3. *Hybomitra bimaculata:* 13—17 mm ($\frac{9}{16}$—$\frac{11}{16}$ in). The Palaearctic region.

1 *Laphria flava* L.   Asilidae
2 *Machimus atricapillus* Fall.
3 *Thereva plebeja* L.   Therevidae

On fine summer days you can find a host of interesting insects in forest clearings. The robber-fly *Laphria flava* is usually among them. With its hairy body it looks a little like a bumblebee, but the similarity vanishes when we watch it pursuing and 'processing' prey such as flies and other insects. Having made a catch, it settles on a stump, a felled tree or a stone and sucks its victim's juices. Its proboscis is so strong that it can even pierce a beetle's thick armour. The imagos fly until September. This species lives in both lowlands and mountains. After flying and hunting all day, it spends the night on plants. The larvae, which are also predacious, live in rotting stumps or in debris behind bark.

Machimus atricapillus is the most common of the few species of robber-flies which closely resemble one another. It occurs from July to September, at low and at high altitudes, has no special environmental requirements and is to be found at the margins of woods and in clearings just as often as in meadows and gardens. It lies in wait for its prey, sitting motionless on a leaf on a bush, a tree or a felled trunk. As soon as some insect approaches, it pounces, seizes it and sits down to suck its juices, often flying somewhere else with it to do so. The whitish larva, which is also predacious, lives and hibernates in the ground and does not pupate until the following summer.

Stiletto-flies (Therevidae) vaguely resemble some robber-flies. *Thereva plebeja,* one of the most common, flies in forest clearings and gardens from May to September. It occurs in lowlands and mountains and in the Alps can still be found at about 2,500 m (8,200 ft). The white, long-bodied larvae live in litter, where they hunt other insect larvae. In turn, however, they themselves fall prey to other predacious insects.

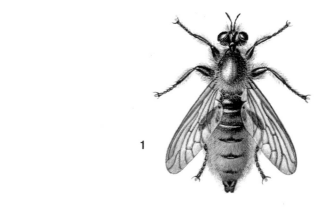

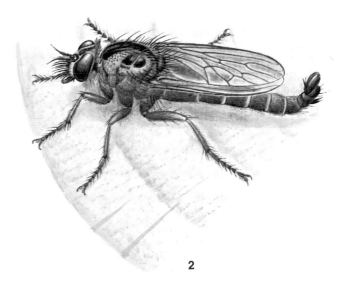

1. *Laphria flava:* 12—25 mm ($\frac{1}{2}$—1 in). Europe, the temperate belt in Asia.
2. *Machimus atricapillus:* 14—18 mm ($\frac{9}{16}$—$\frac{3}{4}$ in). Europe, the Caucasus, the Canary Islands.
3. *Thereva plebeja:* 8—12 mm ($\frac{5}{16}$—$\frac{1}{2}$ in). The Palaearctic region.

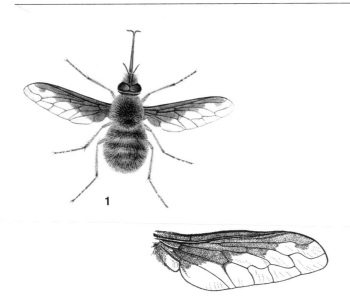

1

Wing of *Bombylius major*

2

3

1 ***Bombylius major*** L.   Bombyliidae
Bee-fly

2 ***Hemipenthes morio*** L.

3 ***Empis livida*** L.   Empididae

The thickly hirsute Bee-fly (*Bombylius major*) looks like a small bumblebee. It likes spring sunshine and visits flowering celandine, anemones, cowslips, dandelions and many other flowers. It lives on hillsides, in open woods, in meadows and on grass borders and is enticed to visit gardens by the many spring flowers. The larva develops in the nest of a solitary bee. It first of all eats the store of pollen prepared by the bee for its own offspring and then sucks the contents of the bee larva's body and finally kills it. Its appearance changes during its development; at first mobile it later becomes sedentary. This species hibernates in the pupal stage. The imagos emerge in March and fly until May or June, depending on conditions.

The development of *Hemipenthes morio* is similarly complicated, but its larva parasitises a parasite. It develops at the expense of various tachinids (Tachinidae), flies which themselves parasitise other insects (most frequently caterpillars). The imagos fly mainly on the outskirts of the deciduous woods frequented by their hosts. They occur from May to August.

Different insects have different nuptial ceremonies. The male dance-fly (*Empis livida*) woos the female with an insect which may be larger than he is himself. The imagos of this dance-fly sit on flowers, drinking the nectar with their long proboscis, but they are also predators. They fly from June to August over fields, along footpaths, on the outskirts of woods and in gardens. The predacious larvae live in the soil and hibernate before pupating.

1. *Bombylius major:* 8—16 mm ($\frac{5}{16}$—$\frac{5}{8}$ in). The Palaearctic region, North America.
2. *Hemipenthes morio:* 5—14 mm ($\frac{3}{16}$—$\frac{9}{16}$ in). Europe, Asia Minor, North America.
3. *Empis livida:* 7—10 mm ($\frac{9}{32}$—$\frac{3}{8}$ in). The whole of Europe.

1 *Baccha elongata* F.
2 *Scaeva pyrastri* L.
3 *Episyrphus balteatus* Deg.

Syrphidae

1

Hover-flies (Syrphidae) may be seen from the spring until late in the autumn. They live in meadows, woods, fields, parks, gardens and cemeteries, near water and in dry regions, in lowlands and in mountains – hover-flies of some kind are to be found everywhere. The imagos sit on flowers and are able to hover (hence their vernacular name). If disturbed, they fly nimbly away, but a moment later return to their hovering. The larvae of some species devour aphids; others are phytophagous or saprophagous. Some species are robustly built and resemble bees, bumble-bees or wasps, while others, like *Baccha elongata,* have a very thin abdomen. This species flies from April to the beginning of October.

Scaeva pyrastri also occurs from the spring to the beginning of the autumn. During this time it forms several generations. The imagos sit on various flowers growing in meadows, on grass verges, along footpaths, at the margins of woods and in gardens and parks. The larvae live on aphids and since they do not specialise in a particular species, they are important predators, especially as they catch a great many aphids which damage crops.

2

Another hover-fly with a long appearance is *Episyrphus balteatus,* which occurs from the spring until late in the autumn. The imagos have a liking for dandelions and hawkweed, etc. and it is not unusual to find several sitting on one flower head. The larvae live on aphids. In prolific aphid years, these hover-flies also multiply more than usual, although they normally form several generations and occur practically everywhere – in meadows, gardens, parks and different types of woods. They are not dependent on the structure of the aphid population and are, so far, known to live on some 40 species of aphids, which makes them all the more important as liquidators of these pests. The adults are good pollinators.

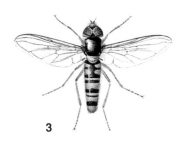

3

1. *Baccha elongata:* 7—11 mm ($\frac{9}{32}$ — $\frac{7}{16}$ in). Europe, the Caucasus, Siberia.
2. *Scaeva pyrastri:* 12—15 mm ($\frac{1}{2}$ — $\frac{5}{8}$ in). The Palaearctic region, North America.
3. *Episyrphus balteatus:* 8—12 mm ($\frac{5}{16}$ — $\frac{1}{2}$ in). The Palaearctic region.

1

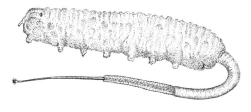

Larva of the Drone-fly (*Eristalis tenax*)

2

1 *Eristalis tenax* L.   Syrphidae
Drone-fly

2 *Myathropa florea* L.

Superficially, the Drone-fly (*Eristalis tenax*) might well be mistaken for a Honeybee. It is the same size, but is more robustly built and, being a dipteran, it has only two membraneous wings. It flies very early in the spring (the first individuals appear in March) and can still be encountered in November, when it visits cemeteries and settles on the flowers placed on the graves. It is most abundant in the summer and the autumn, when, in central Europe, it is joined by hover-flies from the south. It occurs in lowlands, hills and mountains and flies over meadows, hillsides, forests, parks and gardens. In the country it is frequently to be found in the vicinity of people, where there are often very favourable conditions for the development of the larvae. Adults also hibernate in homes. The larva of this hover-fly is very typical; it has a soft, cylindrical body terminating in a partly retractable breathing tube which looks like a tail. The tube is of vital importance to the larva, which lives mostly in foul water, ditches, gutters, choked-up ponds, liquid manure, outdoor privies and latrines, etc. When fully grown, the larvae leave this environment and look for a drier place in which to pupate. The pupa is wrapped in the last larval skin (known as the puparium).

Myathropa florea is a very striking, robust hover-fly which is common from May to September in forest clearings and meadows, on grass verges and beside footpaths in fields. In the spring it frequents flowering blackthorn and hawthorn and later it is a regular visitor on various flowering Umbelliferae and on briar roses. The larva inhabits small patches of stagnant water with sufficient remnants of plants, but it is also common in hollows in deciduous trees (mainly beeches), which contain old leaves decaying in residual water. It is saprophagous.

---

1. *Eristalis tenax:* 15—19 mm ($\frac{5}{8}$—$\frac{3}{4}$ in). Over most of the globe.
2. *Myathropa florea:* 12—15 mm ($\frac{1}{2}$—$\frac{5}{8}$ in). The whole of Europe, the Caucasus.

1 *Volucella pellucens* L. Syrphidae
2 *Volucella bombylans* L.
3 *Volucella inanis* L.
4 *Syritta pipiens* L.

Some hover-flies develop in the nests of social hymenopterans. *Volucella pellucens* develops in the underground nests of wasps of the genus *Vespula*. The imagos are common on various flowering plants from spring to autumn; they mainly frequent umbelliferous plants, thistles and common elder. They are to be found on the outskirts of woods, on grass verges and in gardens and parks. The female makes provision for her brood by entering a wasp's nest and laying her eggs on the protective envelope. The larva, which finds a suitable microclimate in the nest, with a constant temperature and degree of humidity, lives mainly on debris, including dead wasp larvae. It pupates in the ground, below the nest.

In a crowd of small worker bumblebees you would be unable to pick out the furry-bodied hover-fly *Volucella bombylans*. The resemblance is not fortuitous, since the hover-fly generally develops in the nests of *Bombus lapidarius* and *B. terrestris* and imitates the colouring of its hosts.

Volucella inanis, which is characterised by four bands across its abdomen, usually develops in Hornets' (*Vespa crabro*) nests, and also in the nests of *Vespula germanica*.

Syritta pipiens is a small hover-fly with extremely thick hind femurs. It flies from the spring until late in the autumn in meadows, fields, woods and gardens. The imagos are abundant on flowers everywhere, from lowlands to mountains. The whitish larvae live in compost, rotting vegetables and excrement and feed on decomposing organic matter.

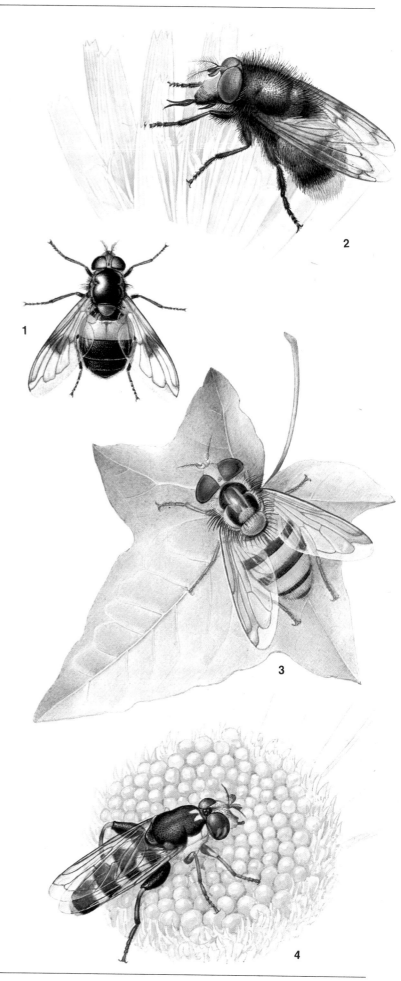

1. *Volucella pellucens:* 15—16 mm ($\frac{5}{8}$ in). Europe, temperate Asia.
2. *Volucella bombylans:* 11—15 mm ($\frac{7}{16}$ — $\frac{5}{8}$ in). Europe, temperate Asia.
3. *Volucella inanis:* 15—16 mm ($\frac{5}{8}$ in). Europe, temperate Asia.
4. *Syritta pipiens:* 6—9 mm ($\frac{1}{4}$ — $\frac{3}{8}$ in). Europe, temperate Asia, North America.

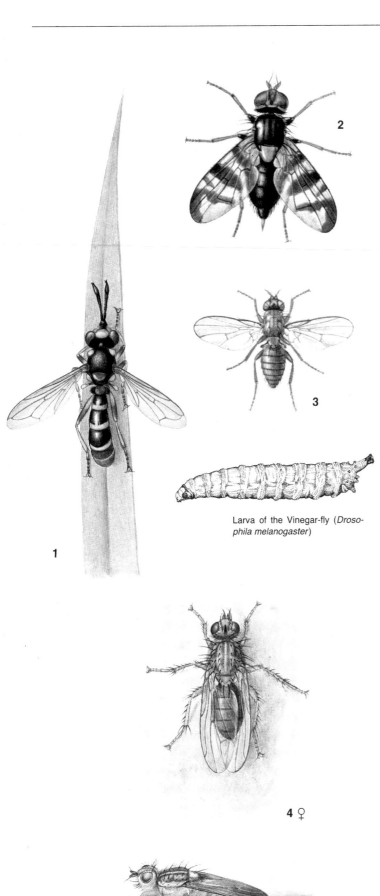

1 Conops flavipes L.   Conopidae

2 Rhagoletis cerasi L.   Tephritidae

3 Drosophila melanogaster Meig.   Drosophilidae
Vinegar-fly

4 Scathophaga stercoraria L.   Scatophagidae
Yellow Dung-fly

Wasp-like colouring is useful in more than one dipteran family. In the thick-headed fly *Conops flavipes* it is very pronounced. This outstanding flier lives almost everywhere – on the outskirts of woods, in damp meadows and in gardens. It is most abundant in July and August. It likes to sit on flowering Umbelliferae or on scabious, sucking nectar. The female makes provision for the next generation in a very original way. As she flies, she sticks an egg to the abdomen of a flying bumblebee or mason bee (of the genus *Osmia*). Bit by bit, the larva consumes its host's tissues and then, when it is dead, pupates and hibernates inside it.

The whitish maggots which are apt to spoil our appetite for cherries are actually the larvae of the large fruit-fly *Rhagoletis cerasi*. The females lay eggs in unripe cherries and the larvae develop in the fleshy part. Before pupating, the larva leaves the fruit and pupates in the ground. This species also lives in other kinds of fruit, such as bird-cherry, Mahaleb cherry and barberry.

The tiny and very abundant Vinegar-fly (*Drosophila melanogaster*) is most common at the height of summer and in the autumn. It occurs wherever rotting fruit or other organic matter is to be found. The Vinegar-fly has also carved a place for itself in genetics, as a satisfactory model for the study of chromosomes.

The Yellow Dung-fly (*Scathophaga stercoraria*) appears on excrement from the spring until the late autumn, but the males frequently also visit flowers. The yellowish-white maggots live in excrement, where they catch the larvae of other (mainly dipteran) insects.

Larva of the Vinegar-fly (*Drosophila melanogaster*)

4 ♀

4 ♂

1. *Conops flavipes:* 9—13 mm ($\frac{3}{8}$—$\frac{9}{16}$ in). Europe, eastern Siberia, North Africa.
2. *Rhagoletis cerasi:* 4—5 mm ($\frac{5}{32}$—$\frac{3}{16}$ in). A large part of Europe, the Caucasus, central Asia, Siberia, northern Africa.
3. *Drosophila melanogaster:* 1.8—2.3 mm ($\frac{1}{16}$ in). Over the entire globe.
4. *Scathophaga stercoraria:* 6—12 mm ($\frac{1}{4}$—$\frac{1}{2}$ in). The Palaearctic and Nearctic regions.

1 ***Delia brassicae*** Bouché   Anthomyiidae
Cabbage Root-fly

2 ***Musca domestica*** L.   Muscidae
Common House-fly

3 ***Stomoxys calcitrans*** L.
Stable-fly

4 ***Fannia canicularis*** L.
Lesser House-fly

The Cabbage Root-fly (*Delia brassicae*), a well-known pest of brassica crops, forms several generations. The first imagos emerge in May from hibernating pupae and are then followed by one or two more generations, depending on the weather. The white eggs are about 1 mm ($\frac{1}{32}$ in) long and have a finely sculptured surface. They are laid at the base of the plant, where the stem joins the root, or quite close to it. The larvae live on the roots, and then pupate in the ground.

The House-fly (*Musca domestica*), the most familiar insect of all, forms several generations in a year and is very closely attached to people. The imagos live on vegetable and animal matter. The larvae live in waste matter, manure and excrement and measure 10–13 mm ($\frac{3}{8} - \frac{9}{16}$ in). The larvae, pupae and adult flies all hibernate. As well as being a nuisance, the House-fly can transmit various infections.

The Stable-fly (*Stomoxys calcitrans*) is much more troublesome than the House-fly. It lives in and around cow-sheds and the male and female both suck animal and human blood. It occurs practically the whole year round. The female lays up to 400 eggs; the larvae develop in manure in cow-sheds, etc. The development of a single generation takes four to five weeks. Stable-flies can transmit various blood-borne infections through their bite.

The Lesser House-fly (*Fannia canicularis*) is very common in dwellings. From the early spring it circles untiringly round lamps. Since it does not bite, it is less unpleasant than the Stable-fly. At night it rests on a chandelier-type light or the ceiling. The larvae develop in decomposing matter.

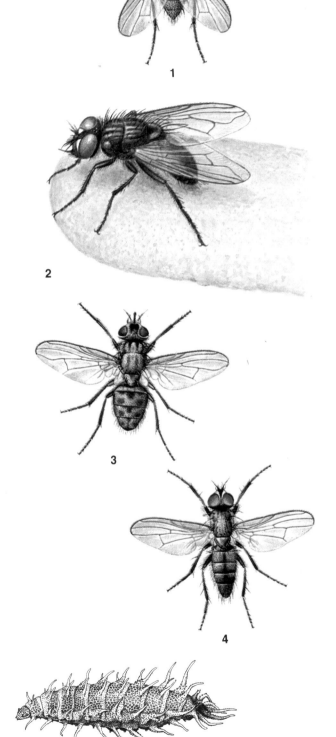

1. *Delia brassicae:* 5.5—7.5 mm ($\frac{7}{32} - \frac{9}{32}$ in). Europe, North America.
2. *Musca domestica:* 7—9 mm ($\frac{9}{32} - \frac{3}{8}$ in). Carried by man over the whole globe.
3. *Stomoxys calcitrans:* 5.5—7 mm ($\frac{7}{32} - \frac{9}{32}$ in). Over the whole globe.
4. *Fannia canicularis:* 5—7 mm ($\frac{3}{16} - \frac{9}{32}$ in). Over the whole globe.

Larva of Lesser House-fly (*Fannia canicularis*)

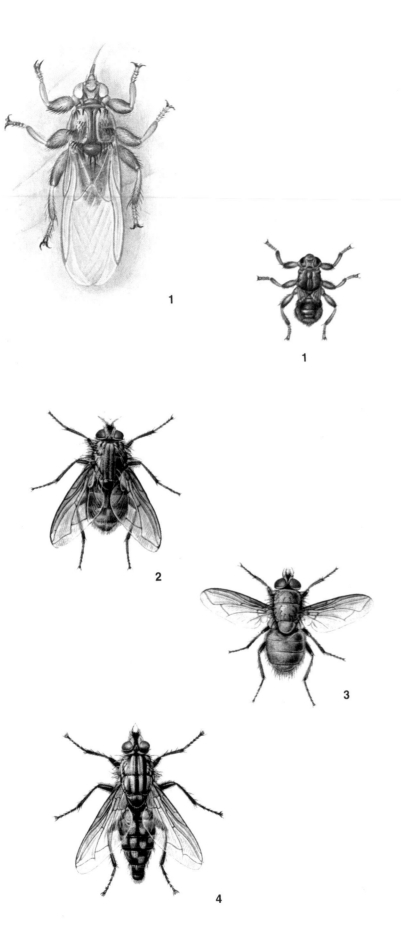

1 ***Lipoptena cervi*** L. Hippoboscidae
Deer-ked, Deer-fly

2 ***Calliphora vicina*** Rob.–Desv. Calliphoridae
Bluebottle

3 ***Lucilia caesar*** L.

4 ***Sarcophaga carnaria*** L. Sarcophagidae
Flesh-fly

The extremely flat-bodied, long-winged Deer-ked (*Lipoptena cervi*) parasitises roe deer, red deer and badgers and lives on their blood. As soon as the female has found a host, she settles on it, preferably on its belly, and since she now no longer needs to fly, she sheds her wings. She spends the winter on the animal and in the spring gives birth to living larvae, which pupate immediately afterwards. The puparium then falls to the ground and the imago emerges in August. Deer-keds also attack humans. They occur in woods from August to October.

The Bluebottle (*Calliphora vicina*) is another synanthropic fly. It flies the whole year round and settles on fresh and decomposing matter, on fruit and on flowers. The larvae develop in meat and in animal cadavers; they pupate in the ground. The generations follow each other in unbroken succession.

It has become customary to describe any gold-green fly as a Greenbottle. There are several such species, however, and it is best to leave their determination to the experts. *Lucilia caesar* lives both in the open and in the company of people. The imagos like to sit on white-flowered umbelliferous plants, but also occur on excrement, on animal cadavers and, in households, on decaying meat. They commonly attack sheep. They live from the spring to the late autumn.

The Flesh-fly (*Sarcophaga carnaria*) is a further markedly synanthropic species. It flies from March to October. The males are to be found on flowers, the females in vegetation, on carcases and on bad meat. In Europe there are many more, very similar species, which are difficult to identify.

1. *Lipoptena cervi:* 4.5—5 mm, wing 6 mm ($\frac{5}{32}$—$\frac{3}{16}$ in, wing $\frac{1}{4}$ in). The Palaearctic region; carried to North America.
2. *Calliphora vicina:* 5—12 mm ($\frac{3}{16}$—$\frac{1}{2}$ in). Over the whole globe.
3. *Lucilia caesar:* 6—12 mm ($\frac{1}{4}$—$\frac{1}{2}$ in). The Palaearctic region.
4. *Sarcophaga carnaria:* 10—18 mm ($\frac{3}{8}$—$\frac{3}{4}$ in). Europe, temperate Asia.

1 *Tachina fera* L.   Tachinidae
2 *Phryxe vulgaris* Fall.
3 *Hypoderma bovis* Deg.   Hypodermatidae
Ox Warble-fly

The very large Tachinidae family is represented by about 500 species in central Europe alone and the red-legged *Tachina fera* is one of the most common. The imagos sit on flowering Umbelliferae and other plants and are to be seen from the spring to the autumn. The female lays her eggs near caterpillars of the Gypsy Moth (*Lymantria dispar*), the Black Arches (*L. monacha*), the Pine Beauty (*Panolis flammea*) and other lepidopteran pests. The larva bores its way into the caterpillar, lives on its tissues and pupates inside its body.

Not all tachinids are as strikingly coloured as *Tachina fera*. *Phryxe vulgaris* is dark and inconspicuous. It also occurs on umbelliferous plants from the spring to the autumn. The eggs are laid on the food host. The larvae can develop on about 80 different species of caterpillars, but very hairy caterpillars are seldom attacked.

Grazing cattle and horses may be disquieted by the attacks of various horse-flies which stab them and suck their blood, but they are far more alarmed by the Ox Warble-fly (*Hypoderma bovis*). When the female flies about among grazing animals, looking for a victim, the cattle show signs of uneasiness and often panic and try to escape. There is no escape, however, and the warble-fly always manages to lay its eggs somewhere on the rear end of the body (usually on the hindlegs). The larva burrows its way into the animal's body and remains there for many months. Then it moves to the back and settles down just under the skin. It forms a capsule round its body and protrudes the tip of its abdomen, with the spiracles, through the skin, so that it is able to breathe oxygen from the air. When the warble-fly larva measures about 30 mm ($1\frac{3}{16}$ in), it leaves its host and pupates in the ground.

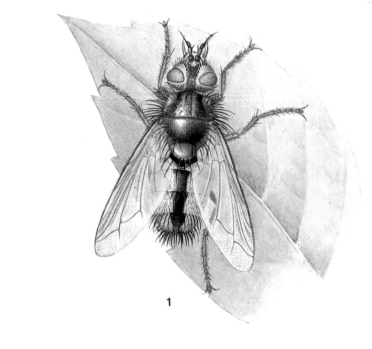

1

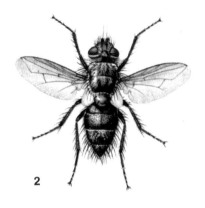

2

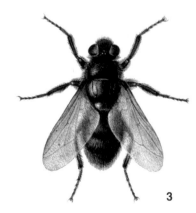

3

1. *Tachina fera:* 9—14 mm ($\frac{3}{8}$ — $\frac{9}{16}$ in). The Palaearctic region.
2. *Phryxe vulgaris:* 5—8 mm ($\frac{3}{16}$ — $\frac{5}{16}$ in). Europe, temperate Asia.
3. *Hypoderma bovis:* 13—15 mm ($\frac{9}{16}$ — $\frac{5}{8}$ in). The Palaearctic region, North America.

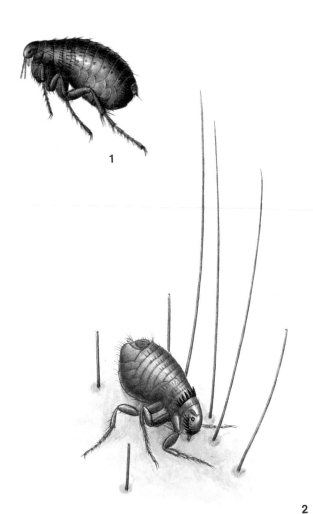

1

2

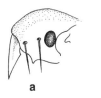

a　　　　　　**b**

Head of Human Flea (*Pulex irri-tans*) (a) and Cat Flea (*Cteno-cephalides felis*) (b)

3

1 *Pulex irritans* L. Pulicidae
Human Flea

2 *Ctenocephalides felis* Bouché
Cat Flea

3 *Hystrichopsylla talpae* Curtis Ctenopsyllidae
Mole Flea

Fleas have been troublesome parasites of man and animals since time immemorial. They suck blood and are vectors of various infections. Some are highly specialised as regards their hosts, but others, like the Human Flea (*Pulex irritans*), live on man, on domestic and wild animals, and breed in their nests or homes. Wherever a flea has sucked blood, it leaves behind it a red spot which remains for several days. The Human Flea forms several generations, whose number and rate of development depend on temperature. One female will lay over 400 eggs, in groups of four to eight, and the laying time may be stretched over three months. The larvae develop in dwellings (usually in chinks in floors and beds) and in the open in birds' nests; they live on small particles of organic matter. In Europe today, the Human Flea is regarded as just another unpleasant parasite.

The Cat Flea (*Ctenocephalides felis*) mainly infests cats, but it also attacks other animals, both domestic and wild, and may even attach itself to people for a while, largely by way of kittens.

From its name, one would expect the Mole Flea (*Hystrichopsylla talpae*) to be parasitic mainly on moles (generic name *Talpa*), but it is hard to say which of its hosts is the chief one, since it also lives on other insectivores (forest shrews and white-toothed shrews) and on rodents (such as house mice, field mice and voles).

1. *Pulex irritans:* ♂ 2—2.5 mm, ♀ 2.5—3.5 mm (♂ $\frac{1}{16}$—$\frac{3}{32}$ in, ♀ $\frac{3}{32}$—$\frac{5}{32}$ in). Over the whole globe.
2. *Ctenocephalides felis:* ♂ 2—2.5 mm, ♀ 2—3.5 mm (♂ $\frac{1}{16}$—$\frac{3}{32}$ in, ♀ $\frac{1}{16}$—$\frac{5}{32}$ in). Over the whole globe.
3. *Hystrichopsylla talpae:* ♂ 3.5—4 mm, ♀ 4.56 mm (♂ $\frac{5}{32}$ in, ♀ $\frac{7}{32}$—$\frac{1}{4}$ in). A large part of temperate Eurasia.

Index of scientific names
Numbers in bold type refer to main entries

Index of common names
Numbers in bold refer to main entries